The Cycles of Sex

The Cycles of Sex

by WARREN J. GADPAILLE, M.D.

edited by Lucy Freeman

Charles Scribner's Sons

New York

Copyright © 1975 Charles Scribner's Sons

The lines quoted on page 440 from "Little Gidding" in
Four Quartets by T. S. Eliot, copyright 1943 by T. S.
Eliot, copyright 1971 by Esme Valerie Eliot, are
reprinted by permission of Harcourt Brace Jovano-
vich, Inc.

Library of Congress Cataloging in Publication Data

Gadpaille, Warren J
  The cycles of sex.

  Bibliography: p.
  Includes index.
  1. Sex (Biology) 2. Sex (Psychology) 3. Sex customs.
I. Title. [DNLM: 1. Psychosexual develop-
ment. 2. Sex behavior. HQ21 G125c]
HQ21.G2   612.6   75-5981
ISBN 0-684-14216-3 (Trade Cloth)
ISBN 0-684-14224-4 (Trade Paper)

1 3 5 7 9 11 13 15 17 19 C/C 20 18 16 14 12 10 8 6 4 2
1 3 5 7 9 11 13 15 17 19 C/P 20 18 16 14 12 10 8 6 4 2

Printed in the United States of America

To Weston LaBarre,
friend and colleague

Contents

Preface

Children of the contemporary western world are most often a blend of enlightenment and ignorance. Many of them acquire more factual knowledge about the external world in their first decade than was available to their great-grandparents in a lifetime. Yet they must essay the task of assimilating this knowledge and budgeting the power that it confers, with little more than a stone-age understanding of the very instrument they must use—their own mental and emotional selves. The disparity in people's capacity to cope with the inner and outer worlds is witnessed in the many who function so well in an occupation or a profession or a hobby but whose personal lives are dull, unhappy, even a shambles. No aspect of personal emotional life suffers more from misunderstanding, anxiety, and the studied neglect of healthful preparation than does sexuality.

I was no exception; my childhood and rearing were neither worse nor better than the middle-class mainstream with regard to sex. I struggled with the same fascinations and confusions and guilts. I was hampered by the same ignorance and secrecy and taboos. It is clear to me now that I responded to this circumstance with an embryonic outrage that developed into a pervading determination to understand, to treat, and to teach. I was not fully aware of it until my own analysis during psychoanalytic training, but my refusal to accept the constricting and disruptive effects of my culture's attitudes toward the sexual development of children and toward adult sexuality in general was a powerful motive directing me into medicine and psychoanalytic psychiatry.

Throughout my experience as a teacher, writer, and practicing psychoanalyst, I have been struck by the fragmented state of source material on human sexual development. The professional literature includes thousands of valuable articles and some specialized books, beginning with Freud's momentous *Three Essays on the Theory of Sexuality*, which first appeared in 1905. But most of these are not easily available to the layman or even the professional nonspecialist, and all of them deal only with limited, specific areas. There is not a single book for either professional or lay readers that attempts to correlate the vast interdisciplinary knowledge on psychosexual development. My increasing focus upon teaching required me first to organize my own notes, and then to revise and expand them continuously. This book is the final outgrowth of the notes relating primarily to normal development and is my effort to fill the existing void in the literature on sexuality.

As a physician and psychoanalyst, I proceed from a broader background in some fields than in others, and on certain basic assumptions. My most important premise is that psychosexual development continues throughout the entire life cycle of the individual, from the time of fetal development until death, and that sexuality cannot be regarded as purely a result of any single facet of a multifaceted process.

My second premise is that of a genetic, developmental psychology. By this I mean that earlier influences affect later behavior and attitudes, that childhood sexuality and experiences are relevant to subsequent sexuality, and that no aspect of human sexual expression can be fully understood without knowing how it developed.

Within this general framework my points of departure are those of the medical biological sciences and modern psychoanalysis. Psychoanalysis, from being a purely individual concept of biologically determined developmental stages that primarily take place internally, at its best now integrates biological, constitutional, interpersonal, cultural, and internal emotional components as they bear upon the development of both health and disturbance.

I have attempted, however, to go far beyond my primary background in the preparation of this book and to integrate the most relevant contributions from sociology, cultural anthropology, evolution, the recent spurt of research in embryology, endocrinology, and neurophysiology, and the applicable research into the sexuality of subhuman primates and other mammals. Obviously the scope of such an effort makes its absolute accomplishment impossible.

The book is arranged in three sections—three "cycles." Psychosexual development not only continues throughout life, but it comes back again and again to similar emotional and developmental tasks, and time and growth will have cast them into somewhat different forms. At each return the person is different, a mixture of what he was at the time of the previous resolution and of all the change and growth that have taken place subsequently. The recurrent echo of earlier phases is one of the most fascinating aspects of a concept of psychosexual development that encompasses the entire life span.

Regardless of the scope I have tried to achieve, the book is intentionally limited to three important dimensions. One is that it focuses exclusively upon sexual development, a limitation that at times seems artificial, since sexual development cannot easily be separated from other equally important aspects of emotional development that are going on simultaneously.

The second major limitation is the focus upon normal development. The definitions of normal and abnormal with regard to sex are both difficult and controversial, but common sense alone validates the fact that sexuality can be abnormal as well as normal. Here the abnormal is treated only in passing and in totally inadequate detail. Hopefully the reader will not perceive the concentration upon normal development as a disregard of its Siamese twin, the abnormal, from which it cannot be separated without obvious scars and some residual damage to each.

Finally, no discussion of normal sexual development can apply equally well to all cultures and subcultures, current and historical. Some aspects of sexual development are shared by all mankind; others are inseparably bound to a specific culture, and I have attempted to distinguish clearly between them. Much of what is discussed in this book applies primarily to the dominant culture of middle- and upper-middle-class United States, and in varying degrees to contemporary Western European or Judeo-Christian culture in general. However, even the United States middle class is not monolithic in its sexual attitudes. I do not attempt to describe the differing effects of even major subcultures, though I recognize their existence and validity. Nonetheless, the white middle class shares certain seminal attitudes toward sexuality that can be identified, and it exerts or even enforces its influence on variant nondominant subcultures more than they influence it.

This book is addressed to two different audiences. The broadest consists of parents, teachers, clergymen, and all questing and curious laymen who want to do better for their own and others' children than was done for them but often do not know where to find the knowledge they need. However, I have been primarily a writer for other professionals, an occupation that fosters a literary style not always appealing to a wide nonprofessional audience. Lucy Freeman, who collaborated with me on style and editing, has done a great deal to smooth the flow of the following pages. If the nonprofessional reader finds the book pleasantly readable, much of the credit belongs to her, but she deserves none of the blame for inaccuracies or for any disagreement the reader may have with my various interpretations, conclusions, or positions.

In addition, this work is designed for every kind of professional in the health, education, and guidance fields who has to cope with developing or disturbed sexuality, whether or not he feels adequately prepared to do so. For such readers I have made the reference notes to original and seminal source materials as comprehensive as possible.

I am indebted to all the creative minds whose work has formed the background for my own understanding of human sexuality and its development. That debt is reflected in every reference and includes equally many scholars and clinicians whose work is not directly concerned with the limited subject of this book. Two men deserve particular acknowledgment. Irwin M. Marcus, M.D., who was my training analyst, is also qualified as a child analyst, and his special understanding contributed greatly to my awareness of the crucial nature of early psychosexual development. I also feel deep obligation to the cultural anthropologist Weston LaBarre, whose book, *The Human Animal*, convinced me of the imperative relevance of a cross-cultural view and also provided the impetus for a close and lasting friendship and professional association that have never ceased to be enriching. Naturally, I alone bear responsibility for the manner in which I have used and integrated his work and that of others and for the interpretations and conclusions I have drawn.

Warren J. Gadpaille

The Cycles
of Sex

What Psychosexual Development Is and How It Happens

There is something unique about sex that has fascinated, confused, delighted, troubled, and obsessed mankind throughout recorded history. No other aspect of human life has given more joy and caused more misery. No other natural bodily and emotional function has been subjected to more divergent means of regulation or been given such a profusion of expressions. No other normal biological activity is at once so personal, and at the same time so unlikely to be left up to each individual.

It cannot help but be so. Sexuality enters into all human relationships, not only the most intimate. It is the fundament of the family and a principal root of self-esteem and identity. Because it has procreative potential, and family or kinship groups are basic to the survival of all societies in the evolution of mankind and of cultures, some form of regulation is inevitable. Total and permanent sexual anarchy would disintegrate a society as surely as political anarchy.

There are further characteristics inherent in human sexual development that tend to evoke irrational and inappropriate approaches to its regulation. The origins of human sexual feelings lie within one's family of rearing, and the earliest attachments of sexual feelings are to one's parents. Those origins contain the seeds of potential emotional conflicts which make mankind prone to fear and overcontrol sex, to inhibit it in himself and prohibit it in others, to hedge it about with taboos and to limit it in accord with rigid and irrational conditions for its expression. When any attitudes, whether constructive or destructive, are shared by a large enough group of people, they become part of that group's culture. They become translated into laws and cultural institutions (such as monogamous marriage, or the unquestioned assumption that sex and love must always go together), and determine child-rearing philosophies and practices designed to prepare each generation to believe in and perpetuate the same system of attitudes and institutions.

Obviously, sexuality does not have to be the object of bizarre and damaging attitudes—it is a natural expression of healthy humanity, and it can be approached with pleasure and good sense—but the potentials for limitlessly distorted sexual emotions are contained in all human psychosexual development, just as surely as the opportunities for making sexuality the supremely rewarding relationship it is capable of being. The subtle obstacles to healthy sexuality must be understood to be avoided.

There is a crucial progression from self-involved sex to love in the normal development of sexual attitudes and behavior. I will not address here the multiple meanings of love, or whether love always involves sexuality. There are obviously many valid and rewarding forms of love. I do mean to imply that mature sexual love between a man and a woman is a culmination of lesser stages of sexual development and interaction. Sex begins in the womb. Sex is present in the hazy genital sensations of infancy and in the solitary and shared sex play and explorations taking place throughout childhood and adolescence. It is present, as I hope to show, in many human interactions that may or may not be thought of as either sexual or loving. But it is what one learns about sex and how he comes to feel about it in himself and in others throughout development that determines whether and to what extent sex comes to be expressed in healthy adult heterosexual love. This particular form of love is seen as an ultimate expression of healthy sexuality. In this sense it is a goal unfortunately never achieved by a dishearteningly large number of people.

Somehow, each individual must *learn* most of the ways of acting and feeling about sex. This book deals with that "somehow"—with the constructive and destructive influences upon psychosexual development and its various outcomes.

Learning never occurs in a vacuum. Every experience becomes part of the background against which new learning takes place, influencing it in complex and often obscure ways. Every aspect of human development is dependent upon what went before, just as it is upon the uniqueness of each new experience.

To comprehend how each person becomes the particular sexual being he is, certain fundamental principles must be understood. The science tracing the influences that shape emotional development is called psychodynamics. Psychosexual development results from the interplay between external and internal forces in the continuous process of forming sexual attitudes and behavior throughout life.

The external forces are broadly termed cultural. They are exerted by parents, other adults, peer groups, religion, the media—any and every agent of influence in the environment. The inner forces are the biological pressures that impel people toward sexual expression and the psychological forces that color the response to outside influences and determine how sexuality will be expressed. The interplay between these forces follows certain basic principles and is often predictable.

The means whereby sexuality may be distorted and disrupted also follow typical patterns. Psychosexual development cannot be understood unless one understands a psychodynamic model of development and the basic principles of mental and emotional function, as well as the predictable ways in which development may be disturbed and forced into abnormal and destructive channels.

Any discussion of the normal implies the abnormal. Not all forms of sexual expression are equally reflective of normal psychosexual development. "Normality" is susceptible to so many interpretations that it is often discarded as fundamentally undefinable. While most definitions of normal merely reflect the bias of the definer, there is a bedrock of behavior for any animal species that cannot safely be violated. Such bedrock, when it can be identified, can be used as a basis for distinctions between normal and abnormal. I use two complementary criteria in the definition of sexual normality.

At the most basic biological level, normal behavior is that which best serves survival of the species and abnormal behavior is any that would threaten such survival if it were followed by the species as a whole. This definition is indeed a rock-bottom one, as only a limited gamut of behaviors would inevitably destroy *Homo sapiens.* Furthermore, there are many forms of sexual behavior—such as homosexuality, fetishism, and sexual acts between adults and children—that might well destroy mankind if followed by the majority, but do not compromise species survival when followed by a minority. How are they to be considered?

My position is that on this most biological level they cannot be regarded as normal. This position is unrelated to the causes of these variant forms of sexuality; it does not matter even whether or not their causes are known. It also implies no value judgment of good or bad nor any psychiatric consideration of healthy or sick. The fact that many people who practice the so-called sexual deviations are creative, productive, warm human beings who are at least as healthy as many of those considered nondeviant is both obvious and irrelevant; any form of sexuality that would threaten the survival of the species can be tolerated only as long as it remains a minority expression. Were it to become the behavioral norm, it would automatically be destructive and therefore, on the biological level, must be classified as abnormal. Only through the great predominance of normal sexual behavior can any species, mankind included, afford its variants.

The occurrence of certain forms of deviant sexual behavior in virtually every culture and every age is sometimes invoked as a basis for considering them normal. That, too, is irrelevant at the biological basis. Such a position would require a totally different definition of normal: Normal would have to include *every* statistically expectable variation in human development and function, such as dwarfism, congenital heart disease, impotence, pneumonia, and heterosexual brutality. There is no disorder that is not statistically expectable to some degree, but any condition that would compromise the survival of the species if it became characteristic of it can never be considered biologically normal.

The complementary definition moves a step above behavior alone and takes emotions into account. With this addition, normality may be defined as functioning in harmonious accord with design. The biological underpinnings are maintained here, too. Normality cannot be equated with what is "average," nor with what happens to be culturally or socially accepted at any particular time, nor even with what seems to "work." Innumerable forms of emotionally distorted sexual interactions—most of them occurring within heterosexual relationships—afford enough truncated or twisted pleasure to maintain themselves. They can continue to exist either because they, too, are a minority form of sexuality, or because their long-range danger to mankind is not immediately apparent. In so flexible a species as man, the tolerable limits of his sexuality may seem deceptively broad.

An aspect of our present technological culture offers an analogy. It is clearly within the scope, and therefore in accord with the design, of man's brain to produce thermonuclear destructive devices. If, however, that technological capacity were to outstrip man's emotional capacity to control the use of such devices, then the biologically fixed species norms would have been exceeded as a result of inadequate emotional maturation. The production of such devices could not be considered to have been normal for mankind if they resulted in his extinction. Thus, while his ability to destroy himself would have been in accord with his mental design, it would not have been in *harmonious* accord with the design of his species. Human harmony demands emotional maturity.

In the realm of sexuality, the concept of harmonious accord also helps to clarify issues of normality. Man's capacity for sexual arousal is nonspecific. A woman does not require a man's penis for sufficient genital stimulation to produce orgasic release. It is in accord with her design to be adequately stimulated, manually or orally, by a stream of water, a mechanical vibrator, thigh pressure—an unlimited variety of stimuli. But if, in order to be aroused, a particular woman requires that a man beat her, hurl obscenities at her, burn her with cigarettes, and urinate upon her, her prerequisites for sexual response cannot be regarded as in accord with her design, as they bear no relationship to the innate mechanisms for sexual stimulation; they expose her to various potential hazards and reveal a derangement of her pattern of arousal. Despite her willingness to accept her pattern, and even her right to do so, such a pattern could not be made to fit into the definition of normal.

This discursion into the issues of normal and abnormal is vital to the understanding of psychosexual development. It is sometimes argued that any form of sexuality is a "normal alternative style." There is also considerable unfortunate confusion between emotional disorder and social or moral "badness." Obviously, disordered development is *not* badness—but it must be recognized as disordered. Realizing the validity of this distinction is crucial. It is true that some variant forms of sexuality do little or no harm to the individual other than to limit his degree or sources of pleasure, and certainly do no harm to others. But the seeming limitlessness of man's emotional flexibility is a deceptive fantasy. Individual constriction and misery is only a part of the consequence of emotional deprivation and sexual mislearning. Sexuality and other aspects of man's emotionality and interpersonal relations are intricately woven together. When inappropriate emotional attitudes governing psychosexual development are sufficiently widespread, society as a whole is threatened by the resultant loss of human warmth and involvement.

How Emotional Learning Takes Place

The mind begins to develop before birth. Normal prenatal development involves various hormonally induced influences upon portions of the fetal brain. These influences prepare the brain to mediate and to express certain attitudes and behavior in later life while inhibiting others. Therefore, part of an infant's *biological* endowment is a particular quality of mind. The newborn is equipped with a mind that is already prepared for appropriate sexual learning.

The biological organism is born into a cultural environment. From the moment of birth, biology and culture influence the infant's development. Biology includes the inborn needs and drives, the genetic endowment, the innate pattern of physical and mental unfolding that are part of the infant's body—all that needs *not* to be learned. Some of the biological drives undergo modifications as the person grows. If he is free of biological defects, his biological development, including the development of his physical drives and desires, will follow certain patterns relatively independent of environmental influence. That is to say, healthy humans everywhere have the same basic biology; they are a single species.

By culture is meant that body of customs, rules, laws, mores, beliefs, social forms, and institutions common to the society into which an infant is born. These shared traditions form the environment out of which come the external influences that are the principal source of the infant's learning.

During the earliest period of life, environment principally means "mother," or the mothering person. She, or her surrogate, is the agent of cultural influence, and is the only part of the cultural environment that counts to the newborn. His senses are too poorly developed to register much beyond immediate physical sensations and ministrations. Initially, a mother's demands upon the infant may be very few, but they are never truly absent. He is never fed simply because he feels hungry. He must indicate hunger, a compromise with the environment's demand that he communicate his need. In addition, he must come to terms with the fact that his mother may be asleep, or his bottle may not be ready, or his mother believes his hunger should be satisfied according to a special schedule. As he grows older, he finds more and more need to compromise between his demands upon the environment and the environment's demands upon him. Either he successfully gets what he needs or some of his needs are neglected, and his development as a happy or a fussy or troubled infant follows almost directly. And just as there are differences between mothers, so there are differences between infants. Though all infants must be fed, there are variations in less basic biological factors, such as stomach size, metabolism, and susceptibility to illness. And culture (mediated through the mother as its agent) is infinitely variable.

The constant interactions between biology and culture produce most of the individual differences between infants in their very early development, but soon—almost from the beginning—a third determinant assumes an importance which increases with time. The infant begins to learn from his very earliest experiences. As soon as learning begins, that which is learned is used to help determine how to respond the next time. Research on infants corroborates what every mother can observe: babies begin to learn within the first week or two.

One example is that how often boy infants smile depends upon how their mothers handle them and how often the mothers smile—the smile on the part of a baby boy is not simply a spasm of facial muscles unrelated to the environment. Some newborn boys learn to smile more quickly than others.

Somewhat later, the infant who learns that it can bury its head in mother's breast and be comforted will seek the same comfort when distressed in various ways. That which has been learned develops into a preexisting attitude to be applied to future situations. From earliest infancy, the developing human does its best never to react to anything as though it were entirely new, whether it is a new demand from the environment (to control his bowels, or to leave his mother and go off to school) or a new drive from within (to say "no" instead of "yes" all the time, or the desire to enjoy the newfound pleasure of rubbing the genitals). Whether consciously or unconsciously, the child calls upon past experience and learning to help determine the most effective way of reacting or behaving or thinking in each new situation.

In addition to the three forces that determine the direction of human development—biological drives, cultural pressures, and the attitudes formed by previous learning—there are three particular qualities of the learning experience that are worth noting. The first is that most learning occurs in completely informal circumstances when neither the learner nor the teacher knows it is going on. Intellectual learning may often be purposeful, but emotional learning seldom is. The learning of attitudes, of what is acceptable and what is not, of how others feel as opposed to what they say, goes on constantly and nonverbally. It evolves from a look, a tone of voice, a silence, an implication from choice of words, the observation of behavior that may be contradictory to a stated attitude—all the omnipresent cues that appear in daily human relationships. It is this aspect of learning that most influences sexuality.

Another significant quality of the learning experience is the existence of critical periods. A critical period is a biologically determined time span during development when an organism is uniquely ready to respond to a specific set of influences with a new maturational achievement. In the instance of specific kinds of learning, it is the time when the individual's maximum capacities—motor, sensory, motivational, and pyschological—are not only present for the first time, but will never again be so ideally combined to facilitate that increment of learning.[1] Prior to the time of the critical period, those same influences would have little effect. After the critical period, whatever has been learned is exceedingly difficult to unlearn.

One can only be tentative about this aspect of learning, but the importance of critical periods has been amply demonstrated in the lower species and evidence is accumulating that such special learning readiness times exist for humans. One example is language readiness. A child will develop its language habits and usage between the ages of two and four. If exposed to a multilingual environment at that time, the child will easily and unselfconsciously become multilingual. After that period, learning to speak differently or learning to think in another language is typically difficult and time-consuming.

Research is scanty in the area of delineating the critical ages in children for the learning of various sexual attitudes, but it is probably a more important factor in the learning process than has been generally recognized.

The third peculiarity of human learning is that what one has truly incorporated into the depth of his being is the strongest and most determinative of the various influences. While cultural and social forces usually determine the broad outlines of what one learns, their influence is not always direct. The younger the child, the more his socialization is mediated through his parents. With the exception of the nonconforming minority, parents generally reflect the culture and function as its agents, but each parent and each family and each little neighborhood minisociety is different from every other, and these differences are what produce individuality. Once this unique combination of individual and culturally shared learning begins to take place, what has been learned can, and often does, become more powerful than either biological pressures or subsequent cultural influence.

The Principles by Which the Mind Functions.

Certain fundamental functional principles can be shown to exist in everyone. What research there is into the deeper subtleties of the operation of the mind and its emotions lends support to these concepts. Without an appreciation of them, much of human behavior is incomprehensible, and the process of psychosexual development cannot be made intelligible.

All human behavior is motivated. There is no true coincidence in anything that anyone—infant, child, or adult—does or says or thinks or feels. Every action or thought has a motive and a goal, often several, however much it may appear to have happened by chance, and whether the person involved is aware of it or not.

For instance, a four-and-a-half-year-old boy "happens" to have nightmares and runs to the safety of his parents' bed—but only on those nights when his father, who travels a lot, is home. At this boy's period of development, he is envious of his mother's attentions to his father and wants to disrupt their peaceful privacy. He may not have any conscious idea of his motive, but his unwitting remarks may reveal that such is indeed the unconscious purpose of his nightmares.

The concept of unconscious thought processes is a major principle of mental function. The vast bulk of mental activities exist and remain largely outside of conscious awareness.

Memory demonstrates one level of the unconscious. It is manifestly impossible to be simultaneously aware of current experiences and of one's whole storehouse of information, yet information can usually be brought into consciousness as needed. Hypnotism demonstrates a deeper level of the unconscious. In spite of every effort to remember, a person may not be able to recall whether or not he had a birthday party when he was five. But under hypnosis he may remember not only that there was a party but who came, what presents they brought, and even what flavor of ice cream was served.

The unconscious has other uses besides the storage of excess information. It is characteristic of the mind to wish to forget any incident or thought that is unacceptable in any way—anything that produces anxiety. The process of making oneself unaware of emotionally painful material is called repression. Once a thought or feeling is repressed, it is impossible to bring it to consciousness by any purposeful effort.

The repressed material, however, does not disappear. The fact that it is now unconscious makes getting rid of it impossible. One can reevaluate and modify, even discard, a conscious attitude or idea on the basis of further experience and increased knowledge, but repressed mental contents remain inaccessible to modification. The conscious mind does not even admit they exist.

The significance of unconscious material lies in its ability to influence subsequent character and behavior regardless of how inappropriate that influence may be. A boy with a harsh, authoritarian father may be afraid to defy him; rage toward such a father would be dangerous, and in addition the boy would often feel guilty over his rage. Consciously he may believe his father to be infallible and righteous, deserving only of deference, but the unconscious rage is not neutralized and the boy manages to retaliate through subtle means, while remaining outwardly compliant. For example, he can disappoint his father's expectations of him by failing in school. And unless some fortuitous experiences with other important males make it possible for him to modify this self-defeating behavior, he may continue this pattern through life, suffering

repeated job failures as each successive employer elicits from him
the old combination of superficial ingratiation and retaliative
incompetence motivated by his repressed rage.

The fact that all behavior is motivated despite unawareness of the
motivation poses a problem for the rational part of the mind.
Actions or attitudes that are unconsciously motivated are not the
considered results of rational, logical thought. But people are
generally made uneasy when they are confronted by something in
themselves that has no rational basis. The mind normally wants a
logical reason for its emotions and attitudes, and this need prompts
it to seek acceptable explanations. Regardless of the fact that a
particular emotional attitude or pattern of behavior existed long
before it was consciously recognized, a subsequent superimposed
explanation may come to be regarded as the prior "reason." This
process is called rationalization. The individual deludes himself into
believing that his later, conscious reasons came first and led in
logical manner to his actually preexisting attitudes and actions. It is
not always possible to credit at face value the explanations people
offer for their sexual behavior, as their "reasons" are often
rationalizations.

An extremely important role in mental life is played by fantasy.
Fantasy springs from the realm of the unconscious. Dreams,
daydreams, and reveries are fantasies. Some fantasies may occur
consciously (such as daydreams), some may originally have been
conscious (perhaps fleetingly) and then repressed, and others may
never have emerged into consciousness at all.

Fantasies are the dramatizations of wishes, fears, and efforts to
cope with conflicts. They are closely related to emotions that are
often unconscious. A mother who unconsciously resents her young
daughter may develop the persistent, distressing fantasy that the girl
will be kidnapped on the way to or from school. The fantasy
represents both her wish to be rid of the girl and her guilty fear that
the wish, unacceptable to her conscience, may come true.

A major importance of fantasy lies in its reality value. Were
fantasies always conscious and always recognized as pure imagination, they would not exert so important an effect upon the mind.
But unconscious fantasies, particularly those of childhood, take on
the value of reality. The mind responds, and the person behaves, as
though the fantasy were fact. This is not a peculiarity of emotional

disturbance, but a normal characteristic of mental function due to the nature of the unconscious: that which is unconscious cannot be evaluated or easily corrected.

Because of the reality value of fantasy much emotional development is shaped not by what actually happened but by what was persistently fantasized and believed to be true. A toddler may so resent his new sister that he wishes she did not even exist. If she gets sick and dies, he may believe his wishes killed her, because his mind still functions on a magical level. He is too young to understand the real reason for her death and will feel as guilty as if he had actually killed her. Because he is likely to repress the unbearable thought of wishing her dead, his intense feeling of guilt may persist indefinitely. It is just such irrational guilt that prompts many of the false confessions that are made when a murder is committed.

On another level of fantasy, a girl with strict morals may wish for sexual intercourse with an attractive man. Such a wish may be so unacceptable to her that she never becomes consciously aware of it and cannot understand why she feels just as sinful and ashamed as if she had actually had an affair. The reality value of fantasy adds in no small measure to the complexity of understanding emotional development.

In the process of development, a person may become fixated at an early stage. Clinically significant fixation occurs for either of two opposite reasons—deprivation (the child has not had enough of his necessary needs met in a given phase to permit development into the next phase) or overgratification (the child finds such complete satisfaction in a given phase that it seems preferable to remain right where he is rather than move on and give up the existing pleasures).

An example of fixation through deprivation is the unwanted and unloved infant who never grows out of the search for a loving mother and whose relationship with everyone is characterized by an infantile longing to be nurtured and cared for. Fixation by overgratification is exemplified by the spoiled child who invariably gets everything he wants. He never learns that he must eventually earn what he wants but continues to act as though he need only demand and his wants will be granted.

When serious fixation occurs, progression to the next developmental stage is either delayed or prevented. An excessively obedient teenager who continues to accept parental authority like an eight- or nine-year-old is obviously fixated. Fixation can also operate subtly: A youngster may appear to outgrow and pass over a disturbed phase into the next one, seemingly making a good adjustment, but perceptive observation of such a youngster will reveal that his emotions are operating at an earlier level. Under stress, his false adjustment will often deteriorate and he will display emotions and behavior characteristic of the phase at which his maturation foundered.

Regression is one of the most important and fascinating characteristics of mental functioning, and it is not always an expression of emotional disorder. During childhood, there is no steady maturational progression in which every newly acquired capacity is permanent, with never any slipping back to prior modes. There are many conditions and periods of life when some regression is normal in the healthiest of people. The normal pattern of maturation involves gaining, then losing, and then gaining again, over and over, each new step in the control of drives, the mastery of oneself, and relations with others. Stress in childhood will intensify regressive tendencies.

It is probably true that no stage of development is ever completely outgrown. To some degree, in every significant phase of life there are always some unfulfilled needs or never-to-be-repeated gratifications that are capable of exerting an emotional pull under conditions of stress or lowered control. Illness, great danger, deprivation—any of the exigencies of life may be accompanied by a return to earlier techniques of coping or of seeking sources of comfort.

The crucial consideration in regression is whether it is temporary or permanent. Temporary regressions are usually insignificant during the developmental years and even in adulthood if they can be correlated with some understandable precipitating circumstance. When development is truly deficient at some stage so that genuine further maturation is effectively crippled, regression may become lasting. It is then evidence of psychiatric disturbance.

The ego is that part of one's mental equipment concerned with the perception of reality and the adaptation to reality—the part most involved in purposeful learning, judgment, decision making, and coping. It is with the capacities of one's ego that one strives to maintain a healthy balance between inner needs and drives and the demands of practical and social reality.

The newborn infant's ego is rudimentary. Ego development takes place as a result of both innate and external influences. There is an innate, though somewhat variable, timetable by which increasingly complex ego capacities unfold. These include thought, perception, the capacity to distinguish fantasy from reality, and a multitude of functions relating to the mastery of oneself and the environment. The rate and quality of ego development depends most heavily upon the learning experiences to which all children are exposed. The growing child's ability to cope effectively with himself and his world is shaped fundamentally by what he learns from his parents and, later, from all other significant interactions. The results of healthy or faulty ego development at every point in one's life history can be seen in the broad sweep of sexual adaptations and maladaptations.

A final vital principle of emotional development is the inevitability of conflict. One kind of conflict arises inescapably in the normal clash between the child's immature and heedless drives and society's responsibility to protect his well-being and to help him learn appropriate and adaptive behavior. Perhaps even more important is that type of conflict which is entirely internal, representing opposing and incompatible drives. The toddler's need for parental love and approval runs headlong into his intense drive for self-determination. Since total permissiveness at such an age would entail a grave threat to the toddler's survival, not even the most sensitive mother can keep these two normal needs from being to some extent irreconcilable. Such stress does not arise out of a conflict between the child and other persons; both the need for love and the need for autonomy are normal and arise within the child, and there is no way that both can be fully gratified simultaneously.

Certain periods throughout the life cycle, from birth to death, impose unique and heightened strain upon human emotions. At such times breakdown of function frequently occurs and symptoms of emotional disorder may surface. But the growth potential of conflict is equally impressive. It is out of the forge of normal developmental conflict that many important facets of ego mastery and character structure are formed. Emotional conflict can be unnecessary and damaging, or it can be natural and beneficent, but it cannot be eliminated from human development. A belief in either the desirability or the possibility of conflict-free child rearing is the result of an inadequate understanding of the developmental process. The misguided efforts by parents to relieve their children of conflict result in emotionally crippled adults.

How Disturbances Develop

It is not possible to trace the influences affecting the course of human sexual development without taking cognizance of the ways in which faulty learning compromises healthy sexuality. Emotional disorder need not be mysterious. Whenever pain, fear, rage, or guilt becomes associated with a healthy mental or physical expression, the groundwork is laid for disturbed development.

This understanding of emotional disorder emerged from a blending of psychoanalytic discoveries and the concept of emergency behavior, first described in animals. Emergency behavior is an organism's response to what it perceives as a threat. Either immediate danger or the anticipation of danger initiates a complex series of hormonal and physiological changes which ready the body to cope.[2] One change is a sharp increase in the amount of adrenalin in the bloodstream, which registers in the brain as a warning sense of anxiety and elicits an emotional response of either fear or rage. These, along with the related feeling of guilt, are the emergency emotions. They prompt emergency behavior, designed to cope with the perceived danger either by preventing it or by repairing any damage suffered from it. A basic principle in the organization of behavior is that the emergency functions take precedence over all other functions in the interest of survival. No matter what other interests engage an organism, emergency coping behavior will take over as soon as danger is perceived.[3]

Humans share this automatic emergency system with other animals that have adrenal glands, but for animals in their natural environment the system is triggered only by genuinely life-threatening dangers. For humans, primitive biological cues such as physical pain, sudden noises, or falling have but limited usefulness. While pain and falling usually signal some degree of real threat, noises generally do not.

Human newborns are equipped with minimal instinctual endowment with which to adapt and survive. They must be taught what to regard as either dangerous or safe; the potential for mislearning is unlimited. There are two basic kinds of mislearning which produce maladaptive behavior: Fear or rage may be aroused by circumstances that are not realistically threatening, and genuine threats to emotional or physical integrity may not be recognized as such. Sexual development most frequently goes awry through learning to react with fear or anger to circumstances that are normal and harmless. Masturbation and childhood sexual curiosity are two examples. Most such mislearning occurs during childhood, but inappropriate associations between emergency emotions and normal functions may continue to be forged throughout life.

The significance of this concept of emotional conflict lies in the fact that the danger need not be real—the person need only believe that it is real. To someone who believes in ghosts, a graveyard at night can be as terrifying as being trapped in a burning building. A child is at the mercy of what he learns, because of his ignorance and inability to fight back against misconceptions.

Parents or other people important in a child's life may so strenuously disapprove of certain expressions of sexuality that he becomes afraid they will reject him and he will lose their love if he expresses his sexual feelings. There is no more serious and genuine threat to a child, since love and acceptance are indispensable to him. His natural sexual drive and his sexual curiosity are usually so strong that he also becomes very angry at his parents for interfering with their expression. But rage, too, is dangerous; it carries the unendurable threat of loss of love. His rage and fear both become inappropriately associated with his sexual feelings so that subsequently all sexual feelings evoke a response related to danger.

As a child internalizes the attitudes and prohibitions of his parents, he learns to disapprove of the same things in himself that were unacceptable to them. He comes to regard himself as someone bad and unlovable as a result of his perfectly normal sexual feelings. Consequently guilt arises whenever he feels a sexual urge or engages in sexual activity. In this manner, guilt joins fear and anger as an emergency emotion which mobilizes emergency behavior.

An example of a serious mental disorder that reflects misdirected emergency behavior related to sexuality and inappropriately associated with a normal function is the illness anorexia nervosa, pathological fear of eating. Eating is obviously not only normal but essential to life. Certain typical childhood fantasies lead children to believe that intercourse and pregnancy involve taking the penis and semen into the mouth and stomach. This fantasy may become inappropriately and unconsciously associated with normal eating. If guilt over sexual desire is great enough (most typically in girls), a young woman may develop anorexia nervosa. This emotional disorder is sometimes so severe that death from starvation results.

Conflicts that are usually a part of normal development may sometimes result in inappropriate reactions—some perfectly normal drives or fantasies may arouse such painful emotions that a person is prompted to undertake defensive measures against them. The toddler who wishes his baby sister dead is such an example. His parents may have no idea of what is going on in his mind and are thus unable to help him overcome his guilt.

Emergency emotions may evoke a wide variety of emergency behavior; any of the mechanisms of defense may be called into play to ward off whatever is perceived as danger. A boy may repress his sexual curiosity and subsequently enter into a marriage with no understanding of his wife's needs—or even of her anatomy. A woman may inhibit her capacity for sexual pleasure out of guilt over sexual desire, or she may rush into repeated disastrous liaisons in the hope that constant exposure to sex will relieve her fear. Some women who had ample reason as children to hate a genuinely punitive and overbearing father may displace their hatred onto all men and mistrust those who wish a close relationship. Often men so fear their normal affection for other men that they deny all feeling and regard any show of tenderness as homosexual. They may even project their own desire for a natural male closeness onto other men and come to imagine that homosexuals pose a personal threat to them.

In time, such complex mental responses become automatic. Their origins are repressed; the motivation behind the defense becomes unconscious. Even the specific conditions which trigger the maladaptive behavior may not register clearly in awareness. Every time the normal thought, attitude, wish, or act occurs, it elicits anxiety so that either constriction of sexuality or inappropriate sexual behavior becomes incorporated into one's character and personality.

The other source of sexual disturbance—ignoring conditions that are genuinely detrimental—is somewhat less common. It often accompanies the kinds of maladaptive behavior already described. The woman who rushes into one unsuitable affair after another is an example. In the effort to rid herself of her unreasoning fear of sex, she ignores the evidences of unsuitability in the men she chooses— signs that healthier women would recognize at once.

In other instances, disturbed sexuality may come about without conflict or distress. A child may learn to respond with pleasure to experiences that will ultimately harm him. Male transsexualism, a condition in which a male believes himself to be a female trapped by a mistake of nature in the wrong body, sometimes develops in this manner. Some mothers keep their male babies constantly and abnormally close to their own nude bodies for hours, days, even months. This sometimes produces no fear or rage or guilt in the infant; it is perfectly pleasureful, but it compromises or destroys the boy's ability during this critical early period to differentiate himself from his mother as a separate individual with his own appropriate body and male sexual identity.[4]

None of these developmental influences take place in isolation. Everything of significance to a human being ultimately proceeds from and involves his relationships with other people. Initially he learns what is accepted and rewarded, and what is disapproved and punished, from his mother and immediate family. Later, the role of "important others" expands widely. Whether healthy or disturbed, development is an expression of interpersonal relationships. Even the pressure of biological drives, and the distressing inner fantasies, are only felt as threatening in terms of their consequences. Consequences inevitably are measured against security and survival in a world of other people, for a child's very survival is impossible in total isolation.

The results of developmental influences are never static. The earliest influences of childhood are more important than any others, and they come very close to being indelible. But these globally perceived influences seldom express themselves in unchangeable ways. They lead to specific character structures and limitations which constantly renew themselves in interactions with others. Even repetitive, self-defeating behavior that represents an early fixation is not a mere mechanical echo of the past. It achieves a new and current reality each time it occurs and produces the predictable results which in turn reinforce it. It is this unending, shifting, dynamic equilibrium between the individual and his human environment that holds out the possibility of change for those crippled by earlier relationships. Positive and constructive relationships can often help repair the damage.

The First Cycle

ONE

Life in the Womb

The fetus floating unselfconsciously in the nirvana of its uterine fortress is not immune to the beginnings of sexual development. Innate biological mechanisms begin almost immediately to differentiate the early embryo into male or female. These earliest biochemical influences may have surprisingly far-reaching effects.

This differentiation is the earliest expression of sexual development. From embryonic beginnings the two sexes take somewhat divergent paths. That a large part of psychosexual development is shared by both males and females will be increasingly clear. But it must not be assumed at the outset that there are no natural differences.

During intrauterine life, it is possible to observe the isolated, uncomplicated operation of the biological vector. Neither culture nor previous learning has any place at this stage. Even the mother's emotional states and attitudes, which will deeply affect her baby after it is born, can now make themselves felt only through biological channels.

This is an interesting subject in itself. There can be no question that a mother's emotional states can be communicated to the fetus she is carrying. Many, if not all, emotions are reflected in changes in blood-borne hormones and other chemicals, which can cross through the placenta into the bloodstream of the fetus. Stress in particular produces body chemistry changes which, if sustained, ultimately alter and disorder many vital functions. A fetus is subject to all the same biochemical influences as its mother whenever she is under stress, whether occasionally or chronically. It has been shown with experimental animals that the adrenal glands of the fetus also respond to stress. The fetus is, therefore, subjected both to its own and to maternal hormones.

Among the reports of research into the effects of maternal stress on the fetus there has been little if any investigation of its influence in humans on the child's later sexual behavior. But one interesting experiment upon rats suggests a possible association between stress

25

and the subsequent sexuality of the affected fetuses. When pregnant rats were subjected to high levels of stressful conditions during the critical period of sexual differentiation, the males born to them were rendered permanently less able to perform normal male sexual behavior, and more prone to respond with female behavior. Severe stress at other times in the developmental history of the rats did not similarly derange their normal sexual behavior patterns.[1]

Rats are not people. It is not possible to make direct application to humans of results obtained in experimenting with laboratory animals. Rats are, nonetheless, surprisingly comparable in many physiological responses and functions. In general, a major difference (other than gross appearance) between lower mammals and humans is in the degree to which postnatal learning modifies the ready-made instinctual patterns that are the newborn's biological endowment at birth. The more highly developed the brain—specifically, the cerebral cortex—the more learning will take precedence over innate patterns. In man, the preeminent influence of learning reaches its presently known peak. But human newborns are not without innate biological endowment, and animal experimentation has often suggested to researchers where to look for better understanding of the complex behavior of mankind.

Sexual Anatomy Begins to Differentiate

The subject matter of sexual differentiation during fetal development is enormously complex.[2] When conception occurs, the future maleness or femaleness of the conceived fetus is fairly well determined under ordinary conditions of unimpaired healthy development. The sex chromosomes of a female are designated XX (female genotype), and those of a male XY (male genotype). Each ovum of the mother contains only one of her sex chromosomes, but since her chromosomes are both the same, every ovum contains one X chromosome. Each of the father's sperm also contains only one of his two sex chromosomes. In his case, half the sperm will contain an X chromosome and the other half a Y. If an androsperm (Y-bearing sperm) fertilizes the ovum, the conceptus has an XY sex chromosome pair, and is destined to be male; if a gynosperm (X-bearing sperm) effects fertilization, a female will normally develop.

But there are many surprises in store for anyone who assumes that sexual differentiation is so simply settled. The fact is that for about its first six weeks of life, the human fetus is totally undifferentiated except for the existence of XX or XY sex chromosomes in the nuclei of its cells. And in spite of the genotype every human embryo is programmed by some unknown mechanism to develop as a female. Male development occurs only if specific and delicately timed influences intervene to preclude female differentiation.

The sex chromosomes appear to determine only whether ovaries or testes are formed. In an embryo with the male genotype, testes begin to develop at about six weeks, and very soon thereafter begin to produce androgen, the major and most potent male sex hormone. In the absence of a Y chromosome testes do not form, and if the embryo has the full female complement of two X chromosomes, ovaries begin to develop distinctly later, sometime around the twelfth week.

Therefore, it is not accurate to describe the human embryo as totally bipotential—having the ability to become either a complete male or a complete female. An embryo cannot survive unless its cells contain at least one X chromosome, so that it has no real "choice" of whether it will have ovaries, testes, or nothing. But in other aspects of maleness or femaleness, it can differentiate in either direction.

Once the sex chromosomes have determined which kind of gonad develops, their influence ends. Further sexual differentiation of the fetus appears to be controlled by the presence or absence of androgen produced by fetal testes. This is a major point. Female anatomy and sex organs (other than ovaries) will inevitably develop if there is no fetal androgen, regardless of whether or not there are any fetal ovaries and circulating female sex hormones. Apparently, the mother's sex hormones, which of course are also in the fetal circulation, are not necessary to bring about the growth of female structures. Experiments have been conducted in which the Müllerian ducts (those primitive embryonic structures that later form some of the female internal sex organs) were removed from very young embryos before differentiation had begun. They were kept alive in the laboratory in nutrient solutions free of any hormones, and still exhibited differentiation in the female direction.

It is in the differentiation of male or female anatomy that the principle of critical periods first comes into play. This concept, previously discussed in its psychological dimension as insecurely validated, is firmly established in its application to sequences of biological maturation. Especially during fetal life, with its rapid series of crucial differentiations of tissues, structures, and organs, any given increment of development must successfully take place during a specific and relatively brief time span if it is to occur at all. Prior to the critical period for each specific maturational step, the organism lacks the requisite readiness to proceed and cannot achieve it regardless of circumstances. After the critical period it is too late, for whatever did or did not occur during that period is then irreversible. The critical periods for various developmental sequences follow a biologically set and inflexible timetable, different in the various species. In some instances the critical period may be as short as a few days.

The timing or duration in the human fetus of the critical period for the differentiation of anatomical sex is not known with absolute certainty. It extends from some time after the sixth week (whenever fetal testes begin to produce androgen) until the twelfth week or shortly thereafter. During those few short weeks male sex organs will begin to form if there is androgen from the fetal testes. In the absence of such androgen, female sexual anatomy will start its growth. The female differentiation begins without any signal from fetal ovarian hormones, since those ovaries do not begin to form until around the twelfth week; naturally, this portion of sexual anatomy can only begin to develop during this time, when the fetus is only about 2.5 inches long. But whichever growth pattern—male or female—is initiated during this critical period, it will continue unalterably from then on. It cannot be interrupted or reversed, even if the hormones to which the fetus is exposed are changed, and it proceeds independently of the sex chromosomes of the fetus.

The consideration of what might happen were fetal hormones to go askew during this critical period is not purely theoretical, nor is the knowledge of the aberrations which occur. In many laboratory animals, including rats, rabbits, hamsters, guinea pigs, and various species of monkeys, experiments confirm this principle of basic female differentiation unless androgen initiates the male direction.

In one experimental approach the androgen effect is removed from genetic (XY) male fetuses, either by removing the fetal testes before the critical period by means of delicate microsurgery or by giving the mother an antiandrogen, a chemical which has been proved to neutralize the effects of androgen on all tissues of the body. In such experiments, despite the male genotype, the male fetuses were born with typical female genitalia and internal sex organs, except of course ovaries, which could not develop in the absence of the XX genotype.

Another series of experiments focuses on the opposite effect— exposing female fetuses to androgen during the critical period. The administration of androgen to pregnant animals results in male anatomical development and inhibits the growth of most of the female anatomical structures. Such female offspring have normal-appearing penises and genitalia, naturally without testes.

These same results may occur in humans. While such experiments are not known to have been purposefully conducted upon human fetuses, natural disorders of development that mimic the conditions of experiment sometimes occur. One is a condition called Turner's syndrome, in which the conceptus begins growth with only one X chromosome. It is therefore genetically neither male nor female, and as a fetus forms neither testes nor ovaries. Consequently, its condition is similar to that of a male fetus whose testes were removed before the critical period, except that it has an X instead of an XY genotype. Turner's syndrome usually carries with it other deformities and abnormal conditions not directly related to sex. But in terms of external genitalia and sex organs babies born with it resemble normal girls without ovaries.

Some children are conceived with an inherent defect which renders the cells of their bodies unable to respond to androgen. This developmental disorder, known as the androgen insensitivity syndrome (also called the testicular feminizing syndrome) is the naturally occurring human equivalent of a male fetus that had been subjected to an antiandrogen chemical during the critical period. Such children have a normal male XY genotype; at six weeks they develop testes which begin on schedule to produce fetal androgen and continue to function normally thereafter. But their bodies cannot respond to the androgen and they differentiate sexually as though none were present. In cases in which the condition is present in its fully developed form, the babies are born as normal-looking girls. They have no penis or scrotum, and the clitoris and labia appear normal, yet they have undescended but function-ing testes instead of ovaries. They lack uterus, fallopian tubes, and vagina because a separate chemical substance produced normally by their testes during fetal life inhibited the development of those organs.

There are also disorders that result when female fetuses are exposed to androgen. One is called the adrenogenital syndrome, in which an inborn defect results in the overproduction of androgen by the adrenal cortex of the female fetus. A similar condition was observed to result from a medical procedure, no longer used, in which substances that could have an androgenic action were given to a mother early in pregnancy to prevent a threatened spontaneous abortion. In both conditions, depending upon the intensity of androgen exposure throughout the critical period of sexual differen-tiation, the girls are born with genitals that look like those of a boy. In the most severe instances, the clitoris was enlarged to the size of a normal infant penis, and the labia were fused, looking like a scrotum into which the testes have not descended. The internal organs, including ovaries, were those of a girl, because the ovaries developed normally as a result of the XX chromosomes and there were no fetal testes to produce the substance that inhibited the growth of the uterus, tubes, and vagina. In these cases the action of androgen during the critical period interfered with female anatomi-cal differentiation, producing male external anatomy instead.

The capacity of the human embryo to develop either male or female anatomy is due to the fact that all embryos have the primitive tissue from which the organs of each sex may be formed. (The exception must be reemphasized: the embryo has only XX or XY chromosomes, and no known circumstances following concep-tion can cause an XX embryo to develop testes or an XY embryo to develop a vagina.) For some sex organs, there are two sets of embryonic structures in all normal fetuses. The Müllerian ducts form female organs and, if they go on to full development, will become the uterus, fallopian tubes, and the upper two-thirds of the vagina. The other embryonic structures, the Wolffian ducts, eventu-ally form the vas deferens, seminal vesicles, and ejaculatory ducts. If the fetus is a male and has developed normal testes, the Müllerian ducts will vestigiate during the third month of fetal life. Their disappearance is believed due to a separate substance, not androgen, produced by the testes. In a female fetus the Wolffian ducts vestigiate during the same period, though the mechanism that causes it is not known.

The external sex organs of males and females develop from the same embryonic tissue rather than from separate structures. Until the fetus is six to eight weeks old, the embryonic genitals of both sexes are identical. There is a genital tubercle behind which is a slit-like opening, the urogenital groove. Immediately on either side are the urogenital folds, and on either side of them are longitudinal swellings, the genital or labioscrotal swellings. In the male, as a result of the action of androgen, the genital tubercle enlarges and becomes the penis. The urogenital folds fuse together enclosing the urethra along the underside of the penis. The genital swellings also come together in the midline and form the scrotum, into which the testes will later descend. These changes are quite evident by the tenth week. The urogenital folds have completely closed over the penile urethra by the twelfth week.

In the female, in the absence of androgen effect, the genital tubercle becomes the clitoris. The urogenital groove remains open, forming the entrance to the vagina. The urogenital folds remain in place as the labia minora, and the labioscrotal swellings increase in size to form the labia majora. These, of course, are the identical structures which respond to androgen by differentiation into male genitalia.

Differentiation in the Brain

Portions of the brain, like the rest of the anatomy, differentiate as male or female during fetal life. Generally speaking, sex-specific brain differences affect two separate areas of later sexuality: hormonal and behavioral.

The elaboration and control of sex hormones is a highly complex and incompletely understood biochemical mechanism in mammals, involving both the central nervous system and endocrine glands, including ovaries, testes, and the adrenal and pituitary glands. Various portions of the brain are implicated in the regulation of sexuality, the most basic of which is the hypothalamus. Research has demonstrated that this portion of the brain is perhaps the crucial center for the integration of emotions and body functions. Sexuality is but one of many areas of human activity mediated through the hypothalamus.

One of its functions is the regulation of sex hormone production and release. In sexually mature female mammals, the ovarian sex hormones (estrogen and progesterone) are elaborated on a cyclic or alternating schedule. This is reflected in estrus or "heat" cycles in lower mammals and in the menstrual cycles of human females. In sexually mature males, the testicular hormone androgen is produced steadily or acyclically, without comparable biologically programmed regular alternations. The hypothalamus accomplishes this through its control of the pituitary gland (hypophysis). The pituitary produces hormones (gonadotrophic hormones) which stimulate the ovaries or testes to produce their appropriate sex hormones. By controlling the pituitary elaboration of gonadotrophic hormones, the hypothalamus regulates the cyclic or acyclic production of sex hormones.

During the same critical period for anatomical sexual differentiation, the developing fetal hypothalamus of either sex is organized so that it will ultimately exercise its regulatory function either cyclically in the mature female or acyclically in the mature male. The biological mechanism for hypothalamic differentiation is the same. In the absence of effective fetal androgen during the critical period, the hypothalamus will subsequently mediate the female pattern of cyclic sex hormone production. In the presence of fetal androgen effect, the hypothalamus is organized for the male acyclic hormone pattern. This is the "inductor" effect of androgen, which operates during the fetal critical period. The type of hypothalamic organization induced by the presence or absence of fetal androgen remains quiescent until puberty. At that time, the presence of adult amounts of male or female sex hormones exert a "releaser" effect upon the hypothalamus, stimulating and releasing it to function in the manner in which it was organized during fetal development.

In lower mammals, the fetal organization of the hypothalamus is irreversible, even when experimentally induced to function inappropriately. Genetic females subjected to androgen during the critical period will produce sex hormones acyclically, and will not have estrus cycles. The hypothalamus of genetic males deprived of androgen effect will function cyclically.

In humans, the derangements produced by fetal endocrine

abnormalities show greater flexibility and do not appear to be irreversible. Girls born with the adrenogenital syndrome do not menstruate at puberty if the condition of excess androgen has not been corrected. But when corrected by proper treatment, the hypothalami of such girls are capable of functioning cyclically, and the girls will menstruate normally.

It is the prenatally organized brain's influence upon later behavior that is of most interest in understanding the normal development of sexual emotions and activity. Here, too, the evidence is more clear-cut in the lower mammals, in which innate biological mechanisms play a greater, and postnatal learning a lesser, role.

In the service of normal procreation, male and female animals must naturally behave in different, sex-specific and sex-appropriate ways toward each other. Females must present themselves in such a manner that copulation is possible and must accept male mounting. Males must desire to copulate, must know how to mount, and must be capable of both copulation and ejaculation. In addition, other actions, such as courtship behavior specific to each sex, signal sexual interest and readiness to the potential partner. Courtship behavior also helps to elicit the appropriate responses from the opposite sex so as to make copulation possible. Further sex-specific behavior includes definite maternal and nurturing behavior that insures survival of the offspring, and, in some species, paternal behavior as well.

In all the lower mammals investigated, each species displays a distinct and separate repertoire of courtship and mating behaviors that are different for the two sexes. This sex-specific behavior is not mutually exclusive. A certain amount of the female pattern may be expressed by males, and a certain amount of the male pattern by females. But mating behavior is never randomly expressed by either sex. Under normal circumstances, the male pattern is usually rare in females and vice versa; an innate and invariable distinction is that a sexual response is more readily elicited to the opposite sex than to the same sex.

Experiments reveal that when genetic males are deprived of the effects of androgen, they display at maturity predominantly the female pattern of mating behavior and sometimes do not display male sex behavior at all. When they do attempt to function as males, their actions lack instinctual sureness. Their behavior is disorganized or incomplete, they mount faultily, and they are incapable of completing the act. Normal males respond to these feminized animals as though they were females. Normal amounts of androgen administered at any time after the critical period are characteristically ineffective as a means of restoring maleness.

Androgenized females show a corresponding shift toward male mating patterns. In addition to all the analogous reversals described for males, their instinctual maternal behavior is adversely affected. If by some means (often artificial) they are made to conceive, they show an abnormally high rate of unsuccessful pregnancies. They do not seem to know how to care for offspring and may destroy those that survive.

Differential behavior in the direct service of procreation and survival of offspring expresses distinctions of maleness and femaleness. Among the subhuman primates, in which evolution has provided increasingly large cerebral cortices and among which, therefore, learned behavior plays an ever expanding role, there also develops an additional dimension of sex-specific behavior—the social dimension. In contrast to qualities of maleness and femaleness, the qualities of masculinity and femininity may be defined as sex-specific social behavior that is not in the direct service of procreation and offspring survival.

The social aspects of sex differences have been studied in several species of monkeys, chimpanzees, and other of the great apes. In rhesus monkeys, for example, there are sharp differences in the juvenile behavior of the two sexes. The males threaten one another and initiate and engage in rough-and-tumble play much more frequently than do females. The males attempt sexual mounting with much greater frequency, and are less likely to withdraw at the threat or approach of other monkeys.

In this same species of monkey, some few critical-period reversal experiments have been carried out. The higher the animal species, the more difficult such experiments are, because external interference with normal endocrine balance is usually not compatible with fetal survival. Thus far, the only successful reversal involves the fetal masculinization of female monkeys. As juveniles, these females display social behavior clearly more typical of males than of females. In other words, they have been masculinized.

Among humans the evidence for such innate influences upon ultimate sexuality must again be sought in the atypical effects of fetal disorders. Evidence is fragmentary and open to differences of opinion, but what there is remains consistent with that learned from animal experiments. Naturally, the conditions cannot be as definitive, since learning plays its greatest role in human development, and learned sexual roles are often difficult to distinguish from innate predispositions.

In Turner's syndrome, the child has neither normal male nor normal female sex chromosomes and is subject to no fetal sex hormones. Since such a child is born a normal-appearing girl and is consequently reared as a girl, the prenatal influences are almost impossible to separate from childhood learning, but inferences can be made from the unusual degree of femininity displayed by this genetically, gonadally, and hormonally sexless child. Several researchers have evolved criteria which reliably measure femininity, at least in modern American culture. When Turner's-syndrome females vary at all from the norm, they are characteristically *more* feminine than normal women, despite the fact that they seem not to be exposed to different or more intense learning to be feminine. It has been suggested, but not proved, that this may be due to their lack of exposure during fetal life to even the small amounts of androgen produced by normal ovaries.

Children with the androgen insensitivity syndrome form a somewhat more striking example. In the full-blown form of this condition, these children are born as completely normal-looking girls, and are so reared. At puberty they develop the normal breasts and other body configurations of girls, under the influence of the small but adequate amounts of estrogen normally elaborated by their functioning testes. Their biological sex is not revealed until their failure to menstruate spurs careful medical examination, when it is discovered they have no vagina, uterus, or tubes, and in place of ovaries have undescended normal testes. Because of their female rearing, their sexual learning is not contrary to the presumed influence of deprivation of androgen effect during the fetal critical period. But unlike Turner's-syndrome girls, in whom biological influences are nonexistent and neutral, these girls are subjected to biological influences discordant with their feminine identity. They have a male (XY) genotype and normal male testes producing normal amounts of androgen, both during intrauterine and postnatal life. However, this chromosomal, gonadal, and hormonal maleness in no way counteracts either the female differentiation resulting from the failure of fetal androgen effect, or the rearing influences toward femininity. These children develop into psychologically typical women.

The most persuasive evidence for the importance of innate influence is presented from the study of girls who were masculinized in the uterus during the critical period, when their mothers were given androgenic substances to prevent spontaneous abortion. When the cause of such virilization became known through medical research, the children were able to be examined and diagnosed at birth, and surgical correction of male-appearing genitalia performed immediately. These girls have no internal disease; their chromosomes, gonads, hormones, and internal sex organs are normally female. When their masculinized genitalia are corrected at birth and their parents, therefore, are in no uncertainty about their daughter's sex, they are reared unambiguously as girls.

Under these conditions, if postnatal learning were the only source of sexual differentiation and sex-linked attitudes, these girls should not differ statistically from other girls reared in similar social and cultural environments. But they do. They show, in childhood and adolescence, a distinct and statistically significant shift toward masculine behavior and preferences.

The delineation of masculine versus feminine behavior and preferences is far from clear. There are enormous differences of opinion as to what is culturally induced and what is innate. At Johns Hopkins School of Medicine, the investigators in one of the largest and oldest of the sex research units have gradually formulated a set of distinctions derived from the many hundreds of patients and nonpatients they have studied for many years. Since their study population has embraced many subcultural groups, the criteria may be considered broadly applicable to Western or Judeo-Christian culture. Briefly stated, the differentiating characteristics are:

• Energy expenditure level (higher in boys).

• Play, toy, and sports preference (boys initiate more play, indulge more in and withdraw less from body contact and rough play, prefer guns and quasiaggressive play, and prefer competitive sports; girls generally have opposite preferences, and enjoy doll and "house" play).

• Clothing preference (shirts, trousers or jeans, and little interest in jewelry or cosmetics in boys; dresses, frilly things, interest in jewelry and cosmetics, and concern with hairdo in girls).

• Maternalism (girls are interested in dolls and doll play and fascinated by infants and infant care; boys usually are not).

• Career ambition (girls rate interest in marriage and family above career, while boys show the opposite preference).

• Body image (each sex conceptualizes itself in drawings consonant with gender orientation).

• Perceptual erotic arousal patterns (males experience genitopelvic arousal from visual and narrative erotic stimuli more easily and fully than do females; females usually require tactile stimuli for maximum arousal).

By these criteria, fetally masculinized girls are more masculine in their behavior than nonmasculinized girls. These girls varied from the norm in two principal areas. They definitely tended to be tomboys, and they were recognized as such by their mothers, themselves, and others. This quality included greater athletic interest and ability with its concomitant higher energy expenditure, a greater preference for male playmates, and a preference for the utilitarian clothes of boys rather than feminine dress. They also varied in their expression of maternalism and in their anticipated future roles. They showed less interest in dolls and doll play, clearly preferring boys' toys of the more aggressive sort, such as guns and toy cars. And they ranked a future career above marriage and family, a reversal of the typical priority.

Their shift toward masculinity is not dramatic, but it is consistent. These girls are not disturbed in their identity as females, do not totally reject maternalism, and do not show any measurable tendency toward lesbianism, but wherever they do differ from the typical girls of their culture, the difference is always toward masculinity.

The masculine shift is even more pronounced in girls with the adrenogenital syndrome. These children are generally subjected to much stronger androgen effects in fetal life. Even those diagnosed at birth and treated successfully are more strongly masculine in more dimensions of comparison than are the normal girls.

Virtually all the evidence of the effects of fetal exposure to hormones typical of the opposite sex has focused upon the androgenization of female fetuses. One recent report describes the development of measurable feminine behavior in the childhood and adolescence of boys who had been fetally exposed to estrogen and progesterone that had been medically prescribed for their mothers.[3] It is difficult to evaluate this finding in the context of simple mammalian logic: Estrogen and progesterone in high concentrations are always present in the circulation of pregnant women and consequently in the fetal circulation of both male and female fetuses. Nonetheless, there exists the possibility that later masculine *or* feminine behavior may be affected by fetal exposure to the hormones characteristic of the opposite sex.

Is Sexuality Innate or Learned?

Many aspects of sexual expression at all ages are given their beginnings in the womb. One rather poorly appreciated difference between men and women is the greater difficulty males have in achieving healthy, functional adult sexuality. This has its beginning in fetal biology, and continues to manifest its far-reaching effects throughout life. The original tendency of the fetus is to develop as a female. Regardless of whether chromosome type is XX, XY, or a single X, female differentiation will take place if there is inadequate androgen in the critical period to initiate male development. Similarly, the fetus will develop as a female in the absence of effective androgen whether there are fetal ovaries, testes, or no gonads at all. Only adequate androgen at just the right time will alter the biologically programmed female differentiation to that of a male.

This preferential development is first heralded by the fact that having only a Y chromosome is incompatible with life, while having only an X chromosome permits a relatively normal life. It is clearly more important in the evolutionary scheme of species survival that females receive first priority.

A consequence of the female-first natural priority is the greater complexity of male differentiation. It is more complex to alter a program than to let it proceed without interference. And complexity multiplies the opportunities for error. This is amply demonstrated even during intrauterine life by the preponderance of spontaneous male deaths. Technical advances have only recently permitted the identification of sex (based on sex chromosome type) of spontaneously aborted fetuses still too young for genital identification. In one study, there were 160 male early fetal deaths for every 100 female. The unequal mortality rate continues, though at a much lower ratio, throughout the life-span of men and women.

This greater male fragility and vulnerability to disorder is not limited to survival. In adult life it is reflected in the ease with which male sexual performance may be impaired, in contrast with the amazing imperviousness to disruption of female procreative capacity. In experimental animals, up through chimpanzees, it has been shown that after the cerebral cortex has been surgically removed, males can no longer copulate but females can both mate and conceive. Since the cerebral cortex is the location of learned behavior, male sexuality is revealed as both more dependent upon learning and more subject to mislearning.

In humans, female sexual durability is reflected in the fact that women are capable of passive intercourse and conception under conditions of boredom, revulsion, physical resistance, and even, unfortunately, unconsciousness. In contrast, men must be able to achieve erection and maintain it long enough for vaginal insertion and ejaculation. At any point from the start of arousal until ejaculation has begun, this chain may be halted abruptly by an endless variety of internal or external events. Inner fear of hostility may render erection hopeless. And as many young men have learned, a night watchman with a flashlight is sufficient cause for temporary impotence.

Men show a higher rate of deviant sexual behavior than do women. Indeed, there are some forms of aberrant sexuality that essentially exist only in men, such as fetishism and transvestism. Only a tiny number of clinical reports of female fetishism exist.[4] And clinical results reveal that a higher proportion of homosexual women than men can shift their sexual preference to heterosexuality when they wish to.[5]

In other words, there is no doubt that innate biological factors exert some pressure on sexual behavior. The real questions are those of degree. How much does innate predisposition literally determine sexuality and how much is the result of rearing and other influences? There are some who maintain that learning has become so preeminent in humans that it completely negates the feebler voice of innate forces, that man is no longer an instinctual animal. The enormously increased cerebral cortex, plus the very long period of childhood dependence and learning, are considered to have usurped totally the role of innate predisposition. Far more of human behavior and adaptation is learned than is that of any other animal.

This position is supported by impressive evidence from the clinical histories of children born with ambiguous genitalia. Such children have often been mistakenly assigned the wrong sex simply because of the uncertain nature of their sex organs. In most recorded cases, the children adopted unwaveringly the gender identity in which they were reared. This has occurred even when all the biological determinants of sex were contrary to the gender of rearing. These people exemplify dramatically the tremendous power of rearing and learning influences. That it often—even usually—transcends contradictory biological forces is unquestionable.

But the evidence is not so conclusive as to negate biology. There are a significant number of cases of children who did *not* permanently accept their misassigned gender of rearing. In those instances, it has often happened that at puberty, when such an adolescent is subject to hormones discordant with the sex of rearing, he or she begins to feel out of place. The urge grows to discard the incorrect sexual identity accepted during childhood and to assume the biologically appropriate identity. There are a significant number of recorded cases of young people who were successfully able to shift gender identity despite all the childhood years of consistent learning to be the opposite sex.[6]

The issue of heredity of sexual tendencies and preferences is unresolved. Research is scanty, often inconclusive, and sometimes conflicting. In obligatory homosexuality, for example, several investigators have reported that in almost every case of identical twins, if one was homosexual, so was the other, even when they were reared in different homes. The validity of these studies has been questioned,[7] but it is not possible to dismiss them out of hand. However questionable the studies may be, the frequency of homosexuality in both identical twins is likely to prove higher than in the general population, as it is not likely that sexuality will prove to be the one area of human life exempt from hereditary influence.

It is unfeasible to consider the infant sexually neutral at birth—a *tabula rasa* on which only the effects of postnatal learning are to be inscribed. On the other hand, a human being is the most intensely learning animal known. He is freer to modify his biological endowment than any existing creature. Compared with other animals, he may easily appear to be released from a thoughtless confinement to instinctual behavior patterns. Nevertheless, man remains an animal. His genetic and constitutional endowment is present at birth and determines the limits—often so broad as to *seem* nonexistent—within which this most malleable of animals may utilize learning and experience to express a not-quite-infinite variety of sexual emotions and interactions.

TWO

All-Encompassing Influences during the First Eighteen Months

What Newborns Are Like

Infants share certain natural characteristics which determine not only the nature of their first unthinking sexual responses but also the kind of nurturing they require for eventual sexual function. The human infant, being altricial (unable to survive without maternal care), contrasts with the newborns of precocial animals (those capable of a high degree of independent activity from birth). The human newborn remains in an unfinished state—an almost "fetal" though extrauterine stage of development—for a considerable time, and does not reach a degree of maturation comparable to that of most precocial newborns until about six years of age.[1] His brain and nervous system are physically incomplete, he has little voluntary muscular control except for sucking and swallowing, and he cannot even distinguish between that which is part of himself and that which is part of his environment.

These characteristics lead his body and brain to respond in all-or-none fashion. He has no capacity to be aware of separate and different experiences at the same time. He does not have the mental sophistication to think, "This tastes good, but that feels bad." If his mother is tense and anxious, he cannot differentiate the good taste of her milk from the bad feeling of her body. Whichever communicates itself most strongly will dominate his awareness and shape his learning about the experience. Therefore early experiences exert the broadest possible effects upon him.

An infant's earliest experiences are very nearly indelible, a characteristic that results from the global nature of infantile responses and from the fact that infants have virtually no inner resources to counterpose against any experience, good or bad. Since they are physically and emotionally helpless, survival is impossible without adequate mothering. Because of the absence of significant past learning, they cannot place the things that happen to them in any perspective. They are at the mercy of whatever befalls them.

The enormous influence of these earliest months is both inevitable and easily comprehensible. Both the firmest emotional security and the most devastating emotional disorders can be traced to this period when psychic vulnerability is greatest.[2] The older a child becomes, the more he develops strengths of his own. He can fight back against disruptive influences, and it takes increasingly more and more severe stress to overwhelm him.

Infantile vulnerability is not, however, evenly distributed between the sexes, at least not at the physical level. In what is already a recurrent theme, males are less hardy.[3] The disproportion of male over female fetal deaths continues in the neonatal period. This difference shows most clearly in susceptibility to certain types of infectious diseases (those caused by gram-negative bacteria) and may be directly linked to the sex of the baby. The regulation of the production of antibodies (one of the body's natural protective mechanisms against bacteria) to these diseases is thought to be controlled by a gene located on the female (X) sex chromosome. Since girls have two X chromosomes, they have a greater capacity to develop protective antibodies.

During the first week or two after birth, there is no difference in the susceptibility of male and female infants, because they both enjoy the protection of maternal antibodies that had been transferred across the placenta during fetal life. But once these disappear, male infants die at a rate from two to four times as frequently as females as a result of infections. The postulated sex-linked character of the protective mechanism would explain both the girl infant's higher immunity and the greater rapidity with which her immunity develops. When antibiotics became available for the treatment of these infections, the disproportion of male to female deaths rose even higher, indicating that more effective treatment is best able to help those who are least vulnerable.[4]

An infant's nutritional and hygienic needs are not the only important concerns in a mother's ministrations. Indeed, it is possible that while they are biologically indispensable, there are even more crucial needs that can be met only through the quality of direct physical and emotional interaction between mother and infant. The need to be touched and held, stroked and cuddled, is vital for a baby's health and ability to function—even his survival.[5]

The Oral Stage

The sucking reflex and the ability to swallow are the only functions of the voluntary muscle system that are fully developed at birth. It will be many months, in some instances years, before the infant has comparable control over other parts of his body. In these early days, the random movements of his eyes and limbs and the involuntary muscle reflexes involved in urination and defecation are at best secondary to his oral activities.

The infant expresses almost all his needs with his mouth. In addition, there is an extraordinarily greater sensation in the newborn's lips, tongue, and mouth than in any other part of his body, enabling him to experience such sensations as cold and heat, shape, and texture with much greater sensitivity with his mouth than with his hands or any other part of himself. Consequently, during the earliest months, the infant experiences his world primarily with his mouth.

This exquisite sensory and muscular oral equipment is necessary for survival, since the infant's oral dependence upon his mother is total: Unless his basic nutritional needs, which he is powerless to get for himself, are given him through his mouth, he will die. He senses his mother's presence and her warmth and love most intensely through the contact of his mouth with his mother's breast. Even children who are bottle-fed detect something of the mother's unique self not only by her personal way of feeding but through nuzzling and mouthing their mother's breasts and body in exploration and in seeking security. Through the quality of his mother's attentions to his oral needs an infant also has a way of becoming sensitive to a *lack* of love and acceptance. While infants may be thoroughly loved and cared for by mothers who bottle-feed them, it is doubtful whether the uniquely reciprocal *need* for one another can be either experienced or conveyed by mother or infant as fully as in the breast-feeding relationship. And beyond the emotional advantages are health benefits for the infant which cannot be duplicated through artificial foods.

For about two days before the first milk is produced, the mother's breast produces a substance known as colostrum. This unique substance cleans out the infant's intestinal tract as a laxative and then acts as the best known preventive of infantile diarrhea. At the same time, it is the richest source of maternal immunizing antibodies. Like those transferred to the fetus from the mother's blood, which disappear within two to four weeks, they provide the newborn with temporary protection against a number of diseases until he can begin to produce his own protective antibodies. The gradual change from colostrum to regular milk takes about ten days, and parallels the infant's gradual capacity to digest the components of human milk. In addition to the early advantages of colostrum, there are statistical differences in many aspects of the health and development of breast-fed and artificially fed children. Artificially fed children have many times more respiratory and other infections, diarrhea, eczema, asthma, and hay fever. Breast-fed children test physically and mentally superior to artificially fed children, and are faster in learning to walk and talk.[6]

The concept of oral dependent needs implies much more than nutrition. The quality of taking in, of incorporating, is characteristic of the infant's whole relationship with his world during this earliest phase of development. His entire skin surface is one unified organ for taking in both the nature and the quality of the sensations impinging upon it, as he gradually acquires the ability to grasp and hold with his hands, to focus his eyes and fix his interest and gaze upon an object or a face, and to listen to the new world's sounds.[7]

The sequence of muscular competence in infancy is first mouth, then eyes, then hands. Eyes are able to focus and to follow objects before arms and hands are muscularly coordinated. Later, the baby can control the larger muscles enough to touch, fondle, and grasp an object within his reach. But even as these abilities evolve, they are subordinated to the primacy of the mouth. Often a baby will try to mouth a visually interesting object. Once his grasping and arm movements are adequately developed, that which is grasped is usually popped into the mouth. Even in toddlers, past the early infancy stage, this same behavior occurs, attesting to the biologically determined supremacy of the infant's mouth as the agent for exploring and sensing his world.

Significantly, his first source of pleasure may also become his first source of normal, self-generated anxiety. The prototype of the anxiety which arises from conflicts in normal development occurs when teeth begin to erupt. To ease and relieve the tension produced by the pain in his gums, the infant naturally wants to bite down. For the nursing infant at least, this poses the real and immediate danger of a mother's startled yelp of pain and the withdrawal of her breast. For many infants this becomes the first experience of inevitable conflicting inner needs. He needs to reduce his inner discomfort and tension by biting, but if he does so, he will lose something else that he also needs and wants. If he acts on his need to bite down it will cause displeasure and disapproval in a person vital to his life.

This may well be the origin of the very earliest sense of inner badness or evil, a source of self-hate toward an inner quality that is believed to drive away needed and loved other persons.[8] This is also the infant's first task of self-regulation. He must learn to suck without biting, to tolerate the discomfort of sore gums to get that which he needs even more, his mother's breast. And mothers need tolerance during the infant's learning period so as to avoid reinforcing their baby's sense of destructive "badness." It is possible that bottle-fed infants are at some disadvantage here, too, and miss out on an important early source of ego development and mastery. They do not have to achieve this accommodation to conflicting inner needs and thus lose the opportunity to benefit by their success.

For all that the oral phase contains sources of conflict and deprivation, it also remains symbolic of what was best and most secure and trouble-free. Under reasonable normal conditions of mother-infant relations, there will never again be a time of such carefree nurturance. In myths of paradise and in dreams, and at times of stress, people always yearn for the passive security of infancy with their mother. And under unbearable stress, or in persons with insufficient ego strength, the most common maladaptive maneuver resorted to for relief of that stress will be the taking in of some substance unconsciously imbued with the magical power to soothe away the distress, be it drugs, cigarettes, alcohol, or excessive food.

Developmental Processes in General

Sexual development does not occur separately from all other aspects of human growth and maturation. To treat it separately is to some degree a distortion. Particularly in earliest childhood, developmental processes occur that are so broad in their implications that they appear unrelated to sexuality. Only later, or on very close scrutiny, do sexual phenomena specifically reflect a relevance to these early, fundamental processes.

Perhaps the crowning mental achievement of early infancy is the gradual capacity to distinguish between self and not-self. This means the ability of the infant to perceive himself and others—at first his mother is the only important "other"—as separate individuals. Newborn babies do not have this capacity, and achieving it takes considerable time and an enormous increase in ego development. Initially, the mother and her breast are perceived as part of the infant's own body. When he cries in hunger and is fed, he does not at first perceive that someone *else* has ministered to his hunger. Everything is part of himself, and his needs are magically met merely by his becoming aware of them. This is the period of primary omnipotence, when the infant is unaware of his helplessness, and imagines that he controls the environment.

The experience of frustration probably sets in motion the gradual process of distinguishing between self and others. There is no need to enforce such frustration; it is inevitable. Even the most normally attentive mother is not always instantly available. She may be asleep, or briefly away from the house, or occupied with some task that cannot immediately be abandoned at the time her baby cries. Slowly the infant comes to the dim realization that feeling wet, or cold, or hungry must wait upon another person to be remedied.

These realizations are paralleled and fostered by the increasing sharpness of his senses and his improving muscular control. Eyes begin to focus, and ocular muscles begin to permit the following of moving objects. Finger and arm coordination for finer and more accurate movements allow tactile exploration of the self and others so that differences in shape and texture are learned. Olfactory development permits the earliest distinction of odors as another means of detecting differentness.

It is during the first half year that an infant slowly learns he is a being separate from others. He is first able to recognize the most important other person—mother—and to distinguish her from other adults at about six to eight months. When this is accomplished, the "eight month anxiety" appears. At this time infants who previously responded to any friendly adult will now spurn strangers in anxiety and prefer to relate only to their mother. This reaction is firm evidence that the child can clearly recognize a person outside himself and prefers to relate specifically to that one person.[9]

The study of object relations aims at understanding the development of relationships between people and of the disturbances that can impair that development. Mother, or the mothering person, is the first object to whom an infant is attached. There can be no mystery why this first nurturing person—usually the mother and almost inevitably female—exerts such profound influences upon a baby.

A part of her all-encompassing power is actually conferred by the infant himself. When the infant discovers his own utter helplessness, his dependence on the care of others, his original sense of omnipotence is shattered. Those gigantic adult "others," especially mother, possess all the power, and the infant now assumes them to be as omnipotent and omniscient as he once believed himself to be. This delegation of omnipotence to the mother—and later to the father as well—will account for many of the exaggerated fantasies the infant will have about them during his sexual development. Not until late adolescence will he finally come to accept their human fallibility.

As the mother is the first source of pleasure, love, and dependence, so is she the earliest potential agent of frustration, deprivation, and hostility. The infant's inability to survive alone and the necessity of this first of many interpersonal relationships to insure survival illustrates the fact that no person's development can be adequately understood except in the context of his relations with others.[10] While internal forces and drives operate from birth to confer an individual quality independent of his environment, it is only in interaction with his mother that the infant begins to savor the emotional climate of his world. Is it accepting, supportive, warm, loving? Or does he feel helpless in a hostile, uncaring world that fails to comprehend or heed his needs? It is in the earliest relationship with his mother that the deepest concepts of himself and his world are laid.

Because of the inescapable importance of early mothering, the influences of fathers have been largely overlooked. The effects of paternal deprivation and of differing paternal character types have been the subject of some research but little, if any, with specific focus upon early infancy. It is known that the earlier effects are more intense and more lasting.[11] In the sexual development of later childhood, the role of fathers will be seen to become of major import. But during the first year or so, one can only sensibly speculate that the father, like the mother, is beginning to influence the infant's sense of being male or female, as a result of his different responses to boy or girl infants.

The Infant Discovers Sex

There is no question about the exposure of male infants to sexual sensations from the time of birth on. A boy baby's penis is fully exposed and immediately susceptible to pleasurable stimulation. It can easily be observed that, however young, stimulation of a baby's penis results in erection and a sense of pleasure. It might be thought that the erection is simply a poorly developed spinal reflex and conveys no special sensation to the infant, but common experience teaches better. In many cultures, including our own, fussy infants may be quieted by genital stroking and tickling. In his earliest weeks, the infant boy probably cannot localize the sensation that pleases him, but the pleasure and the relaxing effect are evident.

Innumerable sources of genital excitation are present in the daily life of every male infant. By its very nature, the diaper changing, the cleaning of the genitals, and the rubbing in of various soothing lotions to protect against diaper rash are directly stimulating to the penis and surrounding sensitive areas. Bathing is accompanied by the similar handling of genitals. Then there are internal, though more vague, sources of excitation. Erections have been observed at times of crying, frustration, and hunger. And even infants show the typical erections during certain stages of sleep. These internal stimuli are not specifically sexual, though those that occur during sleep may sometimes be, but it is likely that there is a feedback of genital sensation as a result of the erection.

Girl infants are exposed to the same opportunities for developing an awareness of genital sensations, at least from their external genitalia, during the processes of maternal care. Their less obvious genital anatomy might suggest that such excitation would occur less often, but that assumption is questionable. When parents are observed cleansing or bathing a female infant, they always seem to be carefully attentive to the genital area between the labial folds, which means inevitable stimulation of the clitoris and the rest of the external genital area. Perhaps the main difference in direct genital stimulation between male and female infants is that females are anatomically less susceptible to inadvertent excitation.

External genital sensations in infant girls have not been a matter of real question. But a significant issue with relevance to subsequent psychosexual development does arise as to whether girl babies have any natural awareness of the vagina. Early psychosexual theory was built upon the premise that female infants and little girls are totally unaware of the existence of this organ.[12] However, this view was questioned on a number of bases quite early in the developing understanding of female sexuality.

For about the first four weeks of life, an infant girl's genitals are swollen and reddened as a result of the remaining presence of maternal estrogen and progesterone that were in her circulation during fetal life.[13] These maternal hormones had the effect of producing a false maturation of the girl's sexually responsive organs. One evidence is the "witch's milk" often present for a few days in the breasts of newborns. The newborn girl's vagina exhibits secretions and microscopic cell structure with similarities to that of an adult. This early hormonal stimulation is one reason to assume that vague but real vaginal sensations are present in the newborn female, just as sensations from other body organs are subject to functional stimulation.

There are many additional sources of infantile vaginal sensations. The musculature surrounding the vagina and that of the anus are similar in embryological derivation and innervation.[14] It is well recognized that reflex anal contractions may occur when an infant is suckling.[15] The similar embryology would explain reports of reflex vaginal contractions during suckling, and it must be assumed that this muscular activity is accompanied by sensations.

Recent research into the physiology of sexual stimulation and response details the vascular and muscular changes in and around the vagina accompanying such stimulation.[16] Since genital stimulation regularly takes place in the normal care of infants, it is reasonable to speculate that even the immature genital tissues of the infant girl respond and that the changes are perceived in some degree.[17]

Evidence also exists in instances of the lack of vaginal awareness.

At least one case has been reported of a girl born without a vagina or uterus, whose total absence of vaginal awareness contrasted sharply with that of normal girls.[18]

Finally, there is the accumulating observation of infant girls. As soon as they are able to direct their hands to their genitals and can govern the movement of their fingers, they are frequently observed to insert their fingers into their vaginas.[19]

From such evidence, it can be assumed that the infantile vagina is subject to and produces sensations, and that the baby registers these feelings. A detailed point is made of this awareness in part to illustrate that both males and females have their own, normal, sex-specific sexual sensations from earliest infancy. The existence and nature of vaginal sensations also is the very earliest forerunner of the awareness of sexual differences, and paves the way for understanding some of the crucially different ways boys and girls come to perceive themselves.

The inevitable and frequent pleasurable genital arousal that all infants naturally receive has only one logical outcome. Infants will want to enjoy more of these pleasing sensations and, as soon as they have the necessary muscular coordination, will begin to manipulate their genitals. This infantile genital fondling of the self is natural and normal, in the healthy service of exploring the body.

In this early exploratory activity, infants are interested not alone in the sense of touch and the different ways in which parts of their bodies respond to touching and squeezing and stroking; they also are fascinated by shape, texture, and appearance. As genital shapes and textures are obviously not the same, boys learn different things than do girls. An important difference is that boys can see the source of their sexual pleasure whereas girls cannot.

At times, the new baby's genital handling is little more than a virtually unselfconscious, absent-minded fingering, but this is by no means always the case. Genital stimulation can also be intentional masturbatory activity with the goal of sexual enjoyment and release in the fullest sense.

The capacity to achieve orgasm begins very early in a baby's development. The earliest observed masturbation to orgasm was in a four-week-old girl.[20] In *Sexual Behavior of the Human Male* ("the Kinsey report"), the American sex researcher Alfred C. Kinsey (1894–1956) and his co-workers reported the observation of repeated complete sequences of sexual excitation and rising tension culminating in orgasm, with rhythmic muscular contractions and pelvic thrusting, and followed by relaxation, in five-month-old males.[21] Children do not all reach orgastic capacity at the same age, and it is not known at what age the "average" child can achieve orgasm. In a group of 317 males, Kinsey reported that 32 percent of those under one year and 57 percent of those between two and five years were observed to have orgasms.[22] There is less statistical data about female infants, but it is likely that they would be capable of at least as early arousal. In support of this supposition is Kinsey's report that more females than males had their first orgastic experience as a result of masturbation.[23] It cannot be overemphasized that these experiences of very early sexual arousal and response predominantly occur in perfectly healthy, normal children.

Boys and Girls Make Different Discoveries

Even in this very earliest phase of life, infants begin to experience their sexual differences from one another. These first perceptions derive from the existence of separate male and female anatomy and physiology. The pioneer Viennese psychoanalyst Sigmund Freud (1856–1938) expressed it in the succinct phrase, "anatomy is destiny." [24] From this inescapable fact, he went on to draw some highly questionable and sometimes biased conclusions about male and female sexuality and character development, many of which, I believe, require revision. The fundamental concept, however, that the possession of one or the other of the two basic body styles available exerts an influence upon subsequent sexual development is valid, and has relevance even to earliest infancy. An infant's body is, of course, a major part of its own environment. Genital differences are by no means the only, nor perhaps even the most important, influence upon psychosexual development. But their significance is sometimes overlooked, and it is a mistake to underestimate their subtle but far-reaching impact.

The visibility of a male's penis and scrotum most unmistakably differentiates them from a female's sexually responsive organs. And vision is one of the infant's major modalities for organizing his environment into comprehensible and familiar patterns. Even though an infant's mouth contains his most discriminatory nerves, it is his sight that produces his first recognizable object, the human face.[25] In forming his concept of himself, visibility is probably essential. Unless the infant is blind, it is necessary that he be able to see an organ in order to incorporate it firmly and sharply into his body image.[26]

A study of children who have been blind from birth reveals a normally developing sexual identity by the time they have become preschoolers providing that they are otherwise mentally normal. It must be assumed that in the absence of sight, other sources of bodily and sexual awareness, such as touch, spontaneous sensations, and language must be more intensely depended upon to furnish the necessary clues for body concept. It is not known, however, whether congenitally blind children develop a sense of anatomical sex identity as readily as sighted children. If language is an important source, that of course becomes intelligibly available much later than vision. It is known that the development of heterosocial confidence is delayed in the congenitally blind.[27]

Because of the capacity for development of an appropriate sexual identity in children blind from birth, one might doubt the psychosexual importance attributed to the visibility of sexual organs. But that would be an unwarranted conclusion. The absence of one sense always heightens the compensatory utilization of others, and the possession of vision, regardless of the contribution of other sensory modalities to body concepts, automatically produces a difference between male and female infants. The very fact of sight determines that boy and girl infants will perceive their genitals differently. Naturally, the feel of a toe or finger or penis or clitoris, and the sensations arising from them either spontaneously or from touch, are also important components of comprehending one's body. The girl infant's inability to see those body parts from which her sexual sensations arise, however, makes it·more difficult for her to have a clear sense of them. This delays her understanding of her genitals and causes her body image to develop later and to be more vague and indefinite.

Not only is the penis visible, it is changeable. Erections occur both spontaneously and as a result of stimulation. At first, the boy baby has neither any control over his erections nor any comprehension of what causes them. With the gradual acquiring of muscular coordination, the learning of cause and effect begins. While the psychosexual consequences of this phenomenon are only beginning to have significance in the first twelve to eighteen months of life, they are not absent. Infant boys can be observed in obviously attentive awareness of their ability to produce penile erections by their own purposeful efforts. Along with the visibility of the penis, this kind of control also fosters their clear sense of body image and body mastery.

Observations of male infants indicate that their most frequent early hand-genital contact is with the scrotum, not the penis, but the difference is only a matter of degree. The scrotum of a newborn is larger than his penis, particularly when filled with one or both descended testicles. The same kinds of nerves, capable of giving the same sense of pleasure, which are most highly concentrated in the penis are also present in varying though lesser numbers in the scrotum, around the anus, and throughout the adjacent skin areas. This makes scrotal fondling a sexually pleasurable act.

The seemingly capricious presence or absence of testicles gives the most meaningful dimension to the appearance of the scrotum to the curious infant. It is not uncommon for one or both testicles to remain undescended for some months after birth. And their descent is not final and permanent for a number of years. Thus the scrotum and testicles, like the penis, are also able to change size and appearance. Initially, these changes are likely to be merely visual and tactile phenomena that the infant registers in the process of becoming familiar with his body. By the second or third year, however, the unpredictable occurrence of testicular retraction can become of considerable emotional consequence.[28]

The location of early sexual sensations has profound implications for the difference in the future emotional development of males and females. The distinctions in the site of sensations that begin in infancy continue to exert influence in the later stages of development. For males, sexual feelings are external, easily identified as arising from a specific, visible organ, and amenable to some voluntary control and purposive activity. The penis is not external in the sense of being a separate object, like the crib rail or mother, but it is external in the sense that it is on the outside of the body and therefore subject to manipulation, scrutiny, and increasing control. Sensory experiences arising in the penis are perceived differently from those arising, for example, in the stomach.

It is quite a different matter for girls. Even the externally evoked feelings are from an invisible site, between fleshy folds. Manipulations of the vaginal opening produce even more vague responses. And the spontaneously occurring vaginal sensations are truly internal. Clinical evidence suggests that although the clitoris is far more sensitive to tactile stimulation, spontaneous genital sensations more commonly arise from the vagina.[29]

In contrast to the genital experience of boys, the internal sensations of girls are diffuse and very difficult to localize. They often arise spontaneously, their source cannot be inspected and easily manipulated, and they are not susceptible to the same degree of voluntary control. Clitoral sensations are localized and can be repeated at will, but they are still subject to the uncertainty of invisibility. All these qualities not only make it more difficult for girls to develop a clear body image, they also determine the nature of their body concepts and influence feminine characteristics and the ways in which girls perceive themselves in general.[30]

Innate sex distinctions other than genital also make their appearance at birth or shortly thereafter. Relatively little research has been done in this area, but there is evidence that some inborn characteristics are specific to one sex or the other. Newborn boys display more muscular activity, are more irritable, and raise their heads higher than girls.[31] The amount of activity shown by girls is less dependent upon maternal handling than that of boys.[32] Girls sleep more and cry less than boys.[33] Boys are more restless before feeding and fall asleep more readily after being satisfied.[34] These are not the sort of findings from which major generalizations can be drawn, but they are consistent with the general data on animals that males are innately more active and show higher expenditure of energy. They do indicate that basic biological factors make some contribution to sexual differentiation.

These early beginnings of psychosexual differentiation are largely private and unselfconscious. That is, most year-old infants are unaware, or at best dimly aware, that others are made differently or have any different feelings and characteristics. The differences described are occurring and producing their inevitable effects but as yet the infants make little active comparison between themselves and the opposite sex.

Infants of this age seldom move around readily enough to observe easily or frequently the sexual behavior or the genitals of other infants or small children. Social interaction with other infants is minimal or nonexistent, and if they happen to observe either of their parents' genitals, it is likely that the visual differences are so massive as to suggest little relationship to their own bodies. These considerations are no longer fully valid for infants near the upper limit of this developmental phase, but essentially the times of comparing and contrasting genitals are yet to come. The kinds of sex-specific qualities considered thus far are largely engendered by innate, biological differences that provide the two sexes with distinct physical experiences and bodily environments with which to identify themselves.

Parents Unwittingly Begin Sex Education

Some of the interactions between parents and infants influence quite directly the infants' emerging and future sexuality. Foremost is the effect of the total behavior of the parents in initiating the child's sexual identity. The knowledge that the new baby is a boy or a girl sets into motion within each parent a complex and never-ending series of differential responses to that child. The various ways in which parents and relatives—indeed, all adults—respond to male or female infants are made up of all the conscious and unconscious preconceptions and expectations they associate with "boy" and "girl."

The difference in approach begins the moment the infant is born. The stereotype of the exuberant father who visits his newborn son for the first time at the hospital, laden with baseball bat and catcher's mitt, is seldom acted out in such amusing exaggeration. But the molding of a boy toward maleness and a girl toward femaleness begins with the choosing of a name and the first moment the infant is held in a parent's arms, and is followed up almost immediately in the choice of the baby's clothes.

Research has demonstrated the existence of a number of early differentiating responses. Mothers relate to their male and female infants in dissimilar ways. Most investigators report that female babies are held, cuddled, talked to, and "fussed over" more than males.[35] In contrast, even when nursing, mothers of boys grant them greater autonomy and freedom. Mothers still touch and talk to their six-month-old daughters more than to their sons. As the infants grow older, boys display more vigorous activity, and more aggressive behavior is tolerated from them.[36]

Such differences in maternal behavior easily help explain the greater degree of compliance and dependency so often seen in girls as well as their greater verbal ability and emotional responsiveness. Independence and aggressive activity is also fostered in boys by the mothers' early attitudes and expectations. In turn, when infants begin to respond with behavior, however subtle, that parents regard as appropriate to their sex, that behavior becomes approved and reinforced.

It is indeed both parents, not the mother alone, who participate in the early foundation of sexual identity. It is inevitable that in most families infants will have more contact with the mother or other female mothering figures. It follows that mothers will naturally exert the strongest early influences. But fathers too will be influential in proportion to the amount of time and loving care they provide for their infants. It is often the father who is most intolerant of deviations from what he believes to be appropriate behavior for a boy or a girl. He may have more narrow concepts of "normal" masculinity and femininity, and be more vigorous in approval or disapproval.[37]

Sexual identity is a highly complex concept, formed of both conscious and unconscious components. Each person's sexual identity contains elements he knowingly associates with his sex (such as gentleness, athletic prowess, or maternal feelings), and elements outside his awareness which may either reinforce or undermine his conscious concept of self. Further, sexual identity is not a unitary mental construct. A number of different components, formed at different times during development and shaped by separate influences, form the final composite called sexual identity.

Most fundamental is *core gender identity,* the deep and unalterable sense of being male or female. As the child identifies with one biological sex or the other, he begins to associate certain behavior and attitudes as appropriate to his sex and avoids and rejects behavior he considers inappropriate. A portion of this *sex role behavior,* is an expression of innate differences, but the bulk is learned through parental and cultural pressures and by observation. *Sex role preference* is another component: a child may ultimately prefer to be a different sex than he knows himself to be. Still another component is *sex role adoption:* a variety of social and intrapsychic pressures may cause a child to adopt a sexual identity and its typical role behavior in spite of his preference or his core gender identity.

The many facets of sexual identity only begin to form in infancy. The most basic—core gender identity—becomes definitively fixed; while others are still in early formative stages. There is a considerable body of evidence that by the age of about three the firm inner sense of being male or female is not only set with incredible solidity but is singularly resistant to subsequent shift.[38] Even those children reared in contradiction to their biological sex adopt and maintain the sex of their rearing.[39] Efforts to reassign sex and train the child to the ways of the new sex are generally unsuccessful unless the change is made before the age of three.[40] Many complex, unanswered scientific questions bear upon the various determinants of core gender identity, but it is fair to generalize that the most important influences are those the parents bring to bear in the earliest rearing.

This concept suggests the enormous importance to the helpless infant of his parents' beliefs and attitudes about what is appropriate for males and females. When it is demonstrably possible to rear a child to accept biologically inappropriate gender attitudes, how much more readily will he adopt those which merely limit or distort his own concepts of himself and others? It is in infancy that the stereotypes of masculinity and femininity are first imposed. When parents' expectations are in accord with innate sex differences, rearing will proceed in harmonious accord with biological design. But when the preconceptions and stereotypes of parents do violence to the broad range of potentials inherently available to males and females alike, limitation and conflict on the part of the child become inevitable.

The impact of parents' attitudes is particularly powerful in direct response to the infant's openly sexual activity. Infantile masturbation is the child's first behavior that parents recognize as sexual. It is therefore the first act that prompts them to express openly to the infant their attitudes toward manifestations of sexuality and sexual pleasure. No possible harm, physically or developmentally, can come from infantile masturbation; it is healthy and beneficial exploratory behavior. In families where this is understood, parental response will convey that message: both mother and father will take masturbation for granted. If the infant's genital fondling is accompanied by smiling and pleasure, the mother will probably smile naturally and automatically along with her baby, as she does whenever he smiles and is happy.

In many families, however, the first sexual taboos are invoked at this time. Though the mother may openly fondle her infant's genitals while cleaning and bathing him, she may firmly remove his hands from his genitals whenever she discovers them there. She may frown disapprovingly, scold him a bit, even slap his hands. Prohibitions, even at this infantile stage, can be severe, from stern scoldings that are incomprehensible to the infant, to hard spankings, and even to pinning the child's sleeves to the crib sheet to prevent the "bad" act. A leading sex educator tells of falling to sleep every night of the first seven or eight years of her life, having to wear aluminum mittens to prevent masturbation.

Sometimes parental disapproval is conveyed more subtly but more confusingly to the infant. Many parents have learned, and consciously accept, that infantile masturbation is harmless, even beneficial, but the new knowledge is not in accord with their emotions. Despite what they know intellectually, they feel disturbed and anxious when confronted by their infant's genital play. They may do nothing overtly to interrupt or discourage it, but their tension and distress communicates itself to the infant through subtle empathic and nonverbal cues. A change of facial expression or tone of voice, a muscular stiffening that alters the way the infant is being handled or touched, will unmistakably signal to him his mother's conflicting emotions. Time and repetition ultimately allow the child to associate his mother's uncomfortable attitude with his masturbation.

An infant can comprehend nothing of what lies behind the display of various attitudes. But he will unerringly sense the emotion expressed. Acceptance poses no problem, but disapproval can have most unfortunate consequences. He discovers that an act as natural to him as feeling his earlobes, and far more pleasant, results in angry disapproval and a loss of the sense of being loved. An infant is too dependent upon his mother to endure disapproval without serious effects: conflict between a pleasure he desires and the pain of disapproval, resentful anger toward the frustrating mother, a decreasing sense of his own worth, and a fear of his own desire for genital pleasure. The last two reactions always occur by virtue of the child's utter, helpless dependence upon his parents. He has no alternative but to yield to them and to fear whatever seems to threaten him with loss of their love. Because he delegates his own sense of omnipotence to them, they are considered all-powerful and all-knowing; they must be right, and he must be at fault.

With the exception of masturbation, which is usually thought of only in terms of its *future* effects, most parents do not think of an infant as sexual at all. This asexual view of infancy is fostered by the child's genuinely primitive level of physical and mental development and by his highly limited capacity to express himself. For this reason, parents often overlook one directly sexual interaction that can have a powerful impact upon their infant—the baby's response to intercourse.

It is not uncommon for a child's crib to be kept in the parents' bedroom for the first months, or even years, of his life. Usually the parents' sex life will begin again within a few weeks after the child is born. Many parents wait until the baby is asleep before beginning their own sex play, or they stop to quiet him if he awakens and fusses, but are likely to become so engrossed in their own uninterrupted pleasure that they fail to be concerned about any detrimental effect upon so small a baby. There is little doubt that infants of almost any age are stimulated by adult sexuality; the older the infant, the more specifically sexual a form that stimulation will take. Children within their first year will sometimes begin to experience specific genital sensations and arousal, and may even masturbate; there may also be signs of rapt curiosity, agitation, or fear.

Psychoanalytic theory has long held that serious developmental disturbance occurs as a result of the witnessing of the "primal scene" (parental intercourse), and clinical material from disturbed children and adults amply verifies the importance of the experience. There are valid reasons, however, to reconsider how universal such disturbing consequences may be.

Only a minority of the world's population is concerned with the need to shield children from adult sexuality. Housing conditions make it impossible in much of the world to provide such protection throughout a child's life. So far as I can determine, no broad cross-cultural studies have been undertaken to find out whether there are specific and predictable developmental disturbances in all primal scene cultures or whether such disturbances, if present, can causally be linked to witnessing the primal scene. I would propose as a self-evident ethological principle that any viable species has the innate capacity to cope successfully with any normally expectable condition of its environment. Childhood exposure to adult sexuality has been the norm throughout almost all the evolutionary history of man. It remains the norm for most of mankind. The fact that infants are stimulated by it is also normally predictable.

Perhaps the most balanced generalizations are, first, that one cannot assume that all children are inevitably damaged by the primal scene experience. Second, the experience likely does exert some developmental effect, and whether it is "harmful" or "beneficial" probably correlates with whether or not early sexual stimulation influences development in a direction consonant with or divergent from later cultural expectations. Third, other aspects of the parental and parent-child relations will color the experience so as to give it unique impact upon the child. Finally, early infancy is not likely to be the time of its maximum impact. Whatever the primal scene influences may be, they are probably more powerful in later stages when children are emotionally occupied with more elaborate and psychologically meaningful fantasies about their own and their parents' sexuality.

While their children are still infants, parent-infant interactions are seldom directly and overtly sexual. The nurturant quality of infant care encompasses most often the whole child and all his overlapping and simultaneous needs. Nonetheless, all these nonspecific interactions have important relevance to sexual development. The most important sexual lessons may be learned simply from the quality of maternal caring.

There is no more vital mode of caring than simple touching, handling, and stroking. Adequate gentle and repeated skin stimulation is essential to more than the infant's comfort and well-being. It is necessary to his physical and mental health, and even his very life. There is an impressive volume of research and clinical data relating to the importance of tactile stimulation of the skin of newborns, among both humans and lower animals. Infants who are handled

gently and lovingly a great deal learn to relate more openly and
warmly to others. Those who are not so handled suffer emotional
handicaps and are subject to more frequent and severe physical
diseases.[41] Studies of infants in foundling homes whose every need
was met except that they were deprived of adequate tactile and
visual stimulation showed they suffered the most extreme detrimental consequences. They became deeply depressed, and normal
development, such as speech, walking, and the capacity to relate to
others, halted in all cases. Minor illnesses such as colds or measles
swept through such institutions with incredibly high mortality
rates.[42]

Insight into the direct sexual significance of general maternal care
came early in the knowledge of childhood sexual development.
Freud stated in 1905:

> As we know, however, the sexual instinct is not aroused only by
> direct excitation of the genital zone. What we call affection will
> unfailingly show its effects one day on the genital zones as well.
> Moreover, if the mother understood more of the high importance of
> the part played by instincts in mental life as a whole—in all its
> ethical and psychical achievements—she would spare herself any
> self-reproaches even after her enlightenment. She is only fulfilling
> her task in teaching the child to love. After all, he is meant to grow
> up into a strong and capable person with vigorous sexual needs and
> to accomplish during his life all the things that human beings are
> urged to do by their instincts.[43]

Recent research has clearly corroborated the connection between
the quality of mothering and the presence or absence of overt
genital sexuality in infants. In extensive observation of infants
throughout their first year of life, it was found that infants who
received virtually no mothering did not develop the capacity for
genital masturbation even though they were exposed to all the usual
hygienic genital stimulation and, in some cases, to more specific
stimulation. Those who were mothered, but whose mothers were
hampered through personal problems in offering the best of care,
displayed retarded forms of erotic activities, such as rocking. Those
given the best of maternal care all developed genital masturbation
by one year of age, even without any unusual genital stimulation.[44]

This most significant study not only correlates good mothering with the spontaneous development of infantile sexuality but unequivocally demonstrates that infantile masturbation is a sign of healthy normality.

The suggestion has been made that in cultures that deprive infants and children of primal scene experience, it is of special importance that maternal care include some genital stimulation. The lack of visual stimulation and learning makes such maternal "priming" of genital response necessary.[45]

The nonspecific maternal influences upon present and future sexuality do not all operate on a one-way street from mother to child. Initially, mother and infant are so nearly literally a part of one another that the relationship is virtually a symbiotic one—one in which each partner requires the other for survival. While this is not strictly the case for the mother, it is true that she grows and benefits and emotionally *receives* from the infant at the same time that she is giving to him. This early mother-infant symbiosis provides increments of psychosexual development for the mother that are not available to her in any other relationship.

As a result, the individual temperamental differences between newborns that are observable from the moment of birth have effects upon their mothers and consequently upon their mothers' responses to them. As time passes, even the most warmly maternal of women will find themselves responding differently to cuddly and responsive infants than to tense, irritable, and physically less pliable infants. When conflicts of which the mother is entirely unaware disrupt her capacity to respond optimally even to a responsive baby, the change communicates itself empathically to her baby and will affect the child's development and ultimately make him less responsive. Whether changes are due to her temperament or disturbed mother-infant relationships, the baby's unique personality has a feedback effect upon the mother. In this manner, at a very early age, the infant begins to play a role in the quality of mothering he receives.

The infant's helplessness and the inevitability of certain interactions with the mother provide the soil in which some future sex-related attitudes and conflicts will grow. To state that all humans have female mothers is a startlingly obvious yet deeply significant truth. Every infant's earliest attachment and most important object is the mother or some other female mothering figure. The effect of this on later psychosexual development is not usually apparent in infancy. This biological truism, however, lays the foundation for some of the sex-specific tasks imposed upon boys and girls in achieving appropriate masculine or feminine identity.

Boys face the more difficult job, since they must learn to become different from the first person with whom they identified in order to achieve a male sexual identity.[46] In fact, as a result of the mother-infant symbiosis, a male infant's earliest sex identity is *female*. It cannot be otherwise, since at first he cannot differentiate himself from his female mother. Thus a male gender identity and masculinity is an achievement, not a given as it is for girls.[47] Girls consolidate their sex identity without shifting away from the first identification. Understandably, the nature and quality of mothering and the role the father plays in the infant's life add many dimensions to this task, either easing or complicating it.

An additional problem for boys is the obvious and total power wielded by the Giantess of the Nursery. Since most males must assimilate healthy aggression and assertiveness into their masculine sex role behavior, this natural maternal power constitutes a threat to the budding infantile masculinity.

An inescapable blow all infants must experience is weaning. Whether breast- or bottle-fed, every baby who grew accustomed to being warmly held as he is fed arrives at the point at which the nipple is withdrawn and milk is supplemented by other foods. This need not be a disastrously painful experience. Weaning may be accomplished gradually and gently, with the mother attentive to signs of readiness from the baby. Often the baby shows some eagerness to assume more independence in feeding, but the transition from being passively loved and fed to the more separate state of being is not without some sense of loss.

This, indeed, is its relation to later sexuality. Weaning is often the infant's first experience of loss. The other loss which may precede weaning is the "loss" of mother when he discovers that she is not part of himself. He knows from these experiences that he can lose or has lost something he once considered a part of himself and always regarded as vital to himself. This feeling is instrumental in the intensity and tenacity of later fantasies in both boys and girls as to how their genital organs were formed and what might happen to them. Again, either the sensitive or harsh quality of the weaning experience will leave its mark on the intensity of the struggle over later castration fantasies. Such natural and inescapable experiences illustrate again that conflict is a normal and unavoidable aspect of human development.

Infantile Experiences and Later Sexuality

As a result of the global nature of infantile responses, the experiences and sensations of this earliest period produce unusually extensive reverberations in the future sexuality of the child, both in subsequent developmental stages and in adulthood. Obviously, the influences may foster sexual behavior covering the entire gamut from the healthiest and most fulfilling interactions to the most crippling and distorted.

The most far-reaching achievement of infancy is the establishment of attitudes toward human bodies and physical closeness. The mother-infant relationship is constantly physical. Almost every interaction involves close physical contact with the mother's body. The infant's happiness or misery is almost always directly associated with maternal ministrations involving body contact.

It is through such closeness that infants learn whether the physical body and physical contact are pleasant or unpleasant, comforting or rejecting, to be trusted or feared, sought after or avoided. Since an infant does not initially differentiate his mother's body from his own, this body contact with the mother is a basic determinant of how he learns to feel about his own body. A physically warm and loving mother builds the infant's inner sense of worth and security. The perception "good mother" is incorporated and comes to equal "good self." If she is distant and ungiving, his sense of himself and his worth is correspondingly compromised through the corollary equation, "bad mother equals bad self."

To this main source of experiencing the environment, his physical relationship with the mother, from which every other future relationship will grow, the infant is exquisitely sensitive. Like a blind man whose hearing is more acute because he lacks sight, the infant must and does perceive all the subtleties of his mother's feelings about him through her touch and her body. The mother who reluctantly picks up her crying baby to comfort him may not be able to stop his crying because he senses her rejection and responds to it with even greater unhappiness. The nursing mother who resents nursing may not be able to persuade the baby to take her breast, or he may get colic, or be unable to be nourished by her milk.

Sex is an inescapably physical relationship. It is impossible to overestimate the importance of this earliest groundwork in providing a healthy or unhealthy basis for future attitudes toward one's own body, toward the bodies of others, and toward what may be expected or hoped for in an intimate physical relationship. When physical contacts with the mother are inadequate or rejecting, there may be permanent inability to trust closeness with anyone for fear the disappointment will be repeated. This destroys the possibility of satisfactory sexual relationships. The mistrust may express itself in wary, hostile avoidance of love involvements. Or there may be a desperate, dependent clinging to any possible love object in a never-ending effort to find the close relationship that never existed with the mother.

Nothing is ever truly simple—there can also be too much of a good thing, even in a mother's bodily contact. Infants need physical love in order to love themselves, but they also need to learn to separate themselves from the mother, to feel worthwhile within their own personal identities. Male transsexualism, and its relationship in some cases to excessive mother-infant nude body contact, has already been mentioned. Such boys never achieve a separate sexual identity from their mothers. This extreme is rare, bespeaking a severely disturbed mother-infant relationship, but it does occur.[48] In this sexual disorder, a physiologically normal boy has a female core gender identity. This type of disturbed background is not found in female transsexuals because such early maternal overcloseness would not disrupt *female* core gender identity.[49]

Like the basic acceptance of the body, which is a more crucial issue in early infancy than at any other time, orality is similarly of central importance. The satisfactions and frustrations of oral needs exert a sweeping effect upon the infant's developing and future sexuality. From this early primacy of the mouth develop the attitudes and emotions about the use of the mouth in the expression of love or hate. Activities of the mouth in lovemaking—the mouth-to-mouth kiss, the affectionate nibble, the enjoyment of kissing the whole body, the man's pleasure at kissing his partner's breast, the exciting use of the mouth in kissing and stimulating the partner's genitals—derive much of their tender and pleasureful and passionate sensations and emotions from the infantile pleasure and security gained through the use of the mouth.

Just as satisfaction of the oral dependent needs of the infant will impart a loving and positive connotation to the use of the mouth in sex, the frustration of these needs may destroy the potential for pleasure, or turn the mouth into a hateful organ, or produce distorted and inappropriate uses of the mouth in lovemaking. A woman may thoroughly dislike, even refuse to permit, a kiss from a man and still be able to accept other expressions of sexual desire. A man whose nursing experience was unsatisfying and led to anger at his mother may be revolted at the idea of kissing a woman's breast.

Other disturbances of the use of the mouth may be more disguised and subtle. Oral frustration may intensify the infant's aggressive wish to devour. He may turn upon the withholding mother in hate and rage with the only weapon he has, his mouth, and in his infant's imagination wish to hurt her, swallow her, bite her, devour her, destroy her. That an infant's fantasies go to such primitive lengths can be illustrated from later memories, fantasies, and dreams.

Such early frustration may produce an inappropriate association between the mouth and rageful, destructive violence. The infant unconsciously becomes terribly frightened of his impulses of fury. He is totally dependent upon his mother; he dares not turn on her. His perception, whether accurate or not, that she has failed to meet his needs has already "proved" to him that her love is untrustworthy. So every time he expresses, or even feels, anger, he is faced with the frightening threat that his mother will retaliate further by withholding her love.

Every time an excessively frustrated child has angry feelings they are accompanied or followed by great anxiety. Such children develop the unconscious fantasy that their mouth is a destructive organ which will harm those they love and thus interfere with their own need for love. The fear of devouring and destroying the breast and the mother, out of either insatiable need or rage, may cause an infant to reject the breast in order to avoid the anxiety-provoking fantasies.

These fantasies may persist into later life and produce disturbances in the use of the mouth in sex and love. The nature of the symptoms depends upon which emotion was stronger—the child's rage or his fear. A child may outgrow biting in anger, but many a woman has been bruised by the violent kisses of a man whose mouth is more an organ of violence than of tenderness, and many a man has been bitten on the shoulders and arms during intercourse with a depth that suggests that violence as well as passion is involved. A man's "biting sarcasm" with his wife or a woman's "cutting tongue" with her husband may be a very thinly disguised expression of oral aggression.

If fear was predominant, the use of the mouth may be inhibited. One teenage girl I treated could kiss only boys she did not care for because her persistent unconscious fear of committing violence with her mouth caused her to "protect" the boys she liked. A young married woman said she felt no taboo about mouth-genital play, but every time her husband's penis was in her mouth she was distracted by the conscious fear that she might somehow "slip" and bite it off.

Deprivation of the infant's oral dependent needs is not the only means whereby fixation at this phase can occur—it may also be caused by overgratification. Children will often progress from one phase to the next only when it becomes necessary for them to do so; if dependency is made too pleasant, such children may not progress further emotionally. In adulthood, they will not seek partners with whom they can exchange love on an equal basis but will need someone who will continue to "feed" them and take care of them, as befits the infants they emotionally remain.

Addictive disorders likewise are traceable to oral disturbances. It is no mystery that virtually every known culture has developed the ability to find or to produce some substance which, when taken by mouth, produces an altered mental state, one that is usually a "good" feeling, at least in moderation, whether it is one of tranquility, nirvana, euphoria, heightened sensory awareness, transcendent experience, or magical power. The ubiquitous use of such substances symbolically echoes the universal human infantile expe-

rience of seemingly magical relief of tension and distress by taking
something into the mouth and body.

Because "magical" oral gratification is part of every person's dim
history, some use of such substances is probably normal, but
addiction to them bespeaks a maladaptive effort to repair some
disturbance that occurred in the fulfillment of early oral needs.
Adaptive efforts to cope effectively with reality are shunted aside in
favor of magical relief through oral intake. The form of what is
taken in, and the manner in which it is incorporated—whether
liquid (such as alcohol) or solid (such as pills) and whether
swallowed, inhaled, or injected—is of secondary importance. The
common denominator is the inappropriate use in later life of
infantile oral techniques to relieve tension and solve conflicts.

In addition to the sexually related developmental issues largely
settled in early infancy are those that only begin to emerge at this
time. They continue into various later periods to exert further or
more definitive influences and to find resolution. Of these, the most
important is sexual identity.

Innate male-female differences begin to manifest themselves in
sex-specific behavior in the neonatal period. The culture, represented by the mother, the father, and all other relevant adults,
begins immediately to respond differently to males and females.
These responses to basic differences in the two sexes are picked up
by infants, who are rewarded when they act in agreement with
parental concepts of masculine and feminine sex role behavior and
punished when they violate parental expectations. A mutually
reinforcing feedback system develops when parental expectations
are in harmony with the genuinely innate characteristics of their
infants.

A seldom considered innate influence upon sexual identity, one
which is not sex-specific, is the child's cognitive development, the
maturation of the ability to conceptualize. As an infant grows, his
capacity to think, to differentiate objects and put them in categories, gradually comes into being. An infant must first be able to
differentiate self from others before he can begin to conceptualize
"boy" and "girl." In addition to the constant teaching that "you
must do girl things because you are a girl," there eventually
develops the cognitive sense that "I am a girl and therefore I want

to do girl things." [50] This innate cognitive contribution to sex identity can be useful only when understood in interaction with the forces of culture and psychology.

A similar feedback system generally develops between the demands of parents and the psychology of the infant—what he learns about responding to his parents' expectations. Ordinarily, each infant learns very early the various sex-related behavior and personality characteristics that bring reward and approval. If his parents are consistent, he gradually adopts such behavior to the exclusion of those acts and characteristics thought inappropriate by his parents.

Most cultures are at least relatively consistent in their implicit assumptions as to what is properly "manly" and "womanly." While wide variations exist from culture to culture, much more general agreement than disagreement is seen if one compares cross-cultural stereotypes of sex-appropriate characteristics.[51] Thus most parents are not in serious doubt about their expectations. They convey relatively consistent messages to their children from infancy on, and the children are therefore relatively confident of their differing sex identities.

The opportunities for disruption in this process, and consequent sexual difficulties, are legion. Most basically, there may be variations in a particular infant's biological endowment that are contradictory to what his parents and the culture expect. Such an underlying biological force may account for those children mistakenly assigned the wrong sex and reared according to this faulty assessment but who steadfastly felt the sex assigned them to be in error and who subsequently made a successful transition to their proper biological sex in spite of their rearing and social learning. Or, for example, an atypically unenergetic boy may find it impossible to live up to his father's athletic expectations. The subsequent conflicts between himself and his father may ruin their relationship, cause the father to withdraw and deprive his son of a necessary male model, and destroy the boy's confidence in his own masculinity.

Parents can also introduce their own conflicts over sex identity, so that the child gets ambivalent or even contradictory messages, one corresponding to the parents' conscious concepts, the other to their unconscious attitudes. Such confusing double messages may begin their disruptive effects while infants are still tiny. Consider the mother who was taught to value the new active assertiveness as the proper feminine role but whose personal nature was never aggressive and who always wished for a more quiet, more receptive role but repressed her wishes as unacceptable. This young mother carefully fostered every independent developmental step her baby daughter made. She praised her for not crying, pressed her to begin cup- and spoon-feeding by herself, and left her alone as long as possible to discourage dependence. But she worried incessantly over her baby's health and lavished attention and affection upon her when she was sick—*only* when she was sick. The little girl was learning that only when she was sick and dependent could she get love, yet only independence and separateness was overtly praised and rewarded. While such a daughter would probably develop no disturbance of core gender identity, the stage was being set for her inevitable confusion about appropriate sex role behavior.

Parents who disagree with each other about sex role behavior may also encourage contradictory sexual behavior in infants. Conflict between the parents may be expressed unconsciously through the child. A crippling kind of sex role confusion may be caused when one or the other parent so rejects the spouse, or the opposite sex in general, that sex-appropriate behavior in the infant is consciously and systematically subverted. An angry, hostile father can, from the very beginning, reject every sign of what he sees as femininity in his daughter. He can make it impossible for her to be feminine and still retain his love. He is inculcating future conflicts that may encompass sex role behavior, sex role preference, and sex role adoption. This kind of early misrearing can be instrumental in homosexual development.

Cultures are sometimes inconsistent in their definitions of masculinity and femininity, and when this occurs sex identity confusions are further confounded. It is characteristic of cultures in transition, such as contemporary Western civilization, that there is a loss of confidence in and unselfconscious allegiance to traditional values. Everything is called into question, and distinctions between valid and arbitrary values are blurred. Parents in such cultures become uncertain of what to expect of their children and of how to rear them. They may express no clear expectations at all, with the result that not only sex role behavior but even core gender identity may be ambiguous.

Even fairly consistent cultural expectations are not immune from the possibility of producing problems related to sexual identity, as the culture itself may demand highly restrictive, inappropriate, and even distorted behavior. "Big boys don't cry" may start in the nursery. This approach to masculinity, carried to an absurd extreme, reaches a peak of constricted personality development in the "machismo" concept of masculine behavior characteristic of many Spanish-American cultures. Clinical studies have shown how much both sexes lose as a result of some of the sex role expectations traditionally implicit in United States middle class culture.[52]

Examples could be multiplied endlessly. There are the men who cannot allow themselves the pleasure of cooking or helping to care for their children because they would be violating their own limited concepts of masculinity. Tenderness and emotional display—even good school grades—are often associated with femininity and are thus off-limits to males. Females fare no better. With athletic interests and outdoor pursuits traditionally reserved for men, many women of conventional rearing are loath to develop their genuine interests in such activities because of their need to live within the stereotypes of femininity they have accepted as "normal."

It should be stressed that when the social pressures that shape sex role conformity are consistently applied, even those that distort or constrict a child's future personality, the child will usually develop without disturbance in his core gender identity. He will probably feel no insecurity in his sexual identity or sex role behavior, even though he may suffer in other ways. Parental consistency and cooperation, especially in the earliest months and years, seem irreducible qualities necessary for a firm foundation to the infant's core gender identity. Additionally, whatever version of sexual identity is valued by the parents, whether traditional or variant, it is necessary that their own sexual identities be clearly differentiated.[53] There is good reason to recognize innate differences in masculine and feminine behavior. Parents who are so confused that they completely blur sexual roles will cause deep future conflicts for their children. The adherence of parents to their own complementary and appropriately different sex role distinctions is a necessary prerequisite if they wish to start their infant off toward a secure sexual identity.[54]

Some less universal circumstances may occur in this early

infantile period that may have repercussions in later psychosexual development. They cannot be considered a part of the normal vicissitudes of development because they happen only in the lives of some children and their effects on development are not always firmly established. For example, clinical observations have led to a possible link between too early and exclusive visual exposure to the genitals of the opposite sex and later disturbances in sexual identity.[55] The data for this relationship are still clinical and speculative, but the suggestion fits well with the known infantile history of some male childhood transsexuals. And since in our culture it is normal for infants of both sexes to be exposed far more to female genitalia, there is some suggestive correlation with the known greater incidence of sexual deviations among men than among women.

Physical injuries and emotional traumas sustained by infants within the first year or so may, in surprising ways, lead to later sexual conflicts. It is during this first year that children are developing a stable sense of their own bodies and of the differences between themselves and others. For healthy development there must be a constancy in what the infant perceives of himself and others. The distinction between self and others is not a suddenly complete and perfect accomplishment; it is evolving and shaky. Also, the infant's perception of body parts and their separateness is incomplete. His perceptions of his genitals and of his whole body may be hazy and intermixed, the part standing for the whole.

Any number of happenings during infancy may disturb the constancy necessary for an infant to develop a firm sense of a dependable self and dependable others. Serious illnesses, accidents, surgery, real or apparent loss of one parent, or serious disturbances in the mother-infant relationship, may produce insecurity about important others. Because self and others are not yet fully separated, the actual or emotional loss of others becomes a threat of dissolution or loss of part of the self.

Initially, these complications of infant development are not specifically sexual (unless injuries or operations involve the genitals), and possible repercussions could extend into any area of subsequent development. It is at the time of discovery of genital difference that the consequences are reflected in psychosexual development. For most children this happens after eighteen months. When such early disturbances have existed, the discovery of genital differences is often accompanied by marked anxiety and regressive behavior. These behavior disorders are indicative that the earlier trauma resulted in a disturbed body image and left the child prone to a heightened and disturbing castration anxiety. When boys and girls discover how differently they are made, the earlier loss will have left them vulnerable to exceptionally frightening fantasies as to how the difference came about and what loss might still occur.[56]

Where is the youngster sexually at the end of eighteen months? A few—very few—things have largely been accomplished. For good or ill, they will be difficult to modify later. Others will have had only their beginnings; further growth and experiences will be necessary before there is even provisional closure.

The basic "gut" sense of whether the body is good or bad is established. This includes whether one's own body is good or bad, and whether other people's bodies are good or bad. The first eighteen months are, possibly, in the true biological sense of the phrase, the critical period for the accomplishment of body acceptance. This is only educated speculation at this time, but there appear to be persuasive considerations. The biological realities of normal infancy make it the time of maximum physical contact between mother and child. At no time is a child more exposed or more vulnerable to physical impressions and their quality. At later periods, different interactions and issues assume stage center and a child's susceptibility to changing perceptions of body acceptance becomes markedly diminished.

Since for the infant his body is himself, this phase provides the foundation for a person's deepest sense of worth, the "goodness" or "badness" of oneself. The American child psychologist and psychoanalyst Erik H. Erikson has characterized this period as the time when the infant decisively learns either basic trust or mistrust. The deepest and most tenacious emotional disturbances can be traced to this period and reflect a basic mistrust of oneself and others.[57]

Attitudes toward sexual pleasure begin in infancy and continue to develop for a long time. Part of the acceptance of one's body as "good" is accepting that the feelings that arise in it and the sensations it produces are good. Genital pleasure is a significant part of an infant's bodily sensations. The mother and other nurturing adults lay the groundwork for the acceptance and "goodness" of sexual pleasure and its pursuit through their reactions to the baby's activity with his own genitals.

Various facets of sexual identity also begin in infancy. Core gender identity, which will become relatively fixed before much more time passes, is already strongly influenced. Sex role behavior, or the distinctions between masculinity and femininity, also begin to be socially enforced. But this is only the small beginning of a long series of influences. An infant is capable of relatively little social behavior and response in comparison with older children and adolescents. Since these distinctions are largely social ones, though interwoven with biological determinants, these social demands are relatively fewer in infancy than in later life.

The anxiety of loss, associated both with weaning and with the repeated disappearance and reappearance of the mother, is first felt in infancy. So, too, is the sense of internal conflict arising out of contradictory needs and drives from within the self. These are but general developmental beginnings. They acquire psychosexual significance only when the anxiety inherent in a loss becomes attached to the fantasy of genital loss or damage, and the conflict between good and bad impulses becomes associated with sexual drives and wishes.

Child rearing should be an extended preparation for adulthood. I urge as a basic philosophical principle that nothing be taught to a child that he must subsequently unlearn for effective adulthood. Implementing this principle best begins at birth. Unfortunately, not all child rearing practices accomplish this goal. Some forms of child rearing produce "good" children but not functioning adults. There may be unnecessary discontinuities introduced between childhood and adulthood, and many of the attitudes inculcated into a child have to be discarded and new attitudes adopted in order for him to become a healthy adult.[58] Nowhere in Western culture is this more true than in adult influences upon sexual attitudes and behavior. Children who are taught that it is bad to pursue sexual pleasure must learn as adults that now sexual pleasure is good—a difficult and sometimes insurmountable task.

The detailed discussion of the complex interactions and potential conflicts arising during this period is not meant to overemphasize the pitfalls; there is probably no time when it is easier for a loving mother to be a good mother than during the oral phase, and the same holds true for the father and other caring adults. The infant's needs are at their simplest, the necessary disciplines and frustrations are minimal, and maternalism is one of the truly innate female characteristics, so getting an infant off to a healthy start is not an impossible task.

THREE

Who Owns a Child's Body?

"No!" With that brave battle cry left ringing in his mother's ears, the toddler trips over the edge of the rug, falls, gets up, and stumbles gamely into unexplored country. Both sides of his world are new to him. His inner world is filled with new drives, emotions, and capacities—not the least of which is the ability to say no and mean it—and the outside world expands to include everything he can get at as his muscular and locomotor skills mature.

There is no sharp time line separating an infant from a toddler, but eighteen months is a meaningful average age at which enormously significant changes take place and an almost bewildering array of new tasks begin to be imposed upon the unsteady adventurer. Roughly speaking, the assimilation of the appropriate development for this stage will occupy the child until he is between three and four years old. The transitions between all stages of psychosexual development will be similarly flexible and indistinct, and the normal age range for the transitions will increase as each phase becomes more complex.

As infancy is left behind, a major biological achievement is the maturation of muscular control and of the nerves that supply the muscles. This interrelated development reflects the gradual completion of myelinization of the nerves, a process of insulation which allows nerve impulses to remain separated and thus permits more discrete and coordinated movements. Muscle and skeletal growth allows more effective physical activity. The combination of more discrete innervation, stronger muscles, and practice at coordination results in the progress from wobbly toddling at the beginning to fairly competent locomotor and manipulative activity by the end of the stage.

Nerve and muscle development combine with the child's intellectual growth to make speech possible. This, too, is a gradual

77

acquisition, and is pursued as enthusiastically as is the rest of his newfound muscular and interactive competence.

These new capacities are imbued with tremendous energy. The typical toddler seldom stops, whether it be running, playing energetically, or talking. All of this is a manifestation of the drive for autonomy, for the independent right to do as he pleases with his own body. Indignant rage ensues if you try to restrain a determined toddler. And as his use and understanding of language improves, the powerful word *no* is added as an audible declaration of independence.

Toddlers, like infants, exhibit prelogical, or magical, thought. It is exemplified in infants by their assumption that mother's breast is a part of themselves which appears in response to their needs or wishes. But because infants cannot talk about what they are thinking and cannot indulge in much play or exploratory activity, their use of magic thought is not as easily seen as in toddlers.

The toddler, as he *very* gradually learns cause and effect and begins to substitute the reality principle for the pleasure principle, is already beginning to move away from magic, but the movement is slow, reluctant, and incomplete and his world is still essentially governed by magic. Anything is possible, good or bad, and the possibilities are enormously multiplied by his belief that there are even more powerful magicians than he—his parents. Thus much of his psychosexual development—what he observes, his fantasies, his comprehension of what he is told, his efforts to comprehend his fragmentary experiences—is colored and embellished by magic.[1]

It has been speculated that early changes and fluctuations in the production of sex hormones may help account for some of the storminess of this period. Sex endocrine data on very young children is scanty and incomplete, inadequate for firm conclusions. What there is suggests that there may be a small increase in the production of both male and female hormones at around two to three years of age and that the production may be sporadic and irregular.[2] Changes in circulating sex hormones exert marked psychological effects, especially during emotionally critical phases of development, such as prepuberty. If such changes, even small ones, can be demonstrated by increasingly refined research to occur during toddlerhood, it is likely that they contribute to the emotional lability characteristic of toddlers.

It is the myelinization of nerves that confers a special capacity for control which has given this stage its most common name, the anal stage. It is not until an average age of fifteen to eighteen months that the nerves to the anal and bladder sphincters are sufficiently myelinated that urinary and bowel control is possible. A few children develop this control earlier, and some mothers, preoccupied by eliminatory cleanliness, train themselves to know when a child will defecate. These are the "stool catchers," who have learned to interpret the concentratedly introspective look on baby's face, and rush him triumphantly to the toilet.

For most children, sphincter control begins to be possible around the beginning of this phase and is not truly secure until the phase is complete. This power is unique: it is one that remains entirely within the toddler's control. His physical mobility can be restrained, objects of his insatiable curiosity can be removed from his reach, even his verbal productions can be inhibited or rendered ineffective; not so his ability to determine when he defecates or urinates. In his drive for autonomy, sphincter control is his prize possession because it is his alone. This unique characteristic, plus the lessening but still significant emphasis placed upon toilet training in Western culture, give this aspect of body control unique significance among the many facets of development occurring at the same time.

There are other characteristics of bowel function which also lend it special meaning in the emotional and sexual development of the toddler. Sensory innervation of the mucosa, the lining of the anus and rectum, produce distinctly pleasureful sensations at the time of a normal bowel movement. The same holds for urination, but urinary control normally does not achieve the same level of emotional importance. One reason is the lesser taboo and shame associated with urine as compared with feces. Another is that no child can exercise the same heady power over urinary function. A full bladder must be emptied regardless, whereas rectal fullness is not so imperative.

Toddlers also are still in the earliest, vague stages of developing an accurate body concept. A bowel movement comes from within the body and is regarded as a part of the body. It is solid, visible, and discretely separate whether in a diaper or in the toilet, and as such is an object of great interest and concern. The anxiety aroused by the loss of what seems to the child a part of himself is a frequent source of the fear of sitting on the toilet or of flushing the feces away and of voluntarily letting go of the bowel movement.[3]

In general, neuromuscular maturation and the concomitant burst of physical activity is as germane to the psychological quality of this period as is anal function, and has prompted the modification of its designation to the "anal-muscular" stage.[4] An overall description of the characteristics of this period of development must encompass all the ways in which physical maturation is swept up into the striving for body mastery and the conflicts over body control.

Children and Parents Become Adversaries

It is precisely because of the toddler's ability to get around plus his fierce drive for independence that there is an inevitable shift in his relationship with his mother and, increasingly, his father. Muscular competence is not matched by judgment, and if only for his own safety the toddler must be restrained under some circumstances; because of his capacity for intrusiveness and disruption, his parents must begin now the process of socialization. They must introduce the requirement that he learn to curb his total freedom in order to function acceptably within the first social unit, the family. Demands for bowel and bladder control are introduced as one specific facet of socialization.

This intersection of inner drives and social controls is biologically related to the simultaneous occurrence of both these aspects of development. This constitutes another normal developmental conflict, inescapable in a child's maturation, even though its manifestations may vary widely in different homes or cultures.

Toilet training is unavoidable in any culture in which the average life style and housing conditions require control of where and when elimination can take place. The style in which the mother goes about it may vary from obsessive to relaxed, but go about it she does, nonetheless, and it is this maternal style that largely determines how well her child will come to accept necessary self-control without loss of necessary self-determination.

Bowel control is usually accomplished only after a period of stubbornness by the child, which is in no way abnormal. He does not easily accept and internalize external control over his bodily functions, and the anxiety over loss of part of himself needs time to overcome. If the mother places excessive emphasis upon the timing of bowel movements, the toddler may not learn that this function is simply something required by his body. He will regard it more in relation to his mother than to himself. When he feels kindly toward her, he will reward her with a gift of the cherished feces. More often, and more disturbingly, his mother's demands may be met by stubborn refusal, and the child develops a sense of physical pleasure in bowel retention. The sensation of holding in the stool in defiance of mother becomes inappropriately associated with the sense of successful self-assertion.

Boys usually give more trouble in toilet training than girls do. This difference between boys and girls is common folk knowledge, and has been verified by child developmental studies.[5] Its possible correlation with the greater compliance noted in girls suggests itself readily, but whether this distinction is related to innate or learned sex differences, or both, is not known.[6]

The mother's style in approaching bowel control is likely to epitomize her style of response to all of her child's independent or obstinate behavior. A mother who needs to maintain close control will usually demonstrate her intolerance of independence in all spheres of her toddler's activity; all increments of body control and ego mastery will be affected by the interaction between child and maternal temperaments.

The child's temperament is now an increasingly significant factor in the relationship. Learning has been going on throughout infancy, and the interaction during this period cannot be simplified into one involving only the child's innate drives and the parental environment's demands. The toddler has a long experience of his mother's response to his earlier needs and to his body. If he carries with him a sense of his mother's acceptance of the goodness of his body, he is more likely to trust both his own and her attitudes toward his body's functions. He will less frequently be fearful, and that will diminish one source of resistance to the acceptance of body control. The infant who learned basic trust is better prepared to assume that his mother's concern with bowel control and other body functions is a loving one, and he is therefore predisposed by his prior learning to easier cooperation.

In contrast, the toddler who has already experienced his mother's repudiation of his body and its processes approaches this new and sharper conflict with distinctly unpropitious psychological preparation. He trusts neither his mother nor himself. If her rejection has been so thorough as to overwhelm him with the fear of her emotional desertion, he may so fear her disapproval as to be already an overcompliant, inhibited child. He dare not give expression to his autonomous needs. If her rejection was inconsistent, or his capacity for anger was not totally destroyed, he can be expected to defy her efforts to impose controls. His earlier learning has prepared him emotionally to regard his relationship with her as a battlefield, to expect distress rather than pleasure. In such ways every child's psychology evolves as a significant influence which colors his response both to his own inner drives and the external demands imposed by other people.

During this stage of development, fathers play a growing role. The father who is at home, and who is not inappropriately oblivious to his offspring, cannot fail to be more drawn into involvement with this active, mobile, verbal youngster. His emotional responses to noise and to the vigorous independent strivings of his child will be added to those of the mother. Since they may well differ in some important respects from the mother's, the little boy or girl has this added complexity (and interpersonal richness) to cope with.

It is probably not an artifact of our cultural attitudes and occupational life styles that fathers become more involved with their children at this stage. Males are not only anatomically unfit for unassisted nurturing of early infants but they also usually lack the true maternal feelings of being engrossed in and devoted to infants. Notwithstanding individual and cultural exceptions, biological, cross-species, and cross-cultural research document the probability that maternalism is an innate female quality.[7] Males generally relate better to increasingly older children. Thus it is a naturally occurring phenomenon that the broadening vista of the toddler comes more and more to encompass the father as a distinct personality.

A major development during this period is the beginning of the earliest form of conscience, the superego. Conscience is essentially an adult property and includes a variety of self-regulatory functions and mechanisms. Superego is the psychodynamic self-control that is internalized by a child. Its consolidation is a major accomplishment of the next phase of development, and will be discussed in more detail in Chapter 6. It is basically childish, however, both because of its origin and because of the simplistic level at which a young child's mind works; to whatever extent it remains an unchanged part of the gradually developing and much more complex conscience, that conscience remains childish.

Arising directly out of the necessity, nonexistent during infancy, to impose social and protective controls upon the toddler, parental prohibitions must be expressed. Initially, these prohibitions are only obeyed, if and when they *are* obeyed, out of the child's fear of disapproval and punishment. Early superego development can be seen to proceed, however, through the gradual internalization of parental prohibitions. Partly through progressive identification with parents and their expectations, and partly because of the child's magical belief that his parents are omniscient and will inevitably know of his wrongdoings, his superego begins to take shape as the punishing agent. It becomes the internal "voice" of real or fantasied parental prohibitions. By three or four years of age, children can often be heard telling *themselves* not to tear up the magazine, or not to hurt the kitty. The development of internal controls, based upon self-imposed punishment by one's own conscience, is on its way.[8]

The characteristics of parent-child interactions during these years are greatly influenced by the culture and its child-rearing emphases and implicit preferences in personality development. In some simple, outdoor societies, the where and when of defecation and urination is a minor issue. The relatively simple matter of going off into the bushes may be left to the teaching of siblings, and the nature of the socializing pressures and demands are infinitely variable, depending upon the desired result.

But there is little or no choice as to whether the developmental tasks involving bodily functions and social controls must be engaged during this period; it is only the manner in which they are approached that varies. There are no physical environments in which a toddler could be totally unrestrained without being exposed to physical danger and death. It is characteristic of all cultures to begin inculcating their behavioral preferences when children become able to walk and talk. Efforts at absolute permissiveness deprive the child of ego development in the areas of impulse mastery, social compromise and conflict resolution, and value formation—deficits that will sorely penalize him in any human community.

And the internal psychological task of assimilating and adapting to the newly acquired muscular and eliminatory controllability devolves upon every child emerging from helpless infancy. Anal functions may not concern parents, but they always concern the child. He must come to terms with the frightening loss of part of himself and must learn to differentiate between the eliminatory and sexual sensations and functions that all seem to localize and concentrate in that one area of his body.

More Sex Differences to Understand

During infancy, males and females begin to sense some different characteristics and qualities about their sexuality, but largely without any awareness of differences. Toward the end of that period, some children begin to register the visual differences between their own genitals and those of the opposite sex, but the crucial combination of inner mental development and external opportunities for observation and comparison generally cannot occur until the toddler stage. The child's mental capacity must reach the point at which he can perceive a reasonably clear body image, his cognitive development must permit meaningful comparisons, and his physical mobility must permit the opportunity for a range of repeated observations of the genitals of both sexes.

The discovery of genital sex differences is utterly fascinating to most children. Their absorption in this amazing fact, and their repetitive focus upon it in order to comprehend it and fix the differences in their minds, are striking. So predictable is both the discovery of and the interest in genital differences in the second half of the first year that it has been referred to as the early genital phase.[9]

The toddler's interest in sex differences may slip by unnoticed in families in which parents are blind to manifestations of childhood sexuality. Since such parental blindness is often an expression of the need to deny and repress children's sexuality, the children in such homes may well also be less overt in their interest—they are quick to pick up their parents' attitudes. Some parents are so determinedly modest in hiding their own and their children's nude bodies that toddlers may sometimes not have had an opportunity to observe the genitals of anyone. Unless such children have playmates whose parents are less watchful, or go to day care centers or nursery schools, their awareness of genital differences may be considerably delayed.

In more casual home conditions, however, there is no mistaking their interest. A little boy will usually ask about his penis. Either as a result of his questions, or in the process of toilet training, he will usually learn some term for it, either the straightforward *penis* or one of the slang-babytalk-circumlocutory terms. A little girl, too, will often have a term, learned during toilet training, with which to refer to her perineal area, but it is more difficult for her to ask a name for something she cannot see.

Upon seeing another naked child, a child's visual interest is clearly genital, and if it is a child of the opposite sex, questions are usually immediate and direct. A little boy will most typically ask, "Where is her penis [or other word]?" or "Why doesn't she have one, too?" or "What happened to it?" or "Will she get one, too?" From little girls, the questions most often take such forms as "What is *that*?" or "Why does he have that?" or "Why don't I have one?" or "What happened to mine?" or "Will I get one, too?" Most frequently, these questions are asked with strong curiosity but with little or no anxiety.

If it is the parent who is unclothed, the child is still more puzzled because the presence of pubic hair and the disparity in size does not admit of such easy personal comparison, but similar questions ensue about the differences, sometimes also focusing upon size. Boys and girls both will often wonder if a penis is hidden within the mother's pubic hair.

Some parents will simply give an answer and nothing more. Many will take the opportunity to explain the differences between boys and girls, also including fathers and mothers. This can lead to an extended period during which the child attempts to corroborate his findings and assimilate the knowledge. He wants to watch whenever anyone is undressed for any reason, and will repeat endlessly the same questions. As the concepts of "boy" and "girl" and "penis" and "vagina" slowly fall into place, children in homes that do not forbid sexual talk will begin running over their store of knowledge as though chanting a litany, "Tony got penuth, Daddy got penuth, Mommy got 'gina, Bob got penuth, Ingrid got bagina, Kathy got 'gina, . . ." and so on through the list of firmly identified acquaint-

ances. Parents may have bemused second thoughts about their
prized openness when a stranger is fixed with an unwavering look
and asked, "You got bagina?" But once the knowledge is secure, the
subject is largely dropped by the child.

Parents often, and wisely, teach more than their child asks when
this curiosity first arises. They point out other sex differences, such
as breasts and, perhaps, beards or moustaches. They may also
emphasize the changes that will occur as the child grows up. This
serves to lessen the impact of size differentials. Even more
importantly, it reinforces the value and significance of the little
girl's genital and sexual status, since at toddler age she has no
equipment as showy as a boy's.

The typical questions of toddlers display variations of two basic
themes. One has to do with how it happens that some people have
penises and some people do not. The other implies the preference
for a penis. These are the child's verbal expressions of castration
anxiety and penis envy. These normal and predictable developmental conflicts are widely misunderstood and have been vigorously
attacked and denied, partly because they remain unconscious in
most adults and thus seem to offend common sense—that vigilant
guardian of the obvious—and partly because penis envy has been
grossly misused as the basis for a thoroughly mistaken and
derogatory theory of female inferiority.

Penis envy, unless complicated by pathogenic circumstances in a
girl's rearing, is as predictably frequent as it is harmless. Every
parent has observed, and certainly every child "knows," that having
something is preferable to not having it. In the simple and
self-evident logic of the toddler's world, this principle virtually
achieves the status of a concrete universal. Toddlers who share toys,
or anything else, do so with the unwavering knowledge that they
are personal possessions which they can snatch back with perfect
right. On this basis alone, penis envy is both understandable and
transient.

Fear of the loss of part of oneself also plays a role. Weaning,
separation from mother, perhaps the beginning of bowel training—
all these have faced the child. Therefore the questions "Where did
mine go?" and "Will I get one too?" implicitly convey the anxiety
that some (necessarily valuable) part of the girl's body is missing or

removed. The envy of those who have not suffered the same fate is to be expected.

Another characteristic of child logic accounts equally well for instances in which penis envy does not occur. That is the tendency to explain the unknown by recourse to the known. Instances have been recorded of little girls, upon first seeing a little boy's penis, asking about the "torn tag of flesh." Apparently knowing only their own body configuration, and presumably having experienced some minor injury during play, they call upon experience for understanding.[10] Such responses, however, are infrequent.

The early experiences of loss that produce penis envy also produce castration anxiety in boys. They, too, know that valued objects, sometimes perceived as parts of themselves, can disappear, and they have been helpless to prevent it. There is also the irrefutable evidence that some people do not have penises. (Child's translation: Some people have lost theirs.) The possibility of loss of this wonderful and pleasure-giving organ can only be anxiety-producing.

That some degree of anxiety attends the discovery of genital differences is inevitable, but at this period it is not great. Girls may try for reassurance that they may grow a penis or that theirs is hidden, boys may persist in the suspicion that mother really has one behind the pubic brush and may even insist that they saw it there, but under ordinary circumstances the concern is minimal. The fantasies which in two or three years will inflame the anxieties to a much higher pitch have not yet occurred. Factual parental reassurance will relieve most of the anxiety and eliminate any sense of real inequality. It is only in families in which there is grossly destructive derogation of women that toddler-age girls will already begin to feel angry jealousy of the penis as the anatomical emblem of might and privilege.

The differing sensations associated with either male or female sex organs that began in a minor way during infancy take on greater emotional importance in the toddler stage and serve as a major point of departure for the increasing psychosexual differentiation of males and females. It will be seen that anxiety typically attends some of these sensations, rendering this issue another of the normal developmental conflicts out of which ego maturation as well as developmental disturbance may result.

It will become increasingly clear that reference to the vagina and to vaginal sensations is simplified and inexact. A female's inner genital sensations may arise from her vagina, uterus, tubes, or ovaries. Her interests, concerns, and fantasies may encompass any or all of her internal organs. A toddler's pregnancy fantasies cannot appropriately be considered vaginal; she has no means of differentiating her separate internal organs, nor does she know in any meaningful way that they exist. Since her initial contact with and hazy concepts of those organs is vaginal, that term will be used in preference to more cumbersome, all-inclusive references. In all further discussions of early psychosexual development, *vaginal* will be understood to refer to any part of the total internal reproductive organ complex unless specifically stated otherwise.

The little girl's awareness of vaginal sensations inside of her, and her discovery of the vaginal opening into the body location of those sensations, poses for her a complex emotional task with respect to her developing body image. As previously indicated, the inability to see an organ compromises a child's ability to incorporate it into his body image; little girls are more often able to name the penis as the source of boys' urine than to name the source of their own.[11] The girl may probe her vagina with her fingers or other objects, specifically to explore it and to make it less unknown, but vaginal sensations remain vague, diffuse, and difficult to localize. She has no control over the spontaneous occurrence of vaginal sensations. In contrast with the easily controlled and localized clitoral sensations, those of the vagina are not only more mysterious, but may even seem to be caused by some outside force simply because she herself has no part in their production.[12]

The various sensory experiences of filling and emptying contribute to learning about an organ as part of one's body. The sensation of air passing through both nose and mouth contributes to a subjective sense of the nature and shape of those cavities. The mouth, in addition, can be sensed through the taste of food and the tactile sensations of holding food in the mouth and chewing and swallowing it. Even though they are out of sight, the anus and the urethra are similarly knowable through the repeated and clearly localized sensations produced by bowel movements and urination. They do not remain entirely mysterious orifices or cavities.

One of the reasons the vagina is difficult to know is that it has no natural contents to aid in its identification and integration.[13] It may be explored by purposely penetrating it, but this mode is potentially anxiety-producing and may cause the little girl to fear that she has done herself irreparable damage.[14]

There is still another anatomical peculiarity that renders the vagina less controllable. Unlike the other two most important body openings—the mouth and the anus—the vagina is not provided with voluntary muscular control for closing it off, at least not in the perception of a little girl.[15]

These normal vaginal characteristics leave the little girl prone to anxieties about her vulnerability. She feels unprotected against the possibility of attack and penetration. And with her grossly insecure sense of bodily integrity, an opening without muscular control poses the threat of loss of body contents.[16] The toddler who has witnessed menstrual bleeding may regard it as further evidence of vulnerability to harm, or of its already having occurred. The diffuse vaginal sensations and the mysteriousness of that organ contribute another source of anxiety. The consequences may motivate a repudiation of the vagina, with preference for the controllable clitoral sensations and a repression of any knowledge of the vagina or its opening.[17]

These are not wild and fanciful speculations, far removed from the actualities of a child's mind. One need not even look into the dreams, fantasies, play behavior, and open statements of young children in analysis in order to verify them, although that rich source of information is unparalleled. There are clear reflections of such emotional responses in the everyday lives of little children. They are much more prone to be upset by a sensation they cannot localize than by one more clearly identifiable. They are most apprehensive—even terrified—at the attempt to insert anything into their bodies even when there is no pain. The fear of loss of what is inside the body is regularly illustrated during bowel training. And it is quite common that girls who have been observed to masturbate with vaginal insertion will later completely forget that they ever knew the vaginal opening existed. The denial of the vagina is so common that many authorities who never observed little girls themselves long believed that females had no knowledge of the vagina until much later in development.

It is equally true that these early childhood concerns are normal and do not lead to disturbed development unless they are aggravated by experiences that reinforce and fix them in the child's unconscious by lending the weight of truth to them. In a healthy family there are no realities to corroborate a small girl's fear that she is peculiarly vulnerable simply because she is a girl. Explanations about sex differences gradually replace mystery with beginning knowledge. Apprehension about her vague inner sexual sensations is slowly balanced by pride in the unique creative potential of her inside organs. And many little girls overcome or do not develop the need to repress vaginal awareness.

But to some extent the anxieties are naturally there. They could not have been prevented, simply because of the reality and inevitability of a girl's increasing awareness of growing up in a female body with female anatomy and sensations. The task of coping healthily with the anxieties of this age is an enriching one. And the struggle with them adds further to the unique qualities of feminine psychology.

Little boys have their own special tasks, based on their own special bodies. Most of their genital sensations are external, easy to localize, control, and repeat. Masturbation for boys does not lead them into invisible areas, unknown cavities, and vulnerable openings. On the contrary, as their masturbation becomes more purposeful, each experience can be increasingly reassuring. Genital stimulation produces erection and enlargement of the penis, so that each easy repetition is a reminder of the presence and dependability of that pleasureful organ.

Superficially, it would appear that nature has tipped the scales in favor of boys, and for this one aspect of psychosexual development, that is true. It is much easier for a boy to integrate his penis and the relative simplicity of its pleasure-giving function into his body image. But there is a major developmental task for boys that girls are spared. The very external existence of this prized organ renders it forever vulnerable to loss. As indicated earlier, the toddler years are not ordinarily those in which castration anxiety is a major source of inner concern for a boy, but the imaginary vulnerability of his penis to loss leads to anxieties and maladaptive defenses that will subsequently cripple the mature sexuality of a surprisingly large number of men.

The discussion of the different sensations inherent in the principal male and female sex organs opens the way for understanding an important and subtle unconscious influence upon psychosexual differentiation. While spontaneous sensations in these major organs are predominantly internal and diffuse for girls, and external and localized for boys, both boys and girls have both internal and external genital sensations.

The nerves responsible for vaginal sensation and movement are also present in the male and innervate the prostate, seminal vesicles, and internal portions of the urethra. The reflex and spontaneous stimulation that accounts for vaginal sensations produce "inner genital" sensations in the male that are as diffuse and difficult to localize as the inner genital sensations of girls.

Likewise, clitoral sensations have the same sharply focused, controllable, and repeatable qualities typical of the "external genital" sensory response of the penis. Both are supplied by the same nerves. Also, there are rich nerve connections, in both sexes, between the inner and external genital organs, so that there is likely to be some reverberation of any excitation that arises either internally or externally, resulting in a combination or even a confusion of the two kinds of sensations.

The significance for children of this age is that this is the time when all children acquire some concept of reproduction and of the role played by the sex organs. This may evolve from observations of pregnancy, of intercourse between humans or animals, from early sexual explanations by adults or other children, or from innate awareness of reproductive function. These early concepts are always to some degree inaccurate and incomplete, but despite the often grotesque anatomical theories of reproduction fantasized by children, two facts are usually accurately perceived: babies grow inside a woman's body, and the penis is somehow involved.

In this very simple manner, inner genital sensations come to be equated with femaleness, and external genital sensations with maleness.[18] This association is, of course, unconscious. All the toddler has is a consciousness of differing qualities and sites of sexual sensations and various poorly formed ideas of reproduction involving the penis and the growth of the baby inside the mother, but the associations between genital sensations and sex-specific reproductive function do form.

The nature and quality of inner genital sensations are as disquieting for little boys as they are for little girls, and for the same reasons. It is easy for a boy to externalize all his sexual excitation onto his clearly defined penis, thus denying the existence of disturbingly vague internal genital stirrings. If he unconsciously perceives girls as being frighteningly penisless, he has further impetus to repress and repudiate this "female" aspect of his sexuality.

Little girls cannot quite as readily externalize their disturbing inner genital sensations, nor do they have as much emotional motivation to do so. The size and invisibility of the clitoris provides some obstacle. More importantly, these sensations are connected with their actual femaleness and the maternal role that they are beginning to conceptualize. For this reason girls during this period usually show signs of working to cope with, rather than completely to deny, their inner sensations. But they can and may be sufficiently anxious to repress vaginal awareness and focus entirely upon the clitoris. If they consider the clitoris a too-small penis, and if they have begun to believe that males are the favored sex, then this female repudiation of internal genitality becomes instrumental in further penis envy and early masculine identification.

Let me anticipate the far distant resolution of these unconscious conflicts and emphasize that the healthy outcome does not entail repression or artificially limited sexual identities. These early childhood unconscious responses are normal and natural, but they also reflect a grossly immature psychosexual state. The clitoris is no more masculine than the prostate is feminine. Years of intrapsychic development will pass, though, before full integration of all aspects of one's sexuality can be accomplished.

There is another peculiarity of the normal male genitalia which affect both his psychosexual development and his response to bowel training: the anatomy of the scrotum and testicles. As already noted, the scrotum filled with both descended testes is larger and more visible than the penis throughout childhood until after puberty and is thus visually important to the toddler. Testicular mobility, however, is unique among visible organs. It is estimated that 90 percent of male infants are born with open inguinal rings (the openings in the abdominal walls through which the testicles descend into the scrotum), and that they remain open at least through age six. The cremasteric muscles will produce testicular retraction into the abdomen and out of sight under various conditions, including cold, anxiety, and in reflex action at the time of closing of the anal sphincter. Thus the testicles are the only visible organs of the body that can and do disappear entirely and involuntarily and cannot be made to reappear voluntarily.

Visualize the little boy sitting gingerly on the toilet seat during the period of bowel training. As rectal activity and the expulsion of the stool begin, he is peering intently between his legs back into the toilet. Looking past his scrotum and testes, with one hanging lower than the other, he sees the fecal mass come into view and begin to drop into the toilet. At the very same time, his testicles move up and disappear into his groin. The stage is set for considerable confusion and anxiety.

There is similar motor and sensory innervation both to the anal muscles and mucosa, and to cremasteric muscles and testicles. In the adult the sensations and movements arising in these body parts will be distinguishable from one another, but this discreteness is incomplete in the toddler. There is spreading of nerve impulses due to incomplete myelinization. These various sensations also tend to be somewhat diffused. All these anatomical conditions, combined with the toddler's very primitive and insecure body image, make it inevitable that he will associate testicular disappearance with evacuation.

Testicular retraction thus becomes one more experience of the apparent loss of a part of oneself and therefore another precursor of castration anxiety—one more example that the loss of a body part can indeed (appear to) happen. At the same time, fear of testicular loss becomes a serious concern in its own right. On the principle that any and every body part is valuable and indispensable to the child striving for a secure sense of self, it is not necessary that testicular retraction be related to possible loss of the penis. It is distressing enough to fear loss of his testicles, a particularly poignant fear in that he cannot make them reappear at will.

A strong indication of the degree of anxiety associated with this "loss" is that conscious interest or concern with the scrotum and its contents is largely repressed by most males. The unconscious association reveals itself in a particularly telltale later development: Research has found that testicular retraction becomes in adult males one of the sharpest and most dependable indicators of repressed anxiety. One of the strongest responses is elicited by questions about bowel training, even when the man is consciously unaware of any anxiety at all.[19]

The visual proximity of the hanging scrotum and the fecal mass, and the confusion of shared anal and testicular sensations, can cause another difficulty in bowel training of boys—the fear that the testicles may fall off into the toilet and be flushed away. This emotional link has been repeatedly demonstrated in boys whose intensely fearful reaction to bowel training led to consultation with a child analyst. Boys without such obvious difficulties will often express the association clearly when they are given the words to do so. This fear may be one reason that toilet training is more difficult for boys than for girls.[20]

A last and most fateful consequence of the genital differences between boys and girls is due to anatomical proximity of the sexual and eliminatory organs. In the case of the penis, they are partially identical. These organs share sensory innervation sufficiently that pleasure developed in the anal region can come to substitute for genital sexual pleasure.

Their proximity contributes to an inappropriate association of emotional attitudes between elimination and sex. Part of toilet training is accomplished by teaching children some degree of disgust for their evacuatory products. As children learn that feces and urine are regarded as dirty, smelly, and nasty, they often apply this attitude to the entire perineal part of the body, which includes the external areas of sexual pleasure.

Because the penis is a distinctly separate organ from the anus, and because of the lesser stigma of "dirtiness" attached to urine, boys are somewhat protected from misassociation. They are less likely to confuse the "nastiness" of bowel function with sexual organs and with the feelings and functions appropriate to them.

A little girl has a more confusing anatomy. With all elimination occuring seemingly from the same fold between legs and buttocks in which her sexual sensations are also felt, she is more likely to lump it all together. Elimination is dirty, the parts of the body associated with elimination are dirty, and therefore the sexual organs and their functions are contaminated and dirty. While such associations are undoubtedly very hazy and often remain unconscious in the minds of toddlers, they can nevertheless be learned.

Sex Play Broadens

Toddlers are far more capable than infants of pursuing anything, including sexual sensations and curiosities. Their better muscular coordination facilitates focused genital exploration, and their more highly developed cognitive and perceptual capacities and peripheral nerves increase their awareness and enjoyment of what they are doing. The result is more purposeful, deliberate masturbation during this period. It is important to realize, however, that masturbation during toddlerhood does not normally have the intensity or importance that it acquires a year or two later. Even though it increases markedly and is highly significant in the toddler's psychosexual development, it remains a relatively casual activity at this time. Its importance will mushroom when the biological maturation necessary for intensely erotic sensation occurs at the oedipal phase.

It is clear from previously cited Kinsey data that a significant proportion of boys between two and four years of age are capable of masturbation to orgasm. (There are no comparable observations of a group of girls.) Some child analysts unaccountably express doubts about whether little boys of this age can achieve orgasm, whereas in their experience girls often can. They draw some interesting conclusions from this presumed differential capacity for the release of sexual tension, but the Kinsey statistics make it impossible to accept those conclusions at face value.

However, there may be some enlightening psychological consequences of possibly differing *qualities* of male and female early masturbation based upon two possibilities. One is that little girls may be able to achieve orgasm more often than boys of similar age; it is entirely within speculative possibility that the greater orgastic capacity of postpubescent females compared with males might hold true at all ages, including early childhood. The other is that the orgastic experience of little girls may be more subjectively satisfying, because it does not differ physiologically very greatly from adult female orgasm. The little boy, on the other hand, can only have the equivalent of a "dry" orgasm, since there is no ejaculate before puberty. Adult males report less full gratification from dry orgasms, and the same may hold true of boys.

If such differences are valid, then it is to be expected that the masturbatory activities of toddler-age boys and girls will have different emotional results. A child of either sex striving unsuccessfully for release of the pleasureful tension of sexual stimulation is likely to be more restless, irritable, and fretful than the child who can achieve the calming aftermath of such release.[21]

One of the most characteristic uses of masturbation is seen when children are falling asleep. As any mother of a toddler knows, this energetic creature often finds it difficult to withdraw his interest from the fascinating outside world at bedtime. Genital fondling during the transition to sleep serves two main purposes: it reinvests the child's body with his greatest attention, easing the withdrawal into himself for sleep, and it reawakens passive infantile memories, as is often evident in the child's talking to himself as he falls asleep, regressed into babyhood, cuddled and rocked by mother in fantasy.[22] Since genital masturbation arises as a result of good maternal care, the facilitation of mothering fantasies through masturbatory play has a naturally preexisting connection.

When given the opportunity, toddlers will avidly pursue their sexual curiosities and activities with other children of their own age and older, and with adults. Their curiosity is not limited solely to appearance; they are curious about how others' genitals feel (to themselves and to the other person), how they taste, how they function, and what changes may or may not occur in them. When they have the necessary words to express themselves, these interests are clearly verbalized.

There is no natural bodily modesty at this age. Little children see no reason to hide their bodies or bodily functions from anyone. Aside from the personal freedom afforded by running about naked, this characteristic affords these natural little exhibitionists with ample opportunity for expressing and satisfying sexual curiosity. It is only through the influence of parental teaching that the beginnings of shame and modesty make their appearance this early.

In permissive societies, interest and curiosity is naturally accompanied by action. Children of this age will play with each other's genitals and masturbate each other, whether of the same sex or opposite sex, will express themselves in both oral-genital and anal-genital play, and attempt to imitate adult intercourse, in which intromission can occur. This range of behavior appears to be a natural and spontaneous developmental expression in the absence of adult intervention.[23] In less permissive societies, however, intervention is usually rather firmly applied and the direct observational evidence of childhood sexuality is rather more sparse.

There is equally active interest in the genitalia of adolescents and adults. Cultural taboos against this kind of curiosity are even stronger, of course, and not only are children more quickly discouraged, but the evidences and memories may be repressed from their conscious recall as adults. Parents can often remember their children's unabashed fascination, though, with everything sexual. Children not only want to look and ask questions, but to touch and feel. They are engrossed by the size and shape of the adult penis and the scrotum with its testicles. The appearance and texture of pubic hair is the focus of much attention, particularly in the mother. In the absence of obvious external genitalia, there is puzzlement about what may be lurking under the hair. And the mother's breasts come in for as much interest as her genitals.

Further Sex Education by Parents

It is during these years of toddlerhood that core gender identity is established and, except in rare instances, closed off to further influence. The nature of the pervasive influences on this component of sexual identity change very little during the year or two of toddlerhood. They remain a constant part of every child's life experiences, both verbal and nonverbal. Statements about what boys or girls "are" or "are not," what they "do" or "don't do," and parental reinforcement or discouragement of various putatively masculine or feminine behavior are omnipresent training influences. Much of what is said to the child refers to sex role behavior. The bedrock assumption that "you are a boy" or "you are a girl" is unmistakably implicit. By no later than the end of the third year, children have normally internalized this knowledge of their unalterable maleness or femaleness with genuine finality.

Under ordinary circumstances, core gender identity reflects a harmonious concordance of all determinants of maleness or femaleness—chromosomal, hormonal, anatomical, and rearing influences. A toddler can hardly be expected to be aware of chromosomes or hormones, but it might be expected that the total absence of a penis or vagina could cripple a child's conception of himself unambivalently as a male or female. Not so. Case reports and follow-up studies of such unfortunate children indicate that the presence of normal genitalia is not essential to the firm establishment of core gender identity.[24] Research evidence is strongly in favor of giving the greatest weight to early parental influences.

While core gender identity is quietly taking its place as a fixed quality of the toddler's self-concept, other facets of his sexual identity are becoming subject to more intense and more varied influences. In particular, sex role behavior and sex role preference are being affected by what his parents and other important adults at this period expect of him. Perhaps even more importantly, these qualities are being molded by the personality characteristics of his mother and father, their availability to him, and the nature of the relationship between them.

There are some intriguing gaps in what is known about the seemingly obvious issue of paternal versus maternal influences. In general, much more attention has been focused upon mother-child relationships than upon father-child relationships. On the other hand, maternal absence or unavailability is virtually unstudied, perhaps because of a paucity of children who were reared from infancy solely by males. Studies of the effects of paternal absence or unavailability do exist and offer some useful insights.

In view of the early determination of core gender identity, it cannot be surprising that the absence of a father during the few early years of childhood handicaps a boy more in developing his fundamental sense of maleness than if the boy suffers the absence of his father somewhat later in childhood.[25] Other aspects of sexual identity, while significantly affected by the nature and availability of both maternal and paternal models, are not so closely and essentially bound to the presence of mother and father. Sex role behavior, preference, and adoption are also meaningfully influenced by later experiences with peers and other adults, in addition to parents.

An additional factor of increasing importance during these years in the early formation of sexual identity is the dynamic force of the child's own previous and present experiences. Beyond the largely biological and cultural-environmental influences during infancy, the child responds more and more on the basis of what he learns from, and about, the differences between his mother and father, or any substitutes for them in his life. Particularly warm relations with the parent of the same sex facilitates acceptance of his own sexuality. Warm relations with both parents increases his integration not only of the value of both sexes but also his valuing of attributes of both parents (both sexes) within himself. His experience of a loving relationship between his parents further reinforces his sense of worth in the eyes of the opposite sex.

Conversely, painful experiences in any of these relationships will mobilize ultimately self-damaging resistances. In the face of a cold, punitive mother, for example, a girl will begin to rebel even against appropriate feminine orientation, not merely against the mother's unpleasant qualities.

These early identifications are quite fluid in the two-to-four year old. The typical family is still one in which, for most of a toddler's waking life, mother is at home and father is at work. Mother is the main model of active productivity in the world of home for the toddler—the boy as well as the girl. She is usually the powerful one in the child's eyes. Mother is actively doing and producing and accomplishing things, most especially if she becomes pregnant during this period. Boys, too, clearly want to be like their mothers and do the things she does, including wanting to have and care for babies. Doll and baby play is common, and generally reflects no ominous confusion in developing sexual identity, as it well might in later stages. At this time, identification with the mother in boys exists comfortably along with, not instead of, being appropriately male.[26]

Were the father's productivity more visible and comprehensible to his small children, the early opportunities for identification would be richer and more varied for both boys and girls. One would see similarly benign—indeed, beneficial—envy and imitation of the father's activities in girls. But there is one unalterable dimension of adult sexual differences which poses problems for boys, with which they will grapple emotionally most of their lives. That is the mother's power to produce a baby. As an innate biological distinction between the sexes, I suggest that envy of the ability to become pregnant proves to be a far greater unconscious dilemma in the psychosexual development of males than penis envy is for females.

During these early years, when parents are first introducing words and verbally expressed ideas to the toddler, parental sex education takes on a new dimension. Many parents are grossly unprepared to supply their children's needs for sexual information. Nevertheless, it cannot be denied that parents and other adults often specifically and *purposefully* take an approach to childhood sexuality that confuses children about sex. They may not recognize the consequences to children of what they do, but what they do is deliberate.

Parents contribute to childhood ignorance and confusion by the ways in which they name, or "label," sex-related functions and behavior. One is by negative labeling. When a child does something the parent perceives as sexual, he may be told unequivocally that it is bad. The child's own awareness of his behavior may not be associated with sex, so that he is not sure what is supposed to be bad, and he is almost never told *why* it is bad. Confusion and anxiety are inevitable.

Then there is nonlabeling. A child may be scolded or spanked without ever being told what his supposedly bad sexual transgression was. Or a girl, discovered masturbating, may be physically stopped or have her attention diverted with no reference whatsoever to her genital play. The result is that children are given no vocabulary for sexuality. No words are provided with which to build concepts and values.

Finally, there is mislabeling. A child may be warned about supposedly harmful effects unrelated to the specifically sexual aspects of a particular behavior. For example, a masturbating girl may be told that she can "hurt herself up inside." It is the sexual act that the adult wants to stop, but he mislabels it as physically dangerous, thus contributing to the child's misconception of sex as violent and harmful. Any false information, such as "God put the seed in Mama's belly," is mislabeling. Another form of mislabeling is the early identification of the sex organ by use of nursery or babytalk words which, in their initial application, refer to excretory functions. These words often are never replaced with sexually accurate words, and constitute a form of mislabeling that fosters the association between sexuality and dirtiness.[27]

The function of language in fostering or crippling a child's development is far broader than that pertaining to psychosexual development. Research has found that appropriate words are indispensable to a child's capacity to comprehend his world and categorize his thoughts so as to function consistently within any social context. Without them, he is as truly deficient and prone to disorder as is the diabetic who is deficient in insulin.[28] The deleterious effects of verbal lacks and distortions in the genesis of sexual difficulties is but one limited illustration.

Negative labeling, nonlabeling, and mislabeling have detrimental effects that influence virtually every aspect of psychosexual development. As sexual fantasies reveal, there are significant limitations upon the accurate sexual knowledge that a small child can assimilate, but this is no excuse to give him misinformation. It is seriously damaging to deprive the child of the verbal means and the emotional right and security to reevaluate and discard his earlier misconceptions as his psychosexual development proceeds. One might be hard put to devise a laboratory experiment better calculated to produce a maximum of crippling handicaps. On the other hand, parents who do provide appropriate labels demonstrate to the child, in that very interaction, the acceptability of thinking about and learning about sexuality.

Some of a toddler's significant interactions with parents involve sexuality more directly. Parents' attitudes toward their own bodies are a major influence upon their children's developing sexuality. Parental nudity around the home has been a controversial issue among child development professionals, especially with regard to a parent and the child of the opposite sex. Some consider that parental nudity is overstimulating, disturbing the child's normal psychosexual development and producing premature interest, anxiety, and emotional conflict. This position has come about chiefly from work with disturbed children who seemed to respond poorly to their parents' nudity.

Others consider the issue vastly overemphasized and point to the lack of evidence of emotional harm when parental nudity is handled casually and naturally. Once again, cross-cultural comparison serves as a useful check against ethnocentricity. Data from other cultures does not support the fear of emotional damage, nor does information gathered informally from sexually well-adjusted Western adults, who frequently recall the bodily freedom of their parents during their early years as a major source of their comfortable acceptance of their own physical sexuality.

The issue appears not to depend so much upon the nudity itself as upon the emotional messages being communicated to the toddler by the *manner* in which the parent uses his nudity. Parents who allow themselves to be self-consciously nude because they believe it is good sex education for the child will more often convey uncertainty and anxiety than easy self-acceptance, and parents are capable of employing nudity in either conscious or unconscious seductiveness toward their children. Nudity in situations where it would not expectably occur, such as preparing dinner, is likely to express motivations other than bodily freedom. Some parents while nude allow their children in bed with them, and some bathe with their three- and four-year-old toddlers. While this kind of child-parent nudity may at times occur as a matter of course, it often involves fostering the child's curiosity and permitting actual sex play with the adult's body and genitals. This kind of parental nudity most often serves the unconscious needs of the adult rather than the child.

Both common sense and authoritative reasoning lead to the conclusion that casual and natural parental nudity is not only harmless but beneficial. Parents' embarrassment about their bodies —if they hide while they get dressed, or lock bathroom and bedroom doors, or rebuke a child for walking in on them while they are unclothed—can do nothing but produce bodily shame in the child. In clinical experience, such a background is found in almost all adults who regard their own bodies with shame and rejection. It is quite appropriate for parents to be nude when dressing or in the private areas of their homes. When they are not embarrassed by a child's presence at such times, no emotional conflict will be engendered in the normal child. Only unnecessarily contrived opportunities for parent-child nudity need be avoided.

The toddler's increasingly obvious and goal-directed masturbation is more difficult than infantile genital handling for parents to ignore. They will be presented with considerably expanded opportunities to convey to the child their attitudes toward genital play. The same is true with respect to the ubiquitous sexual curiosity and sex play of a child of this age. The healthy toddler's interest in the sensations and functions of his own and other people's bodies has burgeoned into an imperative and demanding curiosity. One way or another, with conscious purpose or pervasive indirection, parents must cope with it. The lessons taught and the attitudes learned at this time are decisive in the mastery of body function.

Even the techniques of toilet training become directly sexual under some conditions. When a mother fails to realize the inherent anxiety in a little child associated with the fantasied loss of a part of oneself, she may be uncomprehending and impatient with the resistances, especially in boys, to bowel training. Threats and punishment intensify the child's concern by adding the fear of still further loss—his mother's love. Thus the precursors of castration anxiety are heightened and its subsequent resolution rendered more conflictual. The additional testicular anxieties in boys are also directly subject to eased or added distress, depending upon the mother's understanding and reassurance. Also of direct sexual impact, most particularly for girls, is the mother's communication of acceptance of or revulsion from the perineal region during toilet training.

Awareness of adult intercourse, when such an experience occurs, is evocative of more complex emotions in a child than in an infant. A toddler can more clearly perceive what is occurring and can associate the actions with his own genitals. The primal scene fills him with manifest excitement, of which anxiety can be a significant component. But since this is an everyday occurrence in the lives of a major portion of the world's children, the same cautions that were detailed in the discussion of infants and the primal scene must still be observed in generalizing about its effects.

Some children as young as four are introduced to direct sexual activity by adults. While adult-infant sexual activity is essentially limited to stimulation of the infant's genitals with negligible true participation by the baby, the scope of sexual behavior is much wider with toddlers. The number, though unknown, is probably small, and such sexual interactions are not limited to parents. Baby sitters, adolescent neighbors, and adult relatives and acquaintances, as well as parents, may express their disturbed sexual needs through sexual activity with a child. A surprisingly large number (80 percent) of adult women who recall being forced as a child into sexual activity with an adult, report that the coercion began between three and five years of age. Such sexual activity with so young a child is almost always limited to genital fondling, but instances of penetration of girls and by boys are certainly known. As long as no frightening force is employed, it is often possible for an adult to entice a child into being a willing participant; 23 percent of the women who recall collaborating with an adult sexual partner began this collaboration at the age of five or younger.[29] Genital pleasure and adult affection provide powerful encouragement, and the child's sexual fantasies do not as yet produce the deterrent anxiety characteristic of the oncoming oedipal period.

Widening Implications of Toddlers' Sexuality

Some of the consequences of these years are quite general. They affect character formation and issues of emotional wholeness or disturbed constriction and affect the individual's freedom to enter eventually into a fully participating sexual partnership. The most important general issue is that of bodily autonomy. Out of the conflict between imperative drives for self-determination and the omnipresent need for socialization, the toddler must, in the end, salvage an adequate sense of independent freedom to be and to explore.

Failure to institute gradually appropriate controls prolongs infantile behavior. Excessive disciplinary demands turns the mother, the model of the child's concept of woman, into a powerful and punitive ogre. The solution lies not only in the obvious qualities of patience and sensitivity to the child's level of readiness but in an intelligent assessment of fruitful versus futile endeavors. No one wins when parents become drawn into a battle in which their demands are unenforceable. Bowel control is such an unenforceable issue. Therefore it is prudent to leave it an area of body control over which the child feels maximum autonomy. Toilet training can be gently encouraged, but no effort need be made to invade the child's rights to his sphincter control. The child who is given that kind of basic respect is more able to tolerate restrictions in other aspects of mobility and self-assertion. This is a constructive compromise, because the taming of heedless impulsivity is achieved in just those areas of behavior in which failure of control would entail serious danger to the child or even the environment.

Excessive or inappropriately applied discipline arouses rage or fear or both. Those children in whom fear is stronger resort to fearful compliance and passivity, while inwardly hating and resenting the overcontrolling mother. Children in whom anger predominates become stubbornly defiant and opposed to any controls, meanwhile fearing the eventual consequences of their intense rage. These eventually automatic responses to discipline and to the main disciplinarian—a woman—contaminate a girl's acceptance of her own femaleness and a boy's capacity to allow himself to be emotionally close to women.

When, as still frequently happens, the battle truly centers around anal function, the mother's overconcern for the when, where, and how much of the youngster's bowel movements eventually inculcates into the child some interesting character traits. The mother's preoccupation with evacuatory cleanliness usually prevails, and such children in later life show a constellation of attitudes and behavioral traits sometimes called the anal character. They, too, are fanatical about superficial cleanliness and orderliness. The protracted "battle of the pot" has built into them an obstinacy about everything. They are scrupulous about small and unimportant detail but often ineffective in important matters. They are miserly and stingy, given to hoarding junk as well as things of value. They equate sexuality with dirtiness and are painfully constricted, rigid, and emotionally impoverished in their sexual relations. And they orient their lives around following the rules, more concerned with the letter of the law than its spirit. They are authoritarian towards others in like manner.[30]

Some of these traits can be understood as response to any kind of disciplinary overcontrol, but in its full development, it requires no great stretch of the imagination to detect the consequences of being taught to overvalue something of no real value (feces), to elevate concerns for the unimportant above the important, and to learn disgust for one's bodily functions. Nor does it require trained clinical acumen to recognize the devastating effects of such classically mishandled toilet training upon subsequent sexual adaptation.

Of greatest relevance are the reflections of this period in the directly sexual aspects of the youngster's development. There is a greater difference between the infant and toddler stages than between most stages of human maturation. Proportionately more new capacities, activities, and interactions are available, and this is one reason that these years are so filled with excitement for the toddler. It also explains the vast array of vital influences upon psychosexuality.

Some of these sexual influences are rather general. Both boys and girls have learned a great deal more about their bodies. Beginning with only the vaguest awareness of their own genitals and the associated sensations, they end with fairly sharp perceptions. They know and can verbalize the differences between themselves and others. They have a beginning knowledge of the role of their genitals in sex and reproduction, but in all probability this knowledge is not yet at all clear. Masturbatory activity has sharpened awareness of their sensations and bodily responses and has helped delineate both those responses that are localized and repeatable and those that are less easy to define and control. All these increments of body awareness contribute to clearer body image and more secure body mastery. Those aspects of ego development which relate to knowledge of one's unique body and its boundaries—the more complete separation of self and not-self—are correspondingly strengthened. And to the extent that sexual expression has not been unduly discouraged, self-confidence about one's sexual self has grown.

Many of the lasting sexual impressions from the toddler years derive from both the fact and the discovery of sex differences. This age is by no means too early to discern the beginnings of some of the characteristic differences in interests and personality that emerge from the profound consequences of growing up in one of two different kinds of bodies. As indicated previously, a boy's genitalia, being external and visible, not only facilitate but innately direct him toward external reality and pragmatic, mechanical pursuits. The changes in shape and size of his penis, and the less controllable appearance and disappearance of his testicles, are deeply personal, bodily experiences that serve as forerunners for the boy's later interest in mechanical toys with moving parts that he can control and sometimes take apart.[31] His play with building blocks and other shapes is often characterized by the erection of various structures, their vigorous destruction, and the reconstruction of them. At the mental level, a male's greater ability in dealing with spatial configuration is statistically well documented.[32]

The built-in facility for externalizing his genital interests carries for a boy some potential disadvantages, too. It is reflected in a tendency to more superficial, simplistic thinking, less tempered by intuitive grasp and emotional awareness. His anxiety about internal genital sensations and his association of inside genitals with all that is female cause him to reject that part of himself. That rejection also threatens him, if he does not overcome this anxiety as he grows up, with the loss of his capacity to identify and empathize with women so as to relate to them most fully. These early characterological beginnings, linked to innate genital realities, help to explain why so large a segment of so many men's mental and emotional capacities are relatively undeveloped.

In little girls, the influences are quite the opposite. The persistence of her inner genital sensations and the invisibility of her sex organs predispose her to inner awareness, introspection, and intuitive rather than pragmatic thought.[33] This is her innate tendency, despite the fact that she can externalize and control her most intense sexual sensations, and despite her brain's basic equal competence for any kind of thinking. Little girls of this age are already more verbal, less aggressively active, and less given to mechanical and violent play. They, too, equate inner genital sensations with femaleness and associate these sensations with pregnancy and babies. They express this self-awareness, which is often unconscious, in intense and endlessly varied doll play. While boys, in identification with their mother, also play with dolls, it is seldom as engrossing and dolls are seldom their major choice of toy.

These distinctions are oversimplified in order to draw a statistically typical picture. Most activities and interests are shared by toddlers of both sexes, rather than being the exclusive domain of one or the other, but the anatomically determined tendency toward somewhat divergent paths is a fact of life. There is a remarkably consistent expression of such differences cross-culturally.[34] One suggested explanation for the consistent historical and worldwide tendency toward the derogation of women has been linked to the equation of inner genitality with femaleness and the repudiation of this diffuse and uncontrollable "femaleness" by both males and females.[35] Observations demonstrate that recognizable and characteristic masculine-feminine differences will develop in the most varied kinds of cultural milieus. It therefore requires greater effort in child rearing and education for parents to encourage the development of the various *un*characteristic potentials of each sex.

The normal developmental anxieties related to sex differences seldom lead to serious disturbances among toddlers, but sometimes such disturbances may occur, especially if there has been a predisposing disturbance during infancy, such as surgery, a serious illness or accident, or the loss of an important person. The consequences of such disturbances on the formation of a secure body image were discussed in chapter 2. Ordinarily the discovery of genital differences during the toddler stage is a relatively untroubled one, but when the child's earlier experiences have left him with a defective sense of object constancy, he is likely to interpret sex differences as intensely threatening and may develop severe castration anxiety and regression.

A specific case will illustrate the effects of this combination of circumstances. A female infant was born with a congenital defect that required the wearing of a corrective device in the genital area throughout most of the first year of her life. This also contributed to some difficulties in her relationship with her mother. But in spite of these handicaps she showed relatively normal though slightly delayed development. Around the middle of her second year she began to experience the typical burst of curiosity, motor activity, social interaction, and readiness for toilet training. At about eighteen months, she first became aware of genital differences. She was under particularly close observation during this whole period due to her being in a special nursery, and it was possible to observe her reaction in detail. Her intense sexual curiosity was accompanied by efforts to pretend that she had a penis, to deny the existence of penises, and to destroy or get rid of anything that had a phallic shape. These responses were followed by regression, demonstrated by withdrawal of all genital interest, a return of earlier eating and sleeping difficulties, and the loss of some of her psychosocial progress. Her subsequent character displayed a flattening of normal curiosity. Clearly this little girl reacted to the discovery of sex differences with a rather severe neurotic disturbance characterized by castration anxiety, regression, and ego impairment.[36]

Other disturbances in children during this period are also differentiated by sex. In a sizable series of children brought to a psychiatric clinic for developmental and behavioral disorders, boys and girls presented predominantly different kinds of problems. Boys were typically brought in for excessive aggression, hyperactivity, lack of bowel control, and speech disturbances, girls for overdependency, emotional overcontrol, bowel retention, and sibling rivalry. Differences in impulse control seem central to most of the expressions of sex-linked disorders. Boys with intense emotional ties to their mothers tended to show the female pattern of overcontrol of impulse.[37] In such disorders, it is not possible to demonstrate an unquestionable relationship to genital and sexual differences. But it is possible to recognize exaggerations and distortions of conflicts and characteristics that have been linked to the sex differences.

As soon as the details of parental influences on sexual identity and sex role behavior are discussed, the Pandora's box of masculinity and femininity is opened. I would prefer to avoid the polemics as far as possible and be consistent with the current state of scientific and anthropological knowledge. As phenomena, masculinity and femininity have been defined as sex-specific social behavior not in the direct service of procreation and offspring survival. As aspects of sexual identity, they are defined here, and throughout, in terms of positive attitudes and attributes. Femininity is perceived as a positive attitude toward being female, including all the special capacities and qualities that biological femaleness confers. Masculinity is similarly a positive acceptance of maleness, with its own biological uniqueness. Approached from this position, there is no particular value placed upon any purely culture-produced stereotype.

In the description of parental influences that follows, a number of questions may arise about the value of some aspects of masculinity or femininity that are produced or affected. Studies of masculinity and femininity have generally measured qualities that share two characteristics: they are qualities perceived positively both by the individual and by those of the opposite sex who are comfortably accepting of their own sexual identity, and they are qualities that display very broad cross-cultural agreement.

Even these considerations do not necessarily confer any unassailable value upon specific masculine or feminine traits, unless those traits are consonant with biologic inevitability, and any capricious efforts to modify such traits would constitute a threat to mankind. Such fundamental sex-specific essentials are very few in number. The following discussions of parental factors in sex identity are simply descriptions of which influences tend to produce what results. The interested reader may go to the original studies to reach his own conclusions about the value of the particular traits chosen by the different investigators in rating masculinity or femininity.[38]

A father's absence during the first years of a boy's life interferes not only with the boy's formation of a secure core gender identity but with his formation of a pattern of masculinity. He will be less aggressive, feel himself to be less secure in his masculinity, and will be objectively more dependent. The earlier a boy suffers paternal deprivation, the more severely he will usually be affected. The presence of a surrogate father, such as a brother or uncle, mitigates the effects but does not erase them. A boy's father is clearly most important.

The absence of a father has similar effects upon the sexuality of girls. Girls who are deprived early of their fathers have less satisfactory heterosexual adjustment and tend more to reject the role of wife and mother. They are more uneasy and anxious with males,[39] statistically show lower rates of orgasm in adult heterosexual life,[40] display fewer typically feminine interests, and have less feminine self-concepts.

A father's presence, of course, is even more important to a boy, and investigators have found that the father's perceived masculinity and the quality of the father-son relationship is more important than the amount of time the father spends at home. A boy's sense of masculinity is closely determined by his father's masculinity as expressed at home. Men who consistently take a maternal or traditionally feminine role, or who relate with their wives in such a manner that there is little sex-role differentiation in household activities, will have sons who are not highly masculine in their interests or self-concepts. The most important paternal quality in this context is decision making. Boys whose mothers work and whose fathers stay at home rate lower in the various measures of masculinity than those whose fathers are out working. The father's masculinity as expressed through interests and activities outside the home is relatively ineffective as a model for his son's masculine development unless that quality is visible to the boy in the home.

Perhaps most important is the existence of a warm, caring, affectionate relationship between a father and his son. Boys with fathers who are both traditionally masculine *and* nurturant are more securely masculine in their identity than boys with fathers who are merely masculine but show no caring relationship. The same principle applies in paternal disciplinary function. Firm setting of limits is an important quality in fostering a boy's masculinity, but firm setting of limits without being punitive exerts an even stronger masculine influence.

This discussion of paternal influence is purposely limited to its role in sexual identity, and a pattern of appropriate fathering emerges from the data. It is that of a firm, decisive man with a strong role in family decisions, who uses his strength with gentleness, has a warm and loving relationship with his son, and encourages assertive behavior rather than competing against it. It is not enough for the father to be a domineering he-man; he must form a deeply affectionate bond with his son so that the boy wants to identify with him and is not intimidated.

Similar paternal qualities foster feminine sexual identity. Paternal dominance in family decision making is not so essential for femininity—the mother must obviously be perceived as an important and valued influence—but girls from families dominated by the mother often turn out to be less feminine than those whose fathers had strength in the family. Girls who ultimately choose a career over marriage have been found to have had a less satisfactory relationship with their father than their marriage-oriented counterparts, and highly masculine women actually identify less with their fathers than do feminine women. This is but one evidence of the correlation between inadequate or destructive fathering and female homosexuality.[41] It would seem clear that a father's warmth and masculinity fosters his daughter's femininity not through imitation or identification but by stirring in her the motivation to be an appropriate counterpart of such a man.

Mothers exert their influences upon their children's sexual identity, perhaps more obviously on boys than on girls. A dominating mother is usually either openly or subtly derogatory toward her husband, and this means to a son that his masculinity is not valued. Mothers need to permit and even encourage energetic activity in their sons in order to foster masculine sex identity. Boys whose mothers are overprotective show little masculine interest and behavior; boys who have long, intense, and exclusive relationships with their mothers show confusions and difficulties in their sex roles.

Mothers who are secure and happy in their femininity rear boys who are similarly secure in their masculinity. These mothers encourage complementary, not imitative, behavior in their sons. They can go a long way toward making up the deficit if the boy's father is absent, simply by valuing masculine behavior and imbuing the absent father, or other males, with positive qualities for the boy to strive for. Good mothers recognize, even if unconsciously, a mutually reinforcing difference between masculinity and femininity and help their sons achieve that difference.

It scarcely needs detailing that these same mothers also provide the ideal basis for feminine sexual identity in their daughters. One study of a group of homosexual girls found that they had been unable to find qualities in either parent to which they could trustingly relate. They not only could not learn to trust involvement with a male on the basis of their relationship with their fathers, but they found their mothers equally impossible to identify with warmly.[42]

Fathers are probably more important than mothers in the differentiation of sexual identities of their children. Cross-cultural anthropological studies have found a constant characteristic distinction between maternal and paternal behavior: mothers instinctively know that all children deserve to be equally loved; fathers know that all children will eventually have to earn their love and acceptance. This includes fostering—and demanding—the development of appropriate psychosexual differences. Mothers tend to respond more expressively to children of both sexes. Fathers, even when they are warmly responsive to both daughters and sons, are more concerned with differences between masculinity and femininity and tend to encourage those differences.

Parental influences upon sexual identity are both stronger and more concentrated during toddlerhood than in later years of childhood. Since emotional learning is more deeply ingrained the earlier it occurs, the two or so years after infancy are those when the child is most open to these interactional qualities in his parents. He has had to progress beyond infancy in order to be intensely exposed to, and to begin to comprehend, these characteristics, and if he is reared at home he is exposed to other adults for only a fraction of the time he is with one or both parents; therefore, parental influence is typically almost undiluted and takes hold of the child's mind before many modifying influences or alternative models are available.

The toddler's perception of the relative roles and values of maleness and femaleness is often distorted by the fact that most toddlers live in a female-dominated world. While a toddler picks up many indications of the presence or absence of mutual respect between his mother and father, he can seldom perceive his father's intangible and long-range productive role with the clarity and impact of his mother's immediate power. As long as a child is homebound, the intensity of what he learns about sex-specific roles is not necessarily paralleled by objectivity or cultural accuracy.

In contrast to masculine or feminine behavior, sex role preference is probably more strongly related to interfamily dynamics than to individual qualities of the mother or father. It is in their relationship that the child begins to perceive the environmental attitudes toward each sex and to gauge the activities and opportunities available; these bear forcefully upon whether a boy can look forward to being a man and a girl to being a woman. These impressions continue to be developed, verified, reinforced, and modified during the early school years, when the youngster encounters most intensely the attitudes and expectations of the community in which he must function.

In an effort to discern the basic components of healthy sexual identity that it is the parents' responsibility to provide a child, one finds there are but a few truly indispensable ones, but they are of enormous importance. One is the child's happy acceptance of his biological sexuality and its biological function; another is the secure and trusting enjoyment of the complementary and mutually rein-forcing differences, both physical and emotional, between the sexes. The American sociologist Carlfred Broderick has expressed suc-cinctly the criteria for firm sexual identity leading to healthy psychosexual development: "First, the parent (or parent-surrogate) of the same sex must be neither so punishing nor so weak as to make it impossible for the child to identify with him. Second, the parent or surrogate of the opposite sex must not be so seductive, or so punishing, or so emotionally erratic as to make it impossible for the child to trust members of the opposite sex. Third, the parents or surrogates must not systematically reject the child's biological sex and attempt to teach him cross-sex role behavior." [43] This kind of parenting provides the appropriate background for the eventual emergence of the natural heterosexual preference and performance. Broderick considers that a positive attitude toward eventual heterosexual marriage is also a prerequisite for normal psychosexual development. That appears to be an ethnocentric requirement of a different order, not necessarily of the same basic, cross-cultural validity.

A basic component of healthy sexual identity is the recognition that psychosexual and sociosexual differences between male and female are essential, not optional. I refer here not to any localized, whimsical, and perhaps destructive definition of differences, but to the simple fact that differences exist. Both individuals and society suffer when humans, in their unique capacity to tamper with reality, attempt to negate this biological truism. Clinical experience is replete with examples of disturbances caused by ambiguous sexual identity.[44]

Many of the psychosexual consequences of the sexual development of this period derive from the overt sexual activity of toddlers, particularly masturbation, which is deeply involved in aspects of ego development that extend far beyond the simply sexual.

Virtually all scientific evidence accumulating over the past several generations is in agreement that masturbation is not only harmless but positively beneficial. This is worthy of emphasis in view of the continued widespread taboos based upon antisexual attitudes, religious injunctions, and misinformation. As late as 1939 a widely used textbook of pediatrics was recommending harsh treatments for the "cure" of masturbation,[45] and as recently as 1954 a textbook on urology was attributing such symptoms as mental illness, amnesia, insanity, and circles under the eyes to the "nervous shock of repeated orgasms" brought on by masturbation.[46]

It has already been pointed out that masturbation develops in infancy as a consequence of *good* mothering and that its absence signals a disturbance in the mother-infant relationship. Subsequent masturbatory activity aids in bodily awareness and mastery and enhances the development of object constancy and object relations. Masturbation most often becomes associated with emotional conflict regardless of parental attitudes because of the fantasies that become associated with it during various developmental phases. A major mode of ego development is by learning to cope with conflict by forming defense mechanisms that are adaptive and healthy; a person's ego would be crippled if it had no opportunity to learn to defend itself against the bursting out of primitive drives which, unchecked, could overwhelm his later social behavior. The absence of infantile and childhood sex activity, principally masturbation, disrupts these aspects of essential ego formation.[47]

Quite positive effects of masturbation upon character and personality have been reported. Orgasmic release in girls leads to calmness and an easier capacity to meet stress and to integrate inner sexual drives with external reality demands. Character benefits of this sort are derived only when masturbation occurs in spontaneous response to the girl's own need and readiness. Masturbation that arises defensively or as a result of overstimulation serves different purposes and usually has no such constructive effects.[48] It is likely that boys capable of the same quality of orgasmic release would derive similar benefits.

Masturbation at any age usually elicits some parental response, often a negative one. Because masturbation is more obvious and more frequent in childhood than in infancy, parents may find it more difficult to ignore and may feel their resources for coping with it strained. Many parents have a difficult time putting their own childhood indoctrination behind them and find various rationalizations for distracting a child's attention even when they do not want to appear sexually repressive to the youngster. Their chief motive in interfering with the toddler's genital play may be to relieve the anxiety it arouses in themselves. There is no question that children will perceive the disapproval, however disguised, and while more violent and punitive disciplinary measures will be commensurately more destructive, one must recognize that children do learn how to value their sexual selves from the way in which their parents value the children's sexuality.

"Too much" masturbation is a useless expression, but compulsive masturbation can occur as early as toddlerhood. Even this manifestation is not easy to define, and some parents may display their own anxieties by regarding perfectly normal masturbatory frequency as compulsive. To be considered compulsive, an activity must occur so repetitively and incessantly as to interfere with other normal activities. Compulsive masturbation usually breaks through the beginning boundaries of socially appropriate behavior that even a toddler is starting to learn and manifests itself regardless of the circumstances. At times when he might normally be expected to be engrossed in a new toy, interacting with a playmate, or enjoying an outdoor picnic, his attention appears totally preoccupied with genital manipulation. Genuinely compulsive masturbation may produce genital inflammation, abrasion, and occasionally resulting minor infection, and eventually becomes more tension-producing and exhausting than tension-relieving.

It is only under such circumstances that parents have reason to be concerned, because such genital preoccupation is a symptom (*not* a cause) of some emotional difficulty. The difficulty can be discovered only by study of the particular child, but parents might generally try to be alert to whatever could be overtaxing the youngster's limited ego capacity to cope, such as the arrival of a new sibling, the loss of someone or something important, or a new environmental demand, such as toilet training or nursery school, for which the child is not quite ready or which may be presented too forcefully. Compulsive masturbation is one of a child's ways of withdrawing into his own body and his own capacity to satisfy his primitive needs for comfort and pleasure, away from an external reality he perceives as overwhelming. His activity is self-defeating in that it becomes a substitute for learning to cope with the new demand. If parents can discern what the child is avoiding, they can often either modify the situation or help him to a more constructive approach. When the source eludes the parents, professional counsel from a child psychiatrist should be sought.

At times a child who has been strenuously taught that masturbation is bad and shameful may have difficulties falling asleep. Because of the normal tendency of young children to masturbate during the interval between waking and sleep, the toddler with sleep problems may be expressing conflicts over his genital play. His struggle against it may interfere with going to sleep, or his indulgence may arouse enough fear and guilt to interfere.

A lack of curiosity about sex is another manifestation of excessive and premature repression of the sex drive. There is no question that normal toddlers, given normal opportunities to observe themselves and others, will inevitably express their curiosity about all they see and feel. When they do not, this is clear evidence that something has influenced them to fear, and therefore to suppress, the normal curiosity.[49]

Despite the weight of evidence that masturbation is a normal and necessary part of a child's psychosexual development, some child psychoanalysts believe that children must learn to restrain and control their free expression of sexuality through masturbation on the grounds that in learning to harness and control one's inner drives, ego mastery and defense mechanisms are developed, social existence becomes possible, impulse control is learned, and energies become available for other important pursuits such as intellectual learning and creativity. Such analysts also point out that masturbation can be used as a regressive substitute for coping with reality or learning to relate to external love objects.[50] The maturational goals mentioned are indispensable for ego growth, but their relationship to the control of masturbation is not at all clear, even to those who consider the relationship to be valid, and it must be emphasized that these opinions are not derived from the study of essentially normal children.

It seems likely that the child's masturbatory fantasies, particularly at later stages of development, will provide enough conflict to induce spontaneous efforts at some limiting of his impulsive sexual expression. In addition, sexuality in our culture remains an essentially private expression despite frequent exceptions. As part of every child's general rearing, the pressures of socialization—such as the necessity to renounce totally egocentric gratification and to control unthinking impulsivity—will normally be applied to his sexual and aggressive drives without the necessity of focusing specifically upon masturbation.

The same problems beset the question of permissiveness toward childhood sex play and curiosity. Not only is there a general consensus that our culture has been excessively repressive toward all aspects of childhood sexuality and that the repressive attitude is at least in large part responsible for the high incidence of inadequate and distorted sexual function; there is also cross-cultural evidence suggesting that permissiveness toward childhood sex play is correlated with greater capacity to enjoy adult heterosexuality, fewer adult sexual dysfunctions, and a lower incidence of sexual deviations.[51]

Primate experiments by the American zoologists Harry and

Margaret Harlow, in which they reared rhesus monkeys under conditions of various kinds of deprivation, including a lack of opportunity for maternal and peer group play, produced unexpected data on the significance of peer group play for later sexual function. To the surprise of behavioral scientists, peer-group play was found to be of even greater significance than in the mother-infant interaction in the sociosexual development of the infant monkeys. As long as the monkeys were allowed to play together in mixed groups from "toddlerhood" on, they developed in adulthood the normal capacity for sexual function. But those isolated from peer play did not learn to function normally, regardless of whether they were normally mothered.[52] It must be emphasized that a major component of juvenile monkey play is sexual, involving genital exploration, the imitation of adult heterosexuality, and the learning of the appropriate physical interaction for successful coitus.

It must be emphasized that Harlow's peer-deprived monkeys do not prove anything about human children. It would be an unexpected contradiction, however, if similar behavioral influences proved to result in opposite rather than relatively comparable results; cross-cultural studies suggest that the consequences may indeed be comparable.

As in the case of masturbation, most of the professional cautions against unrestrained childhood sex play assume that intellectual, creative, and other ego maturational components will be crippled unless the sex drive is harnessed and its energies made available for other pursuits. There are innumerable case histories in the literature of Western culture in which sexual impulsiveness and lack of general impulse control is correlated with ego deficits. In many of these cases, therapy resulting in sexual and impulse control was accompanied by ego development which had not previously occurred, but there is some basis for continued reevaluation of the assumed cause and effect relationship. The possibility that impulse control and deficient ego maturation result from earlier deleterious influences has not, to my knowledge, been experimentally studied through systematic research. The fact that most permissive cultures are far less technologically advanced than some repressive cultures is quite suggestive, but the data suffer from two deficiencies, one being that a cause and effect relationship has not been established, the other that some of the most sexually repressive cultures are also among the least technologically advanced.[53]

Until recently, there were no adequate populations for follow-up studies of children reared in a sexually permissive atmosphere within a highly technological society, but that is no longer true. Israeli kibbutzim children are reared in heterosexual groups, there is no interference in sex play, and mixed sex play is frequent and intense during early childhood and the early school years.[54] In several generations of sabras (children of the kibbutzim), the free childhood sexuality has apparently had none of the effects upon intellect or productivity theoretically expected in such a highly technological society. In addition, there is virtually no homosexuality among them.[55]

There is as yet too little data and too many unanswered questions to make it possible to recommend with full confidence the relinquishment of all restraint upon childhood sexuality. Because of the repressive nature of Judeo-Christian culture over many recent generations, the consequences of the prohibition of childhood sexuality are better known than the consequences of its permission, but the known consequences are sufficient to warrant careful reassessment. It is as easy to collect cases in which intellectual and creative impairment are associated with repressiveness toward childhood sexual expression as to find cases in which such ego deficits are associated with unrestrained sexuality.

At this stage of inadequate knowledge, the issue is more philosophical and speculative than scientific. Many people reared in our culture pay a high personal price for the supposed rewards of sexual repression, the price being alienation from one's sexual self, diminished capacity for tenderness and human closeness, a high incidence of sexual conflicts and disordered function, and perhaps the inability to think and feel like a whole person or to relate to others wholly. It is possible that the culture itself pays an unanticipated price. Technocracy has grown in an unchecked manner, largely unguided by wise concern for the human consequences of the technical advance. I am tempted to suspect that the kind of child rearing that trains children to disown so vital and omnipresent a part of themselves as sexuality may be related to the alienated, technologically nearsighted intelligence that reflects itself in the neglect of human values. The evidence available to date is balanced in favor of relaxing the strictures against childhood sex play, both privately and with other children.

Childhood sex play has been discussed in great detail in relation to toddlerhood, not because this is the period in which it occurs most frequently or assumes its greatest psychological significance (it is during the early school years that sexual interaction is most germane), but because it begins in this period, sometimes quite noticeably and with considerable variety. Parents who do not understand the issues involved and who fail to adopt consistent attitudes at the time of these earliest expressions may so strongly influence their impressionable toddlers that they arrive at their early school years with a compromised emotional ability to make use of opportunities for sociosexual learning.

In contrast with sex play among age mates, overt sexual activity with adults is probably, in most instances, emotionally deleterious. Unquestionably, in those instances involving coercion, force, fear, and pain, emotional damage is severe and lasting, and later sexual function may always be haunted and impaired by the enforced association of sex and violence. But even in this area the consequences are not as simply predictable as may at first be expected. In addition to pain and force, some of the variables are the nature and duration of the experience, the adult involved, parental and community handling of the incident, and the toddler's very early level of fantasy development.

An encounter with an exhibitionist outside the home, while sometimes involving a degree of surprise and fear, is more often puzzling (or at most mildly anxiety-producing) than seriously disturbing.[56]

Direct genital sex play, ranging from fondling to purposeful masturbation and penetration, and from passive to active participation by the child, will in most instances provide more intense and premature stimulation than the egos of most children this age are prepared to cope with. This is particularly true if the adult involved is a parent, from whom the child has a right to expect protection from overstimulation. Even if the toddler shows relatively little immediate response, the experience may later be retrospectively invested with great guilt and shame, at a time when the child's sexual fantasies about his parents include the expectation of the most fearful and violent of consequences. Sexual overstimulation typically results in regressive behavior, although evidences of precocious sexual interests may simultaneously be noticeable. Unable to cope with sexual experiences so far beyond his stage of readiness, the toddler will attempt to return to an earlier period when he was more passively cared for and not subjected to such stresses. This can be expressed by a loss of developing bowel control, reversion to earlier eating patterns, sleep disturbances, and generally dependent, clinging, fretful, and fearful behavior; in some cases child-adult and incestuous sexuality results in frankly psychotic responses.[57]

The emotional damage caused by adult-child sexual activity is more easily explained than the fact that some children are apparently unharmed. A gentle approach to a bodily pleasure enjoyed by the child certainly lessens negative response. The fact that the adult is quite often a trusted relative or parent, whose behavior unmistakably conveys permission to the child, may be a factor. A major explanation may involve the relatively benign nature of the very young child's fantasies, so that if the sex activity is of brief duration, it may not become involved in the later guilty incestuous fantasies.

Follow-up studies reporting relatively little subsequent damage to child participants in incest have been rather superficial.[58] An attentive reading of such reports suggests that more careful psychological probing, or more rigorous criteria of healthy response, would more often turn up significant areas of ego and sexual dysfunction. One major follow-up study conducted in Scandinavia, however, cannot be dismissed out of hand. It involved fifty-four adults, women known to have been victims of child assault between the ages of nine and thirteen years; forty-six were functioning normally by community standards, while the status of eight was unsatisfactory. Even among the eight, the causal nature of the child-adult sexuality was subject to question because of evidence of emotional instability prior to the sexual experience.[59]

The weight of knowledgeable evidence remains strongly opposed to adult-child sexuality, but much more research is needed to understand the differences between those whose lives are disrupted or shattered and those who avoid disabling consequences. One decisive factor is the manner in which the child's experience is handled by the adult community. In some instances, the violent nature of the offence demands public efforts to apprehend the offender, and the additional harm done the child by examinations, interrogations, and legal proceedings may be difficult to avoid. But in most cases, the youngster will come to view his experience much the same as his parents and other adults do. Parental and community outrage can transform a minor experience into one with major pathogenic impact. Usually, reassurance and minimizing of the child's reaction can proceed quite apart from quiet efforts to bring corrective measures to bear upon the offending adult.

There is a difference in impact between child-child and child-adult sex activity. The variety of psychodynamic issues involved is endless, but an admittedly overgeneralized distinction may be drawn. Children playing freely within groups of peers will interact, whether sexually or in any other way, at the level of their own spontaneous readiness. With the exception of older bullies ganging up on one or more younger children—a situation akin to child-adult sexuality—little children will express interest according to their own levels of ego and erotic development. Those who are not ready will not participate.

Child-adult sexual activity, however, is enforced or cajoled at the level of the adult's needs. Even though the adult is almost certain to be sexually immature, his need takes no heed of the child's inner level of maturation. The child has little control over what takes place and often little chance to withdraw; the adult's size and authority paralyze the child's feeble capacity for self-assertion.

By the time a child is three to four years old, several aspects of his overall psychosexual development have normally undergone crucially shaping influences. Most important is the sense of autonomy. For healthy psychosexual development to proceed, the question "Who owns my body?" must be answered confidently, "I do." The reason is that the right to personal control over one's body necessarily includes the use of the parts of the body, its products, and its sensations. Ownership of one's body does not mean the refusal to institute appropriate restraints. Autonomy does not deny the right of others to influence behavior. These qualities allow the acquisition of impulse control precisely because the child knows that he, too, has a voice in what he does. Respect for his autonomous drives makes total rebellion against control, or total capitulation to power, unnecessary.

The momentous discovery of genital sex differences is accompanied by relatively little conflict except in exceptional circumstances, but it sets in motion some of the most complex and far-reaching dynamics of psychosexual development. It helps organize the differing sexual sensations arising from the different genital models; it initiates curiosity about origin and function and stimulates fantasies explaining these unknowns. It creates comparison and opens the way to all the consequences of the infinite variety of values assigned to maleness and femaleness.

There is the closure, to all intents and purposes, of core gender identity, at the same time that the range of influences upon other components of sexual identity expands enormously. Not more than a handful of people will ever change their inner sense of maleness or femaleness after this period of childhood. No longer needing to learn which sex he or she is, the toddler has begun to learn what it means to be that sex: what is expected or discouraged, what the advantages and disadvantages are, and whether the adult version is worth looking forward to. Some of the perceptions of the value of being a boy or a girl astutely register the family sexual climate; some reflect continued magical thinking and the unwillingness to accept the biological finality of the capacities and limitations of maleness or femaleness.

There is a spurt of purposive sexual activity and curiosity. Parental influences are more determinative now than they will be at any later time, because of the power of earliest influences, and because parental attitudes are little tempered in the toddler's mind by those of anyone else. Evidence suggests that these years may encompass a major opportunity for learning comfortable, unselfconscious and guilt-free sociosexual interactions with others. The groundwork for untroubled sexual acceptance of oneself and others should be laid at this time.

The anal period is, naturally and inevitably, a more stressful time than the oral period for both parents and children. There is no way to avoid repeated clashes no matter how understanding and reasonable the parents are, because the toddler is neither understanding nor reasonable, and it takes two to avoid conflict unless parents abdicate their responsibilities for rearing and socializing their child. There is no way to skip the normal developmental conflicts every toddler must struggle with and mature from, but the period is an exciting and endlessly rewarding one for both generations. For the child, the entire real world of home comes into focus as he emerges from the nonverbal semiconsciousness of infancy. For parents, there is the delight of encouraging the child's myriad new skills and interests and curiosities.

FOUR

The Riches of Fantasy

It is often difficult for adults to set aside their highly valued logical processes sufficiently to credit the flights of childhood fantasy. A verbatim report may facilitate the willing suspension of disbelief:

> Today William watched his mother empty his bowel movement from the diaper into the toilet. The feces were brownish and ball-shaped. When she flushed the toilet, William commented: "Billy's other penis down the toidet." His mother explained very carefully: "Billy's penis and ballies are right here,"—she had already put on fresh diapers and pointed to the genital area through them—"and *they don't come off!*" On the previous day, while sitting on the toilet, he had leaned over, pointed to the scrotal sac and testicles, and asked: "Dis is?" His mother had explained: "Those are your ballies." [1]

This exchange between a normal boy, aged one year, nine months, and three days, and his mother demonstrates that a young boy cannot clearly distinguish his feces (regarded by the child as part of himself) from his penis or his testicles (recognized as part of himself). Billy had the fantasy that his penis, his scrotum and testicles, and his feces were all the same. As a result of this lack of differentiation, the *fact* that he repeatedly saw his feces flushed away added credibility to the *fantasy* that he could at some time also lose his genitals.

Children make no secret of their sexual fantasies unless they are taught to do so. It requires no sophisticated psychological techniques for one to become aware of fantasies; they have been recognized ever since modern psychodynamics revealed childhood sexuality.[2] One merely has to listen with respect to what children say and to place the child's comments in the context of what is happening to him at that moment, or is important in his life at that time; however nonsensical the toddler's words may seem to an adult, they definitely have meaning for the child. Fantasy is also revealed in a child's actions (especially in his play), dreams, and clinical records of children in analysis. The last source may seem suspect, but emotionally disturbed children do not have entirely different fantasies from those of happy children; they merely react to them and embellish them in more exaggerated and bizarre ways.

It is of course difficult to be sure of the fantasies of preverbal infants—much is conjectural, representing the most logical piecing together of a sequence of actions and emotional responses—but even in such instances the meaning is sometimes impossible to mistake.

Ruth was a toddler of seventeen months when she first clearly focused her attention on her genitals, by way of intense visual inspection and by manual exploration. At the same time she became very interested in looking at the genitals of other children and babies, both boys and girls, as they were being diapered or helped in toilet training in the nursery. At eighteen months, after watching with some apprehension as a boy child was diapered, she sat down on the toilet and held a toy xylophone stick perpendicularly against her genital area.[3] The unspoken fantasy of providing herself with a penis is inescapable.

There have been few if any specific studies of early childhood sexual fantasies, though child developmental and child psychiatric literature abounds with countless direct reports. There have, however, been a few attempts to gather spontaneous stories told by children or to question children about their sexual concepts. Many such efforts have been interpreted to throw doubt upon the importance and ubiquity of childhood sex fantasies; they find few spontaneous stories relating to sexuality, and direct questions often fail to evoke much corroboratory fantasy.[4]

The failure of such studies to find material parallel to that observed routinely by psychodynamically sophisticated child observers is easily understandable. Most importantly, these fantasies rise to a level of overt expression only when stimulated by some associated occurrence of importance to the child; otherwise, a fantasy may not be remembered, even if prompted. Also, most fantasies express themselves in these verbally limited children as a gestalt of communication occurring in a context of behavior, specific but subtle actions, facial expressions, and very few words. When a fantasy exists largely in unverbalized imagery, verbal inquiry may be fruitless. Finally, even toddlers have usually begun to learn that certain words and ideas are taboo, and they adhere to learned taboos no matter how ingratiating the interviewer. One of the early investigators of childhood sexual knowledge found that the child's strongest taboos were against *naming* sex organs and functions, and against genital *seeing*, or being seen, by the opposite sex. These taboos operated even when, under other circumstances, the child seemed relatively accepting of his inner *knowing* of genital differences.[5]

Repression, as a defense against disapproved or unacceptable knowledge and emotion, has already begun to affect the toddler's mental function. This also accounts for some difficulty in eliciting conscious descriptions of children's sex fantasies, whereas under special circumstances fantasies can break through repression or evade the force of repression via nonverbal action, barely disguised play, or dreams.

There are a number of normal tributaries to fantasy formation—characteristics of the small child's experiences and mental processes that can only end up in imaginative and unreal ideas. The first is his process of magical thinking. Logical and scientific concepts of cause and effect have little meaning to an infant or toddler, and when he does think in such terms he is often thoroughly off base. He may be unshakably convinced that "wishing can make it so." He may not even deign to wish; he is omnipotent, and simply by thinking of his toy animals or dolls as alive, they are alive to him. He assumes, following the example of cartoon characters who are alive and well after being flattened by steamrollers, that anything can be undone. Nothing is permanent.

Since he is magically omnipotent, so are others, most particularly his parents, who have magic power and equally magic knowledge. Mother, especially, is forever showing up at the most inopportune times, proving that she knew just what the child was about to do even before he did it. In a world so full of magic, and devoid of inescapable causality, anything is possible; fantasy can run wild, unchecked.

Another characteristic of immaturity that leads to fantasy is the child's defective state of individuation and identity. The separation of himself from others is still incomplete, and the distinctions between the parts and sensations of his own body are still poorly differentiated. He may mistake a feeling arising in one part as belonging to another. The detachable quality of feces may be mistakenly ascribed to a boy's penis; what is going on inside the mother's body may be assumed to be going on inside a little girl's.

Bodily occurrences are not only inadequately integrated but are completely beyond the logical boundaries of cause and effect. To a three-year-old who has just seen a cartoon of a small fish chewing its way out of a whale's belly, a stomach ache may represent a dangerous, toothy baby in his own insides. If at that period a little girl is struggling to accept the baby that her mother says is in her "stomach," it is but the shortest step to fantasizing that a fetus is a dangerous creature who remains alive by eating away at a mother's insides. In the world of bodies—both the child's and the parent's—anything is possible.

A further principal source of fantasy is the youngster's assumption that his parents or other children harbor the same needs and desires that he does. If he wishes to express his anger by biting, he will take it for granted that his target would wish to bite back. When his desire for muscular autonomy makes him wish to destroy anything standing in his path, he feels himself in danger of destruction. In the first few years, the only associations that have meaning in a child's own experiences, between the sensations of a full and bulging stomach, and the perineal area, are those of eating and defecating. Therefore, when told that there is a baby growing inside his mother that will be born through an opening between her legs, the child translates this information into concepts specific to that phase. Because so young a child "knows" only oral and anal sensations and functions, the baby is conceived as growing in the same "stomach" that holds food and is expected to be born through the same opening that produces feces.

The same principle accounts for the seemingly stubborn confusion of three-and-a-half-year-old Jamie. His conscientious mother has carefully explained the special place inside a woman's body where a baby grows, and the separate opening only girls have and through which the baby will emerge. But he still insists, in his envious identification with his mother's productivity, that he wants a baby growing in his inside. This is not merely wishful thinking. It illustrates the developmental fact that normally a child's comprehension proceeds in parallel with his developmental phase. He may know and even use with some accuracy the words *vagina* and *womb*, but in his emotional understanding they have little meaning.

Observation of animals' sexual behavior, and sometimes of humans', is another source of fantasy (as well as a source of learning reality). But the observations are as often puzzling as they are enlightening, unless adults furnish simple, accurate, and nonevasive explanations of what the child has observed—"a consummation devoutly to be wished." Since the information would still be swept up into, and temporarily confused with, the oral and anal concepts specific to the child's phase of development, the same observations provide both learning and fantasy material. The intercourse of dogs, typically accompanied by growling and biting and yelping, will almost invariably be assimilated by the toddler as forceful, dangerous, anal penetration.

In view of the young child's limited capacity to absorb accurate reproductive knowledge, it might not be expected that ignorance or misinformation could have a very strong effect one way or another, but it does and is yet another major tributary of unbridled and uncorrected fantasy. The relevance of miseducative techniques to fantasy is threefold. First, in the absence of understandable knowledge or a usable vocabulary, fantasy overwhelms the child's sex life; even when new information is comprehensible to the child, he has no words with which to organize and assimilate it. Secondly, he lacks mental or vocabulary tools with which to correct misconceptions as his developing mind becomes capable of more accurate perceptions, so that these distorted and conflict-producing fantasies persist into later childhood and even adulthood. Finally, because of the mystery that has been created about the sex organs and their sensations and functions, children are provoked into the eager seeking of answers among the various inadequate sources available to them, though equipped for this quest with grossly inadequate cognitional preparations. Children, no less than adults, will always try to explain the unknown by the known. A ready reservoir of misinformation exists in their equally confused peers.

Parental contributions to sexual ignorance and mislearning do not contradict the principle that very young children can only assimilate knowledge for which their development level prepares them. That remains a valid generalization. But in their anxiety and unpreparedness when confronted with childhood sexuality, adults often misrepresent very simple sexual matters that would otherwise be within the child's grasp.

The most hypothetically ideal parents (even if they could be described!) will never abolish childhood sex fantasies. Given the toddler's inadequate maturation, fantasies are inevitable and, however grotesque, are not to be deplored. They are invaluable exercises in thought and imagination. Even the anxiety-producing fantasies are an inescapable part of normal developmental conflict and are the stuff of which ego strength, healthy defenses, and the ability to cope with conflict and anxiety are formed. But the tools with which fantasies may gradually be replaced by appropriate reality must be provided, and that *is* a parental responsibility.

In the description of sex fantasies typically produced by children up to three or four years old, there are no sharply defined categories. Overlap occurs more frequently than not, because fantasies are sometimes elaborate and touch upon a number of issues related to sex. With the exception of the relatively few truly infantile fantasies, my effort has been to group fantasies according to the central puzzle the fantasy is intended to solve.

In the Oral Phase

It is almost but not entirely true, that those fantasies for which there are some reasonable evidence during the first year or so routinely concern the mouth, its activity, and what goes into it. Perhaps the earliest fantasies that ultimately take on a sexual coloring are those in which the infant appears to attribute certain qualities to his mother's breast, his mother, and himself. In a normally healthy mother-infant relationship, the infant is obviously happy and contented while nursing. In instances of tension between mother and infant, and when there is some difficulty in adequate lactation, the infant is markedly discontented. His is not a whimper or a noisy call for attention or a panicky fearful cry—he is clearly angry, and a sensitive mother can tell the difference. He may orally attack the breast, and if he is teething, bite it.

Infant development specialists postulate that the infant forms a split in his hazy concept of this sometimes rewarding and sometimes frustrating organ—the fantasy of the good nourishing breast and the bad withholding breast. Mother as a whole, as the infant gradually comes to perceive her, is sometimes gratifying and giving, and sometimes withholding, frustrating, and absent. Thus the double fantasy of the good mother and the bad mother develops naturally from the breast fantasies. This elaboration is not dependent upon breast-feeding, however, since the same inevitable maternal qualities would produce the good and bad mother fantasies regardless of feeding procedure.

Beginning with his mother's response to having her nipple bitten, the infant comes to recognize that his mother responds acceptingly to some of his behavior and rejectingly to others. This produces a similar split in his perception of himself. He fantasizes that part of himself is good and part is bad.[6] While the "good mother–bad mother" and "good self–bad self" fantasies are inferential in early infancy, it would require more distortion of the evidence to deny them than to accept them. The evidences from the play and verbalizations of older children clearly document the existence of these dichotomous mental concepts.

In keeping with the principle that children in the oral stage tend to conceive things in oral terms, the penis is also fantasized as a nourishing, fluid-giving organ. It is not clear whether infant boys make this penis-breast equation from the perception of the penis as a bodily protrusion or from its capacity to produce liquid. In girls, of course, it can only occur subsequent to observation of the penis and its function. One of the most significant sexual consequences of the penis-breast equation arises in children who felt the breast to be bad and withholding. They may come to relate to the penis more as a nourishing than as a genital organ, with consequent reverberations in disturbed heterosexual as well as homosexual relationships.

The vagina, too, may be perceived in oral terms and may appear in later fantasies as a devouring, biting, spitting organ or containing a nourishing inner fountain to which only the father has access through sexual intercourse.

A fantasy often arising in infancy is that of intercourse as an act of violence. While foreplay may often express great tenderness, intercourse itself, especially as it builds to climax, seldom appears tender to an observing infant. In some instances, he may assign no emotional value to it other than a contagious sexual excitement, but if he has witnessed or experienced spankings, and if he is both old enough to differentiate facial expressions and in a position to see them, he can only associate intercourse with his own experience and perceive it as an angry, violent act.

It is possible that the sounds of parental intercourse alone can forge a fantasy link between sex and violence. One of the newborn's few reflexes is the Moro reflex, in which the infant responds to a sudden jolt or noise with a startled reaction involving muscular contractions of his whole body and the holding of the breath, which is sometimes followed by crying. The newborn does not distinguish between a loud noise and a physical blow, such as the jarring of his crib. This very primitive association between a noise and a physical blow may be called into play when parents' intercourse is particularly noisy and clearly audible to the child. This innate, reflexive association is most helpful in explaining the widespread fantasy that intercourse is a frightening and violent activity even among children unlikely to have witnessed it.[7]

One more fantasy that probably makes its hazy beginning in infancy is limited to female infants. In their genital explorations and their perceptions of unlocalizable and uncontrollable vaginal sensations, the fantasies of the vagina as a mysterious, anxiety-producing and vulnerable place originate. In their earliest form, the inner female genitals are no more unknown than other bodily parts and sensations, but as the inner female genitalia remain stubbornly unknowable while the girl familiarizes herself with and masters many other parts of her body, anxious fantasies may become associated with them. Males also develop bizarre fantasies about the vagina, but not in infancy when they have no knowledge of it. The assumption is made only through educated speculation that some girls begin to develop fearful vaginal fantasies in infancy because the ingredients for their origin exist that early.

About Intercourse

Fantasies about intercourse really flourish during the toddler years. Most parents, if their living space permits it, become more careful about their sexual privacy at this time. But they are often no match for the toddler's avid curiosity and whirlwind locomotion, which permits him to burst unannounced into the bedroom when parents' alertness to interruption may be blunted by the heat of the moment.

Primal experiences are not the only stimuli for such fantasies, however. Children ask about their genitals and the origin of babies and are often given explanations that include some concept of a mother's and father's coupling in intercourse. An undetermined but considerable proportion of children witness animals mating and are capable of reasonably accurate comparisons of the animals' genitalia and their own, though the vaginal opening may be misidentified. They also learn through all sorts of daily experiences that protrusions fit into openings. And, most fascinatingly of all, close observation of toddlers' play with various toys reveals a knowing and presumably innate preoccupation with activities involving penetration and the fitting together of "male" and "female" shapes.

All this adds up to the fact that many influences, both environmental and innate, come together to produce in the toddler a combination of curiosity and dim knowledge of intercourse. Reasonable comprehension is so far beyond toddlers, however, that they try to fill in the gaps by piecing together whatever fragments of seemingly relevant experience they can think of.

Most early childhood theories of intercourse contain some element of violence. Other than the oral phase fantasies of the father having access to a secret source of nourishment, it could scarcely be otherwise. Perhaps only that small percentage of children who are without any visual or auditory experience of intercourse, either involving humans or animals, and those who have been given no valid explanations at all, may sometimes fantasize about intercourse in ways devoid of physical violence. One such boy announced that "Mommy sucks Daddy's wee-wee to get baby in Mommy's stomach." Boys and girls both will mentally experiment with fantasies of all possible bodily openings as receptacles for the obviously intrusive penis. Folklore and mythology attest to fantasies of anatomically impossible penetrations. One myth of the impregnation of Mary by the Holy Ghost has the Spirit blowing into her ear.

This possibility of violence-free fantasies of intercourse should not be taken as reason to try to preserve the total innocence of children. The natural circumstances in most homes and most cultures is such that innocence does not and can not long exist. Ego development results from learning and being helped to cope with normally expectable experiences, not from sheltering the ego from its appropriate tasks.

And even "innocent" children are not free from anxiety-producing fantasies of intercourse. In their gropings with the ideas of penile penetration and of the body being penetrated, such children bring whatever experience they have to bear upon the puzzle. They know that penetration (enemas, injections, tongue blades) can hurt and that a penetrating object (a probing finger in a feeding cat's mouth) can be hurt. Little girls whose genital explorations have led to discovery of the vaginal opening have expressed the fear that they have injured themselves and produced a "sore" (wound). As soon as there is any association in the child's mind between the vagina and penile insertion, one of the most frequent of all childhood sex fantasies can occur—that the penis produces the vaginal "wound" by forceful penetration.

For the vast majority of children who are less ignorant, there is even more reason to associate some kind of physical, attacking force with intercourse. Animal matings are almost never placid. While in some of the more commonly observable species it is the female who appears to be more angry and vicious, the mounting itself places the male in the position of "doing something to" the female which gives every appearance of being violent even when not accompanied by such reflexes as biting and holding onto the female's neck (as in the cat species).

Human intercourse is also usually vigorous, and while humans display more variety of position than do other animals, the position in which the man is on top is more likely than any other to be observed by a toddler who happens onto the scene. Thus intercourse is not merely a scene of potentially violent interpretation but almost all of the meager experiences in a child's repertoire combine to create the impression that "Daddy is beating the hell out of Mommy." The mother's sounds and both partners' facial expressions do nothing to counteract this impression.

These concepts are by no means adult fantasies about what goes on in a child's mind. Many parents have had the experience of calming the fears of a child who inadvertently interrupted them during intercourse. One three-and-a-half-year-old boy asked in a panicky voice, "Daddy, what you doin'?" and then, becoming quickly more perturbed before his parents could stop, cried several times, "Don't 'pank Mommy!" and flailed away at his father with both hands. He required nearly half an hour of reassurance before he could go back to sleep and in subsequent weeks repeatedly brought up the experience for reassurance.

Children who only hear parental intercourse often fantasize the father in the role of villain. In most reasonably healthy and harmonious homes, the very young child primarily experiences his mother's voice as soft and soothing and his father's voice as sharper, louder, and more explosive. Thus the sounds of coitus, especially if his mother's voice is mistakenly perceived to convey pain or distress, augment the fantasy of his father attacking his mother.[8]

Other aspects of intercourse are similarly difficult for the little child to perceive without the possibility of some anxious fantasy. Girls in particular, who have learned or have seen that intercourse involves penile penetration, cannot help but observe the enormous disparity between their tiny bodies and their father's enormous penis, especially if observed in erection. As they fantasize intercourse involving themselves, the fantasy may include the fear of being ripped and torn asunder by the overwhelming penis. The same observations create in a boy the complementary fantasy that his penis may become a destructive weapon.

At times, a child may be in a position to observe intercourse from beginning to end. Aside from the possibly overstimulating character of such an experience and the possibly reassuring quality of parental tenderness following the apparent battle, this introduces yet another puzzling and sometimes threatening observation. Compared to its erect state, the man's penis usually becomes quite small after coitus. For the boy, this can engender fantasies of losing his penis in the vagina and can be an origin of another common fantasy, one often found still alive in adulthood: the vagina with teeth. In similar circumstances, girls evolve similar fantasies of their genitals as dangerous weapons; the fantasy of possessing mutilating and damaging genitals is not a male monopoly.

It is reasonable, I think, to wonder whether adult sexual privacy actually intensifies the fearful fantasies small children entertain about intercourse. There is no anthropological evidence that children are permanently traumatized in those cultures in which there is constant and free access to observation of adult intercourse. Indeed, various verbatim reports suggest that such children become

free of anxiety remarkably early. One might speculate that when ✓
adult sexuality is as common an experience as any other natural
function of life, there is maximum opportunity for children to lose
their fearful misconceptions of it, because reality will not sustain
most of the distressing childhood fantasies.

This speculation is not to be taken as a cavalier and ill-considered
recommendation for precipitate cultural change. Concepts of
individual and sexual privacy are so interwoven with the whole
fabric of Western culture as to render such a proposition fatuous,
but it is reasonable to consider our tradition of shielding children
from sexuality as playing a supportive role in the predominance and
persistence of fearful childhood fantasies about intercourse.

The Presence or Absence of a Penis

All children wonder about their genitals, as about all parts of
their bodies. Sex organs are especially interesting because of their
enjoyable sensations, but genital fantasies usually do not really
mushroom until genital differences are noted. No other physical
differences between normal toddlers are as unequivocal or dramatic, and genital differences demand explanation.

One group of fantasies focuses upon genital origins. Girls are
more likely than boys to devise fantasies about genital origins—specifically their vaginas—prior to awareness of sex differences. Boys
tend to take their penises for granted as pleasure-giving body parts.
Girls are prone to wonder about the possible ways their vaginas
came into being because of the anxiety that may be stirred by this
hidden and mysterious opening. The result is that, even without
knowledge of male genitalia, little girls may fantasize that some
kind of damaging penetration, caused either by their own explorations or by some other agency, produced this opening. By no means
do all little girls develop fearful vaginal fantasies, but those who do
frequently handle that fear by denying any knowledge of the
vaginal opening. Since this denial can be found in children who
have previously been observed to explore and penetrate their
vaginal openings, the denial is persuasive evidence of anxious
fantasies.

One may safely assume that the original childish expectation in
the child's mind is that all similar creatures are made the same. This

accounts for the boundless curiosity upon discovering differently, and for the fairly narrow range of explanatory theories devised by little children. It also accounts for the complete absence of penis envy in some girls who expect that everyone should look as they do and therefore assume something is wrong with boys' bodies when they first observe a boy's genitals.

Experience has shown, however, that becoming aware of sexual anatomical differences typically excites at least a mild envy in the "have nots" with respect to the "haves," as evidenced by the admiring exclamation of one three-year-old girl: "Look! He's got tassles on!"

If having a penis is usually assumed to be the "normal" state of affairs, then more mental energy will be spent on trying to comprehend its absence than its presence. Both girls and boys will entertain many of the same fantasies—girls might have lost their penises or had them taken away, they may still grow one or grow it back, or it may be hidden inside. Since the mother is usually both disciplinarian and nourisher, she gets blamed by most girls for its loss, and she is also the wishful source for its return. Sometimes there is the fantasy that the mother could, if she wished, provide the proper food to make the little girl's penis grow.

It is partly the mother's power position in the toddler's life that makes her lack of a penis puzzling to a little boy. If a penis is a nice thing to have then she ought to have one. So he imagines that there is one there hiding behind the hair, or tucked away inside. He may even assume that somehow, somewhere, girls actually have something better than he has.

It is worth repeating that at this early age these fantasies are not usually fraught with a great deal of anxiety. The presence or absence of the wondrous penis will, of course, take on more emotional significance in a home in which males are obviously privileged and dominant, but these issues of possible male privilege are not nearly so clear-cut in the mother-dominated world of the two-year-old as they might appear in the culture at large.

In toddler-age children the main source of anxiety about genital origins normally arises from observations and fantasies of intercourse. As already noted, many fantasies about the violent origin of the female genitalia can derive from misconceptions of intercourse. Indeed, the violence mistakenly attributed to penetration may be imagined not only to have produced the female genital "hole," but also to have been the original source of female mutilation and loss of her penis.

Children fantasize not only about the origin but about the nature of their genitals. Just what are these fascinating parts of the body, with their exciting and sometimes confusing sensations? For the boy, his penis may become a separate being, a baby. One not-quite-two-year-old would talk to his penis and try to feed it crackers.[9] The penis may be confused with other body parts or products, such as feces, as in the example which opens this chapter. The fantasy that the penis and the breast may be the same or have something in common is illustrated by the same child when he was one year, ten months, twenty-three days old:

> As William's diaper was being changed, he was kicking his mother's belly, and the following conversation ensued. Mother: "Don't hurt the baby." William patted his mother's bosom and claimed, "Billy no want to hurt the baby." Mother: "You know the baby's in my belly; that's not my belly. What is it?" William: "Finger." Mother: "No!" William: "Penis." Mother: "What is it?" William: "Breastie, breastie hanging down." The mother, struck by the train of thought and description, asked: "What hangs down on Billy?" William: "Billy's penis. Girlies have a penis?" Mother: "You know girls don't have a penis." [10]

There is also considerable fantasy associated with the scrotum and testicles. In addition to those fantasies that equate them with feces and therefore imply a fear of their loss, they are also equated with female structures because of their roundness. The dreams, memories, and associations of adults and older children in analysis suggest strongly that both boys and girls fantasize that the testicles are the equivalent of small breasts. This is another source of a small boy's sense of inferiority to his mother.

The vagina, naturally, is a particularly apt subject for fantasy, because it is so much less clearly knowable. And because the unknown is more anxiety-producing than the known, fantasies about the nature of the vagina tend to have fearful elements. In keeping with the toddler's current anal preoccupations, the vagina is at times fantasized as having the characteristic of that body orifice—holding in, swelling up, busting, foul smelling, and dirty.

Not all vaginal fantasies are distressing. The little girl who associates her vagina with her future capacity to have children equates her vagina in fantasy with the baby itself, thus rendering it a very precious organ. It is similarly precious and enviable to little boys who recognize its creative and productive potential. It is this association of maleness and femaleness with the external and internal genitals that plays such a major role in the unfolding of masculine and feminine characteristics throughout the course of psychosexual development. The unconscious fantasies of both sexes equate inner genital structure and sensations with babies and with femaleness. Similarly, external genital organs and sensations are in fantasy equal to maleness. Even at this early age, these unconscious fantasies have begun to influence how children perceive their own bodies and those of the opposite sex.

Implicit in genital origin fantasies and fantasies about the nature of their genitals are the possible dangers which children imagine may threaten their sex organs. These imaginary dangers grow out of the frightening ways they believe that sexual differences came about, the menacing qualities that they fear sex organs may possess, and the violence inherent in some of their misconceptions about intercourse and reproduction. When a child experiences enough anxiety, there may be a repression of all genital interest and curiosity. A child who truly displays no curiosity about sexual matters and an avoidance of his own genitalia is a child in whom there is already too much sexual fear to allow for normal emotional development. In other children, genital dangers are handled by denial. Denying and "forgetting" the presence of a vaginal opening is one such response to fantasized danger. In boys, the gradually exclusive focus upon the penis (which is reassuringly always there, and can be made to grow at will) may represent a denial of any emotional importance to that other major component of the external sex organs, the testicles (which disappear capriciously and seem in danger of falling off).

The Doll-Baby

For most little girls from about one and a half to four years old, doll play is a major, often the preferred, activity. It is intense, varied, prolonged, and fascinating, both to the child and to the psychodynamically sophisticated observer. A little girl's doll is not merely a favorite toy, it is the means by which she expresses and copes with some of her sexual feeling and anxieties. In a very special way, it becomes the embodiment of many of her genital fantasies.

The poorly localized and uncontrollable vaginal sensations that constitute a source of anxiety and uneasiness for the little girl combine with her subliminal vaginal awareness to become associated with her female productivity. The knowledge that someday a baby may form and grow in her insides is scant comfort to so young a future mother. She has disquieting inner sexual sensations *now*, and her unconscious fantasy is that if she had her own baby now she would have something tangible outside herself which would be far easier for her developing ego to master than those inner genital stirrings. The conscious and visible expression of this fantasy lies in her intense preoccupation with her dolls, in her possessive insistence upon the realness of her "baby," and in the immensely varied ways she uses the doll to cope with her inner needs.

The unconscious association of inside genitals with femaleness and baby, and the child's capacity for magic thinking, combine to provide a fantasy solution. Her doll is her very own real baby, and it is also a symbol of her inner genitals, upon which she can project all those strange and unfulfillable feelings. Her doll becomes one means whereby she can externalize (and thus make more controllable) her inside sexual sensations, as a boy can externalize his sexual stirrings upon his penis. In contrast to a vagina and uterus that she cannot fathom, visualize, or incorporate tangibly into her body image, her doll, which symbolizes her inside genitalia, is admirably concrete and "knowable." Because it represents part of herself, a little girl of this age overwhelmingly prefers girl dolls. Even if the only available doll is male and she is well aware of sex differences, she will often insist it is a girl.

In the projection of her inner feelings upon her doll, it is possible to follow the nature and the changes and the fantasied meanings of those feelings. Her ambivalence about her inner sexual self is continually displayed. One moment her "baby" is real and precious and must be cared for with unimpeachable maternal tenderness, but the next moment she is angry and punitive, even sadistically cruel, to her "baby." Some of this behavior is mere imitation of her mother's mood changes, but not all; doll play shows many of the same patterns of behavior regardless of a mother's temperament. It also represents the little girl's shifting acceptance and rejection of her inner sexuality.

Sometimes the doll is used in other ways to externalize disturbing feelings. The little girl may hold a doll against her genital area, as an object with which to masturbate, fantasizing the doll not as her own inside female genitals but as an imaginary penis. This fantasy represents the same kind of localization and controllability of sexual sensation that is used in clitoral masturbation; it is an effort to "drown out" inner sensations.

In the little girl's further fantasies that equate the doll with a baby, inside genitals, and femaleness, the doll may be treated as if it were her own mother. In such play, the girl enacts with her doll the whole gamut of her emotions toward her mother in this tumultuous period of development. Or the doll may represent both the "good" and "bad" parts of herself. In pretending that her doll embodies her own various characteristics, her play allows her to practice coming to terms with aspects of herself that she is learning to disapprove of, and to work at gradually incorporating the various parts of herself into an integrated whole.

In its symbolic roles as both real baby and penis, the doll is a fantasied means of filling the little girl's empty inner sex organs. Part of the distressing quality of vaginal sensations is that the little girl's vagina has no natural contents to give it shape and form and familiarity. "A hole is to fill" is not a foolish, comic saying. It is an expression of biological and physical logic—a logic innately sensed by the little girl. Woman's lifelong preoccupation with inner space carries with it an inherent need to be filled. Many very early expressions of this need may be traced in the girl child's doll baby fantasies.

This period has sometimes been called the early maternal stage. In all the various forms of doll play, and in the symbolic and fantasy uses to which dolls are put, can be seen the earliest and most unequivocal expression of the maternal instinct in humans. There is no counterpart in normal toddler-age boys, who often play with dolls, but whose interest is typically intermittent, perfunctory, and

easily distracted; their expressed wishes to have babies are identifications with the mother's power and productivity, not with her
inner femaleness.

During this period, the little girl who has not already begun to
have her femaleness discouraged rehearses and reveals her maternalism, but her maternalism is premature. Her psychosexual development must prove itself equal to many maturational tasks before
her maternalism is ready for full expression. One painful blow
comes as this period ends, with her recognition that for all her
magic, her doll is only a doll and not a real baby. As she becomes
more able to distinguish fantasy from reality, she can no longer truly
believe in her doll as a baby. As simply a toy, the doll is less able to
serve as a satisfactory externalization of her inner feelings. Sometimes the early maternal phase is followed by a period of depression,
just as though the little girl had lost a baby. She may lose interest in
dolls for several years. If she continues doll play, it is more the kind
of play in which she knows she is making believe. Such play allows
for the expression of fantasy, but not with the quality of lived-out
reality characteristic of the toddler.[11]

The Watermelon Seed

The origin of babies is one of the most engrossing of the mysteries
that confront little children. The age at which this puzzle bursts
upon the child's horizon varies with exposure to the existence of
offspring. In a minority of children such experience may be delayed,
but most toddlers will have noted or heard talk about the coming of
younger siblings, the arrival of new babies in the neighborhood, the
birth of pets or domestic animals, or have received some explanations in response to other sex questions which then led them to
wonder about conception, gestation, and birth.

Some childhood fantasies are simply adult deceptions, given to
the child to delay sexual awareness, or as a means used by parents to
cope with their own embarrassments and anxieties. "The stork
brought her"; "We found her under a cabbage leaf"; "The doctor
brought her to the hospital in his black bag"—these are examples of
the countless false explanations recorded the world over.

Divine origin fantasies form a special group. In homes and
subcultures where religion is woven into everyday life, parents

frequently resort to these explanations when they want to evade physiological facts. In some older studies, there is quite a high reported frequency of children offering to interrogators such ideas as, "They come down from the Dear Lord," or "It comes from Heaven." [12] One seems to hear these explanations somewhat less frequently today.

In view of the budding innate knowledge of the body and its sexual functions, toddlers' belief in adult-induced deceptions is questionable. On the one hand, magical thinking and the delegation of omniscience to parents make virtually anything believable; on the other hand, observations, overheard conversation, talk with other children (particularly older children), and innate bodily and mental stirrings press for more naturalistic explanations. Clinical and sensitive observational experience, as opposed to contrived questioning, suggest that the child-parent credibility gap begins very early when sexual deceptions are practiced. Divine origin fantasies may resist the erosion of common sense longer because of the parents' own apparent belief in the magical omnipotence of God.

Most fantasies of origin are largely spontaneous rather than entirely parent-induced, though they may be helped along by bits of purposeful or inadvertent parental misinformation. In this class of fantasies, too, will be seen the underlying themes of attempting to explain the unknown by the known, the reflection in fantasy of the developmental readiness of the child, and some confusion of sex and violence. Children with minimal knowledge will sometimes omit the concept of impregnation or conception and fantasize that the baby grows spontaneously inside the mother; such children may have been told, "God plants a seed in mother's stomach."

Other children cannot keep their curiosity away from wondering how the "seed" managed to get there, especially when they have some inkling that the father has a role in producing and delivering the seed. It is in the area of partial parental explanations of reproduction that one is so struck by the literal quality of a little child's mind, a point overlooked by many parents. Such words as *seed, stomach,* and *belly* have specific meanings for a child; a seed is one of those little things that sprout into a plant, and the stomach or belly is the place food goes when it is swallowed.

Parents who, with the best of intentions, offer the explanation,

"Daddy plants a seed in mommy's stomach," often omit telling how daddy does so. The child then fantasizes the process in terms of what he does know—the seed enters mother's mouth. If he doesn't yet associate daddy's penis with the act, he may fantasize that this takes place when his mother and father are kissing or eating together or even when breathing. When he knows or suspects the role of the penis, the most frequent fantasy is still that of oral impregnation, because this is the most familiar route to the stomach.

A serious emotional illness of early adulthood, anorexia nervosa, reflects the unconscious but malignant persistence of the oral impregnation fantasy into adulthood. As described in the Introduction, this rather uncommon disease of young women is associated with deep fear and guilt regarding sexuality, pregnancy, and mothering. When the intense guilty fears exist in a woman who also harbors the strong unresolved fantasies that pregnancy occurs via the mouth, food comes to symbolize semen, and obesity symbolizes pregnancy. Out of unconscious guilt, the patient stops eating, becomes grotesquely emaciated, and may starve to death unless adequate treatment is effectively instituted.[13]

Some children are told about vaginal impregnation, and many witness intercourse. They then add this mode to their store of fantasies but do not necessarily discard the more primitive ones. A sophisticated three-and-a-half-year-old girl may speak of how her father puts a seed in her mother's vagina with his penis and later ask her mother what kind of seed she swallowed to make the baby start growing. Sometimes there are other fantasies about how the seed gets in, as a toddler imagines the use of any and all other bodily openings, and also sometimes thinks that the penis punches a hole where there was none before.

The development of the fetus is inseparable from the mystery of its origin, and the child's mind attempts to link this with how the fetus gets in and how it gets out, within the limits of his cognitive logic. The alimentary theory, combining oral entry and "stomach" growth, is both the most common and the most understandable, as the feeling of fullness that follows eating is a normal childhood experience. Parents' loose use of words that mean "food place" to the child fosters this fantasy. The frequently heard adult reference to a pregnant woman as having "swallowed a watermelon seed" is no product of *adult* imaginativeness; it is the unconscious persistence in jocular form of the earliest and most pervasive childhood impregnation fantasy. Similarly, the expression, "We've got one in the oven," is a reflection of the unconscious association of baby with food or stomach contents.

In considering the baby's existence inside his mother, the child also fantasizes about what this must be like for both the fetus and the mother. It may be assumed (but there are no solid data) that most mothers will reassure children that it is nice to be pregnant, that the baby does not hurt them, and that they will not get sick or die as a result of either pregnancy or delivery.

Unfortunately for many children, what they can observe may undermine that reassurance. The mother may have a difficult pregnancy, with the unpleasant symptoms of morning sickness and fatigue. Some mothers develop severe and life-threatening disorders during pregnancy, and even the healthiest mothers go to the doctor more often than usual for routine prenatal care. The child may well overhear his mother complaining about the physical burdens of pregnancy or the anticipated emotional or financial burden of yet another child, and, rarely, a child may know of someone who dies in childbirth.

For the many who are free of fear, the fantasies are highly pleasant. They identify with the mother and want a baby of their own to be growing in their bodies. They associate growth with flowers and bushes and lovely things, and babies with cuteness and cuddliness (and relief from inner genital tensions). Those with fearful fantasies may imagine the fetus as some gnawing, devouring, destructive creature, somehow harming their mother and sapping her energy.

Other fantasies concern the fetus itself. Some children project upon the growing baby their own shadowy memories of what it felt like to be wholly cared for and dependent. To them the womb is a carefree utopia. To others it can seem a frightening dark prison in which the baby is suffocating and cannot see or communicate. In correlation with the all-embracing attitudes learned by each infant through his experiences with his mother's body, it can reasonably be expected that such distressing fantasies often represent projections of the toddler's own perception of his mother's body as either comfortless or inhospitable.

The existence of frightening fantasies about the fetus was found to be astonishingly high in one study of Israeli children who were slightly older than toddlers (four to five-and-one-half years old). The girls tended to fantasize a miserable state for the fetus; they imagined that it cried, trembled, was lonely and afraid of the dark. Such responses were given by 75 percent of the girls whose parents were of European origin.[14] A similar question asked of a small sample of American Midwestern children elicited, as is typical of American studies, very few such responses.[15] There are no satisfactory explanations for the wide discrepancy, but the Israeli study, despite the shortcomings of conscious questioning, leaves no doubt of the existence of such anxious fantasies.

The process of birth is equally subject to fantasy and completes the triad of conception, gestation, and delivery in the mystery of the origin of a baby. If there is a baby inside the mother, it has to get out in some way, and children return again to the ways in which they are familiar with bodily contents getting out. The anal outlet is most typically fantasized, and the urethral orifice is not at all rare. The more frequent fantasy of an anal "birth canal" is probably traceable to a more widespread knowledge of the association between food in the stomach and feces,[16] and fecal solidity lends itself more easily than does liquid urine to association with a solid object like a baby.

However, the young magic-maker's mind is not likely to be fettered by logic, and any means of emergence may be fantasized. Emergence through the mouth can occur in fantasy but is seldom reported; many children imagine the umbilicus to be where the baby comes out.

Since the umbilicus is not a true orifice, its place in birth fantasies calls attention again to the surprising frequency with which physical damage and violence are associated with procreative functions. The study of Israeli children revealed that 50 percent of the boys and 58 percent of the girls spontaneously said that the baby was born by cutting open the mother's belly.[17] In the comparable American study, most children simply mentioned that the baby came through the stomach, but very few initially expressed the fearful concept of cutting the stomach open. However, when given a series of alternatives including anus and vagina, even the majority of American children (69 percent of boys and 50 percent of girls) chose as one answer "a stomach which has been cut open." [18] Apparently birth lends itself easily to fearful fantasies.

The Grass Is Always Greener

Many children of both sexes fantasize having the sexual attributes of the other sex because they regard it as being in some ways preferable to their own. During this early period of childhood, envy appears to be more a problem for boys than for girls. The flurry of objections to and reevaluations of the concept of penis envy, based upon unsupportable generalizations and extensions of its significance and upon gross misunderstanding of the concept, has obscured the importance of the little boy's envy of his mother. This envy, based as it is upon his mother's power and productivity in the child's home-world, is enormously augmented when the boy discovers his mother's procreative power, especially if she actually becomes pregnant at this time.[19]

The boy's envy of his mother's ability to have a baby, and his identification with her, occur earlier in a child's life than do the issues of intense genital pride and envy. Girls of the same age also envy and identify with the mother, primarily because of emotions relating to the mother-child relationship, which predates concerns about the relationship between the parents. A boy's wishful identification with his pregnant mother often occurs this early:

> In saying a nursery rhyme, "Sing a Song of Sixpence," William jokingly supplied some of his own endings. For "the queen is in the parlor eating milk and honey" he substituted *the baby* for "milk and honey." (Mrs. W. was in the fifth month of a new pregnancy, and William had been told that his mother had a baby in her belly.) Later he referred to "my baby." His mother asked, "Where is your baby?" expecting him to designate one of two dolls he had. Instead he patted his epigastrium and uttered, "In Billy's belly." [20]

Male identification with female childbearing is illustrated in the custom of *couvade*, found in a number of widely scattered preliterate societies. In *couvade*, the husband of a woman in labor also takes to his bed as though about to deliver, usually surrounded by male attendants, and ritually goes through an enactment of labor and childbirth. A number of interpretations have been offered for this custom, which may serve several unconscious motives, but the simplest and most obvious meaning, as well as one of the most persuasive, is that it represents a magical effort on the man's part to pretend that he, too, is capable of creating and giving birth to new life.[21]

It may not be only the mother's ability to create life and her productive activity that impresses boys. The comparison between his mother and father may also be unfortunately impressive. In contrast with his mother, his father's very real contributions may not be very noticeable to the child. Father himself, often enough reduced to a cog in the industrial machine, may well devalue his own importance and productivity. If in addition there is parental strife and the mother is herself derogatory of the father, a little boy is left with little to be proud of in his own masculinity. All these factors may contribute to wishful fantasies of being a girl so as to grow up like mother.

A little girl is characteristically less envious of boys during the stage of toddlerhood and devises fewer fantasies of being a male. A clear exception to this generalization exists in families in which the male is openly privileged and indulged and in which the males are allowed to take ruthless advantage of their privileged status. Such individual family dynamics, and at times the broader social sex-status considerations, do undoubtedly begin to impinge upon the toddler-age child. In such instances, little girls will certainly fantasize the advantages of being little boys and may focus upon penis possession as the obvious badge of membership in the privileged sex, but this is a social status concern, not a spontaneously arising preference for male genitalia. Typical family structure and sexual division of labor in industrial and technological societies make it very difficult for the father's role and prestige to appear to surpass the mother's power in the eyes of an essentially home-bound toddler.[22] If skewed sociosexual attitudes exist, they will not impinge upon a child with full force until he emerges into interaction with the broader community, usually beginning with the primary school years.

Aside from the basic concept that it is preferable to have something than not to have it, the penis is initially envied as a vastly superior urine dispenser. Relatively few toddlers miss some opportunity to observe the other sex urinating. Boys can stand up to urinate, though that is a relatively minor achievement; more intriguingly, they can perform whimsically delightful feats in the process—flooding a bug off a blade of grass with deadly aim, writing their names in the snow, having contests to see who can project the stream highest and farthest. Small children ordinarily have little or no bodily modesty unless it has begun to be drummed into them, and little boys are not hesitant to exploit their superiority by showing off to girls. I have observed small groups of little girls standing with legs spread and bent precariously over backward, valiantly imitating the projectile urination of boys. Ordinarily, however, these cross-sex fantasies are not highly charged emotionally. Most toddlers accept quite easily the existence of two kinds of genitals despite the florid array of fantasies they devise to account for them.

The other normally occurring source of early penis envy is the obvious advantage of visible and tangible male genitalia in externalizing the disquieting fears of inner genital sensations. This may carry a heavier emotional charge. For reasons that are not always clear, some little girls seem more troubled than others by inner genital sensations, and are more pressed to find real or fantasy modes of externalizing them. In addition to doll play, they develop an early preoccupation with purely clitoral masturbation, accompanied by fantasies that the clitoris will eventually grow into a penis or that it really is a penis. Occasionally for such girls these fantasies are inadequate to their needs for externalization, and they develop an attitude of devaluation of the clitoris and a deep, hostile envy of boys and the fantasy of becoming a boy, but these are relatively uncommon developments at this age; penis envy in general is less significant than boys' womb envy.

Only the most typical early childhood sexual fantasies have been mentioned; variations seem, but are not truly, endless. The more unusual a child's experiences, the more atypical his fantasies may be. This could be exemplified in children reared in a primitive culture that practiced such sexual customs as sewing up of the labia, or excision of the clitoris. Childhood sex fantasies elaborating upon such themes might cause concern in some cultures but would reflect reality in others.

Emotional disturbance in early childhood may also contribute unusual characteristics to sexual fantasies. The nature of the child's conflict or fear may cause certain typical elements to be exaggerated or some unusual element to be incorporated. A case concerning a somewhat older boy (six years old) reported by a child analyst, shows the addition of an unusual feature to a typical fantasy. This boy had developed a violent fantasy of intercourse in which the man's penis was damaged—not an unusual fantasy. He also had the more startling idea that the man's penis was cut open in order to get out marble-sized sperm. Treatment eventually uncovered the origin of these elements. At three years of age he had witnessed his baby brother's circumcision, an experience which made a lasting and fearful impression upon him. Later he was shown a sex education book for children which included a microscope-enlarged photograph of a sperm, with the head appearing to be about the size of a marble. In his fantasies, he combined his typical misconception of intercourse with his visual impression of enormous sperm into a highly disturbing fantasy of penile damage.[23]

There are also factors that limit the range of childhood sex fantasies. One is the biological realities of male and female differences and of sexual and reproductive activities; given the opportunity, reality will eventually replace fantasy. Another is the fact that the bodies of most children are normal and must ultimately be perceived as normal despite initial puzzlements and concerns. Perhaps most important is the child's sharply limited mental and emotional capacity to comprehend the complexities of adult sexuality.

The first two limiting factors suggest that in the absence of disruptive influences, and with some reasonable assistance in the replacing of misconceptions with more accurate understanding, reality will ultimately triumph. Children will learn to distinguish the sounds of intercourse from those of violence. They will learn that one sex's genitalia are not, under ordinary circumstances, damaged by the genitalia of the other sex. People are produced with only two basic body styles sexually, and fantasies dependent upon a sense of unique damage or special vulnerability must usually give way to inevitable comparisons and the recognition of similarities. Remnants of early childhood sexual theories will remain in everyone's unconscious, revealing themselves from time to time in dreams, myths, adult fantasies, jokes, and idioms.

The innate limitations of the child's developmental level and mental capacities also set boundaries on the range of fantasy. Because of the biologically determined sequence of stages of immaturity, regardless of the most striking cultural variations, certain fantasies are universal—oral impregnation, anal birth, violently harmful intercourse, genital vulnerability, the whole gamut of fantasies that in one form or another are inevitable because of the stages which all normal human infants must pass.

The ubiquity with which violent elements enter into children's sexual fantasies may seem strange. Why should something normal, natural, and essentially pleasant and good, initially evoke fantasies that are frequently fearful? New experiences *not initiated by the child* are most often regarded with reservation and apprehension. Once children learn that adults can hurt them and each other, the appearance of violence is frightening. For all their magic thinking, children recognize themselves as tiny and vulnerable, and the fantasy of participation in so seemingly violent an adult activity causes deep concern. They have but a limited repertoire of experiences out of which to fantasize what could happen to them, and in almost all instances their experience has been that of a helpless recipient of adult control. When they have managed to elude adult control, that result, too, has often been painful. Thus their fantasies frequently reflect that helpless role—not always a reassuring position.

Even more determinative of frightening sexual fantasies is the adult practice of treating sexuality with secrecy, prohibition, punishment, and purposeful misinformation, as something to be shrouded in mystery. When faced with other kinds of frighteningly new and potentially dangerous aspects of the real world, children are more often helped to cope with them, as adults offer information that overcomes the child's misconceptions as he tries to discard fantasy and to master reality. To a child, that which is hidden—and which arouses as many anxious, negative responses in adults as sex—must surely be something terrifying, not joyous.

The toddler's limited developmental capacity to comprehend accurate sexual knowledge has sometimes been cited as reason not to offer him sexual information. Freud expressed the situation clearly:

> We can have analogous experiences, I think, when we give children sexual enlightenment. I am far from maintaining that this is a harmful or unnecessary thing to do, but it is clear that the prophylactic effect of this liberal measure has been greatly over-esti-mated. After such enlightenment, children know something they did not know before, but they make no use of the new knowledge that has been presented to them. We come to see that they are not even in so great a hurry to sacrifice for this new knowledge the sexual theories which might be described as a natural growth and which they have constructed in harmony with, and dependence on, their imperfect libidinal organization—theories about the part played by the stork, about the nature of sexual intercourse and about the way in which babies are made. For a long time after they have been given sexual enlightenment they behave like primitive races who have had Christianity thrust upon them and who continue to worship their old idols in secret.[24]

It is true that the child will not understand very much about sex and will persist in his childish concepts, but the open proffering of accurate information and accurate words in response to his sexual interests has a far more significant value than replacing, at that moment, his fantasies. It conveys to him the recognition that sexuality is something it is permissible to think about, to experience, and to master. It gives him access to, and the implicit *right* to, the verbal tools and accurate knowledge with which to evaluate his sexual fantasies and ideas.

FIVE

The Impossible Wish

From the age of three or four to about five or six, there is a peak in childhood sexuality that has enormous implications for a child's future sexual life. It is as though all his prior biological maturation, all the subtle and varying qualities of the developing relationships with his parents, and all the emotional attitudes he has been learning toward himself and others, meet (indeed, sometimes clash) in a peculiarly intense manner.

The fact that most of these normal developmental dilemmas occur and are resolved largely out of sight in no way diminishes their crucial importance. The fact that their healthy resolution renders their remnants vestigial in adult life does not warrant dismissing the role of those conflicts in helping produce later health. And the fact that health or disturbance in earlier childhood essentially determines the emotional equipment with which the child enters this stage does not relegate the conflicts to a series of "rigged" encounters with a predetermined outcome.

The psychodynamic term for this period, the "phallic stage," is in some ways a misnomer, echoing the unconstructive notion that female psychosexual development is subordinate to that of males. The term is not entirely inaccurate, however, if one explores it without making value judgments, because, for a time, healthy as well as conflicted girls do adopt an unconsciously male stance in attempting to cope with their heightened sexuality. The healthy ones move through and out of their "phallic" position to a new and further stage of femininity that does not represent a compromise with inaccessible maleness. Those who are less well prepared emotionally have problems with their evolving identities.

This stage is called phallic because it has been universally observed that genital sensations, fantasies, and drives for gratification reach a level of preoccupation in children of this age, most obvious in the intense concern of boys with their penises but, when it is looked for, scarcely less obvious among girls. Freud originated the term phallic stage because of his theory that the penis was the primary sexual organ in the minds of both boys and girls and that girls became (reluctantly) feminine only when forced to relinquish their phallic strivings. For the sake of simplicity, the term can be retained without subscribing to the male dominance theory.

The psychosexual development occurring in this period cannot be accounted for simply through the autonomous evolution of biological sex "instincts." It is questionable whether any development at this time is instinctual in the technical sense of the word, with the possible exception of the initiation of heterosexual responsivity by a newly acquired capacity to detect sexual odors. The child's sexual drive does increase, but what the child, his parents, and his culture do about this increase largely determines the further development of the drive. The quality of earlier preparations and relationships and the attitudes toward childhood sex play strongly influence the child's response to the biologically intensified sexuality, and the biological influences enforce conditions requiring the child to learn more about growing up male or female.

During this time the Oedipus complex develops, and the phallic stage ends when the conflicts inherent in the oedipal situation are resolved. The Oedipus complex is a naturally occurring constellation of emotions in which the child's genital sensations, having become as intense as they are now, become focused upon the most loved, most important, and most logical person—his parent of the opposite sex.[1] The oedipal situation is normal, not pathological; it is only when something goes awry in coping with these normal feelings that emotional trouble develops. The Oedipus complex not only happens, it is essential for normal psychosexual development.

The Oedipus complex was named after the Greek mythological figure Oedipus, whose story was dramatized by Sophocles. Oedipus, not knowing who his parents are, kills his father, marries his mother, and thereby becomes king. When he discovers what he has done, his overwhelming guilt leads to such torment that he puts out his eyes in self-punishment.

The universality of the Oedipus complex has been the subject of controversy and research among anthropologists since it was first described. Without making an exhaustive review of the many different opinions, a few of the basic ones must be considered for the sake of perspective. The biological determinants to be reckoned with are the child's long dependency upon a mothering figure, the emergence of strong sexual urges during childhood, and the possible role of sexual odors in the different quality of sexual responses at this time. The protracted dependency must inevitably produce in the child a sense of possessiveness toward his nurturers and potential jealousy and anger toward any who might seem to come between him and them. The emergence of sexual drives in childhood demands an object.[2]

Varying family configurations produce differing sources of nurture for an infant. Throughout evolution and regardless of culture, the nurturer has almost invariably been female and almost as invariably the child's biological mother. When this is not so, the child's possessiveness may be directed toward the mother surrogate.

Differing attitudes toward childhood sexuality seem further to alter the nature, or even the existence, of the Oedipus complex. Considerable data has been cited to the effect that when pre-oedipal sex play has been culturally accepted, or when sexual outlets with others are permitted during the oedipal period, the exclusive focus upon the mother or father is diminished.[3] Some cultures may traditionally and purposefully redirect the children's sexual interest toward relatives outside the immediate family.[4] Those who argue most strongly against the Oedipus complex as a biologically determined universal phenomenon suggest that only cultures with family structures and child rearing practices which restrict free childhood sexuality and focus dependency upon one person produce the Oedipus complex as generally understood—the fusion of dependency and sexual needs upon the one person of the mother.[5]

While there can be no doubt that cultural variables modify the manifestations of the oedipal situation, they fail to explain the *one* universal human taboo—mother-son incest. The only invariable form of the incest taboo is the prohibition of intercourse between children and their *biological* parents. This is true even when children are not reared by their biological parents and in cultures entirely permissive of childhood sexuality. The universality of this nuclear form of incest taboo is weighty evidence against explaining away the Oedipus complex purely as a cultural artifact.[6]

The origin of nuclear family incest taboos is unclear, extending far into prehistory. Many theories from the ingenious to the fantastic have been proposed.[7] My own study of the alternatives suggests that incest taboos are inseparable from the unique nature of the human family.

The human child remains dependent upon parental nurturance longer, both in absolute terms and in proportion to life span, than do the young of any other species. The roles of being nurtured and of giving nurture are thus biologically distinct throughout a significant portion of the life span. The mother's body is subject to two divergent and incompatible needs, the oral and dependent needs of her child and the genital needs of her spouse. For the family to have been instituted and to remain viable at all, it was imperative that the adult male not regard his offspring as rivals, and thus kill them, as occurs widely in species without the incest taboo. To preserve the family, the rule must be that no male may have the same woman as object of both his oral and his genital needs. There exist no recorded instances of cultural acceptance of mother-son incest.

The issue of homicidal jealousy is not as evident ethnologically between mothers and daughters, but clearly similar issues of family disruption are involved. However, the lesser occurrence of ultimate degrees of female rivalry may help to account both for the rare recorded instances of culturally sanctioned father-daughter incest and for the far greater actual occurrence of father-daughter incest, despite taboos.

Within this framework it can be seen that incest taboos, which of course underlie the Oedipus complex, may have acquired an innate quality through their long association with family survival. The tripartite family structure, consisting of mother, father, and child, is biologically determined by the infant's long dependency upon a mother who is thus unable for long periods to fend for herself. The invariable persistence of incest taboos specifically designating children and their *biological* parents suggests the evolution of innate sexual drives toward one's real parents. This might explain the survival of these drives in spite of the later development of divergent family structures and differing attitudes toward childhood sexuality. In this sense, then, the Oedipus complex is also universal, for despite anthropological findings of varying family configurations, nowhere do sons marry their biological mothers.[8]

Primate research helps to indicate why, in particular, mother-son incest taboos (as well as mother-daughter lesbian taboos) are so very rarely breached, whereas humans are capable of crimes that are by objective evaluation infinitely more ghastly. It has been observed in several species of primates that in the free-ranging state mother-son mating almost never occurs. Primates have a relatively prolonged period of infantile dependency, and sons almost never rise above their mothers in the dominance hierarchy of the group. Heterosexual coitus occurs only with females of lower or sometimes equal dominance rank. There appears to be some quality of relationship inherent in the infantile dependency role that precludes that infant's ever fully losing a sense of subordination to his mother's early dominance.[9]

Always observing the necessary caution in applying animal findings to human situations, it is tempting to see an analogous and even more powerful influence operative in human families. Due to the much longer period of infantile dependency, and assuming that dominance factors also play some role in human matings, it could be even more difficult for a human infant to grow to regard his mother as a woman with whom he could unconsciously feel himself to be equal or dominant.

As stated earlier, much of the important psychosexual development of this period goes on unseen. The general, nonsexual behavior of children often casts little light upon these inner concerns. One exception is the general level of motor excitement and activity.

There is a vast difference between the toddler who seems drunk with locomotor exploration in spite of very uncertain balance and control, and the four- or five-year-old whose motor excitement and sometimes ceaseless activity is supported by remarkably competent coordination. When this older child jumps up and down or runs around until exhausted, he is in control of what his muscles are doing. When he runs directly into furniture or bushes, bursts as noisily as possible through closed doors and into rooms or houses, collides deliberately full-tilt with adults or other children, he is doing so on purpose.

This kind of bulldozer behavior is seen more in boys than in girls. It coincides with a kind of out-of-bounds disequilibrium that may be related to quite small but significant sex hormone changes believed to be taking place at this period. It is a bodily expression of what Erikson has called the dominant mode of male behavior in this stage—the "intrusive" mode. It is as though the heightened genital excitability with its innately associated drive to penetrate is acted out with the boy's whole self, showing his inner grappling with conflicting and unachievable impulses. His behavior represents the fluctuations between sexual drives of an almost adult nature and deflating realizations that he is still just a little boy, between ambivalent desires to be big and independent like daddy and to solve his dilemma by returning to the comforting dependency of earlier childhood.

The same behavior may be seen in girls of this age because they are experiencing some of the same phallic urges as boys, but their phallic behavior does not last as long, and already the innate differences in levels of muscular development and energy expenditure are manifesting themselves. Girls often express their inner conflicts and disequilibrium in moodiness and irritability, directed chiefly toward the mother. They also display their phase-specific mode—"inclusiveness." They learn to act engaging, lovable, and cuddly, even coquettish. This behavior, when not distorted by conflict, is designed to bring something they want and need both to and into themselves—to take in and to fill themselves with love and acceptance. They are generally more verbal and more adept at getting what they want than the rambunctious little boys of the same age.[10]

The New Sexuality

There are biological reasons why this upsurge of sexuality and its psychological consequences occur in this period. Throughout earlier childhood the growth and myelinization of nerves have been proceeding, resulting in progressively better muscular control and sensory acuity. While much of the innervation of the genitals belongs to the autonomic nervous system, which consists generally of unmyelinated nerves, the nerves that transmit the exquisite sexual pleasure sensations from the penis and clitoris are typically myelinated sensory nerves. The development of these sexual sensory nerves becomes complete around the beginning of this stage, making it possible for the growing child to experience genital stimulation at a new intensity.

A second biological basis for the heightened sexuality is suggested but not yet firmly documented by the existing data on the endocrinology of childhood. Until very recent years, methods for measuring human sex hormones were crude and inexact, and therefore unreliable when very small amounts or changes were concerned. Even now, data on circulating sex hormones and their various metabolic fractions are virtually nonexistent for children during the first three to five years of life. What little evidence exists suggests that around three years of age small amounts of both androgenic and estrogenic products begin to occur regularly in the urine of both sexes. Boys are producing more androgen than are girls, and girls are producing more estrogen. It is known that androgen is responsible in both sexes for the intensity of sex drive as well as genital sensitivity. While the known changes are very small, and stand in need of much more detailed research and validation, they do correlate with the stronger genital sexuality of children at this age.[11]

Still more speculative, but supported by significant clinical and animal data, is the possibility that a complex neurochemical maturation of the capacity to detect odors normally occurs at this time. The substances called pheromones, which elicit both sexual response and sexual function, are found in the secretions of various glands and in genital fluids. They exert their effects through the sense of smell, as in the arousal of every male dog within a mile by a bitch in heat, and are known to be essential to adult heterosexual function in many subhuman species. The young of such species show no response to those odors until the necessary biologically determined brain and olfactory maturation permits both their perception and the consequent heterosexual response. Increasing evidence suggests that a similar heterosexual responsivity matures in humans around the end of the anal stage. Further, there may be a unique sensitivity to the odors of one's biological parents, and the distinctive characteristics of those of the mother and the father may produce different emotional reactions in the child.[12] If true, this innate response could shed additional light upon the obscure origins of universal incest taboo as it applies to the specifically biological parents.

Orgasm at an earlier age is possible for an unknown proportion of normal children. The proportion increases at four to five years of age. Whether there is premature neural or hormonal maturation in

children who are orgastic when much younger is not known, and
there is no data demonstrating that all children in the phallic stage
are capable of orgasm; even those who are must be assumed to
experience something different than adult orgasm, if for no other
reason than the pelvic vascular immaturity of both sexes and the
absence of ejaculate in the male. What is observationally certain is
that the intensity of pleasureful response to stimulation becomes
markedly heightened.

The child's sharply increased genital sensations and drives, and
his possibly newly awakened heterosexual responsiveness, has
several important consequences. One is a much stronger urge to
masturbate. Unless a child is already excessively frightened of his
sexuality, this urge is simply carried out in much more frequent
masturbation. Rather than the genital fondling the infant does, or
the more focused genital stimulation of himself by the toddler,
masturbation is now clearly erotic and is associated in the child's
mind with sexual activity.

There is now a desire for an object of the child's sexual drives,
and he begins to have masturbatory fantasies related to that object.
It is this desire that is expressed in the Oedipus complex, the sexual
desire for the mother or father. This is sometimes verbalized in
quite blunt form, but by far most of the wishes and conflicts go on
in the child's fantasies, both those that accompany masturbation
and others without masturbation. If this were not so, the Oedipus
complex would not have such far-reaching impact. If guilt and fear
did not cause the child to repress his urges as completely as possible,
he could benefit sooner from a comparison of his fantasies about his
parents with the real people who are his parents. But this "easier"
solution is itself a fantasy. The nature of the new sexual impulses
and the inescapable fact of his being a small child who still possesses
the magical and irrational child's mentality determine the limits
within which he can operate. Those limits do not include the
common sense rationality that seems so obvious to an adult.

The very intrusiveness that characterizes this new period of life,
even for little girls for a time, also helps to generate fears of
retaliation. The toddler was struggling for autonomy, a right to his
own physical and emotional "turf," which entailed defense against
those who might want to take away what he had, or felt he had a
right to. But now intrusiveness implies displacing and replacing

another. The child's behavior and his wishes naturally create a rival, and even his child's experience tells him that someone who is being forcefully displaced can be expected to fight back. The little boy wants to unseat daddy and occupy first place in *all* his mother's affections. The little girl ultimately wants to be daddy's love not along with, but instead of, mother. Such fantasies cannot be entertained without the accompanying fears of potential retaliation.[13]

During toddlerhood, castration anxiety was not especially intense under normal circumstances. That is different now. One basic condition for the more intense concern is the greater erotic pleasure afforded by the penis. It becomes more precious and important in proportion to the pleasure it gives. Another reason is that the child's genital preoccupations have now shifted to fantasies about the relationship between his parents and to his own wishes to intrude into that relationship. The imagined rivalry and the enhanced pleasure value of the penis combine to make castration a fantasy truly to be feared, and it must not be forgotten that, in the child's "experience," he already knows what it is to "lose part of himself" as he perceived the weaning process and bowel movements, for example. He has also experienced innumerable disciplinary or safety-motivated losses. So the potential loss of his penis is by no means out of the realm of possibility.

Boys and girls use fantasy both to imagine disguised gratification of their wishes (their hostile, murderous ones as well as their incestuous ones) and also to protect themselves from their guilt. Fairy tales—very popular among four and five year olds—fulfill the first purpose admirably. Most of the popular tales throughout the ages have contained a mixture of sentimentality and gory violence. The mixture seems odd, even perhaps harmful, only to those who do not understand the fantasy life of children of this age and who fail to recognize that these stories gratify the child's unconscious wishes. There are always wicked witches, mean stepmothers, male wolves, monsters and ogres—all of whom meet a suitably gruesome end so that the lovers can be united. In fairy tales magical thinking and magical gratification, as well as raw hostility, are honestly expressed.[14]

In a typical protective fantasy, called the family romance, the child imagines that his parents are not his real parents but that he has been adopted, or was a foundling, or was secretly exchanged with another infant at birth. Often the real parents are imagined to be of royal or fantastically wealthy status. Such fantasies may serve many purposes, such as the derogation of a child's frustrating parents or his wish to be infinitely more powerful than they, but its main value is the reduction of guilt. If his parents are really not related to him, although he may still have to cope with retaliatory fears, he need not feel so guilty over either the incestuous or the hostile wishes.

Many parents initially are incredulous at the thought that their little boys' and girls' minds are at times filled with such tortuous and "unchildlike" sexual thoughts. Even the most observant and psychodynamically sophisticated parent usually will see only occasional flashes and hints, because almost everything goes on inside the child's mind, but those times when thoughts do break through are so blatant that parents for their own protection may simply dismiss the literal meaning of the child's words.

When one of my sons was four and a half years old, I had a mild case of the flu and stayed in bed one day. He had been asking about death because there had been talk in the house of a distant relative having died. Suddenly my son asked the housekeeper, "Is daddy going to die?" She assured him that I would not, that all I had was "sort of a bad cold." She then asked why he had thought of my dying. Without hesitation he answered, "Well, when daddy dies and I grow up, I'm going to marry mommy." He was silent a few moments, then, in a noticeably more anxious voice, added, "But that won't happen for a long, long time!"

The four-year-old daughter of a friend announced at the breakfast table one morning, "I'm going to have a baby with daddy, too!" Her mother was noticeably pregnant and this had been the occasion over the previous months for considerable questioning—and sex education. Her father, commenting on her remark, said he was afraid not, that "daddies don't have babies with their own little girls." "Why not?" she demanded. "I've got a vagina, too!"

Such statements and exchanges are not exceptional. They are relatively infrequent only as compared to their importance and to the degree to which the child thinks about such matters. Most families, if they tax their memories, can recall some allusion by one or more of their children to wanting either to marry or to have a baby with their mother or father. There are many more disguised ways in which these fantasies may be expressed, but these are the most unequivocal.

Another way in which parents usually are aware of a change in their children sexually is through the increased frequency and intensity of masturbation. In Judeo-Christian culture, most children at this age have begun to be somewhat secretive about masturbation, but such learning comes slowly, and one of the main reasons for hiding masturbatory activity—guilt over oedipal fantasies—has not made its full impact as yet. So most parents do notice a change, most often struck by the almost adult-like concentration and unmistakably sexual quality of the child's self-stimulation.

It is not easy even for the most liberal of parents to be genuinely unconcerned about masturbation, as it is associated unconsciously with their own childhood sexual training—usually a less permissive one—and their own anxiety-producing oedipal fantasies. Those who were relatively untroubled by the earlier genital play of their child may be unable to withstand the emotions aroused by the different quality they now sense in masturbation and try to find "undamaging" ways to discourage it. The more careless or ignorantly harsh prohibitions are not by any means quaint remnants of the unsophisticated past. Parents still threaten sons with cutting off their penises if they continue to masturbate. Girls are still told how nasty and dirty masturbation is and how they may harm themselves if they indulge in it.

But whether given in a gentle or harsh manner, the prohibition will be heard. A harsh approach is more devastating than a gentle one, but in either case the child assumes that his parents' disapproval of masturbation is disapproval not only of the act but of the oedipal fantasies and wishes. Because of the guilts and fears associated with those fantasies, it is difficult for any child to avoid reading dire threats into even gently expressed masturbatory prohibitions. This is yet another normal and necessary developmental conflict that cannot really be bypassed; every child must cope with the conflict between his impossible wishes and his real role in his family, and the task of coping is significantly different for boys than for girls.

Becoming a Boy

The boy's conflict is relatively simpler than the girl's: he wishes to possess all his mother's love and to gratify his genital urges with her. To do so, he would have to get rid of his father. But he also loves his father dearly, cherishes his father's love in return, and does not want to hurt him. Moreover, he recognizes his puny helplessness, despite his dreams of power, and fears that his father would resent his wish to overthrow him. His father might even "make the punishment fit the crime" and cut off his penis. His castration anxiety, fed by how highly he values his penis and by guilty fear, reaches its most intense pitch. He feels both guilty and angry over the imaginary violent role into which his own fantasies have cast his father. Eventually, he realizes that he cannot compete.

During this time, a boy strenuously externalizes all his genital sensation and interest. His penis has become his most prized possession. Already fearing damage to this wonderful organ, the unconscious association of inside genital sensations with femaleness still further motivates him to value only his external source of pleasure, his penis. His urge is to penetrate, while femaleness is equated with being penetrated, damaged, and penisless. Since he has very much envied his mother's power and procreativity, a genuine and important emotional part of himself must be denied and repressed in order to focus all his genitality on his penis alone. His intrusive behavior also expresses externalization, in which his entire body symbolically represents the penetrating penis.

Sometimes a boy will evidence a more feminine form of castration fear. He fears that masturbation has damaged his penis, that it is in some mysterious way no longer whole or intact, and that this masculine deficit will someday be found out. Instead of being afraid he will lose his maleness, he fears he has already lost it and is essentially a female.

Various aspects of a boy's behavior during these years may be very puzzling to parents who do not recognize the unspoken struggle going on inside. Again, it cannot be emphasized too strongly that these inner conflicts are not always intense and disturbing in a healthy boy growing up in a normal warm and loving family. But they do occur, and evidences of feeling troubled will flare up from time to time in almost all boys during the phallic stage.

One of the facts of a four-year-old boy's life is that when he sees his father naked, which usually happens from time to time, he cannot avoid an ego-deflating comparison between his own and his father's genitals. This experience exerts reality pressure toward relinquishing his impossible fantasies; it also helps account for some of his emotionally labile and changeable behavior. His pride in his penis and his whole effectively aggressive body reflects itself in periods of exuberant self-confidence. At other times moodiness, depression, and babyish behavior may reflect a concept of himself quite the opposite of the victorious gladiator.

An increase in bad dreams and nightmares is another form the conflict may take. Children can be notoriously poor at remembering the content of anxiety dreams, but the dreams they do report on involve violence and physical danger. At times the characters are recognizable: the little boy's daddy may be in danger from thieves with knives or guns who break into his bedroom at night, or the little boy himself may be the victim, chased by giants or monsters or wild animals. At other times, though the theme is one of terrifying physical danger, the child cannot remember who was involved or else the characters were strangers. Children's frightening dreams may have a wide variety of content, but in boys' oedipal nightmares themes of bodily mutilation or penetration are most common, and the dreams usually abound with a variety of phallic, penetrating weapons and other sources of danger, such as teeth and claws. The content of the dreams may also be more typically disguised and not waken the youngster in fear.

Oedipal nightmares may not only reveal the conflicts but may also be a means of acting out oedipal wishes—they provide an excuse for a boy to invade the parents' bedroom in order to be comforted and possibly get into bed with them, preferably between them, thus disrupting their privacy and intimacy. These nightmares are usually real (though occasionally contrived) and they deserve parental reassurance, but at this age it is wiser to insist upon comforting the youngster in his own bed. Allowing him to interfere with his parents' appropriate bedtime privacy will not help him reach a realistic resolution of his oedipal dilemma.

Boys will find other ways to disrupt their parents' nighttime intimacy. It may take the form of an unexpectedly increased resistance to going to bed, or a boy who has gone to sleep without delay for several years will suddenly develop delaying tactics. He gets out of bed and comes to his parents repeatedly with irrelevant and unimportant questions, or he complains that his room is too hot or too cold or that there's a mosquito bothering him, or for the first time since he was two he will call for his mother to bring him a drink of water. Even bouts of sleepwalking sometimes serve intrusive urges.

Irritating and provocative behavior that actually has two quite different goals is often directed at the father, the imaginary rival toward whom the boy feels both guilt and fear. The youngster may become cranky and difficult soon after his father gets home and become even more impossible during the evening. On the one hand, he is expressing vague feelings and probably has no idea why he is angry; on the other hand, the unconscious reasons for his anger make him guilty and he is trying to provoke punishment. If his father does lose patience and spank him or put him firmly to bed, he may actually respond with relief—to the puzzlement of his parents. His father's reaction not only relieved his guilt but also reassured him that his father is strong enough to remain in control. The diminutive Oedipus needs his father's strength in order to resolve his oedipal conflict realistically.

Becoming a Girl

There is both a "phallic" and a feminine component to the psychosexual development of girls when they reach this period. Girls have a double dilemma for the simple and obvious reason that their principal and primary love object, the mother, has also been female. To some extent, they want to turn their newly intensified erotic feelings toward their mother just as boys do, but this first phase, the phallic one, is not of equal importance for all girls. While it undoubtedly plays a role in normal development, it achieves disturbing proportions only in those girls who are already beginning to find their femaleness difficult to accept, or for whom obstacles are provided at this time against their comfortable assumption of a feminine sexual identity. Otherwise, the phallic stage of a girl and its accompanying burst of fairly intense penis envy becomes subordinated to her evolving primary femaleness.

The precipitating condition is the same biological maturation of genital sensation and drive as described for boys. The clitoris becomes the focus of intense erotic pleasure and calls forth a corresponding increase of clitoral masturbation. Since most girls this age are well aware of genital differences, the first source of stronger penis envy may derive from the concrete literalness of the child's mental processes. The penis is bigger, therefore it must afford that much more pleasure. The fact that the clitoris is even more densely innervated cannot be known by a four-year-old and probably would not be believed if she did know it.

It is at this time, too, that the little girl has become disappointed in her inside sexuality. She cannot control it, she cannot have a real baby despite all her magical thinking. She is ready to repudiate her wish and repress it, and the newly erotized clitoris helps her to externalize her sexuality the way boys do. Many girls, in the interest of externalization, repress the knowledge of their vaginal opening and deny awareness of its existence.

The second source of penis envy arises from the little girl's initial desire to continue to focus her love on her mother, where it has always been. Her sexual drive is now erotic, and in order to love her mother as her father does she needs a penis. It is more this *functional* wish than a belief that little boys are naturally superior that endows the penis with its temporarily supreme value.

When the impossibility of her phallic wishes are borne in on her, she turns away from her mother toward her father, in frustration and disappointment. Now begins a crystallizing of the considerable ambivalence that characterizes the feelings of even the happiest and healthiest of little girls toward their mothers. Normally, the mother has been the source of far too much love and pleasure and caring for the little girl to cease loving her; but she is also the source of a myriad real and imaginary disappointments and dissatisfactions, all of which crowd together in the girl's emotions at this time.

In the earlier developmental periods, her mother interfered with her pleasure by weaning her, by toilet-training her, by disciplining her, perhaps by bringing a new sibling rival into the house. Since the mother was always the power figure, and it was the mother who seemingly decided what to give and what to withhold, the mother is unconsciously blamed for not having provided her with the penis she now needs in order to love her mother. To top it all off, her mother obviously prefers her father as a sexual love object. So the little girl "loses" her first love object because she lacks a particular body part.

In turning toward her father, the girl is not impelled solely, or even primarily, by her disappointment over not being a penis-bearing male. She has experienced this frustration, to be sure, but largely, she is prompted by all the normal facets of female identity and preferences that have been developing under the appropriate influences of her parents. If her parents have been exemplifying and fostering an acceptance of rewarding heterosexual complementarity, her phallic interest in her mother will pass relatively quietly. Her sexual drives will turn naturally, not reluctantly and by default, toward her first and most logical heterosexual love object, her father.[15] The shift may be further enabled by the onset of heterosexual responsiveness that may unfold at this time.

Unfortunately, she is still a little girl, and her father's daughter. This second, truly oedipal phase of her dilemma confronts her again with unachievable wishes. Now her position is analogous to the little boy's. Her wish to displace her mother creates a fantasy of rivalry with this powerful giantess whom she loves as well as envies and fears. She could scarcely expect her wish for her father's love and for a baby from her father to go unresented by her rival. So she, too, must finally renounce her oedipal wishes and admit failure. Her father does not fulfill her desires and persists in giving his sexual love and preference to her mother.

During the phallic stage there is a sharp increase in clitoral masturbation—at times almost a preoccupation. Girls' affectionate expressions toward their mothers often have a distinct erotic tinge, such as pressing the pubis against the mother's body when hugging her. They may be angrily and viciously rivalrous toward brothers, especially those near their own age or younger. They may dream of being boys or men, of having control of powerful masculine animals or machines. Dreams that openly or symbolically represent rape, penetration, and mutilation by penetration are frequent anxiety dreams of the phallic period. Dreams and fantasies in which the vagina has teeth may represent a girl's defense against the feared and envied penis or an aggressive expression of penis envy.[16] During both the phallic and oedipal phases, girls use the various available techniques to intrude upon their parents' privacy, since in both phases they want to share in or take over that intimacy.

As the phallic phase succumbs to the weight of reality, the main behavioral expression is irritability and impatience in the girl's relationship with her mother. This may be fleeting or protracted. Within herself, a girl seems disorganized, distracted—at loose ends. Her shift leaves her temporarily uncertain of her direction and her own feelings.

The true oedipal phase is the most obvious. The girl's mother is partly or largely ignored, and her father becomes the object of affectionate attention, coquettishness, even a startlingly obvious seductiveness. Parents may realize for the first time the amazing repertoire of adult mannerisms that their little girl has observed and picked up, as she puts them to use in imitation of being daddy's girl friend. She often makes it quite clear that she thinks she can please him and take care of him with far more loving solicitude than her mother, whom she tries to relegate to the role of housekeeper. She will often verbally rebuke her mother if she thinks her father is being neglected. It is during this time that the classic statements about marrying daddy and having his children are heard.

She shows renewed interest in her father's body, and her efforts to observe him nude may increase. This interest is easily noticed, assuming that parents do not keep bedroom and bathroom doors locked, nor issue such stern prohibitions that the toddler stays out because of fear. In the late toddler stage, the youngster would enter from time to time when parents were unclothed but was usually pursuing her own affairs elsewhere. During the height of oedipal strivings a girl finds many more excuses for having to go to the bathroom or ask a question when daddy is in the bathroom and unclothed. Goodnight kisses develop a flavor of passionate duration.

While the girl's coquettish "little wife" behavior is often thought of as a caricature of adult femininity, and may be genuinely amusing, it should never be ridiculed. Even though its focus on father is unrealistic, it is a serious and essential rehearsal for her future feminine inclusive and actively receptive modes. Parents must know how to handle it; its quality should not be discouraged, because it is an evolving part of feminine identity.

The girl's dreams will reflect both her wishes and her guilts and fears. In this phase, too, her anxiety dreams may reveal an amazing frequency of rape themes, a theme that may turn up in waking fantasies as well. Depending upon the stories she has been read and upon her familiarity with television, the powerful males may be romantic pirates or cowboys. Such dreams frequently contain a mixture of fear and pleasure. The girl has not lost her unconscious fear of mutilative penetration, nor has she failed to be impressed by the awesome contrast between father's big penis and her own small body, but there is also the fantasied pleasure that would fulfill her erotic wishes, with the added bonus that rape absolves her guilt. After all, she was a helpless victim.

At this point, having met with frustration in both phallic and oedipal strivings, a little girl has some realistic, though thoroughly misperceived, reasons to feel temporarily inferior to everyone in her typical family. Her mother has babies, breasts, and her father's sexual love; her father has a large penis and her mother's sexual love; her brother has a penis which gives him a fantasy edge in winning her mother or a substitute, and his equipment more closely resembles her father's than hers resembles her mother's.[17] Children of both sexes, but perhaps especially girls, need helpful and understanding parents to make sure that they garner the many benefits of this crucial stage and avoid its potential hazards.

The Parents' Task in Handling the Oedipal Dilemma

Oedipal attractions are not one-way phenomena. In Sophocles' play, Oedipus did not pine hopelessly for his mother; Jocasta married him willingly and urged him not to feel guilty even after their kinship was revealed to them. In like manner, the sexual feelings of parents are sometimes stirred by their own little children, and they are flattered and pleased by the love turned toward them.

Parental response is not as strong or as fantastically unrealistic as that of their children, but for different reasons it can be quite as guilt-provoking. I have known mothers or fathers to be horrified at becoming aware of a distinct stirring in their own genitals when cuddling or playing with their oedipal-age youngsters. Visions of being perverted fiends flash through their minds. This sense of anxiety and guilt may be so intense that the parent represses all memory of his sexual response and will strenuously deny it, or he may protect himself from his guilt by withdrawing and suddenly becoming distant from the child. Since the reason for such a defense is unconscious or becomes quickly repressed, a parent may not be aware of his disengagement and of its disturbing effect upon the child. The child is prone to assume (correctly) that his oedipal desires caused the withdrawal of his parent and may become guilty about and unaccepting of his budding heterosexual drives.

Such repressive measures by parents are unnecessary. All humans are sexual creatures, and sexual response to a sexual approach is entirely normal. Research has demonstrated that normally heterosexual adult males respond with significantly greater erotic arousal even to very young female children than to males or to sexually neutral stimuli,[18] and there is no reason to assume that findings would be different for adult females. It is how parents cope with the Oedipus complex, both in their children and themselves, not the mere existence of sexual feelings, that has importance to its resolution.

The basic prerequisites of good parenting in this stage are quite simple. The roots of healthy identity in children extend far back into the earliest years. When sex role identifications reach a crux in later years and must be definitively forged out of the conflicts of the Oedipus complex, the same constructive coalition of the mother and father, exemplifying and fostering complementary sex role identities, is essential.

The parental authority to handle oedipal disruptiveness and seductive behavior, if not established earlier, may be more difficult to institute now. Benevolent firmness is necessary to maintain the parents' rights to sexual privacy and intimacy. While the real needs of a youngster need not be neglected, he must learn that he cannot succeed in disrupting his parents' relationship. Seductiveness can be handled similarly. Boys' masculinity and girls' femininity can be happily accepted and encouraged, while making it clear that some forms of love are reserved for the mother and father, which later the child will enjoy with his future partner when he is ready for it. If a little girl is openly and enthusiastically loved for all her healthy, developing feminine traits, she will readily withstand the frustration of their erotic components toward her father. Under analogous emotional conditions, the frustration tolerance of boys will also be adequate.

Sex information and education is especially useful at this time. In particular, explanations of future growth and development help to mitigate the pain of oedipal failure. Children have limited capacity for comprehending the future, and intellectual explanations may provide but cold comfort, the future being too far off to be real. But the parents' concern, the interest and care they take to help with the children's frustrations, and their credibility in their children's minds all gradually have their effect.

By the same token, the uncertainty of parents about their own authority, about their right to privacy, and about whether to be strict or permissive because of the supposed hazards of frustrating a child's wishes or demands can confuse a child just when he needs a confident sense of self conveyed to him by parents to help him find his own sense of self. With insecure parents, oedipal rivalries may be acted out and "won" by the child not only in obvious but in disguised ways. There is the child whose parents back down from a firm insistence that he stay reasonably in bed and the child who insists upon nighttime comforting in his parents' bed. Children may seem—and feel themselves to be—stronger than their parents when they win such battles. This is a distortion of the reality of comparative family positions, a reality the child must learn to accept in order to move on psychosexually. It also intensifies his guilt when family interaction leads him to fear that he really might be more powerful than his fantasied rival, the parent.

The devastating and crippling consequences of seemingly successful oedipal competition are magnified when marital discord or parental psychopathology leads one or both parents literally to encourage the child's rivalrous behavior. A woman who is disdainful of her husband may clearly show her preference for a young son, making him an obvious favorite as she depreciates his father in his eyes. In less blatant pathology, marital dissatisfactions that have not even reached full awareness can result in the subtle preferential treatment by a parent of a child of the opposite sex, combined with resistance against the spouse's effort to insist upon a more appropriate family role for the youngster.

Husbands have frequently been known to encourage their small daughters' coquetry and to flaunt their appreciative response in order to make their wives jealous or to retaliate for mistreatment they feel they have suffered at their wives' hands. Such disturbed paternal behavior intensifies the daughter's oedipal fantasies and the guilty fear attendant upon the successful rivalry.

The ultimately disordered parental response is overt sexual

intimacy with the child. While relatively rare, it is not unheard of, particularly in the form of seductive parental behavior. Despite the greater incidence of overt father-daughter incest than mother-son incest, my clinical experience suggests that mothers are more often involved in clearly seductive interactions short of incest. Some may continue to bathe their sons long after the sons should have been granted that autonomy and privacy. These mothers often rationalize their behavior as concern for the cleanliness of their sons' genitals. The mother of one of my patients would daily retract the foreskin of his uncircumsized penis and assiduously remove any smegma with cotton swabs—and continued this practice until puberty. Some mothers continue to bathe regularly with their four- and five-year-old sons or let their sons sleep with them when both are nude. Some mothers may wear the flimsiest of open robes or negligees or display themselves nude under such intimate circumstances that one can only infer a sexual motive. At the most pathological extreme, some women permit sons to fondle their breasts and genitals, at times attributing this behavior to natural and innocent child's play.

Fathers are at times overtly seductive with their daughters, bathing and fondling them, indulging in prolonged tickling around the genitals, contriving opportunities for contact between their nude bodies, perhaps even purposefully fondling their daughters' genitals.

The study referred to in chapter 3, in which it was found that such a large proportion of both coerced and cooperative sexual encounters between adult males and female children began when the girl was between three and five years of age,[19] attests both to the peak of sexuality in the child in this phase of development and to the responsiveness of adults to children of this age.

As I have already indicated, I have found not just a concern but an overconcern in this culture about parental nudity and bodily modesty. However, our predominant attitudes toward childhood sex play and our most common family configuration are known to focus the Oedipus complex most sharply upon the parents; this should alert adults to situations that intensify the conflict and disturb or disrupt its resolution. It is appropriate that parents should avoid intruding their sexuality upon their oedipal age children and that they take gentle pains to prevent children from intruding into their own intimacy or from forcing their sexuality on them.

Special situations exist for the child in one-parent families, a situation that poses unique tasks for the child in resolving his incestuous urges. If the parent of the same sex is missing, oedipal fantasies may be intensified and also more difficult to relinquish, since there is no real "rival." At the same time, fear and guilt may become more disturbing because in the child's unconscious fantasy he may blame himself for the parent's absence or death. Absence of the parent of the opposite sex can often result in exaggerated idealization of that parent, perhaps making it difficult for anyone else to live up to that idealized model.

The circumstances of the parent's absence help determine how the oedipal dilemma is skewed. Death of the parent of the same sex is especially guilt-provoking because of the child's own unconscious death wishes toward that parent. Desertion or divorce may undermine a realistic resolution of incestuous desires by weakening the love for the missing parent, an important counterbalance against the rivalrous feelings. If the parent of the opposite sex leaves, the child may fantasize that his forbidden wishes were the cause, discoloring future heterosexual drives with inappropriate guilt.[20] When the absence is intermittent, as with the children of Army fathers, the repetitive reaccommodation to the presence and absence of the father has been shown predictably to produce disturbed psychosexual development.[21] These reasons for the absence of one parent produce quite different emotional responses and behavior in the remaining parent, creating another atypical emotional condition that may disturb a young child's ego.

Resolution of the Conflict

It is only through resolution of the oedipal conflict that a child can take his first definitive step toward an integrated sexual identity—a functional and progressive fusion of appropriate facets of his sex role with his established gender identity. The inevitable failure of the oedipal fantasies leads to resignation, guilt, and anxiety. The renunciation of the impossible wish is motivated in part by the need to relieve those unpleasant emotions. It is enforced also by all the positive ties of love for the parent of the same sex, the pressure of innate forces toward healthy sexual identity, the growing power of reality over magical omnipotent thinking, and the influence of healthy sexual self-concepts inculcated by parents throughout childhood thus far. Under the impetus of these forces, the youngster forgoes rivalry with the parent of the same sex and instead identifies with him, accepting the reality that by such means he will ultimately grow up and find his own heterosexual partner. With this step, he gets rid of his guilt, fear, and anger and frees himself for the psychosexual and sociosexual growth of the early school years.

The emotional need to repress the oedipal fantasies is powerful enough to overreach itself and to become overinclusive. Along with the oedipal fantasies are repressed virtually all memory of childhood sexuality and even of the first five or six years of childhood itself. Childhood amnesia presents persuasive supporting evidence for the degree of anxiety produced by the Oedipus complex.

One of the most far-reaching consequences of resolution of the Oedipus complex is further consolidation of the superego, which consists entirely of real or imagined parental prohibitions as perceived by a child of five or younger. Since it can only exist at that level of comprehension, little subtlety or shading is possible; it has a primitive, all-or-none quality, so that actions or thoughts are perceived by the child as "all bad" or "all good."

The character of the superego—its strength and its reasonableness or harshness—is derived, like the superego itself, from various sources. One is the manner in which the parents actually correct and discipline the child; if they sound arbitrary, punitive, and unreasonable, then their child's inner monitor will speak to him in the same tone of voice. Another is the strength of the child's own repudiated impulses. When thoughts and impulses that make him fearful and guilty are very strong, it will require a powerful superego to help him repress and deny them; to bolster their repudiation, he imagines that his parents are sternly forbidding him to entertain such terrible thoughts and feelings. This unconscious projection of the prohibition onto parents makes the child unable to distinguish between those things against which his parents really admonished him and those that arise out of his own fantasies. This unconscious mechanism explains why so many children feel guilty about impulses and thoughts that would never have prompted the disapproval of their parents.

Another source of superego strength is the ego ideal—the set of conscious and unconscious aspirations and standards that each child evolves for himself, demands that he live up to, and from which he cannot deviate without loss of self-esteem. The early unrealistic ego ideals of childhood, based upon infantile omnipotence, are now augmented by internalizing an image of the parents as ideal and all-powerful. Such an ego ideal is a harsh and implacable master and will require reassessment and revision. The reevaluation of one's ego ideal can occur only as the child matures and experiences reality more broadly. He must eventually be able to revise his idealized parental images before he can relax his own overwhelming self-demands.

These internal components of the superego are greatly intensified during the resolution of the Oedipus complex. As a child is torn between his stronger drives and the enormous superstructure of imaginary angry jealousy and retaliation on the part of his parents, he becomes inwardly split into two parts that, in some form, will remain with him always. As Erikson has expressed it, "The instinct fragments which before had enhanced the growth of his infantile body and mind now become divided into an infantile set which perpetuates the exuberance of growth potentials, and a parental set which supports and increases self-observation, self-guidance, and self-punishment." [22]

It has been suggested that a child's superego should guide him as a good parent would, that it is the task of parents to train a child to feel guilty only over attitudes and acts that are truly harmful to himself or others. Since guilt is sometimes appropriate and other times totally misplaced and undeserved, parents must reinforce a child's sexuality and foster his heterosexual responsiveness while gently discouraging its direct expression within the family. They must counteract the potential harshness of his fantasies concerning their terrible retaliatory disapproval with the reality of their loving acceptance of his stronger sexual drive and his appropriate sexual identity.

The built-in danger lies in the fact that the child's superego is inevitably primitive. When the child feels insecure in the control of his inner impulses, his superego will become excessively harsh, making the child overrestrictive to the point that he cannot permit the development and expression of normal sexual interests. The opposite of successful resolution of the oedipal conflict is the inner conviction that one's drives and, consequently, one's basic self are essentially and innately evil.

The resolution of the oedipal dilemma is somewhat different for boys than for girls. Psychosexual differentiation takes now a more sharply divergent path than at any previous stage. Even though in toddlers the core gender identity is fixed, there is still a fluidity in their shifting identifications with one or the other parent and in their imitative experimenting with different sexual roles; by the end of the oedipal period, most of that early childhood fluidity is gone.

In the classic formulation of the boy's unique task, his Oedipus complex is *resolved* by castration fear; the intensity of that fear brings about a rather sudden repression of his incestuous wishes, followed by identification with the father rather than the previous jealous rivalry.[23] It is now known that this theory is oversimplified and overemphasizes the purely conflictual elements. In a healthy and loving family, there are many positive motives, both innately biological and parentally induced, that press toward the boy's identification with his father. Societal pressures reinforce this natural course of events. These considerations do not negate the existence or the power of oedipal guilt and fear, but they help place it in perspective with the child's sociosexual learning and biological predisposition.

A complicating factor in every boy's identification with his father is the fact that he must change his primordial female identity, one that dates back to infantile symbiosis with his mother. Even after that stage passes, his mother remains his first love object and the most important person in his life. She has been his major source of love and comfort and gratification, and disidentifying with her complicates his task. Even in adulthood, the wish to be taken care of without responsibility crops up from time to time in everyone. For a little boy, the regressive pull is strong; it is difficult to relinquish those dependent comforts.

On the other hand, these considerations make his shift to identification with his father easier in some very important ways. The healthy impetus toward greater independence and self-reliance has been growing ever since he learned to move about unassisted; so has the desire to broaden his social world so as to include more people and more experiences outside his home. These growth increments follow a built-in maturational timetable and run strongly counter to the maternal control implicit in infantile dependency. In addition to all the wonderful things his mother was, she was also the main agent of frustration and discipline; her controlling power is closely associated with the pains of earlier childhood. It has been speculated that the original symbiosis leaves unconscious memory traces so deeply threatening to masculine sex identity as to cause an ineradicable symbiosis anxiety—an extremely potent and often misused motivation in distancing oneself from women.[24]

The healthy boy is more impelled to continue maturing than to hold on to infancy, but there can be no doubt that he is pulled in both directions. Thus, in the resolution of his Oedipus complex he rids himself of his unconscious guilt and fear by identifying with his father, and he makes a decisive break with infancy and that level of maternal domination.

The situation just described is more or less ideal, but here again one is brought face to face with another of the less than helpful child-rearing traditions in our culture. The boy differentiates himself significantly from his mother only to find himself thrust under the dominating influence of a succession of other females for the next several crucial years. His identification with his father cannot easily ripen when, as in most homes, his father's work keeps him away much of the time and is also of a nature that makes it impossible for his young son to join in it or contribute to it. By comparison, consider a farm boy: his father's work is not only visible and obvious to him, but by the age of five or six he can begin working along with his father at tasks appropriate to his capabilities.

There are a number of maladaptive resolutions of a boy's Oedipus complex. Some boys regress to infantile behavior and relationships as a means of maintaining their mother's love in a manner less dangerously competitive with the father. This may happen if the pull of infantile gratification is too strong or if the father is seen as too threatening or indifferent or hostile even for identification, much less competition and rivalry. Another possibility is that the desire for the mother is too strong to relinquish and the father is somehow an unacceptable model for identification. Such boys do not cease their rivalry with the father. They maintain an atypical hostile competitiveness with males on into the school years, along with an overclose attachment to their mother and mother substitutes, such as teachers. Such an attachment can easily be distinguished from the quite normal "crush" a boy may develop upon an adult female as part of the healthy resolution of the oedipal conflict, maintaining some of the dependent gratification he still needs and at the same time disguising the object of his interest.

In contrast with the boy's Oedipus complex, which is resolved by castration anxiety, the girl's is said to be *brought on* by the fear of a fantasied castration or resentment over the fantasy of its being already accomplished. The validity of the comparison depends in part upon the intensity of a girl's phallic strivings and subsequent frustration. In those girls with strong penis envy, who resent bitterly their fantasied castration, it is accurate to say that they turn their sexual wishes toward their fathers in genuine disappointment over not being a boy. In a girl whose femaleness has been positively reinforced throughout her earlier childhood, the phallic phase is less intense and she is less driven toward her father by castration anxiety than pulled toward him by developing heterosexual responsiveness. In other words, the oedipal attachments of girls express strong components of natural and positive femininity, not merely reluctant compensations for not having been a boy.

But the facts of life and anatomy are never negligible in shaping psychosexual development. The fact that a little girl has no penis contributes to the slower and sometimes incomplete resolution of her oedipal attachment to her father. Naturally she fears her mother's rivalry and fantasied anger, and she fears losing her mother's love—indeed, fear of her mother's disapproval may be enhanced because her fantasies lead her to believe she deserves it—but these fears are not augmented by the potent additional anxiety over the loss of an especially valuable organ. Her oedipal wishes are gradually given up simply because of lack of fulfillment. Resolution comes about more through disappointment by the father than through fear of the mother.

Because the mother was the important figure all through infancy, girls have a somewhat more difficult task than boys with the identity problems associated with the oedipal resolution. That seems almost contradictory when one realizes that girls can achieve and foster their growing feminine identification without shifting sexes. They are female, and at the end of the oedipal phase they identify with the same female with whom they had always identified—which may be one reason women suffer fewer serious disturbances in sex identity than do men—but realigning themselves with their mothers is not without both conflict and ambivalence. Postoedipal identification with the mother is not simply a matter of remaining identified with her, as the early identification was interrupted by the phallic phase and by the much longer period during which the girl wanted to displace and get rid of the mother in order to have the father to herself.

Girls also experience the same ambivalence as boys about the pleasures of dependent infancy versus the drive for greater independence and self-determination. Remaining childlike is both a temptation and a danger even for the normal girl and her family. It is quite natural for the little girl both to desire and to want to break away from the comfort of infancy. A disturbed mother-child relationship in infancy will complicate any task facing a child, but a happy infancy also creates the desire to retain its pleasures and the fear of forfeiting one's independence in the process.

Therefore, a girl's resolution of the Oedipus complex requires reidentifying with her mother on a new and different level of relationship. She must be able to overcome her various resentments and jealousies. She must allow herself a very close relationship with the same person who totally controlled her for so long, but without fearing that same degree of control now. In her closeness to her mother, she must withstand constant emotional reminders of infantile pleasures without falling back into infantile patterns of behavior. Needless to say, this is no easy task for a little girl's ego. It is not surprising that this new identification with her mother is often an uneasy one, marked by occasional flare-ups, and sometimes not at all satisfactorily achieved.

Where a mother has satisfied her daughter's important needs and at the same time permitted and rewarded appropriate development of individuality and self-determination, the resolution of the oedipal conflict can be accomplished healthily. The girl's own experience will help her realize that her mother will accept her as a separate female individual and will even help her to become one. If their early relationship has been disturbed, this essential step in a girl's development of her own healthy sex identity may be blocked. Girls whose infancy was either unsatisfying or overgratifying, or whose mothers were smothering and controlling, will strongly resist reaccepting the mother as a model for their own developing personalities and will not move appropriately into the next phase of psychosexual maturation. They may return to clinging, babyish behavior and not keep pace with the social growth and interest of their peers. They may continue a running battle with their mothers, constantly seeking to avoid a relationship they see only as unsatisfactory. Sometimes they become tomboys, not out of penis envy and masculine striving, but because it is their way of rejecting their mother as a model.

A different sort of obstacle exists for girls with a pathological degree of penis envy. They have not begun to accept that not having a penis is good—at least as good as having one. The oedipal period is the first crucial opportunity to learn to *like* being a girl. The girl's sexual desire for her father includes pleasure in being his opposite, a female, but the impossibility of satisfying her desire and the disappointment and hurt at her failure can revive her shame over being a girl if this was a serious conflict at an earlier time. Her fantasied humiliation at being female may be such that identification with her mother is impossible and every aspect of femininity must be denied. This is another basis for tomboyism—that persistent and defiant kind that so clearly signals rejection of femaleness. Some girls become little "toughs" in the effort to pretend to themselves that they are really boys, behaving as though they actually possess the coveted penis.

The resolution of the Oedipus complex is more than an end to this particular developmental period; it marks the end of all "infantile" sexual stages of development, during which the child is essentially homebound and parentally dominated. He has been inwardly preoccupied with the various component parts of the sexual drive and bodily and mental maturation, none of which constitute adult sexuality in any sense of the word, but all of which are needed to add up eventually to adult sexuality.

The psychosexual development yet to come is in many ways even more important than that which has gone before. But the child's "basic training" is over. Its excellences and its flaws will favor or plague him as he moves out into the broader community to continue his psychosexual development in the context of increasing social interaction. Many basic character traits have been laid down by this time. They are not absolutely fixed and immutable, but subtly pervasive and highly resistant to change. They remain alive because they have become a functioning part of the personality. They continue to be used in the interaction with others because they are perceived as conferring some benefit or protection, however unconscious or neurotic, against the repetition of the fears or hurts that originally engendered those traits. They will change only under the most felicitous influence of an environment conducive to reparative maturation, or with special personal effort. By now, many of the emotional and characterological consequences of psychosexual development express themselves differently in the two sexes because of the inexorable differentiation brought about by the fact of growing up through these crucial years in two different kinds of bodies, as well as through the capricious dictates of cultural whimsy.

A boy's disidentification from his mother in order to achieve a male sex identity carries with it the potential of some crippling overreactions. If his need, for whatever reasons, to break away from his infantile experiences is especially strong, or his oedipal guilts and fears excessively intense, he may feel threatened by all females. His resulting avoidance of closeness with females can impair his capacity, now or later, to empathize with them and to understand and accept them. Such an outcome is intensified if his earlier identification with his mother was so threatening that he overdid the externalizing of his inner genital sensations, thus denying all the natural "femaleness" in himself. An ultimate expression of the fearful repudiation of "female" qualities in himself is the repudiation of femaleness itself, expressed in the derogation of women. Even under the most healthily normal circumstances, boys need a respite from female control in order to consolidate their sexual identities. Thus for some years following the oedipal resolution, they are largely indifferent to or intolerant of the company of girls in large doses.

The conflicts over maternal identification and disidentification are compounded by the fact that for most boys the mother represented productivity and creativity. During the toddler stage that association was strongly fixed, and if a boy turns too sharply away from his mother and other females, this can destroy the expression of important qualities that are essential for his constructive social participation. Especially where comparable paternal qualities are not easily perceived, male creativity and productivity represent a positive identification with the mother expressed in modalities appropriate to males. This can occur only if normal "female" aspects of the total personality are not perceived as too threatening to integrate into the self. Therefore, boys must preserve many qualities initially associated with their mother when they break away from her and identify with their father. Otherwise they lose a major segment of what is necessary to become a whole person, crippling themselves and their future capacity to relate fully to women.

If a boy is unable to give up competition with his father, the consequences of such fixation may permanently affect character formation. Such boys go through life always competing with other males for women, not because of genuine interest in a particular woman but because of the compulsive need to defeat the rival. They often choose women who are but thinly disguised imitations of their mother. Their relations with such women are full of unconscious guilt and fear, which leads to disturbed sexual function. The reenactment of the oedipal triangle stirs up the original conflict.

One of the most inappropriate endings to the oedipal struggle occurs when the little boy finds it impossible to accept his masculine identity. Sometimes this occurs when his castration anxiety is so great that he unconsciously decides to identify with his mother instead of his father so as to earn his father's love rather than suffer his retaliatory rage. More often, the identification with his mother is less important than the overwhelming fear of attack by all "bigger, stronger" males. Here, the unconscious maladaptive pattern is designed to avoid attack and "protect" his penis by renouncing all competition for women. In many such youngsters, their mothers have so undermined their budding masculinity through overprotection and open derogation of their father as a model that they cannot develop the masculine self-confidence needed for heterosexual competition.

These are grossly oversimplified descriptions of some of the early causes of homosexuality. When the family relationships are not quite disturbed enough to result in overt, clinical homosexuality, there may persist in a boy an unconscious fear of other men and the desire to submit to them rather than to compete. Unconscious conflicts of this nature may be accompanied by fearful antagonism toward homosexuals and pervasive fear of homosexual impulses. The first type of fear dominates those "he-men" who entertain themselves by "beating up queers" or, if they happen to be police officers, by entrapping homosexuals. The "Don Juan" may sometimes have the other type of fear, defending himself against his homosexual impulses by relentlessly pursuing women.

Girls do not have the same task as boys at the end of the oedipal phase. Their attachment to the father is not normally complicated by ambivalence over his role in infantile gratifications and disappointments, because he seldom had that maternal role. Nor has the father usually been as involved in daily issues of discipline and control as the mother. Female identity is not gained by shifting *away* from a primary identification with a male. The result is an easier, more relaxed and unambivalent acceptance of peer group boys and of males in general. Neighborhood and schoolyard observation quickly corroborates the difference in readiness of the two sexes to interact—girls are much more willing and interested, as well as generally physically capable, though they have a difficult time gaining acceptance by boys.

The interest of girls in joining in boys' games is not indiscriminate. By and large they are not drawn to rough-and-tumble body contact play to the same degree as boys, nor is their interest prompted mainly by dissatisfaction with girl-ness and envy of boy-ness. It is more an expression of the readiness for interaction that boys do not as yet share.

Pathological envy sometimes exists and impairs further appropriate sex identity formation. Those girls whose disturbed family situations resulted in exaggerated and unresolved penis envy and the envy of masculine status stand out rather sharply in home and play situations. They are intensely competitive with boys and derogatory toward them. Nature gives them quite an edge, too, when they choose to use it. Girls at this age are statistically taller and heavier than their male age peers, and when they put their mind to it they can sometimes overcome the difference in musculature and energy expenditure. It is a heady experience for a girl to outdo boys in physical feats and quite humiliating to the defeated boy, whose self-esteem may be shakily built upon a disdain for "sissy girls." Boys usually cannot effectively fight back verbally because the possibly innate female superior verbal ability is well established by now. Little girl versions of "castrating women" are often remarkably effective.

Because girls do not have to fear the loss of a penis, that part of their superego which derives its power from castration anxiety is weaker. This fact has unfortunately been used to accuse women of possessing weaker consciences and less firm moral values. The intrapsychic consequence of anatomical difference is probably valid, but I believe that the value judgments drawn from it need rethinking. The rigid and persistently infantile quality of the male superego wreaks much interpersonal and social havoc. In order to keep themselves in line lest their dangerous impulses break through, men are much more likely than women to become authoritarian personalities, to reinforce their own repression by demanding that others hold the same values as they, and to feel threatened by differences. Males kill each other and make wars over the most trivial issues of "honor" and "national pride."

I do not intend to offer an inanely simplistic explanation for complex social phenomena or to suggest that women cannot be rigidly authoritarian or threatened by differences. But the boy is indeed the father of the man, and people are essentially given most of their repertoire of tools for coping with social complexities while they are still children. Clinical experiences and historical evidence suggest an admirable emotional flexibility in women with regard to reaching reasonable and humane adaptations to difficult situations. The probability that one contribution to female flexibility is a woman's less powerful childish superego suggests that this may be an advantage, rather than the handicap it has frequently been labeled.

Another important sex-linked differentiation that crystallizes with the resolution of the Oedipus complex concerns the characteristically different inner sexual fears and insecurities felt by males and females. The evidence has already been discussed for assuming that children of five or six years of age know that intercourse takes place by the penetration of the vagina by the erect penis. They have usually seen the genitals of both children and adults of the opposite sex, and most of the world's children have observed both the erect penis and adult intercourse itself.

In fantasizing themselves in complementary sexual roles with the father or mother, boys and girls are confronted with quite different assessments of their capabilities and of what might happen to them. The little girl knows that she needs the man's penis to fill her inner space and to fulfill her. If she has been frightened and overwhelmed by the size of the erect adult penis in comparison with her little body, her need will be associated with fears of physical damage. On the other hand, she may be aware of her own orgastic capacity as a result of vaginal masturbation and of the capacity of her vagina to distend either through masturbation or by analogy with rectal distension during the passage of stools. In that case she may not be especially fearful, though frustrated at knowing she needs something for fulfillment that her father will not give her.

The little boy's concern is one of narcissistic damage to his ego. He recognizes, as he must, his mother's natural preference for his father as a sexual object. When he compares his own small penis with his father's, he cannot avoid recognizing his disadvantage, and entertains thoroughly realistic doubts that he could possibly satisfy his mother.

Thus woman's basic concern is to have a man who is necessary to fill her and to gratify her; she needs his erect penis. Her innate sexual goal is to attract the man. Her innate sexual fears are of being unattractive, of loss of love, of being left unfulfilled and empty. If she fears man himself, her fear is physical. Man's basic concern is to achieve an adequate erection so as to perform. His innate sexual goal is to penetrate and gratify his partner. His innate sexual fears are of the failure to be able to perform and to satisfy a woman. If he fears woman herself, his fear is of ridicule and humiliation.[25] These differences go back to a child's oedipal wishes and to his unavoidable confrontation with anatomical realities, which imprint themselves forever after as characteristic sexual concerns.

While everything thus far discussed represents important consequences of this crucial period of psychosexual development, it has exerted a more profound impact upon some areas of maturation than upon others. Among the gains made in the healthy resolution of the oedipal conflict is the sense of one's inner right to have sexual drives directed toward the opposite sex. This is the critical period for learning to accept one's heterosexual responsiveness. Until the child matured to the point at which intense genital sensations, and perhaps additional aspects of biological maturation, precipitated him into the desire for a sexual object, and thus into the family triangle, he did not have the interest to make this an issue. Only now can he confront the conflict between heterosexual interest and competitive risks. Out of a healthy family and society he emerges with his right to heterosexuality intact, able to accept the necessity to postpone gratification and to await a suitable love object.

The time of the resolution of the oedipal dilemma is also the critical period for accepting or rejecting sex role identification with others of the same sex. Core gender identity is unaffected by oedipal conflicts. A girl may fail to identify with her mother as a role model of femininity while never questioning that she is female. But if she does fail, or if a boy experiences an analogous failure of identification, the task of achieving appropriate identification will be much more difficult in the future.

In innumerable ways, girls and boys enter the oedipal period as already vastly different beings, but the full import of their differences is not yet entirely real to them. Infants barely register differences, and toddlers' belief in magic makes it possible for them to fantasize that they could really become a different sex if they wished. Not so the child who has emerged successfully from this oedipal period. The issue of sexual differences has been joined, and the die has been cast. The confidently total belief in magic held by the toddler is eroded forever and cannot be called upon to remake reality.

In the process of confronting the pleasures and the limitations of being a girl or a boy, attitudes form that are consonant with one's biological sex. The complementary nature of male and female anatomy and physiology is reflected in the further development of characteristic emotional traits and behavioral characteristics which reinforce that complementarity. This differentiation is initiated by and related to innate sexual distinctions, but they do not operate as do instincts in lower animals. They must be guided and shaped by constructive rearing and cultural reinforcement, and so they are vulnerable to distortion or chaotic disruption. Given a reasonable chance, boys and girls reach the age of five or six with a solid readiness to explore the interlocking intricacies of masculinity and femininity.

SIX

Relative Tranquillity: The Early School Years

As a healthy child enters his early school years, many of his previous imaginary fears and dangers gradually begin to subside. Despite the fact that the slings and arrows he suffered were often of his own unconscious making, the previous phase was nonetheless emotionally taxing. Now the giving up of open sexual interest in the parent of the opposite sex and the acceptance of a working partnership with the parent of the same sex usually leads into a more tranquil period. This new set of relationships will not be achieved without problems and effort, but for most children these will be less-conflicted years.

So much more subdued are the obvious sexual preoccupations during this stage that it has often been thought that the actual strength of the sexual drive diminishes. Freud believed so, for he called this the period of sexual latency, but his experience consisted essentially of the memories, dreams, and associations of adult patients, carefully considered in the perspective of the exhaustive psychological innovation of his amazing self-analysis. He was struck by what seemed to be a regular and predictable phenomenon: the outspoken sexual interests of the oedipal period were abruptly repressed and replaced by prudishness, shame, and guilt. Not only the oedipal desires, but virtually all memories dating from the first five or so years were repressed, resulting in what he called childhood amnesia. A panorama of social preoccupations came to occupy the mind of the growing child.

Freud's metaphor for the sexual drive was that of a physical force. His libido theory was expressed as a literal flow of instinctual energy which could either move unimpeded through normal channels or be dammed up, reversed, diverted, or subjected to other hydrodynamically imaged vicissitudes. When he perceived an apparent quiescence of overt sexuality during latency, unaccompanied by evidences of its bursting out in disguised expressions in other aspects of the personality, he assumed that the actual quantity of sexual energy was diminished. He wrote in 1905 that this development was "organically determined." [1] In other words, he believed latency to be a biologically determined stage of growth, similar to puberty, and true for all children under all circumstances.

The impressive weight of Freud's insight into the existence and crucial importance of childhood sexuality made it difficult for subsequent investigators to question his conclusions and theoretical formulations. Other pioneer psychoanalysts working with adult neurotics made the same observations, but they, too, were operating in early twentieth-century Western European culture, which typically espoused repressive attitudes toward sexuality in general and childhood sexuality in particular. Anthropological study of various cultures was then an infant field, still greatly colored by the ethnocentric bias of the observer. There were no child analysts during those early years to supplement theory with direct observation and objectivity. When, as time progressed, child analysts did begin to work with disturbed children who grew up within the same cultural influences, these analysts came to the same conclusions. So it was easy for an early postulate to be fortified by self-fulfilling expectations, and finally to be regarded as demonstrated fact. Today the "fact" of a sexual latency is often raised as a presumably scientific objection to sex education during the primary school years.

Children pursue the course of their psychosexual development in blithe disregard of an expected sexual latency. Their only nod in the direction of the theoretical expectations is that they have learned to play according to adult rules. They learn to fulfill the letter of the law, even as they proceed secretly in their own ways.

Research has failed to corroborate the fact of a diminution in sexual drive. Data is now available in both areas scanted by the early theorists. A large number of human cultures have now been studied sufficiently to provide a broad spectrum of information about worldwide childhood sexuality. Clellan S. Ford and Frank A. Beach, American anthropologist and psychologist respectively, in *Patterns of Sexual Behavior*, a cross-cultural study of sexual behavior in 190 different cultures, have summed up children's sexual activities during this range of ages:

> In the societies where they are permitted to do so, children gradually increase their sexual activity both as they approach

puberty and during adolescence. . . . Their sex play first includes autogenital stimulation and mutual masturbation with the same and opposite sex, but with increasing age it is characterized more and more by attempts at heterosexual copulation. By the time of puberty in most of these societies expressions of sexuality on the part of older children consist predominantly of the accepted form of heterosexual intercourse.[2]

These are "latency" children. Further anthropological research has offered no serious challenge to these conclusions and has provided much more information about how normal children function in United States middle-class culture. The Kinsey report indicated not only that children indulge in every kind of sexual activity during the gradeschool years but that sexual activity steadily increases rather than becomes dormant.[3] A study of a Midwestern suburb in the early 1940s, probably more accurate because based on interviews with boys whose youth made it more likely that they could recall their erotic experimentation, found that by age eleven, about 53 percent had masturbated, 27 percent had had homosexual play, 52 percent had had sex play with girls, and 26 percent had tried or achieved intercourse.[4] A true diminution of the sexual drive does not appear to exist, even in this culture.

Sex Seems to Disappear

Certainly something happens, in this culture at least, which has led brilliant clinicians to consider latency to be universal, and which permits (or forces) the sexual drive to assume a less obvious place in the child's everyday life. One reason is the result of child-rearing practices; another is genuinely related to biology, but in a different form than was once believed.

There may well be a leveling out of sex hormone production, resulting in less erratic changes during these years. Hormone data is so scanty and inconclusive for the years of childhood that no trustworthy correlations can be drawn from the present stage of knowledge, but there is some indication of a plateau in estrogen production in both sexes throughout this period, and a more gradual increase in androgen production than before. Other studies of the behavioral effects of sex hormones suggest that a steady level of estrogen can exert a calming effect and thus partially account for the more tranquil period as well as aid the organization and consolidation of the ego that must take place.[5] The nature of the estrogen production and the more gentle gradient of androgen production would help to produce the clinical impression that the sexual drives do not increase as sharply in this period as in the phallic phase.

Another biological determinant of this uniquely human stage of development is the long delay in human sexual maturation. Unlike lower animals in general, the human child does not pass rapidly from a state of dependence so total that survival without adult protection would be impossible to a state of reproductive capacity. Far more learning and ego development is both characteristic and required of humans; in fact, it is this delay in sexual maturation that permits the degree and complexity of learning and judgment, and the richness of parent-child relationships, that sets humans apart from other animals.[6]

In humans, much of the physiological maturation that takes place during the fetal period of altricial animals occurs during the first five years of life. In many ways, children arrive at latency in a state of physical maturation similar to that existing very shortly after birth in the altricial species.[7] Though not a true altricial, monkeys have a very short totally helpless infancy. The behavior of juvenile monkeys during their first three years or so is remarkably similar in its social and peer group interaction to that of children from kindergarten to about the fifth grade. An enormous and crucial amount of learning takes place in children during those additional years of life outside the womb. Man's biological evolution has thus provided him with much extra time for learning, regardless of whether one chooses to consider the extra time to be the earliest years or those of latency.[8]

There are thus several internal forces at work to produce the appearance of a lesser sexual drive. There is the psychological force of repression of incestuous desires at the end of the oedipal period, an influence that takes its particular shape from the characteristic family structure and child-rearing practices of this culture and taints much of the child's subsequent overt sexual feelings with some guilt and anxiety. There are the biological facts of extrauterine "fetal" development and delayed sexual maturation that act as a positive force impeding movement into immediate adult sexuality and thus facilitating ego growth. And there is the possible plateau in hormone elaboration. In addition, there are the *external* repressive strictures upon childhood sexuality enforced both by parents and culture.

It must not appear, however, that this entire, enormously important period of childhood development is brought about and maintained chiefly by negative forces. Only the overt sexual interests and activities are affected by repressive influences, and these only in particular cultural and familial environments. In almost every other facet of personality, the normal child blossoms into one of the richest periods of ego maturation in his whole life span.

The major increments of development take place in the social sphere. This is a time to move outside the family and to become acculturated into a broader community. For the first time the typical child, dividing his time between school and peer play, spends more time away from his parents than with them. Thus there are new dimensions of external regulations—nonparental adults and peers.

Social roles are imitated, played at, and acted out in real exchanges. Practical skills and knowledge that will insure a child's future participation in the community are acquired. Learning how to learn hopefully becomes transformed into the enjoyment of learning, and ultimately into pleasure in constructive work and productive effort. The issues of getting along with others, and of cooperation, subordination, leadership, and aggression are worked through. It is during this time that social maladjustment and the earliest manifestations of antisocial behavior first make their appearance. This phase has been characterized as one in which the healthy child acquires a sense of industry, whereas the child whose development falters is infused with a sense of inferiority.[9]

The intrapsychic sexual aspects of these years fall normally into two parts. The earlier phase, lasting two or three years following the oedipal resolution, is somewhat stormier. Children are still struggling against both the resurgence of oedipal impulses and the pull of earlier, infantile gratifications. Their ego defenses against regressive pulls are less firm, and one is apt to see fluctuations and sudden shifts from more mature to very childish behavior. Irritability and mood swings are common, though normally not enough to contradict the characterization of this period as a less conflicted one.

The later phase, extending until the beginning hormonal changes push the child into prepuberty, is smoother and more secure. Ego development is sufficient to quell the echoes of earlier conflicts and urges and to make the interactions with teachers and friends more predictable and satisfying. The rewards of greater maturity and the beginnings of genuine ego mastery weigh more than the pleasures of babyhood.

There is a parallel between the two phases of latency and those of adolescence, important because one is a necessary rehearsal for the other. In the early part of latency the child's ego ideal is not as magically omnipotent as it was at the height of his oedipal struggles, when it was simply an internalization of a fusion of his idealized, all-powerful parent fantasies, but its unreality has only begun to soften because his real world experience is so limited. The child is still prone to sudden despairs over failure to accomplish things easily and perfectly, and to periods of rage over parental imperfections.

By the latter stages of latency, increasing experience with other adults and other children, plus increasing ego maturation, permit an early reevaluation of his parents and, concomitantly, of his own inner expectations of himself.[10] This can only be accomplished at a child's level with a child's mentality, and is naturally incomplete. Nonetheless, it is a vital prerequisite for successful coping with puberty, because a pubescent youngster who is rigidly and unrealistically demanding of himself will lack the tolerance necessary to weather the intensity and unpredictability of the drives and emotions precipitated by pubertal biology. Of equal importance to psychosexual development is this first reassessment of his parents. The quality and stability of his eventual sexual identity depends largely upon his parental models. If now, and in adolescence, his unconscious images of them remain as either unassailably perfect or as contemptibly dethroned hypocrites, his own sexuality will lack a firmly realistic base derived from his parents' essential humanness.

The burgeoning of social interactions and the immense fascination with everything in the new outside world also fosters an impression of diminished sexuality in children. There are simply so many other aspects of life to attend to. From being the major

preoccupation of the oedipal child, sex becomes simply one more
engrossing interest. It is something to master as well as to express.
In the sexually permissive atmosphere of Israeli kibbutzim, sex play
among children of this age predictably continues, though it
decreases to some extent.[11] Since a decrease is not seen in all
preliterate permissive societies, one may speculate that less complexity and development is demanded of the preliterate child's ego
and that he therefore has more emotional energy left over to
continue investing in sexuality. For the kibbutz child, his world is
not only incredibly richer in stimuli but also in its demands upon his
ego in order that he learn to function in a technological world. His
sexual expressions must share his time and energies with a wider
field of interests and learning requirements. This speculative
explanation is not fully satisfactory, however, since it falls short of
explaining the increasing sexual activity found in the equally
technological society of the American middle and upper classes.

Especially in these years of crucial intellectual and social
learning, the recurrent issue of whether it is necessary for sexuality,
including masturbation, to be repressed in order to free a child's
capacity to learn, must be definitely confronted. In other words, is
healthy ego development possible in the face of continued overt
sexual expression, or is it crippled by continued active sexuality?
Many authorities on child development consider that the capacity
to sublimate sexual energy into intellectual and social goals is a
prerequisite for the attainment of those goals, and that children
with adjustment and learning difficulties in their early school years
lack the ego capacity to sublimate. Sublimation means the redirect-
ing of sexual energy away from direct genital preoccupation and
gratification into more socially acceptable and ego maturational
goals, such as finding pleasure in learning, aesthetic creativity, and
social cooperation. The concept is based upon the theory that the
same energy—the libido—drives both the sexual desires and the
other productive capacities of mankind.

These highly theoretical considerations have some very practical
applications for parents, primary school teachers, and other adults
involved with children of this age and especially for the children
themselves. If these considerations are valid, overt sexual expression
during these years should be viewed with some concern because of
its effect on other important aspects of the child's development. The

issue assumes its greatest importance now, at this stage of a child's life when social and intellectual aspects of ego development represent his major maturational task, but the same cautions apply in theorizing about this age as with toddlers. Indeed, the entire concept of sublimation deserves reevaluation.[12] There is no empirical evidence that the same source of energy fires both sexual and social-intellectual pursuits. In addition to the evidence from kibbutzim that childhood sexuality and normal ego development may coexist during the early school years, there is the fact that sexual activity increases throughout this period in children in our own culture along with other learning, and there have been clinical reports of children whose intense sexuality did not interfere with learning.[13]

At the same time that concern has been expressed about the necessity for sublimating sexual energy into other goals, it has been clearly recognized that total suppression of sexual gratification during this period is indicative of serious disorder and is associated with definite neurotic and behavioral disturbances. While it is often true that children in our culture who are very active sexually are also poor achievers in school, it is by no means clear that an inability to control their sexuality is the cause. It is likely that both the problem with impulse control, as manifested in the unusual degree of open sexual activity, and the problem with intellectual or social achievement are symptoms of some deeper and earlier developmental disturbance. It seems most feasible to me that the ability to learn and to achieve the social skills appropriate at this age represents the unfolding of natural ego capacities that are not essentially derived from sexual drives nor sustained by energies that were originally sexual. The gradual emergence of the capacity for new and more complex ego functions probably follows a biologically determined timetable in normal children in much the same way as walking and talking. This timetable can be disrupted by any of the interferences in normal development.

It is clear that the only biological aspect of sexuality that is latent is the advent of adult reproductive capacity, not the sex drives or activities. Using this updated definition, the use of awkward descriptive phrases or the necessity to find another term may be avoided, and this developmental stage can still be referred to accurately as latency.

Sex in the Latency Period

The normal child in Western culture realizes by now that his earlier sexual interests and activities were not warmly received by his parents. He senses that they will be happier and that he will risk less disapproval if he discovers the further fascinations of sex more privately.

His newly acquired superego adds its voice as well. Even when parents do not actively taboo sexual interest, the child's superego will warn him against any display of sexuality in their presence because it is too close to his forbidden incestuous fantasies.

It does not take much experience in the world outside the home for a child to discover his parents are not unique. They share their peculiar aversion to sexual exploration by children with a majority of other grown-ups. To a child, the serious business of anatomical research behind a convenient shrub with the boy or girl down the block can be an unforgettable learning experience. But he must also learn to play a new game with adults. The adult world sets the rule: "We'll agree to leave you to your own devices and pretend you aren't a sexual being, if you'll agree to keep your sexuality out of sight so that we can maintain our pretense." The child is given little choice but to accept this condition, incomprehensible though it seems to him.

The statistics from our own and other cultures make it clear that many children are gathering a great deal of sexual experience throughout these years. Their sexual experiences may be sporadic, and not the most important events in their lives and ego development, but they may encompass every possible form of sexual behavior. Solitary masturbation, self and mutual masturbation in pairs or groups that may be of the same sex, or mixed erotic play with the same sex that may involve oral or anal sex, sex play with animals, heterosexual fondling and imitation of intercourse, sometimes with penetration—all these may be tried by a child at one time or another. This sexual play may often involve siblings—a mind-boggling experience for parents who happen in on the scene.

A patient, the father of nine-year-old twin girls and a seven-year-old son, one day reported an experience that thoroughly unnerved him. It was unusual for him to be home in the afternoon, and when he walked upstairs he was unexpected, though he had made no special effort to be stealthy or to spy. The door to the twins' room was ajar and, in curiosity, he pushed it further open and looked in. The two girls and a neighboring girl friend were seated in a circle on the bed with their legs spread, their skirts up and panties off. A hand mirror was being used for close self-inspection, and two of the girls were giggling and inserting Q-tips into their own and each other's vaginas. His son was standing by the bed, and before the father could utter a word one of the twins said impatiently to her little brother, "Wait a minute! Later you can try to put your wee-wee in!" When the poor man could get his voice, he thoroughly terrified all four children by his loudly shocked and angry reaction. He had considered himself reasonably knowledgeable and tolerant of childhood masturbatory play, but stumbling upon an "incestuous orgy" among his own children was more than he was prepared for. He later realized that he still harbored considerable guilt over his own childhood sexual fantasies about an older sister who had gone through a period when she was very teasingly provocative toward him.

The child, in all this diverse activity, is seeking to explore and acquire increasing anatomical knowledge. When he was younger, he also explored as he felt a great curiosity about the sex organs and bodies of others, but then his research opportunities were largely limited to his family and the social learning element was circumscribed by his developmental readiness. One may observe of nursery school children that they do not really play *together* as much as they play *in each other's presence.*

Now, however, this sex play is avidly comparative. There is still the child's narcissistic need to become acquainted with his own body and its sensations, shapes, and changes, but it is more often expressed in the social intimacy of other youngsters—the natural milieu into which all the ego maturational and conflict-resolving forces have impelled him. These are safe, nonparental chums. This is a time for examining both the similarities and differences of the bodies of others—of both sexes. Everyone is fascinated by the wondrous way in which penises change from small and soft to large and hard and then back to soft. These are the years of playing "doctor," or "papa and mama," or simply "I'll show you mine if you'll show me yours." Unless youngsters have been unusually intimidated by forbidding parents, at this age they display remarkably little modesty over showing their body to other children of either sex. The theoretical expectation that boys will avoid girls because of their castration anxiety does not seem to preclude a considerable amount of spontaneous coed sex education.

Despite the full variety of sex play that is engaged in if the opportunity arises, the major activity remains solitary masturbation. Though there is almost always guilt associated with it, masturbatory relief of sexual tensions is not only normal but necessary for healthy child development.[14]

The primary school child has a rich fantasy life, and it reveals the sexual themes and conflicts that preoccupy him. While there are some times and special circumstances, such as during child analysis, when the youngster will openly reveal his fantasies, an easier source of knowing them is by observing his play and noting the perennially popular books and stories, and their shared themes. Girls return to doll play, and often in their fantasies the dolls are capable of coming to life and doing all kinds of secret and fascinating things, as long as no one is looking. There are many books for girls this age both on the theme of the magic doll and also on dolls that are lost, then found again. Remembering the doll's symbolic equivalence with inside genital sensations and the vagina, it is easy to translate these fantasy stories into their sexual meanings. The secret coming-to-life represents secret masturbation and the hidden, private sexual organs and their sensations. That theme, and the "lost and found" doll stories, also reflect a girl's continued struggle with the unpredictable nature of those perplexing and exciting inner sexual sensations.[15]

Many girls love mystery books, not only for their intrinsic excitement, but also because they symbolically strike a responsive chord with the mystery of their own bodies and their sexual functions, which are never-ending sources of fascination and which express themselves in barely disguised ways. Boys, too, may love mystery stories, but not because their own bodies are so mysterious; for them, the mystery and the hidden treasure is the same as for girls—the secrets and the pleasures (and the titillating dangers) hidden in that mysterious female body. As was true of fairy tales in the oedipal phase, the stories most enjoyed and reread are those that correspond with the unconscious fantasy life of the child.

As children get older and are capable of reading more complex books, the disguised oedipal gratification takes on more subtle coloration than in fairy tales. A widely popular type of girl's story plays upon the theme of the wish for oedipal romance. That wish is not dead, only repressed, and girls love books in which the element of secrecy corresponds to their oedipal wishes. The child heroine often suffers from some bodily handicap or is subject to some danger, from which she is saved by an older man. These stories are never frankly sexual'nor do they involve a romantic ending, but the disguised oedipal wish and the girl's ultimate triumph are clear.

Many popular boys' stories and books are also more disguisedly oedipal. The young protagonists are often orphaned, or living with friends or other relatives. In spite of their extreme youth, these children are unrealistically capable, talented, and incorruptible, and function better than most of the adults in the story. Usually it is the boy who outwits and vanquishes one or more evil men. Sexual material is almost nonexistent, thoroughly subordinated to aggressive interests.

In these books the murderous hostility is more repressed than in fairy tales. Mean stepmothers and wicked witches are replaced by nurses, governesses, and schoolmistresses. The absence (often unexplained) of one or both real parents neatly disposes of incestuous guilt and leaves the road clear for disguised rivalry. Thus the stories can represent ideal fulfillment because both the guilt and the hate are avoided. The invariably unimpeachable moral character of the heroes and heroines also represents the still unrealistic ego ideals of the enthralled readers.

The family romance continues to play an important role in the fantasies, and therefore in the story themes, of latency children. As these youngsters begin to measure their parents with more discerning eyes, they often have periods of resentful disillusionment before working through to acceptance. The changeling and adoption themes, especially those involving vast shifts in social status, unconsciously play into feelings of disappointment with parents, as well as serving the repressed oedipal wishes by displacing them onto strangers.

Interestingly enough, some books appeal to the fantasies of girls who have not worked through and relinquished their penis envy. Many of today's parents will recall the Nancy Drew series, in which the heroine functioned as a loner distinctly doing a man's job.

Carrying a gun, and in her convertible (erectile) roadster, she would overcome dangerous male criminals, showing little interest in romance. The blatant masculine protest of such a popular series suggests how common the continued struggle of girls over genital reality can sometimes be.[16]

Children's play and their special hobbies and interests are often nearly direct translations of their sexual concerns into nonsexual activities. Children have a variety of ways of expressing and trying to cope with their constantly developing sexuality, ways that are not obviously sexual.

Girls continue to project their unconscious feelings about their sexuality and their inner sexual feelings upon their dolls, and one can often gauge the state of a girl's attitudes and emotions about her sexual self by whether she plays with dolls, and how she treats them. Among girls there is also an inordinate delight in sharing secrets. The contents of the secrets are irrelevant compared to having them. Here one sees transparently acted out the secret sexuality which girls do indeed share.[17] This is typically girlish, not boyish, activity. The disdainful exclusiveness of some boys' friendships and groups does not reflect the same unconscious motivation, though that phenomenon may also have a sexual element. Boys are busily and even desperately trying to shake off the female domination that is usually their lot even after getting away from their mother. It is typical for boys to band together and take out their frustrations on females their own size. There are times when boys' avoidance and repudiation of girls also represents unconscious defenses against castration fears, since girls' genitalia represent the "reality" of castration. But it is likely that in normal boys the opposition to female domination is at least as powerful a determinant, and since girls often envy the seeming independence of boys, they can unfortunately be highly sensitive to and greatly influenced by the "castrated" image of themselves and of femininity that boys may impart to them.

Girls, too, must have achieved a reasonably healthy resolution of conflicts over their femaleness in order to show the easier acceptance of boys that is characteristic of normal schoolgirls. If they have not resolved their conflicts, play relationships with boys will reveal definite strain. Most obvious are the desperate efforts on the part of some girls actually to *be* one of the boys, or the opposite extreme—the total rejection of boys.

Boys' typical interest in mechanical gadgets and in various ball sports—most especially baseball—likewise represents more than physical exuberance and muscular energy. Such interests are symbolically linked to the specific sexual anatomy boys must learn to use and to master and the sexual anxieties they must learn to resolve. Anxiety over the retraction and reappearance of the testicles is directly associated with the effort expended learning to handle and control the movements of balls in sports. Baseball and other sports utilizing objects to hit or maneuver the ball add a symbolic penis. It is that organ which boys most need to feel control of, and confident of their ability to "handle and use" effectively and without adverse consequences. Mechanical skills and tool mastery are easily seen to serve the same symbolic purposes. The hobby of magicians' tricks and skills mainly engages the interest of boys, not girls, symbolizing as it does the appearance and disappearance of an erection or of the testicles.[18]

This brief discussion of school children's games and play behavior must not be misread to suggest that everything a child does has sexual significance, or that the sexual drive or conflict is the sole impetus behind the multitude of activities that engross children during latency. Nothing could be further from the facts, nor more alien to my intention. It goes without saying that baseball is principally a sport and that the use of tools and mechanical skills have essentially a practical value. It must be equally obvious that sexuality is only one of the many facets of themselves that children are exploring and learning about and integrating at this or any other time. But singling out and calling attention to sexual symbolism in some of the activities of children illustrates again that everything is motivated. It points up the fact that children can utilize many diverse activities in the service of psychosexual development, and it reminds us always to look beneath the surface if we would truly understand the richness and complexity of the psychosexual development of a child.

Sexual Disturbances in Schoolchildren

Even though the sex drive and sexual activities do not decrease during this period, the behavior itself normally becomes private.

When, in Judeo-Christian culture, this fails to occur, a child is usually expressing a significant disturbance in his psychosexual development. The child who does not, or cannot, keep his sexual interests fairly well hidden from the gaze of adults has been unable to learn the social rules. Because Western culture has never been monolithic, there are certain families, communities, and subcultures in which these prohibitions are modified or absent, but it is usually true that something is amiss in a child's development if the oedipal sexuality persists into the school years or if the exploratory sexuality appropriate to this period is pursued in disregard or defiance of adult disapproval. It is not necessarily the sexual activity itself that is pathological, but its defiant or compulsive expression.

The disturbances which occur at this time may reflect earlier disorders of sexual development or difficulties encountered in tackling the new tasks specific to this phase. Naturally the two overlap at times. The phase-specific tasks involve essentially the social dimensions of sexuality, which will be more fully discussed at the end of this chapter.

Some children may have retreated from the task of mastering their oedipal conflicts and returned to babyish whining and the display of helpless feelings. They show varying degrees of difficulty in moving into the taxing requirements of school and peer group relations; early school phobia is one manifestation. They may withdraw into a stagnating isolation of lonely activities or display their demandingness in futile and unpopular behavior with other children. They may become abnormally compliant, thoroughly intimidated out of the expression of independent impulses.

By definition, this degree of sexual repression forces most of the symptoms of disturbance to express themselves in nonsexual areas of behavior. When the child's overdeveloped superego is unsuccessful in forcing a total renunciation of sexual thoughts or activity, the intensity of his guilt can be tormenting. It may be one source of exaggerated religiosity, sleep disturbances, and learning disorders.

The most common neurosis at this age is the obsessive-compulsive disorder. This neurosis is characterized by compulsive acts, elaborate rituals and obsessive thoughts, sometimes "forbidden" thoughts and sometimes nonsensical ones that cannot be put out of mind. Compulsive acts may consist of endlessly repeated handwashing, or the arrangement of everything in the room in a rigidly proscribed order. Bedtime ceremonies can involve a repetitive series of acts, verbal expressions and prayers that must be performed in unvarying sequence. Failure to complete the compulsive ritual results in intense anxiety. The obsessive thoughts may be the directly guilt-provoking sexual ones, unacceptable impulses of rage usually directed against the prohibiting parents, or disguised expression of such feelings. Obsessive-compulsive childhood neurosis arises from an overly punitive superego which infuses the child with a constant sense of guilt. That guilt is usually related to sexual thoughts or acts, such as masturbation and its accompanying guilt-provoking fantasies. Whenever the forbidden thought or act occurs or threatens to erupt, the symptoms manifest themselves and can sometimes serve to crowd the forbidden urge out of mind. The chief unconscious meaning of obsessive-compulsive symptoms is that they are magically supposed to "undo" or expiate the forbidden impulse.

Some interesting cases have been reported in which total sexual repression has resulted in genital anesthesia in both boys and girls. These children are so fearful of their sexual urges and fantasies, or of the explosive intensity of orgasm, that they lose all genital sensation and the ability to carry masturbation to orgastic release.[19]

The appearance of antisocial behavior at this time may be an expression of completely repressed sexuality. When the sexual drives are deprived of all physical outlet, such as masturbation, the frustrated sexual drive may be turned into aggression. This kind of aggressive acting out against the environment is both a disguised release of blocked sexual drives and an attack of rage against the real or fantasied sources of frustration and inhibition.[20]

At the other end of the spectrum, the apathetic, incurious child may also be a victim of excessive sexual repression. When a child's earlier avid sexual curiosity, interest, and activity is too strongly suppressed and becomes a threat to his security, its subsequent inhibition may constrict all areas of activity and intellectual curiosity.

This is the period in which forerunners of future homosexual adaptations often first appear. In most instances these disturbances in sexual identity were initiated in earlier phases, as a result of family interactions which failed to foster a secure sexual identity that includes a firm expectation of heterosexual involvement. Now there may be evidence of a child's avoiding the usual and expected activities appropriate to his sex.[21]

One needs both wisdom and understanding to avoid premature conclusions. Children will normally experiment with many different social roles, including those typical of the opposite sex. In such child play cultural stereotypes can be particularly constricting. There are far more activities and emotional attitudes that should be open to both sexes than there are those that suggest sexual confusion. Nothing is more foolishly harmful than leading a boy to associate tenderness and emotionality, aesthetic interests, and even learning, with effeminacy. Many emotionally healthy women were tomboys at some time during childhood. Even the overtly homoerotic play that now takes place among so many children usually has no clinical significance; most often it is transient and purely experimental. But the child who consistently avoids the company and activities of his peers of the same sex, and identifies with the attitudes of the opposite sex and chooses them as playmates, is usually signaling that something is going awry in his sexual identity.

One subtle antiheterosexual message may be communicated by a parent's anxiety over opportunities for heterosexual play. It is almost unheard of for children to be permitted to spend the night with friends of the opposite sex. Adults are suspicious of any privacy between a boy and a girl. It is rare that parents fail to show serious disapproval when pairs or groups involving the opposite sex are found examining each other's genitals. Yet frequently having friends of the same sex spend the night together, with uninterrupted opportunities for sex play, is approved and unquestioned by most parents, and part of the normal experience of most school children. The implication that heterosexual activity is more taboo than homoerotic play is clear, and often impresses itself upon the children.

In later years, when youngsters learn of the homosexual taboo, that taboo is likely to be accepted at an intellectual level. Because that taboo is seldom a part of the internalized superego that was formed by early parental prohibitions, homoerotic experiences are less likely to produce an inner sense of guilt than they are to cause shame—a sense of humiliation and degradation in the eyes of others. Many adults will remember that they felt very little guilt at the time of early homoerotic play. They felt far more inhibiting guilt over early heterosexual "transgressions." This in spite of the fact that intellectually they know that heterosexuality is "good" and homosexuality "bad."

Since the bulk of interactions bearing upon developing sexuality are social ones, the overt sexual activity of children exposes them to fewer problems because it is usually so private, although when an adult does discover a child's sexual activity, his reaction becomes part of what the child learns about sex. The private sex play does, however, leave children vulnerable to one peculiar danger. Children talk among themselves at length about their sexual curiosities, sensations, and imaginings but possess very little accurate sex information. All sorts of fantastic stories, myths, and fearful misconceptions are bandied about, and few children have enough knowledge to recognize what is nonsense. Because fantasy thus overruns reality, frightening ideas implanted in this manner may never be thoroughly unlearned.

Sex and Society

Sexual roles within social situations are explored for the first and most important time in these early school years. Many of our cultural stereotypes, such as the protesting submission of females and the bullying aggression of males, are seen in caricatured expression in the sex play of school children. Research has found that in sociosexual interactions during this period, just as with overt sexuality, a steady progression of heterosexual interests normally occurs. There is a gradual shift toward regarding more children of the opposite sex as best friends, toward preferring activities with the opposite sex, and toward romantic thoughts about the opposite sex.[22]

It is in such social interaction that the major maturational changes evolve. Partly as a culmination of all the previously developed physical and mental capacities, partly in response to an apparently inborn timeclock governing the readiness of the ego, and partly in retreat from the fantasied dangers of oedipal strivings, the youngster—hungry for learning—rushes headlong out of the parental cocoon and into apprenticeship to the world outside.

The questing youngster emerges into society quite sure of his or her core gender identity, which was formed indissolubly several years earlier. Both sexes have absorbed the parental patterns that imply what being a boy or a girl connotes. They have even engaged in some preliminary rehearsals, using those roles within the family, but in that earlier development other matters normally took precedence, and now the first real and extended opportunity occurs to discover some of the interpersonal and cultural aspects of one's sex.

It is a commonplace that boys and girls identify with adult male or female roles in their play and in the rich make-believe of this period; the enormous intrapsychic work accomplished through this play is less commonly understood. Since most adult roles are impossible as yet, youngsters must try them on for size in make-believe. Because their level of thinking is still concrete, it is not surprising that their first role playing is with occupations that appear simple to grasp, like fireman, policeman, waitress, and teacher. At the same time that the youngster is identifying with the sex and role of the parent of the same sex, his imaginary occupations may be quite different from that of his parent. This can help in his continuing efforts to repress oedipal desires, as it produces less anxiety to explore his sexual role at some distance from his mother and father.

Woven into the fabric of this imitation of the parent of the same sex are complex learning experiences and feedback mechanisms. As the child pretends to be an airline pilot or a first-grade teacher, the inner sensations that result from acting as a man or woman constantly hone his sense of sex identity and cement its security. Even more important are the responses of others—peers and grownups—to his identifications in whatever role he has chosen to play. The boy whose parents or teachers are more concerned about how dirty he gets, or whether he tears his trousers, than they are with encouraging his real need to find out how it feels to excavate dirt or build treehouses, are teaching him that they do not accept that kind of maleness.

Indeed, it is unusually difficult in an industrial and technological culture for boys to acquire an appropriate and balanced sense of masculine identity. Despite the wide publicity given to obstacles in the path of self-realization as a female, common sense as well as social and clinical experience indicates that the problems for boys are at least as great, though less recognized. Women are the chief bearers of learning and cultural attitudes for children of both sexes, in contradistinction to the traditional patriarchal family of Western culture. Males, including fathers, have played a diminishing role in inculcating values in their sons. The consequences are far from insignificant.

Intellectual achievement, good manners, self-control, aesthetic pursuits and appreciation, tenderness and consideration—the teaching of all these are largely in the hands of the mother at first, and then of a disproportionate preponderance of other females in preschool or day care centers and elementary school. To the lasting impoverishment of the personalities of many boys, these qualities become associated with being like a woman. In their struggle to become secure in their masculinity, and in their strong unconscious motivation to disidentify with their mother, boys often repudiate as "sissy" these facets of human—*not* sex-specific—well-roundedness.

There *are* innate differences between normal boys and girls, and here, too, boys are at a disadvantage. The women in charge of the lives of boys have never had the experience of being a boy. They often tend to see the greater physical aggressiveness and energy expenditure of boys as signs of trouble rather than normal, and to compare the boys unfavorably with the majority of girls, who are quieter, more verbal, and more ready to learn. The result is that the standard of behavior boys are usually expected to live up to is based upon the behavior of normal girls.[23]

Beyond the experiences of play and of school stand the more important learning opportunities of real work. Children can do many tasks, and it is unwise either to deprive them of genuine participation or to patronize their efforts. Appropriate chores sensibly rewarded form a necessary part of childhood. Mothers know how competently little girls can care for younger brothers and sisters. Boys may sometimes be just as capable, though their inclinations toward such tasks are seldom as consistent. If mothers enjoy cooking and other domestic occupations, daughters are not content with playdough and toy stoves—they want to help cook real food, and can learn to do so quite well. An eight-year-old son can be a real assistant in refinishing the basement—the hammer scars on the paneling from missed nail heads are a small price to pay.

A crucial factor in all these experiences of work and play is what the child learns about the value of the various sex roles both to himself and to others. The socializing impact of the culture upon the child is most intense during these years. The relative value and status of males and females is borne in upon the child at every expression of his emerging self. Are girls second-class citizens? Is football or fishing or "man's work" praised and rewarded, whereas the activities of little girls are ignored? Is fighting and girl-baiting regarded with amused tolerance, whereas peacefulness is impugned as somehow the mark of a sissy? Conversely, must a little boy be a non-boy, never rowdy or aggressive, in order to achieve his mother's acceptance?

A fully rounded personality can develop only when sharply exclusive behavior is neither expected nor fostered. Otherwise, a child is forced into a stereotype. Boys may quite normally show a genuine interest in cooking, and will become better fathers if they learn to take care of younger children. Sports offers as much to girls as to boys, and a girl may at times help as much as a boy with a remodeling project, but it remains a fact that in this stage, even when children have free and equal access to all the important modes of identification, girls and boys will typically and healthily display diverging paths of identity.

These social expressions of sexual identity are especially vulnerable now. The child's models—the tradition bearers of his culture, be they parental or otherwise—must reinforce the essential value of his sexuality. They must convey the assurance that involvement with the opposite sex is a warm delight to be happily anticipated. It is at this time that the child's operating society of family, school, and peers can either perpetuate limiting and self-damaging stereotypes of sexual identity and self-esteem or foster the emergence of natural and fulfilling differences.

As a whole, Western civilization has traditionally been less than helpful in fostering equal self-esteem in growing boys and girls. Men and their assumed interests and activities have been much more highly valued than women. Women have had to find their sense of worth too often in the reflected glory of their men—and men do not easily relinquish their imaginary and fantasied superiority. Such subtle, or sometimes not so subtle, attitudes are ubiquitous in the lives of primary school children. As in every human interaction, the attitudes displayed in the ways people behave toward one another carry more weight than their words. No amount of lip service to sexual equality will convince a boy whose father is indifferent to his wife's emotional needs.

Two examples, drawn from families in differing socioeconomic circumstances, will help place these concepts in a real life context.

In one family the father worked as a pipefitter, arriving home from work realistically tired and depressed because of an old, chronic resentment that he had to put in so much effort to make a living. Recent steady wage increases had not erased his resentment. He was not a malcontent, but he felt he deserved whatever he could get, and the needs of his family were secondary. He was not mean to his children nor a poor provider, just an irritable, self-centered man.

His wife was a quiet, gentle woman, as loving as she knew how to be to her six-year-old son, Joel, and eight-year-old daughter, Maureen. She had given up expecting open-handed considerateness from her husband. Her complaints were seldom shrill, but they were steady, expressed largely in a silently suffering demeanor. Both parents were moderately demonstrative toward the children, but the father's physical attentions toward his wife were perfunctory, and she seldom felt roused to show any pleasurable response to him. Not an exemplary family, but certainly not an unusual one.

Neither Joel nor his sister Maureen are learning to be really pleased with themselves or to anticipate their future with much delight. Maureen knows she will grow into a woman, but she sees little to make this an attractive prospect. Her mother's loving qualities save Maureen from repudiating her sexual identity, but she cannot look forward with pleasure to becoming a woman. She has lost respect for her mother for not standing up for herself. Equating weakness with femaleness, she turns this disrespect upon herself, hating herself for being female. She also resents men for their overbearing self-centeredness. As her sexual stirrings foretell that she will inevitably be drawn to a man, she begins to reject her sexuality because it will make her vulnerable to a situation she does not welcome.

Joel is no more comfortable. In spite of his father's apparent strength and his lion's share of the creature comforts, Joel feels an uneasiness about identifying with his father. He loves his mother and feels guilty about his maleness when he sees how his father treats her. Joel also realizes that his mother's personality and disposition are not the most alluring. His expectation of future heterosexual involvement is soured by the assumption that his mother presages women in general.

These distorted psychosexual attitudes are reinforced by the community. The family lives in a city of nearly a million people and their neighborhood is quite homogeneous. Because of the natural tendency for people to group together on the basis of shared attitudes and socioeconomic conditions, this brother and sister play with and attend school with children of fairly similar backgrounds. As they "benefit" from the attitudes of teachers, their friends' families, and their older playmates, certain consistent patterns begin to be established, locking these two youngsters into constricting and unrewarding sexual roles.

Joel learns to hide his concern for his mother and to be ashamed of softness and sentiment, because the narcissistic arrogance of males is labeled manly by his peers, and to show any other attitude is to be a sissy. And there are some self-indulgences to be gleaned from the dominant position granted boys even by most of the adult women they know. Joel gradually closes his eyes to what he is losing and develops a derogatory attitude toward females. This protects him from guilt, rationalizes his exploitive treatment of girls, and allows him to avoid the threatening quicksand of confusion, inherent in having to question and change attitudes that now support his sexual identity. These perceptions, by no means too sophisticated for a grade school boy, are usually not verbalized.

Maureen is trapped too. She realizes the difference in status between boys and girls and sees no real remedy. There is available to her only resigned acceptance or banding together with other bitter and resentful girls. She learns to fight back with sex, transmuting it from a joy she could look forward to sharing, into a commodity that can be withheld so as to exercise power or that can be used for barter. The pretense of not needing males serves few girls for very long; chemistry will usually pull them into an alliance in which the cards are stacked against both partners. While these distorted uses of sex are not often fully acted out at this age, the attitudes and even the techniques are learned, set to be triggered in later years.

In another family, one of four girls, the father was a physician in general practice. In the old tradition of the dedicated general practitioner, his patients came first. Before the last daughter was born, the family was able to move into a comfortably well-to-do suburb of a large Midwestern city, but this had no effect upon the father's attitudes or work habits. His practice was the only thing that engaged his active interest, and the girls saw him only at dinner. Then, and at other rare times when he was at home, the house revolved totally about his needs, and his wife and daughters almost literally tiptoed about so as not to disturb him.

He was a highly reserved and undemonstrative man who admired scholastic achievement and athletic ability. He would like to have had a son who was outstanding in sports. He had no hobbies and apparently little or no ability to relax. Despite his obvious professional self-sufficiency, he remained curiously bound to his mother. He insisted that the very rare vacations he would take with the family be to visit his mother.

His wife was a pleasant and relatively affectionate woman whose life was entirely subjugated to her husband's profession, but she felt resentful and unfulfilled and would talk at length with her daughters about her frustrations.

My principal knowledge of this family came through the third oldest daughter, Beverly, who consulted me in young adulthood when her marriage was failing. I will describe only the sociosexual consequences of that daughter's childhood, although an older sister also had a history of serious emotional conflicts. During her elementary years she became consciously and acutely aware of the inequity between her mother's and father's roles. She was in an emotional bind, however, because her father offered virtually no emotional support or warmth, yet the high moral value of his exemplary behavior as a physician placed him, for a child, beyond reproach. She felt strong ambivalence between her constant but unfulfilled needs to gain his recognition and affection, and her rejection of the kind of heterosexual model he presented. At the same time, she saw nothing in her early family constellation to interfere with her core gender identity as a female.

Beverly's subsequent life course was one of contradictory achievements and self-defeats. While rejecting her father as a heterosexual model, she continued to seek his approval and became quite adept at sports. He was also an effective model of the work ethic and productivity, and she completed college as a registered nurse—again showing greater identification with him than with her mother, and betraying the intensity of her unconscious need for his approval.

He provided so few evident rewards as a heterosexual object, however, that he permanently distorted her choice of boy friends. She associated all professional and occupationally successful men with her father, and studiously and purposefully avoided them. She was never emotionally attracted to any man with a firm occupational identity, and never had a boy friend who could not be classed as a ne'er-do-well, who was having difficulty "finding himself." When she married, her husband fitted this pattern, and she sought help when she realized how unfulfilling her marriage was. She gradually became aware that her early sociosexual learning had betrayed her in two ways. On the one hand she was emotionally incapable of choosing a productive man with a well-functioning masculine identity, and on the other, she still needed her father's love and acceptance, though her ambivalence ruled out her father's chief good quality. Therefore her boy friends and husband were disguisedly similar to her father, narcissistic, ungiving, and dependent men who needed mothering and nursing. Beverly also had difficulty with orgastic response. This was partly because the masculine/feminine roles she had observed, with their greatest emotional impact during latency, impaired her ability to trust herself fully to any man; it was also because the men she chose were subtly so much like the father whose love she still wanted that her relations with them awakened an unconscious guilt that inhibited her sexual response.

It emerged clearly in treatment that it was during the ages of about six to ten or eleven that Beverly first consciously perceived, and felt most strongly affected by, those aspects of sex role and the social and interpersonal dimensions of heterosexual interactions, as exemplified by her parents, that later shaped and distorted her own sex role behavior. The influences upon the more socially interactive aspects of subsequent sexual life encompass those of all periods of development, not only those operative during latency.

With the end of latency, the first cycle of psychosexual development is over. The next is ready to begin with the sharply accelerating hormonal and physiological changes that start in prepuberty. Just as fetal development and birth precipitated the infant into an inevitable series of maturational and developmental tasks, puberty will have a similar effect. Analogous tasks will be encountered. Many of the same intrapsychic and interpersonal issues will be reworked and refined, now enriched by the higher level of development and the new spheres of interaction, inexorably revealing the results of all that has gone before. The relative equilibrium of latency ends when biology again propels the youngster into his second sexual cycle.

If the early school years constitute a dynamically useful subdivision of the stages of psychosexual development, it should be possible, as in the other stages, to discern innate, critical issues in that development which are unique to this period, and which transcend arbitrary cultural differences.

In any setting that permits it, discovery of the full range of possible genital activities occurs after five years of age and before puberty. Regardless of cultural attitude, such experience is not possible until certain biological growth takes place, including the ability to get about without limitation. This sexual development has a certain imperative quality that often seems to achieve its ends even when it is prohibited. So normal is genital curiosity and experimentation that the child in whom it entirely fails to occur must be regarded with definite clinical suspicion. Such a child has learned far too well that sexuality is unacceptable, and he is probably destined to pay the price of inhibited sexual expression in later life.

In any culture, the early school years are the time of the first socialization of a child as a future participating member of his larger social group. In spite of differences, the basic physical and mental timetable of human growth requires roughly the first five years for the child to get fully on his feet. It takes that long to accomplish the internal tasks of trusting, independent functioning, and the feeling of a right to one's own interests. By then, children have the motor coordination and the mental and emotional equipment to address themselves to tasks of social interaction and to learn what the culture requires of a participating member. Even in preliterate cultures, the years between five and puberty are spent playing with and becoming proficient with the tools of future productive membership. It is inevitable that the sexual implications of various work and social roles must be learned at the same time. Experimental sexual and sociosexual interplay with one's peers has had to wait upon both social opportunity and biological readiness.

The unique and staggering volume of practical and interpersonal learning required of every human, merely to survive in even the least sophisticated cultures, is linked evolutionarily to man's long childhood. As man's brain and culture evolved in complexity, it became necessary that sexual maturation be delayed (in comparison, for example, with other primates) so that there be time for that learning. It is in this sense that sexuality is latent during these years. Since there were obvious survival advantages to ample time for cultural apprenticeship and sociosexual learning, natural selection ultimately resulted in this uniquely human phase of psychosexual development. The average child enters the early school years as body and mind are ready to benefit from their opportunities, and approaches the end of these years with his ego hopefully strengthened enough so he can withstand the rising hormonal tides of approaching puberty.

The Second
Cycle

SEVEN

Countdown to
the Biological Implosion

Sometime between the ages of nine and twelve, latency gradually ends and, with it, that period of relative harmony between the child and his parents. The youngster's body begins to prepare itself for sexual maturity through an ever more sharply rising elaboration of sex hormones. Even the fairly wide age range mentioned is only an average, because of the unusually wide normal variability in the onset and achievement of puberty. This biochemical change affects not only the child's body but also his brain and emotions, and sets off a chain of personal and societal responses that will not reach a state of relative equilibrium until the end of adolescence.

Because the same words are used with major or minor differences in meaning by almost everyone who has written on the subject, a few definitions are necessary in introducing this long series of interrelated adolescent developments. The definitions I will use throughout are not necessarily more precise than others—the incomplete state of our current knowledge of the biology of puberty and of the related psychological phenomena do not permit precision—but they seem to me best suited to the specific goal of integrating the biological, psychological, and cultural vectors of psychosexual development. Since preadolescence and prepuberty, considered as facets of a single developmental phase, are intelligible only if one is clear about the meaning of puberty and adolescence, these distinctions are introduced now rather than in the chapters on adolescence.

Puberty refers to the specifically biological and anatomical series of changes which culminate in reproductive capacity. Puberty is panhuman, and except for variations in timing and duration, in healthy humans everywhere it is an innate, inexorable event that occurs at roughly the same time of life and with roughly the same sequence of maturational changes. For the convenience of having an easily recognized midpoint in this extended series of physiological changes, a girl will be considered to have reached puberty at the time of menarche, and a boy when he is capable of ejaculation.

Adolescence is here defined as the psychological and sociocul-
tural response to puberty. Adolescence, then, is almost infinitely
variable, modified by each individual child's emotional development
prior to puberty, by the endless variety of earlier experiences and
child-rearing philosophies and practices, by the whole gamut of
individual parental and familial responses to the child's sexual
maturation, and by the institutionalized as well as the implicit
cultural expectations newly brought to bear on this now procrea-
tively and bodily mature individual.

Prepuberty refers to the one or two years of accelerating
biological changes that take place before the arbitrarily chosen peak
or midpoint marked by menarche or ejaculatory capacity. Preadolescence is the range of emotional and environmental responses to
these preparatory pubertal changes and events.

An advantage of distinguishing adolescent from pubertal phenomena is the opportunity to trace the fascinating and sometimes
individually distressing disjunctions that occur. For example, preadolescence cannot occur in the absence of prepubertal biological
events because there is nothing internally different to initiate a
response. Since one child may normally pubesce as much as four to
six years earlier than another of the same age, youngsters are more
likely to be out of phase with their peers at this time than at any
other period in their lives. The late maturing child continues to
look, and usually to act, like a child in comparison with many of his
classmates. He may attempt to be like them in order not to feel
isolated and abnormal, but his is a pseudo-preadolescence, not
actually responsive to real inner events, and may appear bizarre to
others and feel deeply disturbing to him.

Another disjunction that illustrates with undeniable clarity the
potential extent of mind-body interdependence is psychologically
induced delay of puberty. Clinical experience leaves little doubt
that some children's unconscious fear of full sexuality is capable of
inhibiting the onset or successful completion of pubertal biology.

Neither menarche nor ejaculation announces its coming ahead of
time. Preadolescence is a period of adultlike sexual behavior for
some youngsters in our culture. For an unlucky few girls, the end of
preadolescence may make itself known by pregnancy, even before a
first menstrual period has occurred. Even though this is relatively
rare, one needs to begin considering sexual activity from an

additional perspective, and it emphasizes an imperative obligation of parents to begin providing complete sex education if they have not already begun to do so.

Biological Changes Leading to Puberty

The endocrinology of puberty and its effects upon maturation are highly complex and encompass hundreds of articles and books scattered throughout the literature of various disciplines, with frequent contradictions and differences of opinion.[1]

The exact cause, or chain of events, that precipitates the onset of pubertal changes is unknown, but it is known that the onset is mediated through that part of the brain called the hypothalamus, the same portion implicated so crucially in the whole range of manifestations of sexual maturation and differentiation. Puberty is not merely an independent maturation of the primary and secondary sex organs and other body parts; their maturation is largely dependent upon hormones produced by the anterior pituitary gland which in turn is controlled by the hypothalamus. The essential role played by the hypothalamus, rather than by the level of maturation of the other organs involved, is demonstrated in one way by the fact that the premature circulation of gonadotropins—the pituitary hormones necessary for sexual maturation—will produce precocious puberty regardless of the child's age. Similarly, maturation of the anterior pituitary is shown to be irrelevant by experiments in which the pituitary gland of immature laboratory animals was implanted into the brain of mature animals. If the implantation placed the gland in contact with the hypothalamus, the originally immature pituitary began to produce gonadotropins at the adult level as soon as the blood supply between the two organs was established.[2]

It is considered, therefore, that a certain level of maturation of the hypothalamus is necessary before puberty can begin. As will be seen, mature sex hormone production is controlled by a mutually regulatory feedback mechanism between the gonadal and pituitary hormones, by which increasing amounts of androgens and estrogens influence the hypothalamus to diminish the pituitary's output of gonadotropins, which then diminishes the production of the gonadal hormones. Gonadotropins are required for the growth and maturation of the testes and ovaries in order that they can produce the male and female hormones responsible for most of the sex-related bodily changes of puberty. Without gonadotropins, puberty will not occur. The hypothalamus is thought to be sensitive in infancy and childhood to tiny amounts of estrogens and androgens, so that even the small amounts produced by the adrenals or gonads of children are sufficient to inhibit the production of gonadotropins.

It is probably the gradual maturation of the hypothalamus throughout childhood, with a concomitant decrease of its sensitivity to gonadal hormones, that eventually releases it from the inhibiting effects of childhood levels of these hormones. This release permits it to stimulate the pituitary to begin producing increasing amounts of gonadotropins, thus initiating the onset of pubescent changes. The timing of this maturation, and therefore of sexual maturity, is an innate biological characteristic of each species. It is thought to be the premature maturation of the hypothalamus that is responsible for "normal" (that is, not caused by a disease process) precocious puberty.

One of the mysteries of human maturation is the earlier puberty, averaging about two years, of girls compared with boys. This is not a sudden, unheralded leap, however; there is a close correlation between sexual maturation and bony development, which can be measured through the use of X rays, so that a child's maturational level can be assessed at any stage, beginning even in fetal life. Girls remain more advanced along their physiological lifeline from birth to maturity in this as well as in other measures, such as age of dentition. Their maturational lead over boys accelerates from the equivalent of a few weeks at birth to several months in early childhood, and finally to two years at puberty. Even though the cause of this physiological acceleration is unknown, the earlier puberty of girls is only the rather dramatic culmination of a general and preexisting biological phenomenon.

Even in normally occurring deviations in pubertal onset and duration, the same contrast holds true. Normal precocious puberty is more common in females, whereas delays in pubertal onset unassociated with disease are more frequent in males.[3] Pubertal changes not only start later in boys but generally last longer.

Estrogen is primarily responsible for most of the visible changes that take place during female puberty. It is produced principally by the ovaries and the adrenal cortices. The adrenals are the chief sources of the small amounts of estrogen during childhood. The ovaries become the major source of the great increase in estrogen production at puberty and during reproductive maturity, under the stimulation of the newly available gonadotropins. One of the puzzles of pubertal endocrinology is that estrogen production begins to increase in both sexes at about an average age of eight, and then takes a very sharp upturn in girls at about ten and one-half or eleven, the age when gonadotropins can first be demonstrated. Thus the cause and source of the earlier increase is in question, though it is generally considered to be adrenal, and stimulated by yet a different pituitary hormone.

The two gonadotropins, follicle stimulated hormone (FSH) and luteinizing hormone (LH), are responsible for the real pubertal spurt of sexual changes. They are the same in both sexes, stimulating appropriately different aspects of ovarian or testicular maturation. Contrary to most frequently encountered opinion, recent studies indicate that LH, rather than FSH, is the specific stimulus for ovarian estrogen production, but both working together are required to stimulate maximum and cyclic ovarian estrogen. LH also stimulates ovarian progesterone, the other most important female sex hormone.

Both ovaries and adrenals in the normal female also produce significant amounts of various forms of androgen, the male sex hormone. Androgens, too, begin to increase at about eight to ten years of age in both sexes, and girls ultimately produce a greater proportion of androgen than boys produce estrogens. The action of both estrogen and androgen must be taken into account to understand female puberty.

The first outward sign of female puberty is usually breast budding. It is likely that significant ovarian growth commenced at least a year earlier. Girls' height spurt starts at about the same time that estrogen production becomes cyclic, usually about eighteen months before menarche. Their average greatest increase in height comes between twelve and thirteen years of age and menarche almost always follows the apex of the height spurt. The average age of menarche in the United States is now a bit over twelve years.

Pubertal changes have by no means ended by the time of menarche. The earliest menstrual cycles are often anovulatory and irregular, sometimes for as long as two years. Growth, breast development, completion of female fat distribution and body contours, pubic and axillary hair growth, and other biological changes will continue for several years, but by the time of menarche, most girls look like young women, though still rather immature ones. The typical female pattern of cyclic hormone production is at least partly established, however, and despite the frequency of anovulatory cycles, a significant number can now become pregnant.

In the bodily changes that have begun to occur, estrogens have been responsible for breast development and for the increasingly feminine body contours, including both the sex-typical skeletal changes (such as the broadening of the pelvis) and the fat deposition in breasts and on hips and buttocks. Estrogen has produced growth and maturation of the vagina, uterus, fallopian tubes, and labia minora. Androgens have begun to stimulate early pubic hair growth and are responsible for enlargement of the clitoris and labia majora (analogs of the penis and scrotum). The most frequent sequence of external changes up to this time has been: initial breast budding; appearance of straight, pigmented pubic hair; further breast enlargement and the apex of the height spurt; increase and kinking of the pubic hair; menarche.

Testosterone—the main male sex hormone of many chemically similar androgens—is responsible for essentially all the physical changes of male puberty. Estrogens apparently play a very minor role. As previously noted, less potent forms of androgens, probably of adrenal origin, begin an accelerating rise in both boys and girls at about eight to ten years of age.

In boys there are typically no external signs of change associated with this early rise. Testicular testosterone is needed to produce most of the observable changes, and that depends upon the same gonadotropins that initiated puberty in girls. LH and FSH both stimulate differing facets of testicular growth: LH stimulates maturation of the cells which elaborate testosterone; FSH, in conjunction with thyroid hormone, promotes growth of the seminiferous tubules, with the ultimate production of mature sperm.

The first sign of early pubescent change in boys is noticeable growth of the testes and elongation of the scrotum at an average age of about twelve years. It is only after pubertal enlargement and maturation that the testicles become exquisitely sensitive to pain.

This enlargement undoubtedly occurs under the influence of the gonadotropins, though they may not be present in large enough amounts to be detected until some time after visible testicular growth. After about a year, the testes have matured sufficiently to begin rapidly increasing elaboration of testosterone. This manifests itself in the beginning elongation of the penis, changes in the early pubic hair, and in the initiation of characteristically male skeletal changes. Testosterone also stimulates growth of the prostate and maturation of its secretory function, resulting in ejaculatory capacity at an average age in the United States of just under fourteen years. Ejaculation in boys usually occurs before the apex of their height spurt (between ages fourteen and fifteen), whereas menarche occurs typically after girls' height spurt.

At about the same time as the first genital changes, something causes an early adolescent fat spurt, most noticeably in males. That something is not known, though it is likely related to the increased estrogen production that has already been noted. A concurrent change definitely traceable to estrogen is the transient breast growth that occurs in the majority of boys, analogous to girls' "breast bud" stage. Both of these normal conditions, causing a certain feminized appearance and occurring before any real growth or other obvious masculine body changes, add an extra emotional burden to that of the two-year pubertal delay in boys compared with girls.

The entire subject of pubertal growth is a puzzling one. Estrogen does not promote bone and muscle growth. Androgens do. It is thought that adrenal androgens and pituitary growth hormone are most likely correlated with the height spurt in both sexes, though conflicting evidence exists in the fact that children with nonfunctioning adrenals also have a growth spurt.[4] Testicular testosterone apparently determines a completely different aspect of growth— muscle size and strength as well as skeletal differentiation—and exerts its maximum effect about eighteen months after the peak of boys' height spurt. Boys normally grow tall and gangly, remaining relatively weak, for quite some time before they broaden out and become strong. Both events, however, usually occur after the ability to ejaculate has been achieved.

Major pubescent changes continue to occur following ejaculatory capacity. First ejaculation occurs with prostatic maturation and may not be correlated with sufficient testicular maturation for the production of mature sperm and a normal sperm count. It is reasonable to assume that immediately postpubescent boys have not achieved maximum fertility, in analogy with the frequency of anovulatory cycles in girls.

In boys, the typical sequence of observable prepubescent changes are: testicular and scrotal enlargement; straight, pigmented pubic hair; fat spurt and minor breast enlargement; beginning of growth spurt and elongation of the penis; first kinking of pubic hair; first ejaculation.

Of enormous emotional significance is the wide range of ages, all entirely within the realm of normal, at which pubescent changes may begin, and also the variable length of time required by different children for the completion of pubertal changes. In general, the sequence, once begun, is considerably less variable; it is highly unusual, for example, for menarche to occur before breast budding, or for first ejaculation to precede testicular enlargement.

Aside from sequence, the specific events of puberty are unpredictable in timing. Boys' earliest pubic hair growth may occur at any age between ten and fifteen; their height spurt may start as early as ten and a half, or as late as sixteen; the penis may attain adult size by thirteen and a half, or not until seventeen; first ejaculation comes somewhere between the eleventh and sixteenth birthday for 90 percent of American boys. Girls' breasts may bud at eight or not until thirteen, the peak of their height spurt may occur from nine and a half to fourteen, and the normal range for menarche is from ten to sixteen and a half. One child may burst through puberty, completing all its major changes within a year and a half, while another meanders slowly along the biological path from beginning to end for five or six years.

A final biological factor of major but not fully understood import has been the striking trend toward a progressively earlier growth spurt during the past century or more (earlier records are not generally adequate or available). The earlier age of growth spurt is but one easily recognizable manifestation of a generally younger age of maturity. Nutrition and socioeconomic class have been shown to have some bearing, but since the trend includes all socioeconomic classes, some of which even yet exist at a marginal nutritional status, that explanation is inadequate.

This trend is reflected in the steadily younger age at menarche. The longest series of records, from Norway, demonstrate a change in average age from slightly over seventeen in 1850 to somewhat older than thirteen and a half in 1950. A pooling of all the data indicates that the age of menarche is becoming earlier at the rate of one-third to one-half year per decade. Moreover, there is no indication of leveling off, or that girls are now maturing at the earliest possible age. Data is lacking for males, but since the same trend is shown for males' height spurt, there is no reason to conclude that boys' sexual maturation has followed any different pattern.

This trend has both practical and theoretical consequences. The former encompass the increasingly earlier age at which pregnancy or fathering a child is possible, implying a need for earlier sex education than many parents ordinarily consider necessary.

The theoretical question is: What price, if any, does an individual pay for the shortening of childhood? It is unlikely that the earlier stages of childhood are compressed to the extent that the age of sexual maturation has decreased, because the variability of facets of early childhood growth are more restricted. Consequently, the stage most curtailed is that of latency.[5] The ego maturational tasks of those years are especially wide-ranging and indispensable, and the relative length of time a child has in which to accomplish them may be of critical importance.

Emergence of a Monster

There are similarities and differences in the overt behavior of boys and girls during preadolescence. One of the most painful similarities is that both become increasingly difficult to live with and to communicate with. It is cold comfort to parents that the youngsters are finding *themselves* difficult to live with as well. Even in this characteristic "snottiness," there are differences between the sexes, but it is the shared general recalcitrance that often looms larger to the involved adult.

As a background for a general description of the behavioral changes, it can generally be said that preadolescents are responding in relatively predictable patterns to the sharply increasing amounts of sex hormones in their bodies. This internal biochemical change disrupts the relatively smooth adaptive behavior of the latter part of latency. Preadolescents' coping capacities are further confounded by the fact that until the onset of menarche or ejaculatory capacity, prepubertal endocrine effects are more internal than external. Thus preadolescents are beset by ever intensifying but intangible changes which are disquieting in their effects.

For both girls and boys, there is a gradual breakdown of many of the slowly and painstakingly learned social and "civilized" achievements of latency. Manners, courtesy, eating habits, cleanliness, respect for adults—all gradually sink into the quicksand of the past. The previously considerate young son slowly becomes rude, withdrawn, and unresponsive to overtures of any kind. The happy "young lady" becomes an unpredictable, irritable, aggressively bitchy complainer, especially toward her mother; there are other lovely sides of her personality reserved for her age-mate boy acquaintances. The relative independence of latency gives way to a maddening ambivalence in which, at times, the otherwise parent-avoiding preadolescent will want to be cared for like a small child, all the while managing somehow to convey repudiation of his mother's ministrations. Previously demonstrative children often assiduously avoid physical contact with their parents.

Such behavior is easily seen to be regression, one of the major responses to prepubescent biochemical events shared by both sexes. Under the pressure of both the specifically sexual stimuli and also the nonspecific newness of prepuberty, the majority of children revert, normally and naturally, to earlier modes of behavior. Sleep disturbances may recur for the first time in years, accompanied by nightmares reminiscent of early childhood. Echoes of oral and anal periods are especially evident. Changes in eating habits occur, most usually in the direction of sloppiness and the discarding of table manners. Periods of voracious appetite alternate with finickiness and capricious shifts in what is acceptable and what is revolting. Bedwetting, even occasional soiling, may reappear. More common, especially at home, is a general untidiness shading into actual uncleanliness about the preadolescent's person, clothing, and room. Family battles can erupt over efforts to get the youngster to bathe, allow dirty underwear to be laundered, or discard filthy and tattered clothing. "Bathroom humor" and excretory language enjoy greater popularity than ever before.

Lest it seem these descriptions are overdrawn, it should be recognized that I am describing events of gradual onset and highlighting the changes. Few children act like this all the time. Indeed, it is the disorganized and unpredictable fluctuation between tractability and regressively difficult behavior that is most characteristic of this phase, but it is the rare and atypical child in whom these changes do not occur. Whether parents are acutely aware of the changes or are relatively insensible to them probably reflects differences in parents more than differences in youngsters.

There are characteristic differences between preadolescent boys and girls, in addition to their similarities. Girls appear to become even more emotionally disorganized. Their attention span is often decreased and their ability to express themselves coherently sometimes seems totally lost. Their mood swings are more intense, more frequent, and more unpredictable, and their general sense of dissatisfaction with themselves and others at times seems overwhelming. As they draw closer to menarche, and their estrogen production becomes more regularly cyclic, so may their mood swings. Some premenstrual tension is undoubtedly emotional in origin, but clearly not all of it. Even though the menses have not yet begun, and an important hormone in the biochemistry of premenstrual tension—progesterone—may not be as prominent in prepubertal endocrinology as it will later become, a girl's mood swings may gradually take on a more regular timing. This is not an inevitable occurrence, but a perceptive observer may sometimes discern a faint preview in the rhythm of irritability, peacefulness, moodiness, enthusiasm, and depression.

Most of the ill temper of a prepubescent girl, expressed in interactions with her mother, often overtaxes the mother's patience and understanding. The father is relatively—but only relatively—exempt, and at times can be the only stabilizing influence available. Counterbalancing girls' greater inner disequilibrium, it has frequently been noted that intense regressive phenomena, though they do typically occur, are significantly less characteristic of preadolescent girls than of boys.

Girls do not tend to form peer group gangs as boys do; rather, they form intense twosome friendships, often with overt sexual overtones, and are much given to sharing sexual secrets. These friendships often pursue a stormy course.

Girls at this stage are relatively more at ease and direct in their heterosexual interests than boys—a reflection of their less conflicted heterosexuality since the end of the oedipal stage—but their genuine ease is not untainted by ambivalence and hostility, and they now possess an unparalleled advantage for the expression of any malice they may have been storing up. The two-year lead in growth and sexual maturation that girls normally display allows the average girl literally to leave her male age-mates and classmates behind; she is not only taller and generally bigger, but also blossoming into young womanhood, while they are still little boys. Any reasons, real or fantasied, she may harbor for wanting to get back at boys can now be acted upon with relative impunity. She can outdo many of them in sports and in school performance; teasing boys is characteristically preadolescent feminine behavior.

The boys subject to such treatment are woefully vulnerable. Because their first object of identification was a woman, boys are not as secure in their sexual identity as girls, and overbearing behavior by the more rapidly maturing girls hits them where their defenses are weak and leaves them with little constructive recourse. Their tendency, as in latency but even more strongly, is to band together in mutually reassuring all-boy gangs and make a great show of depreciating and repudiating girls and femaleness. When prepubescent endocrine changes do begin to affect them they are still two years behind, and the emotions and fantasies that are stirred and reawakened make them even more anxious about females and more defensively bonded together in their all-male groups. There is probably no other normal period of maturation for the majority of youngsters in which there is greater disjunction of psychosexual development and disparity of social and heterosexual readiness.[6]

As in all earlier stages, solitary masturbation is the predominate mode of sexual release. The sexual activities of preadolescents in our culture are increasingly varied, as more and more of them become bold enough to experiment in more and more ways, but almost all circumstances in the typical middle-class preadolescent's life—revived unconscious conflicts, the realistic sense of sexual insecurity and unreadiness, limited opportunity—converge to make masturbation the most available sexual outlet.

It is in preadolescence that the incidence and frequency of normal homoerotic play reach their peak. The use of "normal" in this context deserves comment. Whatever attitude one holds regarding the normality or abnormality of preferential or exclusive adult homosexuality, it is clear that the vast majority of instances of erotic play among members of the same sex occurring in preadolescence and early adolescence is of a totally different character. The expression "homoerotic play" is used specifically to avoid confusion with the clinical term homosexuality.

Although girls are less threatened by their heterosexual interests than boys, they are similarly more comfortable with friends of the same sex. When the rising tides of prepubertal sex hormones make themselves felt in stronger sex urges, children in our American middle-class culture find it generally less threatening to explore and experience those feelings with the friends with whom they are most comfortable.[7]

Kinsey's data showed that among girls the active incidence of homoerotic play reaches its peak at ages nine to eleven and remains more common than heterosexual play through age thirteen; among boys it peaks at twelve and remains more common through age fifteen.[8] During preadolescence, homoerotic play is chiefly exploratory and masturbatory, but may not be so limited. What is most important for parents and other involved adults to realize is that this play very seldom has prognostic significance. It is a frequent part of psychosexual development in this culture and gives way to heterosexual involvements as soon as any youngster overcomes the conflict and self-consciousness of puberty sufficiently to risk sexual experimentation with the opposite sex.

Sexual activity involving animals also has its peak incidence in preadolescence; it varies from masturbating pets during sexual arousal to penile insertion in the vagina or anus of pets and domestic animals. Sex with animals is limited almost exclusively to rural boys and to city boys during rural visits. Six percent of all preadolescent males and 11 percent of rural preadolescent males are reported to have had at least one sexual experience involving an animal that resulted in orgasm.[9] Despite the horror with which many adults regard this form of sexual activity, there is no evidence that it has any more significance than homoerotic play for any but an infinitesimal number of permanently disturbed youngsters. It is no more than making do with what is available at a time when drives are increasingly pressing and heterosexual outlets are scarce, frightening, and prohibited.

These general trends vary from one locale to another, and according to subculture, education, and other types of demographic categorization. Clearly, heterosexual experimentation was not so threatening to the group of boys mentioned in chapter 6, of whom 54 percent had had sex play with girls and 26 percent had attempted or achieved intercourse by age eleven.[10] Another study suggests that black preadolescent boys do not display the heterosexual reserve of preadolescent whites.[11] Kinsey's figures indicate that preadolescent coitus has been attempted by only 26 percent of males who go to college but by 74 percent of those with an eighth grade or lower maximum education.[12]

Despite the fact that mutual avoidance is the most characteristic public stance of preadolescents, some early heterosexual interaction is beginning. In urban settings, 28 percent to 40 percent of ten- to eleven-year-olds claim already to have had a date.[13] A survey of adolescents which made a conscientious effort to obtain a representative sample of all socioeconomic and subcultural groups in the United States reports that 10 percent of boys and somewhat more than 3 percent of girls have their first intercourse before they are twelve years old.[14]

Even more meaningful is the preparation for ultimate heterosexual liaison that is taking place in the minds of preadolescents regardless of how they characteristically act toward one another. In an extended series of studies of the sociosexual development of youngsters between the ages of ten to seventeen, it was found that already at ages ten to eleven, 30 percent of boys and 57 percent of girls had positive responses to romantic scenes in movies. One of the most striking and significant findings was that at the same age, 61 percent of boys and 79 percent of girls want to get married some day.[15] These investigators consider that recognition by preadolescents of the desirability of a permanent marital relationship is truly a fundamental point in their psychosexual development, virtually a prerequisite emotional position before further heterosocial development can proceed during the preadolescent and early adolescent years.[16]

Both the inner preparation and the outward reserve and antagonism are going on simultaneously in the majority of preadolescents
in our dominant middle-class subculture. There is some indication
that the once very typical heterosocial and heterosexual avoidance
may be giving way to some degree, but the data are far from
conclusive. In both adolescence and preadolescence, it is difficult
for youngsters not to be increasingly ruled, in a sense, by their
biological changes. These changes essentially drive them apart, even
though to different degrees and for different reasons in the two sexes
and in individual children, until they have begun to come to terms
intrapsychically with the new aspects of themselves.

It has been found that the peak age of social exclusion of the
opposite sex is twelve. This correlates well both with the preadolescent predominance of homoerotic play and with the time when the
differential physiologic maturation of the two sexes is most dramatically visible.

Adults too often like to blind themselves to the occurrence and
incidence of youthful sexual activity. No matter how different one
community may be from another, it is only realistic for adults to
recognize that a variety of sexual experiences—probably more than
they would choose to believe—is a part of life for a variable but
significant proportion of preadolescents.

Growing Inner Turmoil

Despite the naturally increasing differences in the psychology and
in the emotional tasks of boys and girls, it is a human characteristic
to regress under stress when better mechanisms of adaptation are
not available. Pubescent biological changes constitute such stress
because they are puzzlingly new—it is impossible to have learned to
cope with something that has never before happened. Added to its
newness is the fact that most of our youth are singularly unprepared, even handicapped, for the comfortable acceptance of mature
sexuality by traditional adult sexual attitudes and child-rearing
practices.

Furthermore, each sex in its own way must accomplish the same
unfinished job, that is, separation from the emotional ties with, and
unconscious attitudes toward, the mother of infancy. Final and
definitive resolution of the oedipal phase must wait for both sexual

maturation and the capacity for a more genuine kind of independence. The true resolution of this second edition of the Oedipus complex is one of the major tasks of adolescence. Only begun in preadolescence, this intrapsychic task relates more to the mother than to the father. The efforts to cope with increasing sexual tension and to resolve the remaining unconscious ties with the mother provide the major intràpsychic motives underlying most preadolescent emotions and behavior.

The experiences and unresolved conflicts of previous developmental stages may be resolved either progressively or regressively. The progressive mode incorporates the past experiences in progressively higher and more complex and effective levels of behavior and ego function. This is quite typical of the latter parts of latency, as, for example, when a girl's increasing mastery of real maternal or domestic tasks reinforces her initially shaky independence of her mother. The progressive mode is also more characteristic of girls than of boys in preadolescence, though girls certainly do not escape regression.

The regressive mode, while often indicative of emotional disorder, is by no means always pathological. Regression often serves constructive ends. By reactivating (in a sense reexperiencing and reliving) old unresolved conflicts, there is new opportunity with a now stronger and more mature ego to stabilize the unfinished emotional business and to reach new and more appropriate resolutions. Much of preadolescent regression is of this healthy kind. There is little doubt that it is the hormonally induced sharp intensification of sexual drive that "pushes" a child out of latency. The regression to and reactivation of very early attitudes and conflicts is usually a necessity before a child can cope with puberty because the ego and other mental capacities were simply not mature enough at the earlier age to achieve valid resolutions.

The tables are now turned. In the initial oedipal period it was the boy who severed his infantile dependence upon his mother, renounced his sexual fantasies for her, and began masculine identification by allying himself with his father—all with one internal emotional adjustment. Now the boy has a contrastingly more difficult task. He must reattach his sexual feelings to a female while avoiding the pull back to dependency on his mother and his oedipal wishes for her and, at the same time, maintaining his male identity. The task is not easy.

Since a boy's ego is not fully prepared to cope with pubertal changes, he will naturally regress. But the increasing sexual drive at this time makes regression to the oedipal phase intolerable, so he regresses defensively to preoedipal levels. This enforces a further working through of earlier conflicts because, in so defending himself from intensified oedipal desires, he has jumped out of the incestuous fat into the dependency fire—an equally threatening position. Oral and anal needs reawaken his conflicts between the pleasures of dependency and the resentments of subjugation to the powerful, dominating, and (in fantasy) castrating mother, and bid fair to undermine both his independence and his masculinity.

It may well be that this fairly sudden appearance of regressive behavior marks the beginning of preadolescence in boys.[17] Preadolescent boys are not, and cannot be, secure in their masculinity and therefore retreat into all-male peer groups for mutual support and reassurance. It is in these groups that the frequent occurrence of homoerotic play serves a number of temporarily defensive and supportive purposes. Beginning now and extending into early adolescence, the exploration of sexual sensations and genital changes in the company of friends of the same sex clarifies a boy's understanding of the normality of his own body and its urges, and reassures him that nothing is wrong. His infantile regressions have unconsciously revived his childish fantasies of castration and of the genitals of females as proof of castration, and such activities as group or mutual masturbation are graphic demonstrations of male intactness. These groups often thoroughly exclude and derogate girls, not only because they unconsciously represent castration but because of all the many anxiety and guilt-provoking fantasies aroused by females, equated with the childhood mother.

A favorite book of preadolescent boys has long been Robert Louis Stevenson's *Treasure Island*, which is also popular in the latter part of latency, when the safety of the oedipal struggle (Jim Hawkins has no father) allows the wish to be enjoyed in disguised form. Now and during early adolescence the oedipal challenge is every bit as clear, but it may well be that fantasied success of the challenge, rather than its disguise, accounts for its fantasy-gratifying popularity.

Young Jim measures his strength and wit against a wide gamut of father images, represented by all manner of good and evil characters. Out of this contest Jim emerges as an acknowledged rival on an equal footing with the men.[18]

The growing sex drive of prepuberty also reawakens a boy's conflicts between internal and external genital sensations. Some of the beginning sex hormone stimulation is vague and internal, associated with growth of the prostate and seminal vesicles and with beginning prostatic secretions. The largest subjective hormonal effect, however, is increased penile erotic sensitivity to stimulation. The established unconscious equations of inside equals female and outside equals male join the other unconscious motives for a flight from femaleness. Abetted by the much stronger concentration of pleasureful sensations in his external organ, his penis, the boy repudiates his inner genital sensations and externalizes his sexual interests almost totally onto his penis, with increasingly intense masturbation. Eventual ejaculation will, hopefully, enforce his having to begin to integrate the external and internal, masculine and feminine aspects of himself.[19]

The marked increase in testicular sensitivity to pain is yet another push in the direction of focusing sexuality almost exclusively upon the penis. Testicular retraction, even with disappearance into the inguinal canal, in many boys still remains an involuntary response to such stimuli as cold, anxiety, closure of the anal sphincter, and sexual arousal. Unconsciously associated with castration and body-part loss since toddlerhood, the new exquisite pain sensitivity intensifies the fear of damage and loss. Additionally, spontaneous testicular sensations and movements are sensed as internal, uncontrolled, and female. Again biological and intrapsychic circumstances combine to encourage a rejection and repression of the uncontrollable, the damaging, and the feminine, in favor of the comforting, repeatable pleasure and presence of the essential male organ, the penis. These feelings and involuntary movements and sensations, together with the anxieties and needs for mastery they engender, continue to serve as the unconscious motivation for the lifelong male fascination with games involving balls and sticks or bats, with mechanics, spatial control, the hunting use of penetrating objects, and other external control activities. Such interest derives from these unconscious motivations blended with men's higher activity and aggression level, innate properties bred into them from eons of evolution in which survival of self and family depended upon such abilities.

The dynamics described explain aspects of boys' preadolescence which are regressive, troubled, withdrawn and female-avoidant; such behavior normally alternates with more mature, reality-oriented behavior. It is the repeated emerging from fantasied infantile dangers into the real interaction with the real mother, from heterosocial avoidance to heterosocial and heterosexual experimentation, that allows reality to be compared with fantasy and finally to replace it.

Not all of a preadolescent boy's apprehensions about maintaining his masculinity and independence against threats posed by females are entirely unrealistic fantasies. Many boys have had ample proof of some of their larger, more mature female age-mates' capacity for spite and malice. Concerns about the mother also contain a germ or more of truth. A little boy's mother did have nearly absolute power over him, and many mothers are reluctant to let their boys grow up and move away from them.

Nor are his sexual fears always groundless. His oedipal conflicts gain a quality of reality now that he is really starting to mature, and sex will not long remain academic. He is, of course, not in danger of anatomical castration but he may be in danger of functional castration—a form of emasculation that may have begun in early childhood. He may have a long and accurate perception that his mother or father, but more likely females in general, did not welcome and foster his genital sexuality or other masculine characteristics. The behavior and qualities of girls have generally been preferred, especially in school, and maleness may have been actively derogated, both at home and elsewhere. Some boys may see clear signs, as puberty progresses, of a mother's distress or even disgust over their oncoming adult sexuality.

There is no denying that the beginning of puberty precipitates a boy into a real life struggle with the real people in his family and his life; it is not imaginary jousting with the windmills of childhood fantasy.

Girls, in contrast to their original oedipal dilemma, now move more easily than boys into the heterosocial and heterosexual interactions instigated by pubescent maturation. The difference is relative only, and they are not spared all the problems of regression or their own brands of turmoil, but they have a major advantage in that they have been enabled under healthy circumstances to become quite secure in their female identity. They have not had to shift; they have remained in a kind of apprenticeship-identification with a female since birth. Unlike boys, whose specifically masculine qualities have been appreciated mainly by other males, the feminine identity of girls has been fostered by adults of both sexes. Girls have significantly consolidated their feminine role identity by the latter part of latency because of considerable experience in performing the feminine role so that the natural heterosexual impulsion of pubertal biology is not threatening to the same degree or in the same fashion as to boys.

I am well aware that there are certain cultural and individual parental attitudes that can lead girls to feel like second-class citizens, that do not foster the development of some aspects of feminine identity nor promote the enjoyment of being female. But the basic biological realities of female function and the feminine, maternal role are usually fostered, and it is this area of identity that is practiced during childhood and about which confidence most predictably develops. Evidence continues to build up throughout the stages of psychosexual development that boys often suffer greater discrimination, and more distortion and curtailment of their natural sex identities than girls.

The reemergence of oedipal feelings is not usually felt to be so dangerous to girls because they never had to give up their attachment to their father as fully as boys had to renounce their mother. Their castration anxiety has not been as intense, and they need not defend themselves so strongly against a resurgence, but they do face the analogous problem of discovering that sexual attraction and sexual activity are becoming a potential reality, sometimes expressed directly by a girl in surprisingly adult seductiveness and attentiveness toward the father, in a frank bid to outdo her mother. This characteristic of preadolescence tends to yield to more defensive techniques after the burgeoning of true young womanhood in early adolescence. The same intrapsychic conditions will allow the girl to focus her heterosexual interests upon her peers with fewer anxieties and conflicts.

The newness of inner biological changes, and the fact that girls' earlier oedipal attachments were not entirely without guilt and conflict, do produce some regression, which is especially threatening to preadolescent girls because their principal intrapsychic task is to free themselves from early childhood ties to someone of the same sex, the mother, rather than to defend themselves against emotions toward the parent of the opposite sex. In the effort to draw away from her mother, a girl at this stage displays a thrust of activity and a turn toward reality, essentially a progressive rather than a regressive attempt to deal with old conflicts. She would like to demonstrate, mainly to herself, that she is already fully grown, adult, and competent, no longer in need of her mother's ministrations or guidance.

Her mother represents so much of what is both good and bad, in her fantasies and in her past, that the intensity of her struggle is commensurate with the degree of her ambivalence. Her mother was the succorer and the punisher, the giver of love and the disciplinarian. In the girl's childish mind she once blamed her mother for not giving her a penis with which to win her mother's love, and for keeping her from winning her father's exclusive affection. Her mother is both the model of femaleness and the one who keeps the full female sexual function for herself. To whatever extent the girl has learned to regard her own sexuality with fear and guilt, the growing inner insistence of her sexual drive makes her reject as bad and debased the sexual aspects of her mother.[20] Through all this, the girl cannot reject her mother entirely without rejecting her own femaleness. As one solution to the conflict, girls probably repress infantile (pre-oedipal) sexuality, that period most filled with unrealistic and conflicted fantasy, more totally than do boys. A later reflection of this may be expressed in adult patterns of heterosexual foreplay, which consists largely of acting out infantile sexual expressions in preparation for intercourse. Women consistently reject a wider range of foreplay techniques—oral-genital sex, for example—than men do.

One means of a girl's breaking away from her mother is by transferring her affections to another adult female, such as a teacher or a friend's mother. Another is the formation of girls' secret-sharing, best-friend twosomes. The secrets that were a major part of girls' friendships during latency could be about anything; now the secrets are essentially sexual. There is a quality of excluding the mother in these pairings, as though in retaliation for all the sexuality that mother had "withheld" during childhood.

These twosomes often serve the same sexually reassuring purposes through homoerotic play as do the gangs of boys. The greater readiness of girls for heterosexual interaction is only relative. They, too, need and can find comforting support in exploring their own genitals and genital sensations with someone who is experiencing the same feelings.

Girls, more than boys, must now begin to learn to cope with the inevitable predominance of their inner genital sensations. With the onset of puberty and ovarian maturation, estrogen stimulates rapid and massive pelvic changes including uterine and vaginal growth with accompanying cellular and secretory maturation, and markedly increased vascularization of the network of vessels in and surrounding the sex organs. At the same time, testosterone initiates final development of the clitoris, including its vastly increased erotic sensitivity, and growth of the perineal and perivaginal musculature.

In prepuberty, these changes are just beginning, but the magnitude and rapidity of the changes, and the amount of circulating sex hormones, far exceed anything the girl has previously experienced. Inner genital sensations are correspondingly increased, and they are just as diffuse and uncontrollable as ever, only more and more insistent. Until menarche, there is no recurrent, predictable genital event around which to organize the naggingly tantalizing sensations. It has been suggested that it is as though her inner genitals are teasing her and that to try to rid herself of the sensation she turns to teasing boys, perhaps a significant unconscious motivation behind this characteristic preadolescent feminine behavior.[21]

Under the impact of this prepubescent inner genital surge, much of which takes place before major sexual changes are apparent, the girl's previous mental and emotional organization becomes loose and disorganized, in a state of lability and disequilibrium which manifests itself in poor concentration, irritability, dissatisfaction, indecision, fragmented thought, and endlessly meandering and never-to-the-point verbalizations that masquerade as communication. Menarche, when it occurs, will serve as a concrete bodily and sexual focus around which the girl's psyche can begin to reorganize.[22]

Girls who have been healthily prepared for joyous acceptance of their sexual selves have a less troublesome time than their poorly prepared peers but still find this a difficult time because the subtle and diffuse nature of what is happening gives them little to hold onto. They give the general impression of flailing distractedly and aimlessly about under the push of disintegrating pressures.

This is the second period in a girl's psychosexual development when she makes an intense effort to externalize her inner genital sensations, simply because she cannot do anything with them internally. There may be frantic periods of clitoral masturbation, both to find relief from the tension and to externalize and thus control the excitation. There may be a fervent return to doll play, in unconscious remembrance of the doll's earlier capacity to assist in externalization. In girls with excessive fear of genital penetration and damage, there may be a renewed denial of awareness of the vaginal opening. Further externalization may be expressed by obsessive preoccupation with barely beginning secondary sexual characteristics such as budding breasts and when and whether to wear a brassiere, or hip size and contour, or—even further removed—problems of complexion or hairdo. Underlying all this concern is the inescapable awareness that her inner destiny exists and will ultimately have to be confronted.

Such unconscious emotions account in large part for the pre-adolescent horse craze which, contrary to what might be expected, is more typical of girls than of boys. Among girls whose life circumstances permit it, their preoccupation with horses may assume the proportions of a monomania. A full-grown horse is usually a masculine symbol, regardless of the horse's sex, and the sexual meaning of having control of this powerful, rhythmically surging, living object between one's legs is obvious. Direct genital stimulation received during the act of riding is often fully conscious, and the passion for horses can serve many symbolic sexual purposes. The horse is a substitute penis for girls who are conflicted over their femaleness, it is an object on which girls can externalize their inner sexual sensations, and learning to control so powerful a male symbol is tantamount to feeling that they can control men. This need may express no more than the normal apprehension over penetration and injury, though it can assume great intensity in girls who misperceive the sexual act as violent and mutilating.

Unconscious psychodynamics and their almost magical reflections in behavior and thought are a constant source of bewildered skepticism to people who have not become familiar with the cryptic logic of unconscious processes. It is always gratifying to have a means of demonstrating those processes in some readily recognizable fashion. The characteristic organization of each sex's mental life around static inner or dynamic outer concepts has been classically illustrated in an extended study of the spontaneous configuration of structures produced during play by preadolescent children, age ten to twelve. Girls typically built static, peaceful enclosures with people inside, often with elaborate doorways; frequently the interior was intruded upon, but this did not lead to the erection of defensive walls, and the intrusions tended to have an element of humor or pleasant excitement. Boys' constructions abounded with cones or cylinders and high towers, with people or animals outside the enclosures; there were many moving objects and automotive accidents, with traffic often being channeled or stopped by police; there was much play with collapse, and the danger of downfall of high structures. Only the boys built ruins. The differences were so consistent that independent evaluators could accurately distinguish male from female constructions.[23]

Charlotte Brontë's novel *Jane Eyre*, long a favorite among preadolescent girls, reveals oedipal fantasies in virtually undisguised form. The "family romance" persists, the young governess eventually becomes the wife of a man a generation older who could possibly be her father, and his first wife dies, completely vanquished.[24]

The onset of puberty in comparison with one's age peers has significant and fairly consistent intrapsychic consequences. A truly early-maturing boy or girl is no longer preadolescent whereas the majority of his peers still are, a state of affairs which, at its beginning, has different consequences for each sex.

It is the late-maturing girls who have the greatest peer prestige and social acceptance, at least through sixth grade (average age twelve) and perhaps longer. These girls seem to be more vivacious and outgoing, with more drive to achieve—as indicated, for example, by more frequent mention in school newspapers and elections to class and extracurricular offices.[25] An early-maturing girl who reaches menarche by age ten and is a fully developed young woman by twelve is not only markedly ahead of her own sex but fully four to five years ahead of most boys. This is enough to make her initially a real outsider.

Early-maturing girls are also rated more negatively by adult observers, but it is difficult to be sure what part of that evaluation reflects adult anxiety over early female sexual flowering.[26] It is no myth that early maturers, at least those who pubesce by age eleven, begin sexual activity earlier than the later maturers.[27]

The social effects of early maturation are different for boys. At the time, at least, there appear to be few obvious drawbacks. They are not only ahead of their admiring peers of the same sex but they are more up with the typical girl. Sooner than typical or late-maturing boys, they begin to manifest self-confidence, independence, and heterosexual readiness.[28] Earlier sexual activity is strongly correlated with early pubescence in boys.[29] Such boys are more popular and generally enjoy greater social prestige.

One potential social disadvantage is that adult society, while approving of these boys, tends to require them to meet expectations determined more by their size and appearance than by the more important inner developmental criteria. And for both male and female early maturers, there may be highly important, long-term consequences to the curtailment of latency.[30]

Puzzled Parents

Preadolescence catches many adults as much off-guard as the youngsters. Most adults have only sketchy recall of their own behavior during that brief period. They may remember specific events or particular grades in school but not their state of mind. This is only partly due to repression—such diffuse and unorganized emotions and interactions offer poor subject matter for clear recall. For the same reasons that puzzle the child—the acceleration of major internal changes well before clear external signs of maturation—parents are taken aback by the seemingly unprovoked behavioral and mood changes in their children. While mothers find themselves most severely taxed, fathers, too, are struck by the ricocheting emotions of their children, catch the backlash from exasperated wives, and experience a few conflictual interactions of their own.

It is difficult for even the most forewarned and psychodynamically sophisticated parent to maintain equanimity and to roll with
the gradual crescendo of regressive and disorganized punches. The
day-to-day interaction with a preadolescent in full bloom is no
picnic, but a long-term comprehension of how absolutely necessary
it is that he begin to distance himself from his parents, even though
he may go about it tactlessly and grossly, can help maintain
patience. Unfortunately, it is likely to get worse, in early adolescence, before it gets better.

In addition to the stress of being unable to predict her
preadolescent's response to anything, a mother must herself begin
to cope with a sense of inevitable loss as it gradually dawns upon
her that puberty, growing up, and growing away has begun. Her
response will depend upon her own emotional health, her security
in the job of child rearing she has done, in her own life and marital
relationship, and her readiness to begin to hold with a releasing
hand. There are those mothers whose sense of meaning is vested too
fully in their children and who will try to keep them dependent too
long—perhaps successfully. Others will be envious of their daughters' burgeoning sexual attractiveness and feel threatened by it.
They may derogate their daughters' halting and clumsy attempts to
look grown up, prematurely suspect them of sexual activity, or erect
barriers between the girls and their fathers.

Some mothers try to make up for what they themselves have
missed by pressing a patently unready preadolescent into heterosocial maturity. Others, chronically dissatisfied with their own
femaleness, will undermine a daughter's acceptance of her sexual
identity, and still others are simply afraid of a daughter's oncoming
sexual maturity and try to close their eyes to it, to delay it as long as
possible. This fear also affects many mothers of preadolescent sons.
While a mother cannot really impede the steady march of biology
unless she has already helped instill such deep sexual conflicts as to
disrupt physiological maturation, she can surely impair her child's
emotional preparedness for puberty. When either parent is apprehensive about the coming of adult sexuality, the fears are conveyed
in innumerable nonverbal ways and add to the youngster's own
anxieties.

Fathers and mothers both may be made uncomfortable by their
own inevitable sexual responsiveness to a maturing child. This is

another phenomenon that does not reach its peak in preadolescence, though some anthropological studies indicate that institutionalized incest taboos may be most strenuously imposed at this period.[31] The parents' erotic arousal is inevitable and normal (though it may be kept carefully out of conscious awareness), and it parallels the youngster's reawakened oedipal yearnings.

This arousal is often a greater emotional problem for fathers than for mothers because girls are less threatened by their attachment to their fathers and hence more open in their affectionate and seductive displays. Mothers feel the conflict also when, often to their shocked dismay, they are stirred by sexual feelings for their maturing sons, but sons are less likely than daughters to heap fuel on the fire by acting provocatively.

These conflicts, when they occur at all, are less intense at this time than after the full sexual maturation of children, but can be more confusing and more disruptive at this early stage because the cause is so much less obvious. Both parents and youngsters may be afflicted by the same vague guilt. When the parents do not understand the source, they may employ the same defensive tactics as their children and cause real damage to the relationship. Fathers may suddenly break off all affectionate physical warmth toward their daughters. Either parent may become hostile toward any sexual manifestations in order to defend himself from guilt-producing arousal. Even though the preadolescent youngsters do the same thing, they cannot healthily tolerate having it done to them. However crudely they may disdain parental affection, they read a sudden, distant avoidance as rejection of themselves as persons, and specifically as rejection of their maturing sexuality.

Preadolescence is the beginning of the span of several years when being a parent often seems dishearteningly unrewarding. While it is difficult to be a good parent during this period—one whose calmness reflects dependable security and understanding rather than indifference and unresponsiveness—it can be done, and there are some relatively simple measures that are helpful and reassuring for both generations.

One is simply to choose a quiet time in between (or perhaps just following) flare-ups or uncommunicative moods, and talk to the youngster frankly and openly about what is happening to him, and how typical his responses are. I have found children, my own included, gratefully receptive at such times. It makes no difference if the parent has also been explosive or uncommunicative. The preadolescent is far more puzzled and frightened than his parents and is expressing only one side of his ambivalent feelings; the love and respect and need for the parents has not disappeared. This nearly grown, awkward-looking youngster needs to know that his uncontrollably volatile emotions cannot destroy the love nor deprive him of the guidance he still desperately needs.

The youngster's active participation is not necessary. Unless he stalks away—in which case the parent has chosen the wrong time or is conveying a negative message that the youngster is picking up—the words will be heard and will help. Long, detailed biological lectures are not necessary (although at times they may be appropriate), but the parent should indicate that he is aware of the chemical changes beginning to take place in the youngster's body and that he understands that these changes are both exciting and disquieting, producing unexpected moods and impelling him toward a new relationship with his parents. Such reassuring talks will have to be held over and over through the next few years, and none of them are wasted.

Even more specifically, preadolescents need to know that their developing sexuality is welcomed. A girl must know that her father accepts and likes her oncoming young womanhood. He can reinforce her attractive and womanly qualities even though he must also add his voice to help discourage slovenly and unappealing behavior. When he is unafraid of his own responses, he can appreciate his daughter's affection at the same time that he avoids and gently deflects the overtly erotic overtones. A warm and good-natured comment such as "Don't worry, one of these days you'll have a real boy friend of your own" is both an acceptance of a girl's sexual self and a noncritical reminder of its appropriate focus.

Complete sex education is imperative in preadolescence, as many youngsters will be seriously damaged by their ignorance if they remain unprepared. Not only must information be provided but it must be offered repeatedly. Children often unconsciously retain infantile sexual theories into preadolescence as a means of defending themselves against the anxieties associated with adult sexuality. This causes frequent forgetting (repressing) of factual information and innocent or indignant claims that "You've never talked about that before!"

Complete sex education, including full information about intercourse, contraception, abortion, and venereal disease, is frightening to conservative parents. They fear that information—especially contraceptive knowledge—will lead to sexual experimentation that would not otherwise have occurred. These fears are not rational. Ignorance has not kept adolescents from experimenting sexually but has merely made their activity more dangerous. The fears about the effect of contraceptive knowledge and availability have been shown to be invalid. A major study reveals that a girl's or woman's decision for or against intercourse is based on her entire background of attitudes, maturity, and value systems; contraceptive availability is simply incorporated into that value system without changing it.[32]

It is my considered opinion, as a clinician and teacher who works constantly with both healthy and disturbed adolescents, that the withholding of sexual knowledge, whether from fear or any other motive, is neglect of parental responsibility. Accurate and full sexual information is not a guarantee against sexual misuse and misadventure—sex education is not disaster insurance—but ignorance inevitably leaves one more vulnerable than knowledge. Preadolescence is the last chance one has to provide children with the protection of knowledge before that knowledge may come too late.

One of the most vitally reassuring preparations all children need for puberty and adolescence is an understanding of their variability. No matter when the bodily changes of puberty begin to show, there will always be friends and acquaintances in whom the changes began earlier, or have not begun yet, or may somehow appear different. The newness of the changes, and the unconscious fantasies that may be called upon to account for them and their timing, make for inner puzzlement and uncertainty in most children. Whether an early, average, or late maturer, no youngster is immune from fearing that something is wrong with him because he is different from some of his friends. Repeated preparation for variations in pubertal timing will not eliminate all anxiety but will reduce it reassuringly. There is even an excellent series of photographs of nude (male) pubescents available, all the same age yet varying from child to adult in bodily appearance, that carry a reassuring impact words alone cannot have.[33]

Because of the more intense conflicts on the part of the child surrounding the mother, she needs much greater patience than the father and can profitably avail herself of any opportunity to keep lines of communication open. Her greatest way of showing pleased anticipation of her daughter's approaching womanhood is conveyed in the way she prepares her daughter for menarche. It makes no difference that a girl may defend herself against the knowledge. Obviously such preparation must be given, and preferably by the mother, assuming a healthily feminine mother; it should not be left to the school, older sisters, relatives, friends, or a physician. Such avoidance implies only negative attitudes. A discouragingly large number of girls are totally unprepared by their mothers and the consequences are not minor. Many women who suffer excessive premenstrual distress in adult life have had poor relationships with their mothers and have been inadequately or negatively prepared for menarche by them.[34]

Menarche and preparation for it should not be secret women's business that excludes the father. He may not have the intimate personal experience to instruct a daughter about what to do when she discovers her first period, but there is no reason that discussions should not include him. Preadolescent daughters may display some embarrassment, but the more important message—that open sexual discussions between the sexes is healthy and normal—will get through. Fathers should definitely be told when menarche occurs so they have the opportunity to express their own happiness at their daughter's maturation.

Boys need the same kind of reassurance, but they offer fewer opportunities because of their withdrawal into all-male peer groups and their greater avoidance of the mother. Nonetheless, any opportunities for supportive discussion should be sought and used. This may be easier for a father to do (though mothers should make the effort, too), assuming that the father is knowledgeable and comfortable talking about sex. Too much teasing about a boy's beginning or future interest in girls often has a nonconstructive effect, making the boy too self-conscious to come to his parent when he really needs to talk something over.

Boys are the forgotten sex when it comes to preparation for puberty. While girls' preparation for menarche is often inadequate, boys' comparable preparation for frequent spontaneous erections and eventual masturbatory ejaculation and nocturnal emissions (wet dreams) is virtually nonexistent. These events are not quite as dramatic as menarche, but an unanticipated first ejaculation has been very frightening for many a boy. When it occurs as a result of masturbation (about which he usually still has much guilt), he is prone to anxious fantasies about possibly having damaged himself inside, loss of vitality and fertility, equation of semen with pus, and all manner of other guilty misconceptions. The same is true when earliest ejaculations occur as wet dreams.

His increasing sex hormones also render him subject to frequent erotic arousal at times that he may find embarrassing, and to spontaneous erections under totally unexpected circumstances. It is easy to help a boy anticipate these normal events as normal, yet it is seldom done. Foreknowledge will not eliminate his conflicts in learning to cope with these events, since those conflicts are largely rooted in unconscious fantasies unaffected by conscious reason, but it does give him some reality to counterpose against his fantasies. Knowledge of these inner sexual phenomena help in his ultimate and difficult intrapsychic task of integrating internal and external sexuality.

Disruptions of Preadolescence

"Tomboyism" has many meanings, some of them entirely normal. In a society that has historically limited or depreciated the athletic interests of girls, those who pursue such interests regardless of the stereotypes may be falsely stigmatized as tomboys. At an age during which boys are threatened by femininity, a girl's effort to gain acceptance to the boys' groups by being "one of the boys" may be one of her very limited routes for expressing her need for her normal heterosocial readiness. But preadolescent tomboyism can also be a repudiation of femaleness, a pathological envy of males, or an effort to deny the reality of the female biological changes. Even though conflict may have been building for years, it sometimes requires the inexorable march of pubescent biology to flush the repudiation of femaleness out into overt and easily recognizable behavior.

Some girls may simply try to deny that anything is happening to them and cling to both the behavioral adaptations and mannerisms of latency. They continue wearing little-girl clothing despite its increasingly anachronistic appearance on a maturing body. Denial of puberty is usually indicative of severe sexual disturbance. So intimately are the mind and body integrated in pubertal processes that intense unconscious fear of sexual adulthood is capable of deranging the complex endocrinology of adolescence and can literally delay puberty indefinitely.[35]

Boys are as often afflicted by similar fears of growing up sexually, though they may express them differently. The counterpart of the healthy tomboy is unusual. Boys will seldom adopt obviously feminine roles and companions except in the presence of serious sex role conflict. Such boys are clearly signaling that they face the risk of developing lasting homosexual preferences.

Others with conflicts about adult male sexuality, or their own masculinity, may gradually withdraw from masculine competitive activities. While not choosing to identify with girls, they are indicating some significant unease about and rejection of the preadolescent mainstream. This cannot categorically be labeled sick; there may be extraordinarily healthy reasons for unusually mature or perceptive young men to repudiate some of the disordered and regressive aspects of that mainstream, especially in some of the more sexually exploitive subcultures. But whether due to health or conflict such boys are outsiders, and that is a difficult added burden. Those who withdraw because of intrapsychic conflict may be afraid that they are not manly enough to be one of the gang or may have more than the usual degree of conflict about their own developing sexuality.

Some children may express their fear of sexual maturity by remaining fixated at some regressive level which originally seemed only typical. This is not the healthy use of regression to tie up loose ends emotionally, but a retreat from a maturational task to which the child feels utterly inadequate. One girl suddenly became obese at age eleven and remained so throughout adolescence; she maintained an unusually intense and clinging dependence upon her mother, and did not proceed with increasing dating activity along with her classmates.

On the other end of the spectrum are those who rush prematurely into heterosexual behavior. Before examining such behavior, it is necessary to consider the meaning of "premature," which cannot be defined with assuredness. Cross-cultural data demonstrates that in permissive societies children of eleven are finished with experimenting and have already adopted the preferred form of adult heterosexual intercourse. Is that premature? How do their normal unconscious conflicts manifest themselves? Are there ways to rear children so that they will *not* be afraid of their own sexual maturation? What is premature heterosexuality in our culture for a boy or girl who was somehow reared not to be afraid? Can it be that those who mature early also sometimes have more mature brains and emotions so that they are sexually ready sooner? It is not possible to answer all—perhaps any—of these questions, but I would like to propose some working hypotheses. I cannot equally support them all, and future research may require that some be discarded, but an effort must be made to establish a baseline about which the innumerable issues subsumed under the elusive concept "premature sexuality" can be grouped.

One hypothesis is that some kinds of intrapsychic conflict are innate and inevitable in psychosexual development. Cultural and child-rearing attitudes do not create all conflicts.

A second is that cultural institutions and child-rearing practices can and do exert enormous effect upon psychosexual development, either intensifying, ameliorating, or creating entirely avoidable conflicts, depending upon their multivariant forms.

A third is that any person, child or adult, can bring to any sexual interaction only as much as his innate maturation and learned development has provided him.

A fourth is that maturational level is more important than chronological age.

A fifth is that when young people suffer mild to devastating emotional damage from various forms of sexual activity, the damage can be traced to some kind or level of unreadiness.

A sixth is that in order to learn to function at higher levels of human interaction, people may first have to interact at the only level at their command—in other words, in more primitive and less mature emotional involvements.

There appear to be roughly two different sources of emotional unreadiness for sexual behavior. One relates to the innate timetable of brain maturation as more complex capacities unfold and become available for development, and which, thus far, cannot be accelerated outside a certain normal range (an eleven-year-old Pilagá Indian may be perfectly comfortable with heterosexual coitus but still cannot bring to that relationship emotional qualities unavailable to normal eleven-year-olds). The other relates to those learned emotional and intrapsychic qualities—such as fear, guilt, ego mastery and coping capacity, the ability to trust and to love, security of sexual identity—which are so vulnerable to the impact of parental and cultural influences, and which can affect so strongly (more to retard than to accelerate) the individual's innate timetable.

None of these working hypotheses directly addresses itself to the recurrent question of whether or not a person will *inevitably* harm himself or others, and cripple further emotional development if he becomes active in involvements for which he is emotionally unprepared, but they provide bases upon which prematurity can be considered.

Out of all this, I believe that one tentative definition of premature sexual activity may be proposed: Sexual activity of any kind or degree is probably premature when it expresses serious emotional conflict, when its chief motive is to resolve conflict, or when it is associated with strong emergency emotions. In such circumstances it will more likely result in psychological damage rather than growth. A corollary principle is that to whatever degree children's rearing and interpersonal experiences lead them to fear or to be guilty about their normal sexual impulses, they can be expected to misuse early active heterosexuality and to risk harm from it. The tacit assumption is that with more time for ego maturation and corrective emotional experiences, they would be less vulnerable to sexual misuse and harm, but this assumption does not necessarily follow. Time may merely rigidify the inappropriate attitudes. By adulthood the concept of prematurity may no longer apply, but disordered sexuality that is damaging to oneself and to others may certainly exist.

It is important to establish some guidelines for sexual prematurity, in the sense of being emotionally harmful, in discussing preadolescence, because this is when adultlike sexuality begins among some youngsters in our culture, and it is also when sexuality begins to become a major concern of parents and other adults.

I cannot define the conditions under which preadolescent sexual activity, up to and including intercourse, is harmless or perhaps even growth-promoting. I know that it frequently occurs without demonstrable damage. In such cases, which are not rare, I must give principal credit to an upbringing free of fear and guilt over sex, so that early experience could be positive and could be utilized emotionally to help allay and resolve the normal sexual conflicts of this phase.

It is much easier to define the typical conditions under which preadolescent sex is premature and harmful. First and foremost is any sexuality into which a preadolescent is pressured or coerced. A preadolescent who must be truly pressured knows he is not ready for the emotional repercussions of sexual intimacy. Even though his body may respond with arousal, fear and guilt will predominate. Future sexual trust may be seriously compromised, or the experience may become the prototype for a pattern that requires force and submission as a prerequisite for arousal.

When a seemingly preadolescent girl becomes pregnant, premature sexuality was obviously involved. One or both partners were insufficiently educated or too immature to guard against such a consequence.

Among girls, a common form of premature heterosexuality is one unconsciously used as a defense against an overly strong dependent attachment to the mother. These girls are so threatened by the intensity of their dependent yearnings that they feel in danger both of losing their shaky independence and of becoming homosexually attracted to the mother. Their heterosexual activity has a frantic, compulsive quality because of its defensive nature. It does not arise from a relatively uncomplicated attraction to males.[36]

Paradoxically, some girls actually use premature heterosexuality as a defense against further heterosexual development. Such girls are both deeply conflicted about heterosexuality and, at the same time, highly erotic and curious. They may subtly but actively provoke a sexual encounter, usually with an adult, and then utilize the enormous anxiety aroused as a defense against further psychosexual development. In these girls there may be an abrupt halt in heterosocial involvements that essentially paralyzes their sexual and social development in adolescence, and puberty itself may be disrupted or delayed.[37]

Boys most commonly become involved in inappropriate early heterosexuality out of insecurity about their masculinity. Not only is sexual identity inevitably incomplete in preadolescence, but any involvement in homoerotic play may further undermine a boy's confidence. Notwithstanding the actual peer group support of homoerotic activity implicit in peer participation, there is usually awareness of strong social stigma. Even the boys involved may project their own sense of shame and tease others mercilessly. Unfortunately, the heterosexual activity motivated by such causes often backfires. A frightened and insecure preadolescent boy is not likely to obtain the cooperation of the healthiest (most considerate and supportive) girls and will find himself experimenting with those least likely to reassure him. To the malicious derision of such girls add the inhibiting power of a boy's fears and self-doubts, and the result is often a most unsatisfactory experience, if he can perform at all. If he cannot perform, or is inept and is ridiculed, his self-esteem is terribly diminished. If he is successful, it proves a hollow victory, the beginning of the shallow pattern of using sex to prove his manhood.

Either sex will misuse sexuality if there is inadequate superego or conscience development so that there is no concern about the partner. Exploitive sexuality of this nature is only premature if normal conscience development is on its way and only delayed or immature. Where conscience formation is genuinely impaired, sexuality will remain exploitive at all ages.

In describing preadolescence less has been said about cultural and interpersonal influences than in earlier phases. The shift in emphasis is not an oversight; it corresponds to a shift in the relative potency of the various shaping vectors. During the early school years the relatively gradual rise and steady rate of sex hormone production probably contributed to the relative stability of the child's sex life. By no means did his sexuality stop—in an absolute sense, it actually increased—but it was not normally preoccupying. The social, cultural, and interpersonal aspects of learning and of intrapsychic ego development had an opportunity not only to occupy the emotional center stage but to overshadow the overtly sexual in the child's development.

Now, in preadolescence, the tables are turned. The current motive force behind most of what goes on is the beginning surge of sexual maturation, as it confronts, interacts with, and is modified by what has gone before. Pubertal biology is essentially sexual, and its impact now overshadows other influences just as the societal influence took precedence in latency.

Under the impact of prepubertal biology, the influences of ten to twelve years of prior psychosexual development begin to reveal themselves more clearly perhaps than in earlier years. To make an overbroad generalization, the younger child has normally been busier absorbing influences than in displaying major and lasting adaptations to them. All the prior phases have been building up to puberty and its ultimate culmination in adult sexuality. The excellences and flaws in that early preparation will begin to reveal themselves more and more sharply as the final product begins to take its first dim shape. Not that psychosexual development is essentially complete—some of the most telling influences take place in adolescence, and throughout adulthood such events as marriage, parenthood, and loss of reproductive capacity all keep sexuality a changing and dynamic quality until death—but the time has come when the visible consequences of previous psychosexual development begin to balance the input of new psychodynamic influences.

One consequence typical of our culture has been mentioned— mutual fear and mistrust between the sexes and the predominance of homoerotic play are regarded as normal for preadolescents. This is not true of all cultures, particularly those that do not inculcate fear and guilt about sexuality. Children cannot grow up conflict- free, but it may be a pathogenic characteristic of our culture that elaborately rationalized theories must be erected to account for the "normality" of behavioral phases that reflect distorted rearing and may also presage future sexual dysfunction. Most preadolescents seem to come through these phases with little or no obvious harm, but since these phases are considered normal, the subtler, less visible prices that restrictive sexual attitudes may exact from all or most of the adults in our culture cannot be known. It is entirely credible that an unnecessary degree of fear and mistrust of the opposite sex is built into our cultural character and that this fear and mistrust, first shown so blatantly during preadolescence, later makes genuine and caring intimacy more difficult to achieve.

Preadolescence is different in cultures with, for example, variant family structures which diffuse oedipal attachments, or in which sibling incest taboos are cruelly strict. The unique effects of variations in rearing and externally imposed expectations are in this phase more and more evident. Infants who were psychologically virtually identical the world over are now preadolescents who would barely recognize those from another culture as belonging to the same species. Shared qualities diminish proportionately as learned qualities and divergent expectations multiply. Increasingly, I will be describing the psychosexual development of an ever narrowing group—the dominant, white subculture of Judeo-Christian culture—because only its members share enough of the truly basic influences to form an even tenuously homogeneous group. I am aware of the existence of endless subcultural variations and will try to be clear about those issues I consider to be part of the human condition and which therefore transcend culture.

Psychosexual development should, at each phase, contain a critical period for further growth. In preadolescence, it is difficult to tease out an easily expressed increment of emotional growth. Perhaps what is critical is best stated in negative terms: In order to get on with the job of adolescence, it is crucial that the youngster not deny what is beginning to happen to his body. He may temporarily use any number of defenses against the new feelings and the sexual anxieties, but he may not healthily pretend that changes are not happening. Adolescence cannot be successfully negotiated by anyone who emotionally insists that he is still sexually a child.

EIGHT

Early Adolescence: Self-Centered Sex

Early adolescence reflects the sharpest impact of pubertal changes. During preadolescence, the upheaval is not so great in the youngster, nor the societal response so massive, as it is after most of the pubertal changes have taken place and the young adolescent has essentially assumed the appearance, at least, of a full-grown sexual adult. The rather sudden convergence of massive and imperative biological changes and wrenchingly new social and cultural expectations combine to make adolescence potentially one of the most unstable and tumultuous periods of life.

Some authorities have made a three-fold division of adolescence, including a period of middle adolescence, and in such instances the distinctions become delicate and the overlapping of phase-specific characteristics blur the boundaries. I prefer a two-fold division, relegating to preadolescence the period that some writers describe as early adolescence. There is still an inevitable blending of characteristics rather than sharply defined boundaries, even though for simplicity I have chosen definite physiological events to signal the beginning of early adolescence. In general, early adolescence in girls lasts until about age fifteen or sixteen, and in boys until about seventeen or eighteen, but the normal range may be anywhere within at least two years on either side of those ages.

Adolescence must be distinguished from pseudo-adolescence. A teenager who has not reached puberty may try to act like his adolescent peers and will certainly be involved in some of the same activities, especially in a school system in which groupings are determined by chronological age, but he will usually feel like an outsider and be treated as one, because he literally cannot perceive or inwardly participate in an adolescent's psychosocial world. On the other hand, once puberty has taken place, adolescence must follow, however distorted or disguised. Even if a girl denies the implications of her menstrual periods and steadfastly persists in the pretense that she is still a child, she is an adolescent, though a disturbed one. Her denial itself is a response initiated by puberty.

With the coming of adolescence, societal pressures now reassert themselves in a major way. While the inner pressures toward adolescent change and development are essentially sexual, the cultural environment now assumes a greatly intensified role in trying to mold and direct the youngster. Cultural influences vary so widely that it is feasible to discuss the universal bases first and later to be more specific about the impact of our own dominant subculture upon its adolescents. Many of the manifestations of adolescence are caused by the culture and may be unique to it. Comparisons with other cultures illustrate the arbitrary quality of many of the ways every society has of coping with adolescence. Adolescents as a group, and adolescence as a phase, are comprehensible only in their cultural matrix.

Cultural institutions represent the dominant society's consensus about the means of regulating matters and events deemed important to the group. Institutions as divergent as formalized schooling alternating with vacation periods, dating, and marriage may be seen as group-sanctioned adaptive-defensive techniques designed to maintain a working compromise between the gratification of individual needs and group survival and values. Unbridled individual license is incompatible with group life and cooperation.

The universality of the major physiological events in the human life cycle, such as birth, death, puberty, and senescence, impels each society to adopt a group position about them. The group positions become formalized into institutionalized practices, such as the puberty rites of some cultures. Puberty is one of the most powerful stimulants of group attitudes and cultural institutions.

All societies have assumed the necessity of regulating sexual behavior, at least of its adult members, however diverse and however relaxed or stringent those regulations may be. Puberty initiates adult sexuality and society asserts its traditional efforts at control. It should be clear that the consistency or inconsistency of cultural mores about sexuality in general, and adolescent sexuality in particular, will have crucial consequences for the psychosexual development and emotional health of adolescents. It is also implicit that our own culture embodies its unique regulatory attitudes toward adolescent sexuality which impart a special flavor to the developmental tasks of youngsters.

Puberty imposes upon virtually all adolescents certain universal, culture-transcendent tasks that must be accomplished if healthy adulthood is to be attained. One such task is that during this period the adolescent must move, emotionally and often physically, away from his family of origin (the family into which he was born) to a different family of procreation (that in which he will produce offspring). This functional and emotional shift is an expression of the universal incest taboo. Nowhere is the same person both child and parent within the same nuclear family (the family that consists of biological mother, biological father, and their offspring).

A second task facing the adolescent is to change his position, both within the family and within society, from one of being nurtured to one of providing nurture. Whether or not he literally produces children, it is an adult's role to help provide for others, not to remain in childlike dependence.

A third task is to become finally able to work and to love, both tenderly and sexually. Obviously, many aspects of development are subsumed under so broad a statement, and by no means do they spring suddenly anew at adolescence. At least from the moment of birth every child has been learning, within each important human relationship, the precursors of adult love, but only after puberty can the ingredients of adult sexuality and independent caring be added, and these must be integrated with earlier learning in order to qualify as fully manifested adult love.

Pleasure in being a productive member of a group—an essential facet of work within a society—was a critical developmental task of the early school years. The meaning of work in the context of an adolescent task, however, implies finding and applying oneself to a realistic and rewarding occupational identity. Again, this level of function is accessible only after maturation of all physical and mental-emotional capacities permits the recognition and constructive development of one's genuine abilities, and when society is ready to accord a fully participatory role.

This third task has been stated somewhat differently in Erikson's progressive schema of phase-specific developmental crises. He characterizes adolescence as the period during which a person must achieve a firm and stable sense of identity or become lost in what he calls identity diffusion.[1] In this sense, identity is a rich and complex concept, including such considerations as secure adult sexual identity, ideological and value system identity, occupational identity, and a social identity in which one's self-concept is reasonably in accord with how one is perceived by responsible others. Sexuality is only one facet of the total panoply of adolescent developmental tasks, but it is a truly critical facet, and discussion of equally germane issues must be limited here to indicating only some of the more important points of integration and overlap.

Biological Changes Become More Visible

The basic endocrinology of puberty was outlined in the preceding chapter. Most of the changes begun in prepuberty continue, at least through early adolescence, the phase during which most of the visible bodily changes stimulated by pubertal endocrines take place. Early adolescence, therefore, is usually the period when youngsters are most intensely preoccupied with their bodies and during which concerns, delights, and disappointments over those bodily changes are most deeply felt.

Menarche, which marks the beginning of early female adolescence, is characterized in its early stages by menstrual periods that are frequently irregular and more often than not anovulatory. The hormonal reasons for the delay in maximal fertility are not agreed upon. It is possible that the optimal production of the pituitary gonadotropin LH occurs later than that of FSH. Without a fully mature cyclic interaction between both of them and the ovarian hormones estrogen and progesterone, normal ovulation does not occur. There is some evidence that progesterone may not be elaborated in adult quantities until one or two years after menarche. The full explanation remains to be researched.

The frequency of anovulatory periods has given rise to a concept of early adolescent infertility. That very indefinite period of diminished fertility (*not* infertility) is not true of all girls, and taking it too literally has had disastrous consequences for countless youngsters. Without complex medical and laboratory tests one cannot be reasonably sure whether a young girl has ovulated, even in that very first cycle before the first menstrual flow, but regular ovulatory (fertile) cycles have usually been established by the end of early adolescence.

Estrogen production, mainly due to ovarian stimulation by LH and FSH, continues to rise steeply (though in cycles) throughout this period. Androgens, from both adrenal and ovarian sources, also continue to rise in about the same degree and amounts as in boys, until an average age of fourteen to fifteen years, at which time androgen production begins to level off.

Throughout early adolescence, under the influence of estrogen, the uterus and vagina continue to increase in size and in the maturation of their various component parts and cellular composition. Breasts show their major maturing in both shape and size, and the feminine pattern of fat distribution resulting in the typical feminine rounded body configuration is largely accomplished. Skeletal differentiation, as in pelvic broadening, is similarly nearly complete. At the same time, androgenic effects are becoming more noticeable. About two years after the beginning growth of pubic hair, underarm hair starts to grow, and at the same time adult-type sweat glands and sebaceous (oil-producing) glands develop. This produces the characteristic adult odor of perspiration and accounts for the fact that children normally lack that odor. The height spurt, which began before menarche, has nearly run its course.

The characteristic postmenarcheal sequence has been: further breast development, near-adult type of pubic hair, axillary hair growth and sweat gland development, and regular ovulatory periods. By the end of early adolescence, most of the normal bodily changes associated with sexual maturation are almost complete. An individual girl may not look as she will at twenty-five or thirty—further important changes in appearance, barring illness and accidental influences, are probably hereditary—but she now looks like a woman, not a child.

In the average boy, already two years older than girls in reaching his point of early adolescent onset—ejaculatory capacity—the pubertal transformations continue to move more slowly. Early ejaculations produce relatively few mature, healthy sperm, but absence of fertility is not to be assumed. Characteristically, boys' sperm counts continue to rise in both quantity and quality throughout early adolescence but have not reached their peak by late adolescence.

At puberty perhaps as many as 2 percent of boys' testicles have not descended into the scrotum, a condition known as cryptorchidism. The temperature inside the body is too high to permit sperm to mature, and the result of cryptorchidism affecting both testicles is sterility. There is also evidence that cancer of the testicles, though rare, is much more common in undescended testicles. The condition is easily repaired, and any boy who is manifesting other pubertal changes but whose testes remain undescended should be brought to medical attention.

Testicular testosterone begins to increase greatly at about fourteen years, which probably accounts for the larger total amount of androgens in males compared with females and for the fact that male testosterone production continues its rapid rise at the time it is leveling off in girls. Under its influence, boys' peak height spurt occurs during early adolescence. Most height has been gained by about seventeen or eighteen, but height continues to increase in boys longer into late adolescence than in girls.

Because many visible pubertal changes in males are related to testicular testosterone, which is a relatively late addition to the circulating androgenic substances, those changes are late in appearing. By the end of early adolescence, most boys are just in the midst of broadening out in the shoulders and of muscle growth and strength increase. Major voice changes are now taking place, and beard growth is only beginning. Penis, scrotum, testes, and pubic hair are nearly adult in size and configuration, but some development will continue for a few years. Following a schedule analogous to that of girls, axillary hair and sweat and sebaceous gland growth begin about two years after pubic hair development.

Most typically, the male early adolescent sequence has been: more marked kinking of pubic hair, maximum increase both in height and penis size, axillary hair appearance, and the beginning of major voice changes, facial hair growth, and adult male body configuration. By the end of early adolescence boys' pubescent changes are nearly complete but not to the same extent as those of girls. As they pass into late adolescence, boys look somewhat less like their final adult selves than girls do.

Early adolescence, like preadolescence, remains a period of marked dissonance in the timing of biological changes, both between the sexes and between different youngsters of the same sex. In some ways this asynchrony is even more noticeable now. The physiological changes are producing more visible effects, and differences seem more marked when a fully pubescent youngster compares himself with one who has still not begun, than when comparisons of pubertal beginnings are made. This intensifies various kinds of anxieties in adolescents at all levels of maturation and has significant social repercussions. Comparable maturational levels are an important basis of friendship and peer groups, which means that earlier—sometimes long-lasting—alliances and groups may be broken up and realigned.

One hormone effect that depends on an identical endocrine in both sexes is the intensity of sexual desire. The subjective sense of sexual interest and urgency is dependent upon androgen. The intensity of sexual drive is not solely dependent upon the actual amount of androgen present, though there is some relationship. Males do not necessarily have greater sexual drive even though they produce more androgens, though women with a pathological excess of androgen often complain of unbearably intense sex urges.[2] Sexual desire, however, is dependent upon the action of androgen; males without functional androgen gradually lose their sexual drive and females respond exactly the same way. Giving large doses of estrogen to males also decreases their sexual interest whereas large amounts of normally produced estrogen does not inhibit desire in women as long as androgen is also present.

Another, and far less welcome effect of androgen in both sexes is acne. Androgen stimulates the growth of sebaceous glands, and acne is essentially an overgrowth of the glands that produce sebum, a thick waxlike substance, while there is insufficient concomitant growth of the ducts of the glands so that the sebum can come to the surface. The glands thus become swollen, plugged, red, and painful, and sometimes infected. Acne seems to be more common in girls with irregular menses, and additional estrogen is often helpful. But it is really not known why acne afflicts some adolescents more than others and some not at all, or why it lasts longer in some, or why it completely subsides with time for almost all adolescents. Acne is actually a normal and natural condition at this age, but no one can convince a youngster with a bad case of acne that it is anything less than the plague.

In addition to variations in the timing and duration of puberty, further endocrinological effects may begin to appear that are probably due to hereditary or constitutional differences. One example is the total amount of body hair. The existence and distribution of pubic, axillary, and facial hair is dependent upon normal endocrinological differences between the sexes, but overall body hairiness is probably most influenced by heredity. Another, less well understood difference that may be genetic or constitutional, or both, is the permanent development of physical characteristics which tend in the direction of those more typical of the opposite sex. One example is the girl who appears somewhat virilized or masculine—that is, whose body is more than typically muscular or broad-shouldered, has more body hair in a masculine distribution, or who has a larger clitoris. Such a condition is in no way pathological (unless it is grossly excessive or progressive), nor does it make her less of a woman. She is most likely producing a form of adrenal or ovarian androgen which is biochemically a closer relative to testosterone and which is more virilizing than that produced by most women. These individual variations usually begin to manifest themselves, if they do so at all, in early adolescence, and are rarely a factor in the biological portion of psychosexual development.

Big Brother Steps In

With respect to early adolescence, I have shifted the usual order of discussing psychosexual developmental influences from what might be thought of as "from inside to outside" to its opposite. The shift reflects my emphasis that any aspect of adolescence, sexual or otherwise, can be made intelligible only by considering it within its cultural matrix.

During the early childhood years, even though the child moved out into a wider social area, his family remained dominant, at least at deeper intrapsychic levels. He expanded the ranks of influential others, but the school and neighborhood were perceived essentially as extended family—in a sense, his life space became a larger front yard. Not so for adolescents, at least in large, nontribal cultures. Though different cultural attitudes provide for varying ways in which an adolescent can perceive and assimilate the entire gestalt of culture, parents now come to be seen in a different perspective. They are no longer really central; at the very least, they are seen as assimilated into the overall social group, sometimes as extensions of the culture rather than the other way around, as in childhood.

All cultures assume the responsibility for regulating the sexuality of its members, and Judeo-Christian culture has its own unique approaches. There are certain characteristics of the dominant subculture—that of the white middle class—that particularly impinge upon early adolescent psychosexual development:

Sexual Values. Most specifically, and all publicity to the contrary, Western culture's official value system is still sexually prohibitive. Any changes taking place are doing so slowly—more slowly among adults than among young people. "Official morality" is that set of values which the recognized adult arbiters of social mores openly and publicly encourage and reward. It is not the same as what adults may do, or what they may close their eyes to when others do it. Those adults who favor significantly greater sexual permissiveness are those who would like to see change, rather than those who are the true spokesmen for the broad middle class.

The durability of this sexually prohibitive stance is attested to by large, cross-sectional population samplings made in 1973. In one, the large majority disapproved of almost all forms of nonmarital sex,[3] and in another, 80 percent flatly declared sex before marriage to be wrong.[4] Masturbation is not yet generally accepted—in the random sampling questioned almost 50 percent condemned it.[5] Data from a study of Philadelphia medical school graduates and faculty in 1959 revealed that half of the newly graduated physicians and 20 percent of their faculty still believed the hoary myth that masturbation was instrumental in causing mental illness.[6] Other research has shown that prohibitive sexual attitudes particularly focus upon adolescence because at that time sexuality has potential procreative consequences and parents still consider themselves responsible for adolescents' sexual behavior.[7]

Repressive sexual attitudes are not new in adolescence. What is new is that adolescents can now engage in and enjoy sex in exactly the same ways adults can, and their sexuality has adult procreative potential with its attendant liabilities. Although it is the adults' clear responsibility to help guide adolescents into both responsible and enjoyable sexuality, an opposing adult attitude makes its appearance. This is the pervasive adult stance that adults own all sexual rights, that they alone possess the right to decide the conditions under which youths may have access to their sexuality. The complications that this authoritarian position introduces into adult-adolescent relationships can be grossly disruptive.[8]

The extraordinary durability of official middle-class morality has been made possible, at least in large part, by the taboo that has existed for so long on open discussion of sexuality, either privately or in the communications media. The ease with which people compare notes about various foods or different political candidates has not existed with respect to sexual attitudes and practices. With each person thus isolated from any broad sexual consensus, many individuals fear that their private urges and preferences are bizarre and deviant. Whatever anyone says openly about sex is regarded as a personal statement of his sexual ideology. The result is that most people are reluctant to voice any but the most conservative views. Even when some of these are minority attitudes, they represent and perpetuate the traditional cultural mores because they remain practically the only voiced and encouraged positions. Thus it frequently happens that adults in our culture will staunchly advocate sexual attitudes that barely coincide with their private behavior.[9]

The effect of isolation from reality testing and consensual validation about sexual matters is well known to clinicians and sex educators who work with groups. Once sufficient trust develops that individuals will venture to share some of their sexual experiences and feelings, there ensues a nearly magical release of tension. Without exaggeration, a chorus of relieved sighs accompanies the sudden recognition by many that they are not depraved sex fiends after all.

It is possible that this basis of spurious cultural unanimity may be changing. Recent years have brought about considerable relaxation in the strictures against open discussion of sexuality and its treatment in the media, but such changes, regardless of their ultimate value or harm, are slow to reach the grassroots majority of our dominant subculture, and have so far influenced primarily the urban centers. Also, there is recent evidence of a significant swing of the pendulum back toward media control. This peculiar characteristic of our culture which bears so directly upon the early adolescent's sexual world remains a contemporary and potent force.

A further directly sexual characteristic of our culture is the frequently mentioned discontinuity between childhood training and the ultimately desired adult adaptation. Overt sexuality is seldom condoned and usually consistently discouraged among children. This attitude extends to factual education and a usable vocabulary. Adolescents, especially young ones, are even more strongly enjoined not to engage in orgastic sexuality, yet they are expected to achieve a stable sexual identity, and at adulthood suddenly to become able to enjoy all the mutual delights of sexual partnership as soon as they comply with the cultural institution of marriage which confers the rights of sexuality upon them. Massive numbers of men and women are simply unable to shed their years of contradictory rearing.

Another, and virtually unique, attribute of our sociosexual mores is the manner in which sexual regulation is approached. As indicated, all cultures must and do undertake some kind of sexual regulation, differing only in the forms of control, but our form is distinctly atypical. Our culture attempts to control and regulate *whether* a person may have any orgastic sexual outlet at all. Almost all other cultures, major and minor alike, regulate *when* and *with whom* orgastic sexual gratification is permissible—kinship taboos may be mind-staggeringly complex, and various ritual considerations may introduce many strictures—but with all the restrictions, there are always *some* circumstances in which sexual gratification is entirely permissible for any biologically mature person. When restrictions extend even to masturbation, cultural regulation becomes cultural prohibition.

The end result of the official sexual attitudes of white middle class culture is failure to provide any form of openly approved, guilt-free, orgastic sexual gratification between puberty and marriage.

General Value System. Cultural mores other than the specifically sexual ones strongly affect the adolescent's efforts and resources to master his sexuality. Perhaps most blatant are the contradictory messages from the adult world to which no mentally competent adolescent can be oblivious.

The communications media bombard the young teenager with sexuality and its desirability. Teenagers know that adults control the media and that it is the adults' own preoccupation that they reveal. Many parents push their daughters and sons toward earlier and earlier dating. They carefully teach them how to be "sexy," at the same time sharply forbidding them to be sexual. Adolescents quickly recognize the disparity between adults' public attitudes and private behavior. Such conflicting cues offer them no help at all with their own problems of coping with urgent and ambivalent sexual feelings.

There is ambivalence, too, in society's valuing of individuality. Particularly in the United States, the national ideal and its culture heroes are rugged individualists who follow their own paths without yielding to the conventional and timorous many. Every schoolchild grows up immersed in this ideal, and it may well be that before puberty this ideal is practiced in the rearing philosophies for children. Erikson has maintained that American elementary schools are quite effective in training children to display initiative, self-reliance, individuality, and a remarkable lack of prejudice. It is after puberty that individualism becomes suspect, if not actually illegal, and the pressure shifts, suddenly and shockingly to the adolescent, toward conformity and intolerance of differences.[10] Adolescents display their own need for peer group conformity, but these adult discontinuities and inconsistencies increase the task imposed upon the adolescent ego.

Family Structure. Western society is also characterized by its almost exclusive composition of nuclear family units. Geographical mobility has quickened the dissolution of extended families, and a saddening intolerance across generational lines is generally evident. Even within the nuclear family, responsibilities are rarely spread among the older and more capable children. Both authority and the nurturing functions remain vested in mother and father, while siblings of all ages remain essentially equal, dependent, and without genuine responsibility for one another. Thus each sibling is a competitor, a situation that engenders an emotional set that is carried into the outside world. All emotions—loving, angry, dependent, rebellious—remain focused upon the parents. The family structure of contemporary Western culture is one which both fosters and intensifies adolescent oedipal conflicts.

Associated with the nuclear family pattern are particular difficulties adolescents have in realistically encountering the culture as a whole. Because authority has not been diffused among many adults and older relatives but associated almost exclusively with parents, they become the paradigms of all adults and all authority. Adolescents reared in this manner often find it difficult to perceive the new adults and social authorities they now must deal with as genuinely individual, with their own special qualities and differences. There is a strong bent toward projecting parental images upon cultural institutions and the "establishment." Such adolescents respond stereotypically, shaping expectations and responses according to their parental models rather than in an accurate reflection of external reality. Adult culture tends to be perceived as an extension of their own particular parents, more in the manner of an early school child than an adolescent.

Discrepancy Between Biological and Cultural Demands. One of the most crucial features of modern culture, in conjunction with its essentially prohibitive position, represents man's unique and disquieting capacity to become out of phase with his biological self. As a result of our increasingly technological and complex culture, more and more is required of the typical adolescent to be able to "make it" in the western world. There is a constantly widening span of years between biological sexual readiness and socioeconomic and even psychological readiness for self-sufficiency and family responsibility. Even a century ago, taking into account the much later age of puberty at that time, most youths in that agrarian and craft-oriented world were ready to assume a beginning place in the adult community within two or three years after the first intense stirrings of puberty. Not so any longer. At the least, three or four years typically elapse between puberty and even high school graduation, well known to be inadequate preparation for all but a marginal economic existence. College-bound youth add four more years, and those with professional ambitions may not be fully on their own until their thirties. During this span, young people must marry while remaining dependent upon parental subsidies, or try to cope with the culture's biologically unrealistic dictum that sexuality should be postponed until marriage. This long dry period between biological and socioeconomic sexual readiness does not directly impinge upon early adolescents, because their life has not yet extended into its future unrealistic reaches, but they do become aware of what kinds of expectations lie in store for them, both educationally and sexually, and it aggravates their impatience even in prospect.

Rapidity of Social Change. Finally, there is the rapid, disorganized, and unpredictable social change that extends its effects into every corner of the adolescent's being. Culture has always been changing to some extent, but it is no shortsighted, ethnocentric myth that, amid historic cycles of relative cultural equilibrium and transitional upheaval, the present age is one of the latter. It is difficult, or impossible, for an adolescent to anticipate his own future based upon what his parents' world was like when they were young. Many adults are equally demoralized by seeing the ground of secure life being eroded from under them by forces they neither understand nor believe they can control. Even though parents can be perfectly good models for their youngsters, however chaotic the world, the parents often lose confidence in their ability and their right to guide, and as a result the adolescents lose their most vital island of security and enduring reality.

A unique aspect of today's social change is the shifting and realigning of sex roles and the blurring of previously clearer sex distinctions. No doubt some of this has been long overdue, though it is a transition susceptible to species-threatening misapplication. Whether an ultimate redefinition is predominantly more or less humane and realistic, it is an additional burden as well as a potential benefit to adolescents. Clear-cut distinctions, even when simplistic or false, make firmer anchoring places when one is lost in the sexual fog of adolescence.

The characteristics of white middle-class culture remain the most pervasive influences on adolescents, despite the infinitely more visible and widely reported exceptions, such as swinging singles, communes, group sex, and mate-swapping. Without attempting to judge ultimate effects, what are some of the more readily observable consequences to early adolescents who experience their first years of an adult level of sex drive in this particular kind of cultural milieu?

One is that there is no emotional and behavioral sexual route open to adolescents that does not incur a culturally induced burden. I am not alluding to any of the probably innate maturational conflicts that might be expected, even if only in small degree, to accompany the major life cycle event of puberty, but to those added, like a surtax, by the culture. To whatever extent a youngster has been molded by middle-class values, he is "damned if he does and damned if he doesn't." There is the double burden of attempting to suppress his increasingly urgent sexual desires and the weight of guilt when he almost inevitably fails to do so. Where the attitudes of middle-class culture have determined a child's rearing, they make healthy adolescent use of any sexual outlet very nearly impossible. This is equally true of masturbation and sexual intimacies with the opposite sex, no matter what the degree of appropriateness to the individual's age and level of emotional maturity.

The appearance many adolescents give of blithely living by their own codes, unaffected by the official mores, does not reflect reality. Perhaps the clearest evidence that so few have escaped the guilt, despite their denials, is the fact that the main reason adolescent girls give for purposely avoiding the use of contraception is that it would signify that their sexual activity is premeditated. They must rationalize their sexuality by regarding themselves as swept away by unexpected passion (even when being "swept away" has become a familiar experience). Guilt over recognizing their own sexuality paralyzes more rational decision making. The same loudly disclaimed guilt is still attached to masturbation. A number of years spent as consultant in sex education for a large school district has consistently revealed to me that by far the most difficult topic for adolescents to discuss is masturbation. It remains taboo and shameful even though young people can talk about other typical and even atypical sexual activity.

The unique configuration of cultural ground rules for sex that the early adolescent finds applied to him determines a predictable gamut of responses. Most numerous are the adolescents who do try to accept and comply with what they are taught, at least with regard to heterosexual activity. These are the ones who must cope with the guilt that attaches to their natural and inevitable failure to live up to their own standards. Among this group are those who continue their early erotic experimentation with same-sex peers, finding homoeroticism a lesser violation of conscience than heterosexuality. Also included is that particularly unfortunate group who totally repress *all* sexuality, including masturbation and the awareness of their urges. If they are successful in their repressive efforts, these youngsters always have difficulty adapting to adult sex roles, and they risk serious emotional disturbances since such massive repression is a symptom of abnormal emotional development.

Those who try to live relatively within society's dictates are surely the majority, particularly in early adolescence, and among them, those who run into obvious and serious difficulties are a small proportion. This overall group of youngsters forms a majority analogous to the large majority of adults who try to live up to the social consensus and for whom conformity in most matters is a virtue with tangible rewards. Such adolescents, even though they must struggle with their guilt-producing lapses, generally succeed adequately at both tasks. Most of them reach adulthood without obvious disturbance and without any conscious sense of deprivation or constriction. Whether they have paid a price of which they remain unaware will be a recurring theme as adolescence, and continuing adult psychosexuality, is discussed. This may seem to be a moot point if a person feels himself to be sexually satisfied and healthy, but unperceived sexual constrictions can contribute to less rewarding adult relationships and marriages, less effective parent-hood, and a less fulfilling later life.

In a second typical pattern fall those youngsters who seriously and sincerely question the traditional values and try to live by a different personal value system, one they consider both more appro-priate and more moral. The fortunate ones who were reared to be ready for such a degree of autonomy and to be capable of early development of nonexploitive relationships seem to be successful, but probably the majority underestimate the emotional power of their rearing and find themselves enmeshed in guilt after all. Be-cause they feel that their sincerity should protect them, they often do not recognize the guilt; instead, they are puzzled by all manner of disguised self-defeating manifestations, such as an inability to enjoy sex, difficulties in choosing appropriate partners and main-taining satisfying relationships, inexplicable underachievement at school, and the loss of interest in things they genuinely care about.

Because adolescents must usually fight adults for the right to some sexuality, their sexuality understandably becomes contami-nated with competitiveness. This contamination may endure and produce a disruptive element in all future alliances.

The dictum that sex and marriage go together "like a horse and carriage" is instrumental in many very early marriages, sometimes even in early adolescence. By such means, sex becomes available without guilt, but marriages on this basis are usually ill conceived and premature, because the multitude of other necessary considerations for an enduring partnership are either ignored or not even as yet available to the pair. In some instances, the couple remains socioeconomically dependent upon their families, often with disruptive consequences; in others, they withdraw from economic competition in a premature effort at self-sufficiency, a maneuver most likely to result in financial suicide and stultification of further educational and personality development.

Finally, there are the frank rebels, that most eye-catching minority, who openly repudiate the relevance of traditional standards to their life style, some of whom in the process deny the existence of any kind of conscience. In terms of emotional maturity, this group is a mixed bag, extending from some of the most disturbed adolescents to some of the strongest and most autonomous who somehow seem to make the rebellion work. At the most distressing end, it includes those who have in essence dropped out from the world, repudiating everything their culture stands for, without discrimination. Unless this is a very transient phase, or unless intervention is instituted successfully, these lost youngsters remain lost, fading eventually into the anonymous adult mass of the world's losers, hangers-on, and petty criminals.

At the other end of the rebel spectrum are healthy, intelligent youngsters (usually in late adolescence, although the rebellion sometimes begins to make itself evident earlier), perhaps ahead of their peers in some ways, who by no means are dropouts. They may fulfill exceptionally well many of society's expectations, accepting much of the implicit value system, but choose open rebellion against sexual restrictions. Their expressions of rebellion may sometimes assume interesting and amusing forms. In not keeping their sexuality secret, they are refusing to pretend to wait for adult society's blessings. If this group comprises even a reasonably sized minority, and if a significant proportion of them are functioning well at school and in other areas of typical adolescent activity, they effectively undermine the conventional adult assumption that sexually active teenagers are highly unusual and "sick." At other times the rebels make clever use of some of the cultural inconsistencies, turning them against the "establishment": for example, when they actually live according to the saying "make love, not war," outraged and disapproving adults are made to seem foolish and hypocritical.

However effective these rebels sometimes appear, their unconscious reasons for rebelling and their modes of rebellion may arise from grossly inappropriate perceptions and fantasies about sexuality, about their parents, and about social regulations. The passage of time may prove many of them to have been unable to manage their rebellion without damaging consequences. It cannot yet be known, however, whether early adolescent sexual activity, regardless of its motives, is intrinsically damaging. It is not possible, from the standpoint of mental health, to disapprove of the rebels totally. Some of the successful, healthy, impatient adolescents even seem to benefit from their sexual experiences. In some instances they have shown a more than usually mature awareness of genuine cultural inconsistencies and an earlier than usual capacity for autonomous decision making.

The institutions of white middle-class culture do not provide any approved and encouraged avenues for adolescents gradually and appropriately to join and become part of adult culture with its adult sexual prerogatives *while they are still adolescents* and therefore still have much to learn from adults. Such a gap totally ignores the essentially adult bodies, sex drives, and sex needs of adolescents. A result, extending far beyond its purely sexual consequences, is to help drive adolescents into an oppositional, resentful group position, further isolating them in their peer groups, and unnecessarily intensifying the polarization between the generations. Adolescent peer group formation is a natural transitional stage in maturation, but instead of easing their eventual acceptance of the value of working within adult culture, and easing the bridge to adulthood, this particular characteristic fosters opposition. It helps to create an "us against them" coalition among adolescents and erects additional obstacles to communication.

Puberty is always a time of physiological turmoil. Culture plays a determining role in whether, and to what degree, it is a time of psychological and social crisis. Even without value judgments about its long-range benefits or damages, it is clear that the particular idiosyncrasies of our culture make of adolescence a period of considerable stress.

Neither Child nor Adult

The physiological events that signal early adolescence do not produce sudden behavioral transformations, though menarche usually has some fairly dramatic and rapidly occurring sequelae. Preadolescent behavior and personality changes continue with markedly greater intensity. New qualities also become manifest under pressure from the dominant theme of early adolescence—disengagement. The many aspects of beginning to find an appropriate adult identity and of becoming adapted to an adult physical self require at least a temporary disengagement from the past. Unless he is to perpetuate his childhood into adulthood, the adolescent must disengage himself from earlier attachments and values and attitudes sufficiently to reevaluate their applicability to his real self in the real world in which he must function. His parents and his culture may facilitate or hinder this process, but it is a time of stress and pain, joy and creativity, in any culture that provides him with the alternatives to become different from his elders.

Early adolescents continue to show frequent regressive behavior, which continues to be more typical of boys than girls. They are characterized by unpredictable wide mood swings from euphoria to seemingly suicidal depression—a painful intensity of transient and shallow emotions. Their unpredictability and experimental behavior extends in all directions. This is accompanied, and to some extent impelled, by an increased sensitivity of their sensory organs, more intense perceptions of their emotions and sensations, and the newly available mental capacity for abstract thought. This latter maturational step is not normally available until adolescence, and unfortunately does not always develop even then.

The development of the capacity to think in ever more logical, complex, and abstract ways, called cognitive development, depends upon a variety of fortuitous maturational circumstances throughout childhood, including good nutrition and physical health, and emotional and educational influences. Though the increasing levels of cognitive development unfold in a logical and unvarying sequence, it is not inevitable that everyone achieves the highest cognitive level. Some studies have shown that nearly 50 percent of the people of the United States never achieve the ability to use abstract thought.[11] When adolescents do achieve it, it precipitates them into recurring preoccupations with ideals, morals, values, and the meaning of life.

There is a great surge of physical energy, perhaps related in ways that are not well understood, to pubertal endocrinology. When cultural stereotypes do not distort its manifestations, the increased energy is seen in both sexes, though the expressions may not be identical. Aggressive drives are also increased and push for expression in action and activity. Various sports, some determined by sex appropriateness, are vigorously pursued. Social activities that more often seem to interest girls than boys may be more physically taxing than a boxing match. This penchant for physical action may sometimes backfire. Successful adolescence entails struggles with conflicts and anxieties that can only be resolved appropriately on the mental and emotional level. Compulsive and impulsive activity can be used to avoid confronting essential issues.

Bodily preoccupation reaches its normal peak at this time. It is related to both inner sensations and external changes and focuses not only on sexual organs and characteristics but upon every conceivable manifestation of size, shape, and proportion, on complexion, hair style and grooming, on clothing, fashion, adornment and, cosmetics, as well as on bodily function. Early adolescents are notorious hypochondriacs, not only because of their general preoccupation with their body and its mysterious workings but as a result of continuing unconscious fantasies about such problems as sexual vulnerability and masturbatory consequences.

Boy-girl differences noticeable in preadolescence continue and in some ways increase. Because this is the period of maximum maturational disjunction between typical age-mates of the opposite sex, girls can be expected to be more openly heterosocial, and boys can be expected to insulate themselves more defensively in all-male gangs. Heterosocial as well as heterosexual activity increases as sexual identity becomes more secure and acceptance by the opposite sex more confidently anticipated. Late pubescence continues to pose social problems for boys, and now for girls as well. By seventh or eighth grade, early maturing girls have begun to equal and surpass the later maturers in peer popularity and prestige.[12]

Some of the most dramatic manifestations of early adolescence derive from the necessity to begin the final individuation from one's parents. This is a predominantly healthy and positive movement, necessary for optimum self-actualization, but the characteristics of our culture not only intensify the struggle, but make the process a more painful and hostile one for both generations.

This process of adolescent disengagement, individuation, and rapprochement with parents and the past is similar to the stages a toddler goes through when he first walks and must begin to trust himself to leave his mother's immediate presence, feels confident to move about on his own and out of her sight, and then is able to return to her because he wants to, rather than because he is afraid to be away from her. Except that now, in early adolescence, the recapitulation that begins is an enormously complex and multifaceted process that takes place in the real world with real adult consequences, and eventuates in real adult independence, often with permanent separation. At this time the process is emotionally fired by both progressive and regressive motives. The normal adolescent has a strong drive toward increasing independence and self-determination; at the same time he hears the siren call of enticing but threatening continued dependency, and, most imperatively, the revived oedipal drives now operate with adult intensity in an adultlike body. Because of the solely parental focus built into our adolescents, these emotions may be intolerable, especially for boys, and adolescents will employ any methods available, however crude and inconsiderate, to put an end to them. Early adolescents run toward some things and away from others in desperately ambivalent efforts at independence. The multiple sources of emotional fuel that propel an adolescent make it easy to understand why he so often seems to demand an autonomy for which he is unready and which reaches almost comically beyond his capacities.

Perhaps most difficult for parents to tolerate with patience and minimally bruised egos is one of the early adolescent's favorite techniques for distancing himself from his "threatening" parents— that of derogating them. This is an essentially "sour grapes" maneuver in which that which is desired but unattainable is rationalized as being unworthy of desiring. All of a sudden, neither a mother nor a father can do anything right. They are both unspeakably dense and humiliatingly square, incapable of understanding anything at all of the youngter's feelings, aspirations, friends, problems, or life style. Previously delightful family jokes become gauche and embarrassing, attempts at affection may be met with a literal shudder of revulsion, and even idiosyncrasies of speech become a major breach of taste.

Adding to the parents' discomfort is his new and sometimes accurate weapon, abstract thought. If he acquires the capacity for it and becomes fascinated with ideals and values, he also acquires the heady ability to perceive with growing accuracy some of the culture's contradictions, double messages, and arbitrariness. Since his parents almost inevitably reflect and perpetuate some of the cultural imperfections—who can escape being caught in some of them?—he draws an exultant bead upon his hapless targets. When his humanly fallible parents have contributed some of their natural uncertainty and confusion—as, for example, when their behavior differs from their professed standards—he feels inwardly triumphant. He now has something real to complain about, and can displace all his inner turmoil onto external realities. These realities may have little to do with what is really troubling him, but when neither he nor his parents recognize the displacement, they can be drawn into endless and unproductive conflict.

Early adolescent rebellion is at first mainly verbal, because carrying out real independent action is still too risky. By the end of this phase, as the teenager has become more confident and as he has learned in spite of himself that his abominable parents actually foster his growing self-reliance, the rebellion is more often tried out in action.

The wide mood swings of this period are closely related to adolescents' ambivalent detachment from their parents. The repudiation of a parent, while grossly exaggerated, is nonetheless real. It entails a real loss, because never again will an adolescent's relationship with those parents be the same. Adolescent depression is akin to mourning for the lost nurturing parent of childhood, but this feeling is difficult to sustain unless the childhood has been very traumatic, and through much of early adolescence there is oscillation between disdainful withdrawal and impulsive affection, reminiscent of late childhood. The same sixteen-year-old-boy who made a ghastly scene at the dinner table over the unavailability of the family car, may that very night ask his mother to put a Band-Aid on some minor scratch and show affectionate gratitude to her for doing so.

Distancing oneself from parents leaves a void that must be filled.

One way of filling it is to turn to the peer group, probably one of the most easily recognized patterns characteristic of this phase. The peer group not only provides support and a set of values to replace those of the abandoned parents but provides a sense of belonging, enhanced by the pressing need to be like everyone else. It serves as a valuable source in the young person's effort to know himself in all of his shared and unique qualities; by comparing himself and his reactions with his friends, he is reassured that many of his puzzling feelings are quite normal and acceptable, and he also begins to perceive those ways in which he is a unique individual.

Another effort to fill the parental void is to substitute other adults—teachers, famous personages, the parents of friends—in their place. At some mental level, often consciously, early adolescents know full well that they are not prepared for the hard reality of self-sufficiency and that they still need guidance and limits. Some adolescents' most bitter resentment against parents is that they did not continue to function with an appropriate degree of authority and responsibility, despite the adolescents' noisy objections. Since inner conflicts make it difficult to accept the parents' help, adolescents turn to other adults who are not contaminated by childhood memories and oedipal fantasies.

Even these attachments are ambivalent, however. There is some association between a parent and any adult of parental age, and therefore the latter are not immune from stirring up oedipal conflicts. Perhaps even more important, the young adolescent's identity is amorphous and shaky, and the very qualities that are likely to attract him to another adult—self-confidence, effective function in important areas of his life, a secure sense of who he is and what he is doing—may also be felt as a threat. The adolescent, determined to shed the expectations of others and to find his own individuality, is afraid to come too closely or too long under the influence of someone with an ego that is so much stronger than his own. He is often afraid that he will end up being like this other person, not like his still undetermined self. Acting upon this fear of identity capture, he may suddenly break off a warm relationship. Many an adult has been left puzzled and hurt, wondering if he did something to offend an adolescent.

Having at least temporarily forsaken his parents and their values as models, the young adolescent seems to start afresh looking for

other and different models for identification. In searching for what
he is like, and what fits him, he tries identifying with a wide and
often motley variety of incompatible types. Considering again the
wide mood fluctuations, depression can reflect the loss of any
important object of love and identification, though the most intense
mourning reactions are usually related to parental disengagement.
Likewise, euphoric periods attend the finding of new love objects,
which need not be sexual objects.

A most important psychological process that is facilitated
throughout all the turmoil is the eventual shift from superego to
conscience. The youngster enters early adolescence with a superego
that is still largely childlike. Though his early school years were
accompanied by a limited opportunity to reevaluate his parents and
see them as more human, imperfect beings, they normally remain
supreme in a reasonably healthy, intact family. They are not quite
the gods they once were, but their authority is generally unquestioned, and the superego, composed as it is of highly oversimplified
parental prohibitions and values, is not much modified.

A successful adolescence changes this. Though only begun in
early adolescence, the disengagement from parental models and
values is necessary in order for an adolescent to be able to bring his
own judgment to bear upon the things that he was taught were right
or wrong, good or bad, valuable or worthless. This is no mere formal
exercise, because the world changes, cultures can promote some
amazingly wrongheaded attitudes, and the values of parents may
sometimes be inappropriate. It is equally true that values inculcated
early may be solid and constructive, able to withstand objective
scrutiny. This shift from values imposed by others to self-deter-
mined values is primarily a late adolescent process, but the stressful
loosening of parental ties is its early adolescent prerequisite.

Along with recognition of the many steps toward maturity made
by these youngsters, some cognizance must be taken of their glaring
immaturities. Their frequent oscillations between defiance and
dependency is one obvious, though minor, example.

The capacity for abstract thought, unaccompanied by either
wisdom or experience, leaves adolescents prone to gross oversimpli-
fications and black-or-white judgments. Their criticism of adults is
untempered by any recognition of the inapplicability of sweepingly

simple—indeed, magical—solutions. Lacking the dimension conferred by experience, they often refuse to grant its importance.

Their narcissistic self-preoccupation further cripples their objectivity and judgment. The internal and external changes and consequences of puberty overwhelm their minds and usurp their attention. The intrapsychic infantile and oedipal conflicts centering upon their parents blind them to all but the need to detach themselves, and they lose sight, at least temporarily, of the realities of the parental relationship. These preeminent psychodynamic influences cause them to withdraw their focus of attention from the real external world and into their inner world of intrapsychic concerns. One must be sharply and objectively aware of the real world in order for one's ego to function at its best. The emotional withdrawal into self in early adolescence produces a period of impoverishment of ego capacities and results in poor reality testing. Inevitably, there is a compromised ability to assess cause and effect or to judge the long-range consequences of behavior, a predominance of impulsive action and short-range thinking, the inability to perceive oneself accurately in relationships with others, and an insensitivity to the reality and needs of others—in general, defective judgment.[13] All these deficiencies, however maddening, are normal and hopefully transient manifestations.

The Selfish Experimenters

Although it is not entirely just to label all early adolescents as selfish, it is true that most of them are too busy discovering themselves to have much emotional energy left over for anyone else—even when one is in the throes of over-romanticized infatuation and insists he would die (like Romeo or Juliet) for his love. The exceptions to this narcissism are just that—exceptions.

This discussion will compare those who are roughly at equivalent stages of psychosexual development regardless of their ages. This means a two- to three-year average age difference between girls and boys. This discrepancy in age obviously poses a serious dilemma for the average girl. Common sense dictates, and research has corroborated, that postpubescent girls have distinctly different, more mature, and more heterosexually oriented interests than boys of the same age. Boy companions who would both interest them and be at a comparable stage of muturity are usually two or three years older, perhaps in senior high while the girls are still in junior high. But to many parents, dating "older boys" conjures up lurid fantasies of smooth-operating sexual predators—a complete misunderstanding that is the ground of many a family battle.

Despite the increasing sex drive and heterosexual interest, the major sexual outlet of early adolescents is masturbation. In terms of frequency, other forms of sexual activity are minimal. Most studies show that boys masturbate more than girls, but there is little agreement as to why. In all likelihood, traditionally greater sexual freedom generally accorded boys, despite the overall prohibitive stance, plays a major role. The disparity would probably narrow were sexuality as (relatively) condoned for girls, and the little specific cross-cultural data available lends support to this observation; but there are intrapsychic male and female differences that also give different meanings to masturbation, and the observed differences are probably a combination of various insufficiently understood factors.

Because adolescents find it more difficult to discuss masturbation than any other sexual topic, the figures, regardless of source, are highly suspect. Depending upon the study, the percentage of boys with masturbatory experience by the end of early adolescence varies from 43 percent[14] to 90 percent[15] to over 98 percent.[16] For girls, comparable figures in two studies are approximately 25 percent[17] and 36 percent.[18] Personal contacts with adolescents lead me to believe that the higher figures for boys are more accurate, and that both of the quoted figures for girls are somewhat low. What is important is that masturbation is the chief sexual expression, and that its frequency varies enormously from time to time and from youngster to youngster.

During these years there also develops a great deal of heterosexual sex play short of intercourse. Figures here, even if of any value, are hard to come by, because the kind of behavior is so varied. One study, using age rather than maturational categories, suggests that 30 to 50 percent of early adolescents involve themselves in this kind of sex play, which includes kissing, all manner of physical contact and embracing, fondling of breasts and male and female genitalia either clothed or unclothed, and petting to orgasm. This kind of sexual activity does not usually continue over a long span of time for most adolescents. Once serious sex play begins, it tends rather soon to progress to intercourse.[19]

Heterosexual play of this sort is very hesitantly begun. In our culture, there is a great deal to overcome, especially for boys, before they take the risk of exposing their ineptness and inexperience, and also risk incurring ego-shattering rejection. Returning to the sexual traits of the culture in which middle-class adolescents have grown up, it is not surprising that it requires considerable time for them to become openly sexual—to get rid of the long-entrenched sexual repressions and all the oedipal and infantile anxiety-producing and guilt-laden fantasies.

While the popular stereotype places boys in the role of aggressor, this is frequently not true. It may fit situations involving boys who are already experienced enough to feel some security and to have learned they can withstand some rejection and failure, but it does not typically hold true for inexperienced boys, or for sex play arising in mixed groups that are determined by age equality, such as school classes and class-oriented social activities. Pairs that form out of these very common groupings usually find the girl, naturally, both more sexually mature and less heterosexually apprehensive. As a result, girls may often be the instigators of these earliest heterosexual experimentations.

Early adolescents—in numbers surprising to many parents—also experiment with intercourse. Here, it would be either useless or endless to try to give accurate estimates of the number of early adolescents who have already become coitally active. Despite the large number of surveys attempted, each has tapped a different kind of population and it is possible to find published statistics that seemingly support any preexisting opinion. In one study of conservative white middle-class high school boys, only 10 percent had had intercourse by the time they left high school.[20] In another, twenty years earlier, of a different group of suburban middle-class white boys, 26 percent had already attempted intercourse by age eleven.[21] Both studies were probably accurate. One can only assume that there are unexpectedly large peer group differences.

The age at which active intercourse begins, as well as its frequency, has been found to be influenced not only by the broad cultural variables already detailed, but by such disparate variables as degree of religious affiliation, socioeconomic level, urban or rural environment, ethnic subculture, age at reaching puberty, and educational level. A study of a statistically representative cross section of United States adolescents reports that 37 percent of those aged thirteen through fifteen have experienced intercourse. Even though this means of dividing the sample would not include most early adolescent boys (to do so, it would have to include sixteen- and seventeen-year-olds), 44 percent of the boys and 30 percent of the girls in this age range had experienced intercourse.[22]

There are two reasons for this excursion into the tangled maze of sexual statistics. One is to caution the reader to beware of any dogmatic pronouncements "proved" by a set of statistics that either proclaim or deny the existence of a "sexual revolution." When all the available studies are carefully evaluated, the overall impression is that there is some increase in adolescent intercourse, especially among girls, and some lowering of the average age at first experience,[23] the increase is not great enough to justify so dramatic a term as revolution. The second reason is to dispel any notion that early adolescent intercourse is rare. However divergent the findings, the consensus of those that are representative, rather than being derived from limited groups, is that intercourse among younger teenagers is *not* rare, and any knowledgeable approach to adolescent psychosexual development must keep this in mind.

Early teenage pregnancy is also not rare, as all junior and senior high school personnel know. Pregnancy in early adolescence is almost always emotionally damaging, and almost sure to be disastrous if carried to term. It must be regarded as a problem, regardless of its resulting from what might be considered normal experimentation.

Homoerotic play remains a major source of self-exploration and sexual gratification because our culture makes heterosexual experimentation the most anxiety-producing of all available routes of sexual expression. Since the biological push for sexual activity outstrips heterosexual readiness in most youngsters, those youngsters who are not too guilty or anxious to find some release will find it wherever it is safest and most available. For many youngsters, this remains homoerotic through at least the early part of this period of adolescence, and regardless of what this fact may imply about our culture itself, it is a fact that homoerotic play arising out of this motivational background hardly ever has prognostic significance in terms of adult sexual preference. While it may be making the best out of the kind of cultural pathogenicity the youngster is stuck with, it also serves some useful purposes.

Early adolescents are frequently preoccupied with and apprehensive about their body changes, anatomical differences, ejaculation, menstruation, masturbation—anything to do with this pleasureful, guilt-ridden, scary-exhilarating part of the self. Sexual activity among boys is usually mutual masturbation, or even merely self-masturbation in a group, but it may also include oral-genital and anal-genital activity. Among girls there is breast fondling and kissing, mutual clitoral masturbation, and the insertion of various objects, both for exploratory and erotic purposes, in the vagina and occasionally the anus. "Play-acting" the typical male-female roles and positions of intercourse is common, but penis substitutes (dildoes) are seldom used. Sexual experimentation with peers of the same sex can be enormously reassuring of one's normality and of the shared nature of both sensations and concerns.[24] If it were not for the heavy taboo we place on the expression of all physical affection between members of the same sex, especially males and regardless of whether or not it is sexual, this "normal" homoerotic period could lay the foundation for an acceptance of warmth and tenderness between adults of the same sex that is too rarely encountered.

Where possible, these group explorations of sexuality might achieve even greater sexual self-acceptance and assurance if the groups include both sexes. In my clinical experience I have found this to occur with beneficial results. Acceptance of, and by, the opposite sex occurs more readily in groups with less conflict. But in our culture, one is forced to regard preadolescent and early adolescent homoerotic experimentation as a normal way station, occupied by a considerable proportion of youngsters for shorter or longer periods, along the route to normal adult heterosexuality.

In this highly driven and heavily repressed period of life, it should not be surprising that sex involving animals continues to be fairly common, especially among boys. The same activities described for preadolescents are indulged in. Both boys and girls sometimes pursue their curiosities by masturbating their pets—mainly dogs— who are more often than not thoroughly bored. Some girls encourage exploration of their genitals by pets, but it is very rare for such exploration to become more than a desultory licking or at most a slightly different form of masturbation. Perhaps it is the difficulty a girl has in cross-species sexual pursuits that accounts for the small incidence of reported experience—3.8 percent.[25]

Among boys, however, the experimentation is often quite active, especially among farm-reared boys. Kinsey found that 17 percent of all rural boys had some sexual contact with animals resulting in orgasm, and as many as 40 to 50 percent had sexual contact with or without orgasm. Only 4 percent of urban boys report this, and only during visits to the country. The incidence is not as high as in the preadolescent years, and varies widely according to area and to educational level—the higher the level, the higher the incidence of animal contact.[26] Such contact most typically involves penile insertion in the vagina of a domestic animal.

Throughout these years, and progressing along with heterosexual experimentation, heterosocial interaction is also moving forward. The preadolescent kept his positive heterosocial responses largely hidden under a mask of cross-sex avoidance in public. Early adolescence is the main period of transition in this dimension of sexual development. During these three or four years, the public social ostracism breaks down; gradually it becomes more acceptable not only to be seen with someone of the opposite sex, but to prefer to be with a partner of the opposite sex and even to proclaim members of the opposite sex as among one's best friends.[27] Group dating becomes very common, then groups of pairs and double dating, and some youngsters begin to go steady. In fact, one criterion of the end of early adolescence is the establishment of the heterosexual dating pattern.

A major characteristic of the overt sexual behavior of early adolescents is its ineptness. Not only are most early adolescents, by definition, grossly inexperienced, but they are also afraid, usually guilty, perhaps desperately importunate, and lost in the flood of their own emotions and sensations. Even when they want to be considerate, there is little emotional energy left to devote to practicing the art of love. There are exceptions and "quick studies," and adolescents do begin to learn with practice, but there are few good lovers among them.

Even more fascinating than the budding sexual behavior of adolescents are the hidden, intrapsychic, and unconscious shifts,

changes, and developments that are taking place, and the enormously important tasks in the course of becoming fully human that
are being quietly carried on out of sight. It is not a smooth process,
but even when all that shows is tumult and obstreperousness, normal conflicts are being resolved and psychic progress is being made.

Some of these growth tasks are simply human, that is, they are
part of the necessary growing up shared by both sexes, such as
further major solidification of one's sexual identity, which includes
learning to accept the *differences* in the identity of the opposite sex.
After all the layers of tradition and false stereotyping are stripped
away, there remain essential ways in which males and females feel
and respond differently. Knowing, respecting, and valuing these
differences is an indispensable part of one's own sense of self as a
man or woman. But in this early phase self comes first. Though a
youngster may be pouring out his tender concern in reams of bad
poetry, the important questions inside are, "What does it *feel* like
to . . . ?" "What will happen to *me* if I . . . ?"

Accompanying all this is a voracious sexual curiosity, the
satisfaction of which is crucial to normal psychosexual development.
Even the crudest and most tasteless of explicit sexual pictures,
stories, and movies—so-called pornography—is used in this quest.
This is not the appropriate forum for considering the complexities of
the pornography issue, but it is directly to the point that the
President's Commission on Obscenity and Pornography found
unequivocally that sex offenders had less experience with erotica as
adolescents than is typical of the general population or nonoffen-
der.[28] This is not an endorsement of pornography but an indication
that the satisfaction of sexual curiosity is necessary and beneficial
and that even means which would be considered offensive to many
people can be used constructively toward this end.

Learning to be in love is not easy. Love is as risky as it is
enriching, in that one hands over a considerable part of his sense of
well-being to another person. To let another person into the self is
to feel strong enough to be vulnerable and to believe that one can
recover if the alliance fails. To care is to risk loss and rejection. At
least the readiness for such risking should be achieved in early
adolescence, and the transience of self-preoccupied young teen
pairs gives a lot of painful practice in learning to continue valuing
oneself despite repeated hurts.

Boys and girls alike must learn to incorporate their new, sexually adult bodies into their general body image and sense of self. Tight, exhibitionistic clothing alternates with loose garments in which sex is virtually indistinguishable as youngsters struggle with their ambivalence. At the same time, bodies that somehow fail to conform to the current standards of sexual attractiveness can be a source of personal despair, social withdrawal, and emotional illness.

At times, the integration of this new body image can be made more difficult because of the simple fact that the disturbing oedipal fantasies are no longer childs' play—they could perhaps be realized in actual behavior. A sixteen-year-old son may be bigger and stronger than the "rival" father; a sixteen-year-old girl may be more sparklingly attractive, at least on the visible surface, than her mother. Compounding this dilemma is the fact that it is in early adolescence that oedipal wishes are most likely to become shockingly conscious under the impact of the mushrooming sexual drive that catches the youngster's ego by surprise. Thoughts that at other times would be repressed from conscious awareness burst through the repressive barriers in frank incestuous dreams and conscious incestuous fantasies. These wishes may complicate the acceptance of oneself as an attractive sexual being, and, still more, acceptance that it is *good* to be so.

A strenuous intrapsychic task necessary in becoming a healthily functioning sexual adult is learning to identify with one's parents as sexually functioning people. This may sound easy, but the internal shifts and reperceptions required are formidable. In teaching about the tasks involved in shifting from child to sexual adult and the added complications caused by the oedipal dilemma in coming to comfortable terms with one's personal and parental sexual equality, I can always bring the point home with two simple questions. I ask how many are thoroughly uninhibited about making love in the same house with their parents and knowing that their parents know they are doing so. And I ask how many can literally visualize their parents naked and having intercourse. Many people find the first situation very difficult, and the second is too much for almost anyone from our typical middle class; in fact, it arouses so much anxiety that many people simply cannot focus their minds upon it.

This new *sexual* identification with parents involves realignments within almost the total psychic structure. It requires humanizing parents rather than seeing them as godlike creatures who never indulge in activities the child has been led to believe are bad. And to humanize parents, they must be "forgiven" for whatever sexual deceptions and false teachings they may have perpetrated in their usually well-meaning efforts to rear a "good, moral child." Comfort with parental sexuality means enough comfort with one's own peer sexual relations so that sexually active parents do not stir unbearable oedipal desires. Ultimately, more so in later adolescence, it demands the security to allow loosening of both the ego and the superego. The ego must be loosened and expanded to permit behavior previously kept under stricter control, and the superego must relax its early childhood inflexible prohibitions to permit both a more rational reassessment of one's parents and more autonomy in evolving personal value systems.[29]

Inner perceptions of and emotions about parents are typically ambivalent. At the age of five, a girl's resentful perception of her mother as a "bad, mean, sexual woman" who keeps the father for herself becomes an indelible portion of her unconscious store of emotions about her mother. In adolescence such feelings must change radically if that girl is to consider her own future female sexuality, marriage, and maternity as good. At every turn there are obstacles fabricated by unnecessary discontinuities in child rearing, making it necessary to unlearn much in order to leave unconstructive childhood attitudes behind. Furthermore, it is important to remember that children not reared in primal scene cultures need special training to learn to accept sexuality as a natural part of all human life.

Both sexes—boys, especially—have to learn to separate sex from aggression, especially violent aggression. All the inner drives are strengthened at puberty, and it is easy for them to flow into and contaminate one another. One must remember that this potential mixture of generally incompatible drives does not arise at puberty in emotionally virgin soil: throughout childhood perfectly normal sexuality is repeatedly misperceived as violent, and a considerable number of youngsters grow up in disturbed families in which the hurtful or even violent use of sex is not a misperception. Early adolescence is the time to begin learning to separate inner drives so that they are expressed toward appropriately different objects. In what is naturally a slow process, this intrapsychic confusion of drives adds another source to the conspicuous lack of tenderness— indeed the crudity and roughness—in so much heterosexual activity. The fusion of drives does not operate in only one direction, as evidenced by the frequency with which an erection will occur in boys who are wrestling without any homoerotic component to their physical contact.

Along with other reasons for the increase of homoerotic activity in preadolescence and early adolescence, there is some suggestion that identification with the opposite sex is heightened at this time both by the normal regression to developmental periods when such identifications were fairly characteristic, and by the fact that it is only as early adolescence gets well underway that male and female hormones begin to differentiate sharply.[30] It is fascinating to speculate where, in this constellation of behaviors, the phenomenon of "unisex" fits. There are familiar and probably valid sociopsychological explanations that relate it to such factors as youthful rebellion against parental expectations in general and against sexual stereotyping in particular. A blurring of sex roles goes on in the adult culture as well. The fact that the early adolescent effort to blur sexual distinctions is not a ubiquitous phenomenon in other cultures and other ages makes it clear that some universal psychodynamic determinant is not likely to be found.

But there is a seldom discussed intrapsychic concern, more or less characteristic of this phase, that may add its weight to the particular unisex feature once it has been engendered by other determinants. That is the early adolescent's preoccupation with death, immortality, soul, afterlife, and other aspects of his own personal mortality. In a number of young people studied in depth, there existed the fantasy that if one could somehow be both sexes rolled up in one, then immortality would become available. Unisex would allow for a magical self-regeneration which neither required another person nor inevitably ended in personal death. In these youngsters the unisex look was a symbolic expression of this fantasy. This wish is both reminiscent of, and closely tied in with, the little boy's womb envy, in which he deeply envied his mother's ability to create life, and the little girl's fantasy that equated a baby inside with her own hidden penis. Both instances show early wishes to be capable of both functions.[31]

The early adolescent is caught off guard by the relative suddenness of the sexual drives of puberty. Anna Freud described this situation succinctly in psychoanalytic language: "a relatively strong id confronts a relatively weak ego." [32] The anxiety prompted by such a situation reflects the inner fear that one will be overwhelmed by the power of his biological drives and lose all rational and social control. Some of the typical behavior is partly defense against this kind of fear, such as the derogation of elders and distancing oneself from parents.

Other defenses are quite typical of early adolescence, such as asceticism. Everyone is familiar with adolescents who massively try to deny the existence of all drives, sexual and aggressive, and for a period try to live almost a monkish or cloistered life. In most instances, the effort at total denial fails and the youngster may swing to the opposite extreme of impulsive gratification, or may return to more normal and less excessive adolescent behavior, or may feel pressed to find some more effective defense.

One then often sees a second characteristic defense against drive strength—intellectualization, an attempt to avoid acting through obsessive thinking, preoccupation with abstruse philosophical considerations, and endless talking about highly abstract matters.[33] There is a driven quality about such intellectualization that differentiates it from the relatively conflict-free exercise of a good mind and healthy curiosity by an adolescent who is also allowing himself to experience and cope with basic drives.

Masturbation fantasies reveal typical sex-specific differences, but a task that both sexes share is to cope with the anxiety some of those fantasies arouse. As noted, oedipal wishes are close to the surface, and often emerge during masturbation. Contamination of sexuality with violence gives rise to grossly violent fantasies involving rape, torture, beating, murder, rendering victims helpless. Though it is normal, at least in our culture, to find sex and violent aggression not yet separate in the unconscious perceptions of early adolescents, the deeds these fantasies depict would be ghastly if acted out, and frequently arouse guilt. Contrariwise, rape fantasies often serve a special guilt-relieving function for girls by removing the element of willing participation from their imagined activity.

Even the more "normal" adolescent masturbatory fantasies are often lurid testimonies to genital preoccupations and wishes for superhuman sexual prowess. There are visions of an endless variety of magnificent men or gorgeous beauty queens, orgies involving crowds engaged in every imaginable sexual act, feats of sexual athleticism that leave countless partners in exhausted ecstasy. It is probably accurate to regard hard-core pornography as the literal expression of adolescent masturbatory fantasies.

As always, each sex has its unique developmental tasks. For girls, many of these tasks are closely related to menarche and the subsequent menstrual cycle and predictable menstrual flow. It has been suggested that menarche functions as a biologically imposed puberty rite.[34] Menstruation acts as an organizer of women's emotional and biological life. It is especially important in helping a woman integrate and accept her inner genitality. All the diffuse and unpredictable inner sensations she has had while growing up, and which intensified and disorganized her during preadolescence, now have a concrete focus. All the aspects of menstruation, most especially its regular predictability and the flow itself, help a girl finally to define and "know" her inner genitalia. Even the cramping, when normal and not excessive or severe, aids the development of a secure body image that could never before be fully integrated.

Reflections of the organizing and integrating effects of menstruation may be seen in numerous areas of the typical adolescent girl's personality. The scattered quality of the preadolescent's mental and emotional function, her unpredictable restless and complaining lability, her difficulties in concentration—all start slowly to settle down. Her verbal expressions become intelligible and it may be possible to get a coherent answer to a simple question. Mother-daughter conflicts may continue but they are of a different order, and the girl can often be clearly articulate about their causes, whether or not they are objectively valid.[35]

Typical feminine characteristics are fostered and show themselves more firmly following the healthy integration of a girl's inner sexuality and its undeniable implications for her future sexual function. She *knows*—Zero Population Growth, dissatisfaction with today's world, and feminist disenchantment with masculine stereotypes notwithstanding—that her biological destiny is to create and enfold and nurture a new life. And she *knows*—sperm banks, eugenic artificial insemination, and fantasies of relegating males to stud service also notwithstanding—that it requires the complementarity of a man to fulfill her destiny in its most deeply rewarding sense. As part of this inner knowledge, and in the interest of the most effective maternal function, girls typically become more settled than boys and are generally more conservative. Their long having to cope with their less definable inner sexuality has prepared them to use their intuition more effectively. The repeated experience of menstruation, even when *not* seriously uncomfortable, is instrumental in a greater capacity to tolerate pain, and contributes to the frequently repeated observation that women often function better than men in stressful emergencies. And girls begin to look toward males with an eye toward total, not merely genital fulfillment, though in early adolescence the purely genital needs may overshadow broader needs that must be considered characteristic of mature adulthood.

As one examines closely the intrapsychic dynamics of adolescent girls, it is easier than ever to trace the continuity that exists throughout each sex's psychosexual development. When the resolution of the oedipus complex was detailed, it was possible to see inexorably being laid down the precursors of the source of women's most characteristic intrapsychic sexual anxiety—the lack or loss of love. Tracing now the influence of her adult menstruating body upon her sense of her role and her needs, those early intimations begin to find full expression.

Many girls have fears of performance, too, as peer pressure mounts to denigrate virginity, and girls may seek through sexual activity to prove their liberated equality rather than to express their natural readiness. Some fear success as well as failure as sexual objects if community pressure and their guilt combine to punish them for being sexual. Community and peer pressures vary, however, and are not inherent—and girls can fake performance if need be. For those who are not so defensive as to deny the man-woman reciprocity essential for optimal fulfillment, adolescence is the time when the innate feminine anxiety over attracting and holding a man becomes intensely felt and starts to play a determining role in a woman's entire life style.

Menarche only initiates this integration and organization, which is not nearly completed even by the end of early adolescence, and menarche is not the only organizing force by far. The mother is a most important "organizer" of a girl's womanhood, despite the ambivalence of their relationship. The mother remains the important model she has always been; her emotional "style," her ways of functioning and coping, her female self-esteem, can facilitate or defeat her daughter's access to healthy womanhood. It has already been pointed out that poor or negative preparation for menarche is correlated with increased menstrual disturbances.

Many girls masturbate, usually clitorally, and probably more and more will do so as the sexual double standard continues to decline in importance. Masturbation operates, especially in adolescence, to aid in gaining a sense of mastery of sexual sensations and a knowledge of one's own body. The ability to initiate, predict, and control sexual arousal, and the physiological participation of inner as well as outer sex organs in orgastic release, joins with menstruation in bringing about a clearer and more anxiety-free sexual body image.

Masturbation by early adolescent boys serves many of the same developmental ends that, in girls, are served by both menarche and masturbation. Unfortunately, masturbation is not as naturally adapted to serve all those tasks as effectively. In its usefulness in securing a boy's sense of body mastery, the unique anatomical and physiological characteristics of his penis probably make that easier for him. The repetitive and controllable quality of stimulation, arousal, orgasm, and tension release are accompanied by easily visible effects and may therefore be more reassuring. The fact that nothing calamitous happens to the precious organ, and that it always remains available for the same pleasure, is a reality that eventually resolves infantile castration fears and is a source of increasing ego development and self-esteem as a boy cements his sexual identity and learns to master his sex drive.

Ejaculation and associated accompaniments of orgasm are another matter. When masturbation is as guilt-ridden as it so often is, ejaculation can arouse deep anxieties. Especially when unprepared for its occurrence, boys may misperceive it as evidence of the irreparable damage they had always feared would catch up with them as punishment for masturbating. They may associate the ejaculate with pus and believe they are diseased inside. They may assume that they possess a finite virility—just so much semen or so many sperm to last a lifetime—and that masturbation will deplete them and leave them infertile or impotent or both.

Testicular retraction, sometimes completely into the inguinal canal, accompanies arousal and orgasm. Unlike penile changes, this is uncontrollable and has been associated since toddler days with bodily loss and castration fear. Additionally, the testes are now excruciatingly sensitive to pain. These factors tend to add up to a repression of emotional investment in the scrotum and testes, and a focus, consciously at least, of genital interest upon the penis alone.

Ejaculation, testicular movement, and other internal concomitants of orgasm have important positive contributions to make to psychosexual development that are impaired when the anxiety they engender is too strong. These are all inner genital events and sensations, contrasted with external penile stimulation and movement. They should, and could, facilitate the ability of males to integrate their own inner genitality. It is this intrapsychic function for which ejaculation is less effective than menstruation; in contrast with the regularity and predictability of menstrual events, erections come unbidden and there is always a question about when and how much one will ejaculate. One motive underlying the high frequency of masturbation by early adolescent boys is their desire to reduce the level of unpredictability and uncertain control. Ejaculatory control sometimes becomes a neurotic preoccupation as some boys experiment with bizarre and possibly harmful means of retarding or preventing ejaculation because they cannot tolerate losing control.

Ejaculation can help to give some organization to the mysterious inner pubertal changes, as does menarche. With preparation and reassurance, all the internal sensations can help boys to accept their inner genitality—as indeed they must for healthy adult sexual function. Male sexuality is predominantly external and female sexuality internal, but both aspects are normal in both sexes. Only when males learn to accept the internal and vague sensations and movements, the loss of control during ejaculation, as a normal part of their maleness can they lose their fear of female insides and identify fully with their female partners. Much of this essential capacity begins during early adolescence through the ego-maturing qualities of masturbation.

The response of early adolescent boys to menstruation is a measure of how far they have progressed in resolving their childish castration fears (the "bleeding hole" is "proof" of genital mutilation) and in resolving their fear of their own and of girls' inside sexuality. As might be expected, the younger the boy, the greater the anxiety. Negative feelings may be expressed openly or masked by crude jokes and derogatory references ("she's got the rag on"). Menstruation has normally become a less anxiety-producing fact of life by the time of transition to late adolescence.

It is in this period that the characteristic masculine fear of performance ceases to be academic. Initially, boys are at least as insecure about their ability to attract and be loved by a girl as girls are about boys. Some, sadly, do not overcome this insecurity, but most do—only to come face to face with man's prime sexual disadvantage: there is no way he can fake performance. Many young adolescents, even many with no coital experience, have begun to learn that an erection cannot always be willed into existence and that a surprising array of circumstances interfere with arousal. Whether experienced or not, adolescent males begin a lifelong acquaintance with an unwelcome mental intruder—the question, "Will I be able to, or won't I?

Life with the Monster

Early adolescents are often not easy to get along with, much less be parents to. Since these youngsters are doing their best to break loose from the parents they still need, and are using both fair and foul means of doing so, it is a trying period. To give them the freedom they demand would be to desert them with disastrous effects, but since their cooperation with continued parenting can scarcely be counted on, parents must be stable and mature enough to supply almost all the rationality and tolerance with little immediate return, trusting in its long-range value.

There is no way to be unaware of—or unaffected by—adolescents. Puberty literally coerces adult attention and apprehension. In this young person who is soon to be a full member of society, adults sense both the constructive and destructive potential. The cultural institutions specifically bearing upon adolescence—such as minimum schooling requirements, age-graded access to certain rights and privileges, sexual restrictiveness—may be viewed as defensive and adaptive efforts of adults to cope with the new generation. Most adults and most cultural traditions are directed toward molding adolescents to fit into, support, and perpetuate the culture as it is, and to pose as small a threat as possible to the myriad vested interests. Parents' vested interests in the status quo are probably far more emotional and attitudinal than material. Many adolescents, content to trade autonomy for conformity, follow the route the culture has laid out for them, but many do not, and of those who do, many do not give up without a struggle.

One reason that it is difficult to be a parent to a nonconforming early adolescent is that adult culture itself is in transition and many parents are not sure of their positions. The narrow and ever shifting area between overparenting and neglectful permissiveness is difficult to define, and even in basically confident parents adolescents reawaken early and perhaps poorly resolved conflicts. As youngsters noisily question parental standards and flamboyantly experiment with all kinds of social and sexual behavior, adults find it difficult to maintain repression of some of their own questions and unfulfilled longings. Parents' sexual response to children is but one of many discomforting emotions that the challenging attitude of adolescents may stir into life.[36]

It is not easy for parents to recognize that they can no longer simply enforce their will upon their children; it is difficult to shift from authoritarianism to reason, especially when the youngster often seems to reject reason as well. It is a rare parent who does not find it painful to be challenged about many of the basic values and attitudes on which he has built his own self-concept and self-esteem. This is especially true when he is ambivalent about some of his life solutions, or when he has given them relatively little thought and now, called upon to validate them, finds himself unable to do so. To consider this questioning a basic, healthy adolescent *right* requires a strong parent.

The emotional task imposed upon adults by adolescents fosters a stereotyping of adolescents into a few oversimplified—usually negative—types. This superficially easy way out is thoroughly maladaptive and damaging to all concerned. Parents, imbued with media-propagated generalizations, slip unawares into viewing a youngster not as an individual, real person but as an embodiment of one of the stereotypes—delinquent, emotionally disturbed, sexually promiscuous, or drug-prone. In turn, the adolescent comes to regard the stereotype as a valid statement of what he is or should be and proceeds to fit himself to it.[37]

The older generation—not the adolescent—is the group in power and is responsible for modifying the traditional values to which adolescents are exposed. It behooves adults to accept that responsibility and the parallel responsibility of helping youngsters cope with the overwhelming ego task of growing up into a world they did not create. It is worth reasserting that when a discrepancy exists it is how the parent lives, not what he says, that is the effective model.

It is possible only to touch upon some of the less constructive interactions that parents inadvertently find themselves engaged in as they struggle with the genuine difficulties presented by adolescents. The living model—the life style of the adolescent's home—is emphatically the most powerful influence. Many youngsters have had little experience or practice at home with real human warmth. Parental indifference or discord have, in addition, interfered with the resolution of oedipal conflicts, since it is parents' solidarity and love that enables the resolution of these conflicts and the child's turn toward appropriate love objects. The child of indifferent or angry parents is trapped. He can either stay home, bound by his oedipal dilemma, or go out into the world with little preparation for true warmth and relationship.

Parents who are made too anxious by the sexual feelings aroused by their attractive youngsters may withdraw in self-protection. This response usually occurs without the parent's conscious awareness. The youngster is usually busily doing the same thing, but however unfair it may seem, parents do not have the same right: they need to be careful not to be overtly sexual in their responses and to respect the teenager's right to privacy and distance. But uneasy withdrawal of physical contact and warmth is another matter. When it coincides with pubescent budding sexuality, it never escapes the youngster's notice, and it is always read as rejection of that sexuality, implying that sexual maturity is bad and that the adolescent has to renounce sexuality if he is to retain his parents' love.

Parents who are unconsciously disturbed by their own repressed sexual response to an adolescent may project such feelings onto their youngsters or their dates, a typical reaction in many a father. The father becomes acutely and angrily suspicious of the designs of every boy who shows interest in his daughter. He may find fault with any boy she begins to like and look for rationalizations to interfere with the relationship, or he may set thoroughly unrealistic restrictions on whom she dates and the hours she must keep. When his sexual feelings are projected on his daughter, he is driven by curiosity about her every action, convinced that at any opportunity she will act out the sexual urges he is repressing in himself. Boys are by no means exempt from the effects of identical projections by their mother.

Adolescents may be the targets of parental jealousy which may also be expressed in excessive restrictiveness, derogation of the adolescents' attractiveness and the quality of their dates, or obsessive suspiciousness. In direct contrast, parents who feel they missed a lot in their youth and who envy the seemingly freer sex life of contemporary adolescents may often seek vicarious gratification of their own unsatisfied needs. They push their youngsters into early dating and sexually conducive situations without regard for the individual adolescent's own timetable of sexual readiness.

A most destructive double bind exists when one or both parents are sexually unfulfilled and inhibited but have repressed all awareness of their own wishes and replaced them with puritan values. This kind of parent often gives strong contradictory messages. The overt injunction is to stay away from all sexuality, but the covert, nonverbal message is to act out the parent's own repressed sexual desire. This message is often conveyed by the driven suspiciousness which translates as "I suspect you of being sexually active because I expect you to be." The adolescent reads the unspoken expectation clearly and accurately, and this covert cue is usually much stronger than the overt prohibition. The response is "Since that is what you expect, and I am given no credit for being any different, I may as well comply." Unfortunately, compliance brings nothing but grief to everyone involved. The youngster is guilty because the only overt injunctions have been prohibitive. The parent, most often a mother, cannot recognize her role, is righteously horrified, and then displaces the guilt over her own sexual desires by heaping blame and disapproval upon the youngster.[38]

Their envy of youth, plus the uncertainty many parents feel that their own values and attitudes have really paid off in happiness and emotional contentment, has contributed to a subtle reversal of roles in many families. Adolescents are, in a sense, parentified. At one time, children were spectators of their parents and learned how to become adults. Now it often happens that parents are imitators of their children and strive to remain adolescent. When parents abdicate their roles, their children are deprived of the emotional tools necessary to become adult, condemned to perennial adolescence.[39]

Despite the obstacles it is possible to be a good parent to an early adolescent. Many mothers and fathers succeed quite well, and the examples of failure I have given are not designed to terrify those who have the job to do. No one escapes conflicts, and no one has ever succeeded in resolving all conflicts ideally. The parent who knows enough about adolescents to be forewarned that his own will likely lift the emotional rug—and expose much of what he has so painstakingly swept under it for years—will be better prepared for a rocky time. If he is able to accept the imperfections of some of his own solutions, he will be more able to deal with some of the difficulties as essentially his own problems and not blame everything upon the adolescent. The adult who is lucky enough to remain able to question and to grow emotionally, and also lucky enough to have a normal adolescent, can gain tremendously from the encounter.

Patience and a belief in the future are indispensable. The adolescent's attacks and seeming rejection are not truly personal, assuming reasonably healthy and loving parents. Some of the barbs hurt, especially when they accurately penetrate an area of real mistake, poor judgment, or emotional failure, but most critical and withdrawing behavior is motivated by the youngster's own inner need to counteract his love and attachment in order to get on with the business of making his way among his peers. They are not usually true assessments of the parent, and he deeply hopes the parent will have the wisdom to help him apply the brakes to his own excesses. He does not really want to risk alienating the parent. This is difficult to keep in mind in the sweat of the fray, but doing so will help preserve sanity.

Equally important is respecting the youngster's right to question, to challenge, to criticize, to recognize the parent's real and inevitable flaws and imperfections, to be credited with being right about them when he is, and to benefit from a reevaluation by learning from the parent's mistakes. This, too, is difficult to keep in mind, because even the most inadequate solutions to inner problems are strongly defended and there is little assurance that the grossly inexperienced and immature early adolescent is really more likely than the parent to find a better way. But he might. And his right, his obligation, to question is his only means of doing so.

Absolutely complete, no-holds-barred sex education is a moral imperative. The dangers inherent in its omission make it immoral to keep any adolescent in ignorance. Sex education beginning at this time is irresponsibly late, but no matter how much prior sex education a youngster has had, he needs it all over again now and in just as complete detail—physical and physiological information (the "plumbing courses" and "organ recitals") as well as information on the details of intercourse, contraception and its techniques, venereal disease, sexual variations and deviations, abortion, masturbation and everything else related to sex.

Since reassurances are especially needed at this time, it is necessary to anticipate adolescents' apprehensions and irrational guilts, especially about masturbation. A physically normal adolescent boy who truly does not masturbate is without exception a sexually disturbed boy. All the normal physiological accompaniments of postpubescent sexual function call for repeated reassurance. A girl cannot too often be reassured about the normality of all the events of the menstrual cycle, including variations in physical sensations and flow and irregularities in timing. The same is true for boys' ejaculation, spontaneous erections and unexpected orgasms, and nocturnal emissions.

All adolescents are concerned about their anatomical endowments, and many must eventually (though not usually until late adolescence) face the fact that their secondary sexual characteristics may not be what they had hoped. Some girls, for example, will always be flat-chested (unless they give nature artificial assistance). Such youngsters need the reassurance that fads in body shape change; more importantly, all youngsters need reassurance that they will not ultimately be valued on the basis of anatomy.

Boys are vulnerable to an almost invariably unwarranted worry—anxiety about penis size. The myth that bigger is better persists—and it is a myth (with the rare exception of a truly pathological condition called *microphallus*, abnormally small penis). It is perpetuated by surreptitious comparisons in locker rooms and showers, and a strange quirk of anatomy that reinforces the myth as a result of these observations. There are considerable differences in penis size in its limp state, but these differences almost completely disappear with erection. With few exceptions, there is little variation in length or circumference of normal erect penises, no matter how great the difference when flaccid. This information can be very helpful. The males in pornographic movies and magazines are exceptions who are often chosen for their abnormally large penises, and should not be used as standards of comparison.

At least as important now as in preadolescence is the need to keep reminding youngsters of the wide normal range of ages at which sexual maturation occurs, and also the equally varied pace of that maturation. Since the criterion for the beginning of early adolescence is menarche or ejaculation, one would not strictly be concerned now with youngsters in whom pubertal onset has not yet occurred, but variations in maturation pace can arouse equally strong concerns.

Because of the widespread difficulty that adolescents have in talking with their parents about detailed and personal sexual matters, sex education must frequently be taken over by schools, churches, or special programs under various other auspices. Nevertheless the belief that adolescents are unable to discuss such matters with their parents is largely a myth; it is the parents who cannot speak openly. When parents are genuinely comfortable, both consciously and unconsciously, with their own and their offsprings' sexuality, discussion is possible. There will be unpredictable fluctuations in the youngster's willingness or accessibility, but there is no inevitable block, and the youngsters are relieved and grateful when their parents can be open about sex with them.

Early adolescence is a period when the parent of the same sex is particularly important for psychosexual development. The presence of an emotionally strong, admired, and respected parent of the same sex is of great help in the final resolution of oedipal wishes. A weak and ineffectual parent, one who is emotionally unavailable, or one who is constantly being derogated by the other parent, is a liability, fostering unconscious fantasies of successful rivalry. It may be unavoidable that a boy is reared by a mother alone at this age, but it does add an extra burden to his oedipal resolution. Such a mother can help him by trying to provide surrogate adult males, by open and unequivocal expression of her own admiration and respect for adult males of her own generation, and by avoiding the temptation to make her son "the man of the house."

Each sex probably learns the capacity for sexual response from the parent of the opposite sex. How this is so is not really understood, since overt sexual interaction is obviously not involved. It is probably a matter of the loving acceptance of the blooming sexuality, the sense of being welcomed into becoming a woman or a man, as well as a firmly established respect for the opposite sex as exemplified by the parent. Research data about boys is unavailable, but there is data correlating adult female response with paternal relationship. Adult females with a high capacity for orgasmic response are typically those who describe their fathers as men who cared about them and were concerned with their upbringing. Their fathers had definite views, and took a definite role in the conduct of their adolescent lives. By contrast, low orgasmic women usually had physically or emotionally absent, or indifferent, fathers.[40]

Several basic factors enter into an adult's interaction with an adolescent. There is that part controlled unconsciously by the adult's earlier life and conflicts stirred by the adolescent, there is the distortion introduced by stereotyping, and there is the direct, personal response based on the real personalities and the shared experiences. Constructive parental interaction is characterized by minimal contamination by stereotypes, a perception of the youngster as the unique individual he is, an ability to free oneself from one's own conflicts so as to deal directly with the adolescent's needs, and the capacity for empathic understanding that derives from a satisfactory adolescent experience of one's own. All this involves not a "best answer" for any particular adolescent situation or dilemma but a process of relating. While not abdicating appropriate authority, the parent must teach the young person to have more and more of a voice in his own affairs. Most parent-adolescent interactions require negotiation more often than rules, a process which simultaneously teaches the adolescent something about how to acquire authority and about its rational, legitimate use.

Common Problems

For most parents, the most common problem of early adolescent sexual development is intercourse. Whether or not it is a problem for the adolescent is a totally different question. It raises all the same issues of potential ego damage as in previous phases, and one finds the same array of conflicting evidence from other cultures. There is a qualitative difference now, the possibility of pregnancy, but that is preventable and therefore another matter. Some youngsters seem ready for the various implications of full heterosexual gratification earlier than others. A more detailed discussion of adolescent intercourse will be found in chapter 10. Here it is sufficient to indicate how intercourse may either be indicative of a problem or may lead to problems.

There is almost no behavior that cannot be misused, however inherently normal it may be, and intercourse is no exception. Most instances of its misuse may be characterized as the use of sex for nonsexual purposes. Unless anyone, no matter what age, engages in sex primarily because of genuine erotic urge and arousal, there is some suggestion that emotional conflict is being expressed. This may be minimal or even normal in such typical behavior as the use of masturbation for release of tension, but it is the more obvious symptomatic use of sex in adolescence that is really worth attention.

Sexual activity may reveal a severely disturbed parent-adolescent relationship. It is very often used, especially by young girls, as an act of hostility or of vengeful retaliation against one or both parents. A young girl knows it will anger and hurt her parents. Either sex may use it as a gesture of rebellion and defiance against the entire adult establishment. Intercourse is often equated with maturity and adulthood, and adolescents may seek to gain maturity via sexual activity—a form of playacting that is immediately indicative of the very opposite quality, immaturity. Sex may be used to gain status among one's peers. Intercourse may become a truly compulsive preoccupation, usurping attention and energy from all the other learning and maturational tasks necessary in adolescence. It may also be used, again most often by girls, as a means of getting boy friends. When sex is used in such ways, it is always symptomatic of some kind of emotional disturbance, either within the family, the community, or inside the youngster, who lacks self-esteem or has too great a need for the approval of others. These youngsters are disturbed, but the sexual activity is not the problem. The problem is whatever is causing the misuse of sexuality.

Early adolescent intercourse may certainly lead to serious problems, of which pregnancy is the most obvious. The younger the girl, the greater the role played by childish failure to consider consequences and genuine ignorance of contraceptive techniques and their availability. The element of acting out unconscious feelings is sometimes significant, especially in girls approaching late adolescence. A study of such girls found their motivations for being pregnant to be fulfillment of blatant incestuous wishes. In younger girls, the baby's father is usually a nonentity in their minds, barely associated with their pregnancy. The older girls had a much firmer grasp of the boy's existence but tended to deny their own role and blame their entire plight upon him or their parents. These girls also felt their pregnancy to be a powerful weapon against their parents.[41] What is seen here is a double problem—sex and pregnancy used for grossly distorted reasons plus the irresponsible sexuality itself.

It is doubtful whether most early adolescent pregnancies are actually motivated in this way, and it is impossible to estimate what proportion results from genuine contraceptive ignorance or unavailability, but there is no doubt that a major proportion are the result of sexual conflicts. The most frequently reported reason for lack of contraception by girls is that they would feel guilty over premeditated intercourse: in other words, sex for its own sake is bad. A slightly different version of the same guilt that affects both boys and girls is that sex for kicks is unacceptable, whereas sex with love is all right. They convince themselves that it is love rather than pleasure alone that motivates them by the purposeful avoidance of contraception; since they "love" one another they would marry in the event of pregnancy—a feckless fantasy at such an age. A pervasive sexual guilt has many subtle ways of wreaking its damage.

An unconscious theme that contributes to contraceptive reluctance in both sexes is the early established equation that *inside* equals *female* equals *baby*. Contraception in such a context is infanticide, and since inside sex organs and baby are equated, a woman may unconsciously fear that contraception ("killing the baby") also means destruction of her inside genitals, the very core of her female body ego. Ultimate resolution of the complex unconscious meanings of internal and external sexuality comes only with true maturity. Fantasies of this order may contribute to dogmatic repudiation of abortion, especially among early adolescents.

Pregnancy is not the sole problematic consequence of early intercourse. Guilt alone may do serious damage. Despite their defiance, adolescents cannot wish away their conditioning for guilt when it has been a ubiquitous ingredient of the social waters through which they have swum. Free sexual behavior does not always signify sexual freedom, as many youngsters discover to their chagrin. Until the ego is sufficiently mature to handle the loss of adult support, violations will evoke punishment by the superego. Depending upon its intensity, the guilt may produce an endless spectrum of disturbances, from mild uneasiness to neurotic symptoms, persistent adult sexual inhibitions, and even psychotic episodes.

Venereal disease, an ugly spectre that hovers over all sexual activity, is all the more menacing for early adolescents because their greater immaturity makes them less thoughtful of consequences; they are likely to be grossly ignorant of its dangers and symptoms, prone to be secretive when they are sexually active, and guiltily afraid to seek treatment.

Only recently has it become relatively well accepted that cancer of the uterine cervix is probably a venereal disease, in that its probable and most common cause is a virus transmitted through intercourse. Closely related to the kind of virus that causes cold sores, this specific viral disease *(Herpes genitalis)* may occur in sexual partners of any age, but in males and adult women it amounts to little more than an annoyance with no known serious effects. It is young women who run a particular risk. One possibility is that until about the age of twenty, a girl's body is less capable of mobilizing the specific blood-borne defenses against its effects; another is that the youthful cervix is more susceptible to the initiation of early cellular changes that become cancerous in later years. Whatever the exact pathological factors, it seems established that early infection is associated with a much higher risk of cervical carcinoma. It follows that early intercourse provides an opportunity for this venereal infection, and that the greater the frequency of intercourse and the larger the number of partners during the teens, the greater the possibility of infection.[42] There are, of course, some differences of opinion, many aspects of the exact pathogenesis need further research, and it is certainly known that cancer of the cervix appears capable of occurring in women without such a history, but the summary given represents the general consensus of current knowledge about its frequent relationship to early sexual exposure.

Masturbation, principal sexual outlet of early adolescents, although both normal and beneficial is associated with various untoward consequences. Compulsive masturbation at any age is a symptom of disturbance. Masturbation may be employed by insecure youngsters as a means of avoiding heterosocial and heterosexual progress. By turning to themselves for total gratification, they deny their need for others, and may so fall behind their peers in sociosexual development as to find themselves increasingly handicapped. In some adolescents it may arouse as much guilt as intercourse, with the same potential for inhibition, neurosis, or psychosis. The severity of mental illness is not determined by the true seriousness of an action but by the degree of emotional danger that an individual assigns to it.

The unconscious fantasies associated with internal sexual sensations, and the anxieties aroused by them in both sexes, means that some people will not succeed in integrating the totality of their sexuality. Menstruation and ejaculation make it impossible to delay forever some resolution, whether healthy or faulty, and in early adolescence it is already possible to distinguish some who are having difficulty. The persistent tomboy whose friends have left her behind in their feminine and heterosocial development may be one who cannot yet accept her inner sexuality. She externalizes her feelings in imitation of boys, in their interests, mannerisms, and personality characteristics. Such girls may not only masturbate clitorally—the typical manner—but allow themselves to value only the sharp intensity and localizability of that sensation and successfully keep themselves from sensing or enjoying the full participation of all their inner sex organs in the orgastic experience.

Boys who are also unable to begin to accept their own inner sexual sensations are those who still fear the inner sexuality of females. As young as they are, they begin to show a preference for girls who also deny their inner sexuality through continued externalization. These budding mutual attractions are defensively non-threatening to both because they reinforce each other's denial. Unless fortuitous circumstances foster later integration of their total sexuality, these youngsters are on the path to limited and unfulfilling sexual partnerships even though they may be able to function sufficiently to be orgastic.

Although normal homoerotic activity remains common in early adolescence, many of those who risk developing true homosexual preferences begin to be more clearly discernable after puberty. Homosexuals of either sex do not follow any one, easily recognizable path. They do not have one "type" of personality, nor are they a homogeneous group set apart by mannerisms, appearance, or obvious and severe emotional disturbance. They share only one thing in common—a sexual preference for their own sex accompanied by a relative or total sexual avoidance of the opposite sex.

Heterosocial pairing and heterosexual attraction are competitive activities. An adolescent interested in a particular partner must make some effort to attract and to be attractive, and must be prepared to persist despite real or potential rivals. The future male homosexual will not engage in this competition with other males. Again, it is essential to avoid socially destructive labeling on this basis alone—there are too many normal variations in maturational pace and ego readiness that can delay a youngster's entry into the lists—but a persistent backing away from heterosocial competitiveness indicates the likelihood of sex role identity conflicts.

The end of early adolescence is almost imperceptible. The differences between young people in the early and late phases usually become obvious only in retrospect, or in comparing large groups so that their typical characteristics stand out. The subtlety of the shift makes it difficult to define. It is possible only to describe it in general terms and to speculate about what makes it possible. It is essentially a shift of sexual feelings from parents to peers of the opposite sex. By its end, the heterosexual dating pattern is usually established. Sexual behavior within the pair is still crude and self-centered and sexual feelings are still conflicted, insecure, and contaminated by guilt and anxiety, but the shift has been made to a person outside the family and of one's own age. This is both an accomplishment and an enabler of further emotional growth. Because this new person affords relief from the dependent and incestuous urges that plagued the early response to puberty, the adolescent can now focus his energies on the new relationship.

At the same time, relations with parents have begun to change. Noisy, irrational battles have given way to more serious efforts to think and to use reason. The issues become more serious, too, as the adolescent comes nearer to independence, and they may therefore be more, not less, distressing to some parents who find it increasingly untenable to dismiss differences as childish. When these somewhat older and more secure adolescents and their parents cannot rationally discuss and negotiate their differences, the young person begins more and more to act upon his own decisions instead of merely ranting about them. This may mean tension at home, sometimes even disruption of parental relationships for a time, but the increased confidence derived from acceptance by his peers makes the adolescent willing to begin to risk the consequences.

In general, the adolescent has now had time to get used to the impact of puberty and all the accompanying changes. His ego has begun to gain mastery over his drives, and he is less afraid of going out of control. It is possible that there is some correlation between ego maturation and the regularization and stabilization of male and female hormone patterns, but such correlations are tenuous. The transition is principally marked by the establishment of a nonincestuous love object choice, and an increasing capacity to cope with the changes that have taken place since puberty first disrupted childhood equilibrium.

NINE

Late Adolescence: Other People Become Important

Late adolescence is perhaps best characterized as a time of consolidation. It has no dramatic biological onset as does early adolescence, although adult-type hormonal regularization and full reproductive capacity may correlate roughly with the transition, and it has, if anything, even a less well defined psychosocial offset in the gradual movement into adulthood. Nonetheless, it is a definite and unmistakable phase, a time for pulling together the "loose ends" of psychosexual development, not only from early adolescence but from one's entire previous life, in order to begin adulthood with sexual attitudes and emotions relatively settled. Hopefully, by the end of late adolescence the psychological disequilibrium of adolescence will be replaced by a relatively stable equilibrium, an emotional state of dynamic tension, but not of rigidity and stasis.

Adolescence will be over when (1) a person has formed stable behavioral and emotional patterns, regardless of whether or not they are healthy, neurotic and maladaptive, or a unique mixture; (2) when the fluid and shifting quality of identity experimentation has passed and in essence the young person has closed off or abandoned many of his previously open alternatives; (3) when he has adopted an irreversible (except under extraordinary conditions) sexual position; (4) when he has revised his internal value system to fit his unique self; and (5) when he has—in the resolution of a *healthy* adolescence—achieved a reasonable balance between his biological drives, his conscience, and his ego, with his ego basically in control so that the exercise of judgment is paramount.[1]

The thread that runs throughout adolescence is the acquisition of a reasonably stable identity, as contrasted, using Erikson's phrase, with "role diffusion," a mentally painful state in which one has been unable to find himself, or has been deprived of the opportunities for valid self-actualization. Identity is a larger concept and a much greater accomplishment than identification. It is more than the sum of earlier identifications. It is the ego's integration of all previous identifications with one's individual quality and quantity of basic drives, genuine aptitudes, and socially available role opportunities, resulting in an inner sense of unity and continuity that matches reasonably well with the meaning one has for others.[2]

The prolonged adolescence of our culture, while it engenders endless problems, compensates partially by providing a psychosocial moratorium for the accomplishment of these goals. The extra time is required to find one's proper niche in a society offering many alternatives, as an appropriate identity can be found only through time-consuming exploration and experimentation.[3]

Identity implies and requires choice and commitment, requirements that frighten many adolescents. One cannot choose an occupation, a value system, or a sexual role without some elimination of other possible choices. The adolescent moratorium is normally most pronounced in highly gifted youngsters who could validly make a number of successful choices, and it is most pathologically misused by those who are afraid of the responsibilities of adult commitment. It cannot be denied that the ending of adolescence involves a narrowing down, a channeling and delimiting process. Identity has its price.

Taming the Monster

Some biological changes continue at least into this period, especially in boys. Height continues to increase, though much more slowly, long bone growth finally being inhibited by an action of testosterone at about twenty-one years. Full muscle size and strength is not usually achieved until some time in this phase, as is also true of final voice change and complete development of facial and other body hair. The bone growth of girls is inhibited by estrogen usually by eighteen years, and there is relatively little change in body configuration.

All the most important biological changes have normally taken place by now, including fully fertile, adult capacity for both sexual response and procreation. However, even though the late adolescent does not have to cope with an unstable pubertal biology, he is still getting used to its effects. It is the continuing psychological response to the physiology and the implications of a now stabilized puberty that characterizes late adolescence.

Among the most interesting responses to puberty are those correlated with early or late maturation, a theme first encountered in preadolescence. In order now to compare early and late maturers, it is necessary to make age comparisons; a boy who reaches puberty at seventeen or eighteen, for example, is not a late adolescent, and many of the phenomena discussed in this chapter are inapplicable. Within the general age range of late adolescence, however, all physiologically normal youngsters will have pubesced, and some further comparisons of the two extremes can be made.

As suggested earlier, peer and social prestige for girls shifts from the late to the early maturer over the junior and senior high school years. Different studies find different average grade levels in which the shift becomes obvious, some suggesting that it occurs as late as the tenth to twelfth grades.[4] One rather sizable study found that as early as the first year of junior high school, girls who mature early become socially more sought after, a situation with interesting consequences. Since biological puberty always takes longer than a three-month summer vacation, it would be hardly possible for the same girl to be preadolescent in the sixth grade and physically mature in the seventh. On the basis of physical maturation alone, therefore, it is unlikely that the same girl could be highly popular throughout high school; different girls would benefit either from maturing late while early in their school careers or from maturing early in later school years.[5] There is some evidence that girls who mature late compensate for their loss of status by a continuing drive for and success in achievement and recognition, which is less obvious among the early maturers, but high test results in the area of self-concept among those who matured early indicates an inner assurance in their progress toward the goal of adulthood.[6]

There is no shift in prestige and social achievement among the two groups of boys. Throughout most of adolescence, late maturation carries few if any advantages in the social area, other than lesser social pressure to "act like an adult," but intensive research carried out with respect to the intrapsychic and long-term consequences of maturational timing in boys reveals some unique emotional advantages for those who are late. The relevant factor appears to be the length of time a boy has in which to achieve the ego maturation and strength that is both characteristic and necessary during latency, before he must cope with the sexual drives of puberty. The early maturer has had much less time, and with his less mature ego, he is more likely unconsciously to regard his drives as uncontrollable and dangerous to his security. The late maturer is more ready to cope with them and to regard them as constructive and positive.[7]

By the late adolescent years, different character structures can already be discerned in the two groups of boys, which follow-up studies have been able to trace into their thirties and forties. The premature identity formation of boys who mature early, and their relative fear of their impulses, has led to emotional overcontrol, greater conservatism and social conformity, less creativity and exploratory, self-initiated behavior, and more orientation toward power and conformity. By contrast, the late maturers, while still manifesting *social* insecurity and negative self-concepts, are more independent, more insightful and psychologically minded, more flexible and tolerant of ambiguities, and give freer play to their curiosities and creative initiative. These differential characteristics correlate highly with the relative fear and mistrust, or acceptance and utilization, of one's drives and impulses. The differences express themselves more in character structure than in relative psychological health.[8]

Late adolescence usually brings less contact with parents. Other activities realistically keep adolescents away from home and busy. Many are off at college or have moved out and are working and self-sufficient. This makes the emotional loss of being separated from parents more real, and accounts for even more intense periods of "mourning" and depression—a common experience among college freshmen. They compensate for this loss with deeper and more meaningful involvements with friends and lovers.

Paralleling the subsiding of physiological lability, emotional fluctuations become less violent, rapid, and extensive. This also reflects growing awareness that independence is, after all, possible and soon within grasp, so that it does not have to be fought for so noisily, but immaturity combines with the almost-adult status to make of this a very dangerous period. Most adolescents are impatient for adult status and prerogatives yet bitterly resist the requirement that many of those prerogatives must be earned. Even so, the average late adolescent already possesses many of the powers and privileges of adulthood though he fails to recognize the permanency of consequences that accompany adult power. The persistence of infantile omnipotence leads him to treat behavior in the real world—speeding, drunken driving, or unprotected intercourse, for example—as a form of play, with reversible outcomes, or to assume that he is immune from danger. Often such behavior masks an unconsciously suicidal depression resulting from parental loss and isolation. It is not surprising that these factors combine to make accidents and suicide the first and second most frequent causes of death during this phase.

At times, all these influences combine to produce extremes of behavior, a phenomenon often dramatically visible in the first year or two of college. This is still, after all, an immature stage, and the intrapsychic and external circumstances at this time often provide the first relatively unimpeded opportunity to act out many adolescent emotions. It may be difficult to correlate such behavior with the characterization of these youngsters as showing less violent, rapid, and extensive emotional fluctuations, but regressive periods throughout the transition are to be expected. Observation corroborates the assertion that even the extremes of late adolescence are identity experimentations explored at greater length and depth than the earlier, more shallow vacillations.

Older adolescents gradually become aware that their personal pasts are real, as those pasts begin to catch up to them in various ways. Past school performance, or police records, determine some of their academic and social options. Past developmental influences manifest themselves in unexpected character traits, behavior patterns, or inhibitions. Predictably, there is a wide gamut of response to the inexorable ascendence of reality. For many, the ground rules of reality constitute a further prod to pull themselves together to meet challenges and avoid defeats. Some are furiously resentful at being judged by their performance, attack society for not accepting them as they are (as their mother did in infancy), try to deny the implacability of reality, attempt to form countercultures that have a different reality, or make a life style of adolescence so as to stave off confrontation with the adult world. The final rule of reality is a potent factor in separating those who are prepared for adulthood from those who are not.

Late adolescence is the time of life when revision of the childhood superego into the adult conscience is best achieved. This requires realistic reevaluation of what one was taught by parents and by the culture, and also of what one childishly imagined his parents and the real world to be. Although one never loses all the automatic prohibitions of the childish superego, most of them are ideally replaced by rational judgment and decision. An adult conscience is based upon an objective perception of one's relationship and responsibilities to other people and to society as well as to oneself, not a set of inflexible moral rules imposed by others. A healthy conscience allows the flexibility to modify values as one becomes wiser or encounters situations for which previous standards are inapplicable.

A crucial aspect of this modification concerns the ego ideal. By now, it has come to be influenced and determined not only by infantile onmipotence and idealized parental images, but also by the oversimplified and mythical perfections attributed to one's culture by one's parents. A successful latency sees the first incomplete reassessment of parents and self. The ego ideal, too, needs to be definitively revised in late adolescence so that one's aspirations correspond with real capacities and the ego ideal is sufficiently realistic to spur constructive striving instead of serving as a constant reminder of one's failure to reach impossible goals.[9]

Masculine-feminine differences now settle into their more or less final expressions. These are always a varying blend of innate propensities and capacities with idiosyncratic and capricious culturally socialized stereotypes. These differences manifest themselves in all areas of life and in all cultures. In some present and past societies there have been crippling and inappropriate sex role constrictions that invariably have resulted in an emotional loss to both sexes regardless of which sex appears to be the more obvious victim; some differences, however, are universal and biologically determined.[10] They begin with the different organization of the brain of the two sexes in fetal life, are augmented when these brain centers are activated by pubertal hormones, and are further defined by the relationship between male aggressiveness and the biological characteristic of higher testosterone levels.[11]

It cannot be stated too often that the recognition of innate masculine-feminine differences—a common-sense realization documented by research from a number of scientific disciplines—is not a disguised implication of superiority of either sex. This simple, inescapable biological fact is often misread or baldly misrepresented to imply such irrelevant issues. The majority of social roles can be equally well performed by either sex. Some social roles can best, or only, be performed by one or the other sex as a result of differential embryological development and adult hormone status. None of these roles is better than another. Societies, for all their frequent and blatant wrongheadedness about what is "manly" and what is "womanly," usually succeed in socializing the majority of each sex toward the roles for which they are best suited. In late adolescence the behavioral and temperamental patterns of masculinity and femininity, displaying in any culture both unique and universal characteristics, assume their definitive forms.

Society's Influence Strengthens

The impact of culture upon the adolescent is stronger and more pervasive now than at any earlier time. Society expects more of the late adolescent; he is expected to begin getting down to the business of life. He is held responsible for more of what he does, though not quite to the extent of an adult (for example, an eighteen-year-old burglar is handled quite differently in the courts than is a twenty-five-year-old). More adult privileges are granted (in some states a seventeen-year-old girl may marry of her own volition) though others are still withheld (that same girl is virtually unemployable in most states and in many occupations).

In other words, our culture has its own jerry-built and often confusing set of gradations in according adulthood. Much of the confusion results from the fact that there really are two kinds of adulthood—adult function and adult status. The differences come to have considerable meaning to late adolescents. Adult status is acquired or conferred usually according to relatively arbitrary criteria, such as age, which are not related to individual differences and may only be tenuously correlated with maturity. Adult function—living and performing in a responsible and contributory fashion—may be achieved individually according to maturation rather than age. Adult function may be either thrust upon or required of an adolescent by the society, or withheld from him, without regard to corresponding adult or subadult status.[12]

The two aspects of progress toward adulthood are often bizarrely out of phase, a situation that contributes much to adolescent resentment and frustration. On the simplest level, society is characteristically much freer in its demand for adult function and much stingier in its granting of adult status, whereas adolescents are much more vociferous in their demand for adult status but far more reluctant to display adult function.

In many other instances, functional and status adulthood are not so easily linked to conflicts of interests between generations and are often most confusing and frustrating to adolescents. Depending upon the legal age of consent in different states, a delinquent, promiscuous, and precociously mature-looking girl may misrepresent her age and aggressively seduce a young adult man. Yet he can be convicted of rape because the law does not grant her sufficient adult status to decide about intercourse for herself. Equally irrational is the plight of the eighteen-year-old draftee who is told to defend his country and is even given the right to kill, but who may not marry without his parents' consent, or be served in a bar, or vote in some elections.

Clearly, the culture exerts both constructive and negative influences upon the adolescent's development. The fact that more and more is expected of him, providing that those expectations are appropriate and humanistically oriented, is definitely constructive. An infant can be loved and accepted by merely existing, but an adult must earn his rewards. When the culture's value system is consistent with clearly predictable rewards and punishments, that, too, is overwhelmingly positive. Even if the cultural mores are highly questionable, they provide a solid rather than a shifting and unfocused background against which an adolescent can formulate his questions and doubts and evaluate the probable consequences of any life styles he may choose for himself. Such cultural qualities provide something firm for him to push against emotionally, both testing its strength and quality and sharpening his own perceptions of what dissent would be like.

There are certainly some negative potentials in the culture's arbitrary efforts to prevent the adolescent from growing up "too fast." Neither the laws nor the traditional mores regarding sexuality bear any relationship to psychosexual development in general or to individual variations in maturity. The inevitable conflict engenders a widening gulf of antagonism and poor communication between the generations that need not exist. A relatively recent phenomenon—the adult culture's creation of a separate and unassimilated youth culture, isolated and stereotyped as a subculture with interests inimical to those of adults—achieves a similar unfortunate end. The adolescents are forced to define antagonistic boundaries between themselves and the adult establishment. The position of "us" versus "them" associates the identity and loyalty of adolescents with youth and antiestablishment values, rendering assimilation into adult culture the equivalent of betrayal to the enemy, instead of a natural act of joining and taking an effective role in the adult world.[13]

An adolescent's responses to the effort to acculturate him are determined not only by actual interactions and external pressures but also by the difficult intrapsychic readjustments he must make before he is able to reach a working agreement with the adult world. These readjustments derive mainly from efforts at resolving his attitudes toward his parents. But the culture too—often equated with parents—may be seen as hypocritical and disillusioningly imperfect. Again, this is sharply felt in the sexual sphere. Why should society demand adherence to values of abstinence from him when its adults fail so miserably to live up to the standards it sets? Cynicism and moral anarchy may rule his life for a time. His criticisms may hold much truth, but his own simplistic and idealistic "solutions" reveal the immaturity inherent in his inexperience. Free love will not solve the economic, ecological, and political problems of the world.

Nonetheless, adolescents, especially older ones, have a vital role in the very culture they struggle with. Their dissatisfactions push their creativity to its extreme. Their increasingly open and unrestrained challenging of traditional sexual attitudes has had an important part in forcing many adults out of unthinking complacency about their sexual attitudes. The attempts by adolescents to explore and live by alternative sexual values are not all hedonistic, immature, and impractical. They are helping to force sexuality out of the closet and to bring into the light the contrast between what people say and what they do. It is unlikely that adolescents will provide a sexually confused culture with final and universal answers, but in the interface of their struggle with the parental generation, both participants can learn and grow.

From Sex to Love

During late adolescence, the most important shift in the attainment of sexual maturity takes place—the shift from self-centered sexual sensation to couple-centered involvement in both sex and love. I define adult sexual love as the capacity to invest both sexual and tender feelings in the same person and to hold that person's well-being as important as one's own.

This is an enormous step. The outcome is a long way from the beginning of late adolescence, when a heterosexual dating pattern is barely established, when only a minority have had intercourse, and when the chief focus is exploring the personal experience of sex. The shift from "What does sex feel like to *me*, and what does it tell me about *myself?*" to "What is involved in a sexually intimate *relationship?*" is the ideal endpoint of late adolescence. It is achieved slowly, sooner by some than others, and, sadly, never achieved at all by a disheartening many.

Love during adolescence can be real and intense, but still show the immature adolescent qualities of shallowness, evanescence, undependability, and narcissism. These are not contradictions. It can be intense *and* shallow, because depth comes only from experience of the multiple faces and ramifications of love in a relationship with another person. It can be real *and* narcissistic, when one of its purposes is to reassure the self that he is lovable. The lover is often idealized in order to make oneself feel good at being loved by one so perfect. Permanence is not a necessary quality of genuine love. Stability and dependability are, hopefully, qualities of the kind of love that leads to lasting relationships, marriage, and taking on the awesome responsibility of rearing a child, but that is only one kind of sexual love, and many brief relationships can be characterized by sexuality, tenderness, and genuine considerateness.

Adolescent loves break up for many reasons, many of them entirely normal and expectable. Principally there is the inevitability of changing attractions as the young person changes and grows and achieves an identity.

Since incestuous conflicts are not fully resolved until adolescence is successfully over, many breakups reflect unresolved oedipal remnants. The boy friend or girl friend may resemble the father or mother either too much or too little. A bested rival may be a prerequisite to developing interest in a partner, a poor basis for choice and one that predisposes the love affair to failure. As long as all girls are associated with the mother, guilt will prevent any alliance from enduring. The need to win out in oedipal rivalry can lead boys to choose partners who are emotionally disturbed and stir the boys' need to rescue the girls from a fantasied intolerable situation—"rescuing" mother from father. Conversely, inappropriate attachments may be prolonged for unconscious oedipal reasons. An adolescent who persists in pursuing an unrequited love arouses a suspicion that oedipal guilt drives him to experience repeatedly the frustration of his incestuous wishes.

Independence may be too precious still. Career choice may be too pressing. There is also the desire for varying experiences—a healthy urge because experience often operates to protect against poor judgment in later choosing a mate. It is generally more appropriate that adolescent loves be trial courtships rather than permanent commitments.

In general, it is accurate to say that in late adolescence masturbation and all heterosexual activities increase in incidence and frequency, while homoerotic activity and atypical activities such as sexuality with animals decrease. Once again, figures and percentages lead to more confusion than clarity.

Two studies in 1972 and 1973 indicated that barely more than half the girls in the United States are still virgins at nineteen,[14] and that by age twenty 45 percent of girls and 59 percent of boys are nonvirgins.[15] These figures, even if roughly accurate, are not to be taken as representative of all groups of adolescents. There are enormous variations between subcultural groups, sections of the country, and urban versus rural adolescents. Some careful studies of sexual trends over a period of years have demonstrated that the major changes in sexual activity have been shown by young women, not young men. Between 1958 and 1968 there was little change in the premarital coital activity or the attitudes of the late adolescent males studied, but there was a sharp increase in premarital intercourse among the females, plus a corresponding increase in their acceptance of intercourse without guilt. It appears that the differences between the sexes in sexual experience is narrowing, and that fewer late adolescent girls who have intercourse feel guilty about it.[16]

Relatively few late adolescents have the necessary opportunities or accommodations readily available for intercourse, so that even for most of those with experience in intercourse and regular sexual partners, masturbation remains the chief sexual outlet. Many late adolescents, for many different reasons, have not yet begun to have intercourse; probably most have boy friends or girl friends with whom they engage in a great deal of sexual activity, but stop short of intercourse.

Among those who have intercourse, there is every shade of attitude and activity, from complete license to a totally exclusive and monogamous relationship. Promiscuity is difficult to define and has pejorative connotations. A more useful term is "sexual adventurer," which is not limited to any special age group. Adventurers have intercourse for pleasure only and do not associate it with love or involvement. They have as many partners as they want or can find. Desire is reason enough for intercourse whether or not they know the partner. About four times as many boys as girls are adventurers. This sexual style is not the principal one in the United States, even among characteristically narcissistic and experimental adolescents; only 15 percent of those who have had intercourse fall into this category.[17]

There appears to be a new sexual ethic emerging among young people that is already predominant during the teens. It regards intercourse as morally acceptable when accompanied by affection. This trend has been documented by various researchers.[18] It is accompanied by a real freedom and openness in discussing sexual feelings and values, in making intercourse a mutual, thought-out decision. This approach to sexuality has a number of ramifications. One is a decrease in the double standard, with much less concern about virginity as a prerequisite for marriage; as long as the girl has had intercourse with boys whom she loved, more and more young men find this experience quite acceptable, and an even larger proportion of girls find it acceptable in themselves.[19] Another ramification is that fewer males have their first intercourse with a prostitute.[20] Increasing sexual permissiveness among girls and the greater frankness of sexual discussion makes it more possible for the experience of first intercourse to occur with a known and meaningful partner. Among adolescents up to the age of twenty, 40 percent of those who have experienced intercourse are reported to confine their sexual experience to one, loved partner over an extended period of time. This appears now to be the predominant pattern of active sexuality. Almost twice as many girls as boys show this type of sexual behavior.[21]

With the emergence of permissiveness with affection as the major ethic of adolescent intercourse, it is probable that the capacity for intimacy develops hand-in-hand with adult sexual identity, rather than coming about only after identity has been fully achieved. Since females are always well ahead of males in maturation, and since the average age of marriage for girls in this country is twenty, it is understandable that their concern about intimacy is more pressing and comes sooner than in males.[22]

In the area of sexual behavior, I would like to call attention to a few beliefs about adolescent male-female differences that need some revision. One has to do with the kinds of sexual stimuli to which males and females are supposed to respond differently. It is generally thought that only males are aroused sexually by looking at the opposite sex nude or partially clothed, or by visual and narrative erotica, such as sexually explicit photographs, movies, and stories. Women are considered generally unresponsive to such stimuli, requiring instead a romantic and loving element of mutual caring, and responding more to touch than to the other senses. Kinsey's statistics seemed to validate this clearly,[23] and the predominantly male audience toward which most pornography is directed seems further evidence. There is little doubt that some difference in sexual arousal must exist because of the different innate needs and roles of men and women, but such a wide disparity is more apparent than real. Recent research has revealed that while women are less aware consciously of being sexually excited by explicit sexual materials, their sexual physiologic responses, such as vaginal lubrication, occurred quite regularly, and their subsequent sexual activity increased just as the males' did.[24] If it were not that women were culturally conditioned to be less open than men in their response to frankly erotic stimuli, the difference would be much less than it is consciously imagined to be.

Another changing concept is the difference in the ages at which men's and women's sexual drive and responsiveness reaches its peak. Males are supposed to be at their highest level in the late teens, showing a very gradual, steady decline thereafter; women's responsivity is believed to be relatively low in the teens, and to rise steadily into their forties and fifties. Again, data on frequency and incidence of orgastic response seemed to corroborate this view,[25] but once more we seem to have been partly misled by cultural influences. Cross-cultural data from permissive societies indicate a far greater sexual readiness in adolescent girls than has previously been seen in this culture. There is reason to recognize that there are two qualities of sexual response possible in women, and that one (masturbatory) may be easier to develop than the other (coital), but the growing knowledge about sexually active teenagers indicates that there is no reason to assume a lesser or later sex drive in females. Were it not for the double standard, there probably *would* be a difference, but in the opposite direction—the woman's drive and responsiveness would probably come earlier, in keeping with her earlier maturation, and be stronger, in keeping with her greater capacity for orgasmic response, than the man's.

As is always true, the variations in sexual behavior reflect not only differences in biological drive and environmental influences, but also the intrapsychic processes. I have tried to differentiate between those processes which result simply from being human and therefore apply to both sexes, such as the crucial need to develop basic trust as an infant, and those that evolve from the differences between the sexes and are therefore not the same in both sexes, such as the difference consequent upon growing up in different bodies. These differences continue to sharpen in late adolescence.

While emotional phenomena cannot easily be quantified, the shared aspects of psychosexual development probably far outweigh those that differentiate males and females. Even the physiology of orgasm is nearly identical, despite anatomical differences and the fact that only males ejaculate.[26] By now the shared psychodynamics have been traced sufficiently so that they may be taken as understood. The need to develop trust and a positive feeling for bodily contact, to understand that one has a right to one's body and to genital feelings, to learn to value one's body and to lose early fears that it had been or could be sexually damaged, to find that each sex is equally valued by society, to cope with the biological surge of puberty and to resolve incestuous wishes, to solidify one's sexual identity by becoming confident one is acceptable to the opposite sex—these underlie any differences, and are prerequisite to healthy adult sexual function.

Early adolescence brings the typical youngster to the point where he can begin to develop heterosexual confidence and competence because it has taken that long to get past the emotional preliminaries to the opportunities provided by regular pairing and dating. Now, in late adolescence, both girls and boys need to learn to risk entrusting themselves to another person. They must learn what a member of the opposite sex is really like and how to love and care for him or her, and to learn to complement each other's emotional needs—the simply human ones and the ones that are unique to the opposite sex. The intrapsychic development necessary to accomplish this complementarity entails sex-specific differences.

Paradoxically, an essential facet of psychosexual differentiation is learning to identify some of one's own sensations and emotions with those of the opposite sex. This requires getting to understand and to be unafraid of those aspects, both of oneself and the partner. It is in this process that the different quality of male and female responses helps fulfill the different needs of each sex. Increasing length of attachment and concern for one another allows a boy to teach a girl something about her body, at the same time learning about it and about his own. Girls are naturally fearful and protective of their own delicate internal organs, and their own explorations are insufficient to reassure them that a male will not harm them. The rate of progress that many adolescents make in proceeding farther and farther with petting is usually determined by the girl. Her inner space is her unique property, and while she needs a male to help her know it fully, she must also be sure that he respects it. When genital petting is gentle and sensitive—something most late adolescents come to experience fairly frequently—this can reassure a girl that males are not the ogres of her infantile fantasies, determined to damage and mutilate her vulnerable wound. Remembering those ubiquitous fantasies of sex as violence, it is not surprising that most girls can trust a boy's fingers before they can trust his penis.

The boy receives at least as much reassurance through petting for his particular concerns. He has always unconsciously associated inside genitals with femaleness, with danger (his own childish fantasies were no less fraught with possible violence to his penis), with his powerful and dominating and deeply envied mother, and he has feared and rejected his own inner sexual sensations accordingly. As he comes to explore those female insides with a caring partner, he learns what they are really like, in contrast to his fantasies. As his girl both welcomes his caresses and responds with pleasure, he eventually loses his fears of damaging her, as well as his fear of woman's mysterious inner sex organs. As he comes to perceive a woman's inner sexual sensations as psychologically acceptable and "good," he can cease to fear his own inner sexual sensations and in this way begin to identify with her so that he can eventually share with a girl that orgastic loss of control characteristically felt as internal and, therefore, as female.[27]

Genital petting experiences also lessen the boy's fear of menstruation. As the organs lose their mystery, there is no need to harbor dire fantasies about the bloody flow that naturally arises in them. In petting, boys can learn that they are capable of more control of their seemingly imperative sexual drives than they may have thought possible. Thus simultaneously they develop more control and less fear of uncontrol.

The analogous benefits of diminished fear and identification also accrue to girls from these mutual explorations. Familiarity with the penis robs it of the misconceptions and fantasies of violence that can only flourish when there is no corrective reality. Mutual masturbatory activity allows a girl to understand a boy's quick and sharp arousability by recognizing its similarity to her own clitoral response. If mutually satisfying and orgastic intercourse occurs between such couples in late adolescence, the girl can further relinquish any vestiges of penis envy because she has every reason to be perfectly delighted with her own equipment and recognizes that the boy *must* have the penis for her own fulfillment to be realized.

Healthy psychosexual development can take place—excepting the final understanding and achievement of adult sexual reciprocity —whether or not adolescents proceed to intercourse, but probably not if they are too inhibited to engage in heavy petting. Petting is likely to be the principal source of such emotional growth in either case. Not only does it afford learning opportunities that quick intercourse without much petting experience cannot, but also, despite the increasing frequency of adolescent intercourse, the opportunities for petting far outnumber those for intercourse for the average young person.

I have described the outcome of health-producing experiences. In any adolescent's experience, one or more partners may behave so as to verify every horrible and frightening childhood fantasy. Most adolescents do have some such terrifying experiences, and even though it is probably natural and unavoidable—no one is gentle and sensitive and reassuring without first having been clumsy and rough and self-concerned—it is one more of an entire childhood full of reasons why few people come to adult sexuality unscarred and without some defensive walls. If the good experiences outweigh the bad, young people can emotionally overcome most of the damaging effects.

And, of course, the effects of prolonged genital petting—or of any prolonged sexual arousal without orgasm—are not always beneficial. Pelvic blood vessels and those of the scrotum and testes become normally engorged with blood during sexual stimulation. Prolonged engorgement is painful, as girls who have had pelvic aching and cramping and boys who have suffered "lover's nuts" will remember. The congestion and the discomfort caused can only be relieved by orgasm, in which the accompanying contractions of the perineal muscles squeeze the blood back out of the swollen vessels.[28] When, for whatever reason, couples regularly refrain from petting to orgasm, the discomfort can easily keep alive some of the fantasies that sex is damaging and harmful—the very opposite of reassurance and relief of fears.

All menstruating women have normal emotional fluctuations that accompany their menstrual cycles. This emotional obbligato is as normal and natural as menstruation itself, though for various physiological and psychopathological reasons some women suffer grossly abnormal distress. If adolescents are together long enough and closely enough, the boy also begins to learn something about a girl's emotional changes. At first her mood swings and her fluctuations from irritability to increased sexual interest to quiet maternal introspectiveness may bewilder and disturb him (or even drive him away if they are excessive or he is too intolerant), but if he allows himself to observe and understand, this experience has a unique value in leading him to a realistic reassessment of his mother. As he learns to understand some of her previously puzzling but normal mood changes and no longer takes them personally, he is further freed from anachronistic responses toward her.

Most of the differences in masculine and feminine sexual behavior—both culturally determined and innate—should begin to crystallize during late adolescence, although some of those differences do not come to the fore until the later stages of lasting adult sexual relations, marriage, and parenthood. Even in a culture that grossly distorts or limits the sex role options open to each sex, distortions normally have been socialized into the youngster and become a part of his behavior by the time he is ready to assume adulthood.

For truly normal psychosexual development to occur, socializing influences should emphasize only those aspects of masculinity and femininity which correspond to innate propensities and capacities, and which are necessary for the health of the individual and the species. All others should depend upon individual interest and ability and not be subject to arbitrarily sex-defined limitations. I am unfamiliar with such an ideal society.

The opposite extreme of cultural caprice—that of erasing all differences—is at least as damaging. Mankind cannot discard its mammalian heritage, nor negate the behavioral and attitudinal consequences of sex-specific hormones, physiology, and anatomy. Each sex is programmed toward behavior which facilitates its procreative and protective survival role within a nuclear family group. That is a general principle whether or not any specific individual opts out of his biological role, or has been subjected to destructive family experiences that cripple his ability to perform that role, curtail his capacity to comprehend its validity, or even turn him against it.

Normally, either sex feels incomplete, empty, and unfulfilled when alone, and looks for completion in a relationship with someone of the opposite sex whose ways of loving are complementary, not identical.[29] Normal young women welcome a man's sexual aggressiveness as long as it is loving, and not used to hurt, dominate, or constrain them. Normal young men who have successfully resolved their dependency conflicts enjoy the caring and comforting quality of a woman's love, so long as it is not engulfing and infantilizing.

In sexual behavior, these normal and healthy differences are not at all equivalent to masculine activity and feminine passivity. Those concepts are destructive caricatures of masculinity and femininity. Each sex in its own way is naturally active, both in seeking sexual pleasure and in the sexual act itself. This is something many late adolescents seem to know better than the older generation. Nonetheless, there is an active assertiveness in healthy males and an active receptivity in healthy females that provides the mutual complementarity both seek, and is in harmony with their predominantly external or internal genitality, their hormonally determined temperaments, and the social roles consequent upon their different procreative responsibilities. These characteristic ways in which males and females relate to one another are normally in operation by the successful end of late adolescence, whether or not any young person has yet begun active intercourse.

Equally active sexuality for males and females has not been the norm in our culture and is only beginning to be seen as appropriate. The young man who is threatened by it probably is unsure of his masculinity, but there are predictable and probably natural hazards as this new standard of behavior becomes the norm. One is the necessary attitudinal shift from traditional concepts, which is neither easy nor free from potential emotional conflict. Far more significant is the fact that sexual participation on demand is only possible for females, never for males. Male coital capacity is limited, female capacity is not. Even in a loving relationship, a man may not be physically or emotionally capable of having an erection and maintaining it long enough to satisfy his partner at the specific time she wants him, though he may wish it just as strongly as she does, to please her. He may do so with nongenital techniques, and often does. But the woman, with her unlimited capacity for arousal, is infinitely more able to respond to her lover's timing if she wants to, and can even participate lovingly at less than orgastic levels of arousal. This simple fact of universal biology is explanation enough why active sexuality cannot express itself identically in both men and women.

Some young women do not understand this difference, especially when they are just beginning to explore their newfound sexual equality. Their demands may be ill-timed, importunate, and challenging. When their young man is put off by their manner, or simply is unable to respond, they may belittle his manhood or accuse him of refusing them an equally active role. He, too, may blame himself, and begin to doubt his virility in what may be the beginning of a downward spiral of both masculine self-esteem and actual potency. Such problems are more typically adult, but can arise between late adolescents engaged in regular intercourse.

Parents Become People

Many late adolescents fail to recognize a difference between parental and cultural values. Even though it is the culture at large that now takes precedence over parents in the relative influence in the lives of adolescents, the emotional basis for the rational or irrational interaction with society has been laid at home throughout childhood.

An infant's earliest relationship with his mother determined whether or not he was able to internalize a sense of trust and a feeling of relatedness to people and to life influences outside himself. This earliest prototype remains amazingly viable in determining the prejudices with which he will later approach other outside influences—neighbors and friends, school, the "establishment." The infant's sense of omnipotence, which he later delegates (but never fully relinquishes) to his parents dates from the same early period. Different kinds of parents, usually unaware of the meaning of this fantasy power, either attempt to remain the Olympian authority as long as possible or, from the beginning, are unafraid to admit their own humanness and mistakes in judgment, and let children take an increasing, age-appropriate role in family decision making.

A second ingredient in future constructive cultural interaction derives from two essential facets of rearing, one essentially maternal, the other paternal. Healthy mothers innately love all their children with relatively little distinction, simply because they exist. Fathers know that the world is not the nursery, and that in adulthood one must earn love and respect and acceptance, or do without them. From the beginning, paternal love tends to be more contingent upon behavior, and becomes more so with age. Any child deprived of this element of love in rearing will be unprepared for reality.

These aspects of rearing bear directly upon the ease or difficulty, the success or failure, of the adolescent's ability to achieve a firm and valued sexual identity, because to do so, he must correct his childish and magical overvaluation of his parents and come to see them as real people. He may be disillusioned and derogatory for a time because the parents seem to have been hypocritical and to have let him down, but if they have helped to foster his sense of their reality and his own, and to prepare him for the real world, the disillusionment will pass. Before a girl can become a healthy woman, she must come to terms with the good qualities of her mother as a model in order to make any appropriate modifications to fit her own individual feminine qualities in a constructive rather than in a rebellious or defiant manner. And she must be able to identify with her father's love and concern for her as a young woman in order to approach young men with warm anticipation and with adequate judgment to discriminate against those whose masculine love is immature or destructive. Complementary conditions underlie a boy's capacity for sexual identity and function.

In the absence of childhood-long preparation—and no family can ever be ideal—the late adolescent has some degree of difficulty, often serious, with himself, his parents, and society. Parents may struggle against losing their godlike status, making it difficult for the youngster to accept his own human imperfections and still regard himself as acceptable, and the opposite sex as accepting and attainable. Without that early incorporation of trust and relatedness, there is a wariness in relations with others that impedes real involvement. Heterosexual relationships are doomed to dissension for anyone who has not learned he must earn and deserve love, steadily, as long as a partnership lasts.

The struggle for realistic perception of parents, and therefore of the self, is often intense and painful on both sides. The adolescent gives up his exaggerated expectations very reluctantly because, with them, he must also lose the remnants of his own onmipotence, his magical belief and expectation that he is capable of anything and everything. He is also still contending against—and against giving up—strong dependent ties. At times the disparity between what is true and what he wishes were true is projected onto the culture, and the adolescent becomes preoccupied with the imperfection of society. So long as an adolescent must invest intense emotion in his claims and demonstrations of independence, the old ties are still strong, and his "independence" is more rebellion than autonomy. The final attainment of a realistic rapprochement with one's parents—both in reality and with their internalized images—is a mark of adulthood, not late adolescence. By the time it is well begun, the young person is more adult than adolescent.

Failures of Adolescence

Since sexuality never exists separately from a person's functioning wholeness, any falling short of the tasks of adolescence invariably reflects itself in erotic relationships. The most obvious failure of all is simply not to experience adolescence. It is possible to have such fear and guilt over adult sexuality that puberty is emotionally denied. Childhood relationships with parents are maintained with minimal upheaval and questioning, eventually to be transferred to all authority figures. The superego never becomes a conscience, and the individual remains emotionally a child. Such adolescents are often thought of as "model youngsters" but they are, in fact, crippled. They can usually function sexually, but their relationships are unimaginative, provide only a fraction of their potential joy, and are usually contaminated by the unconscious identification of the spouse with the parent.

"Refused" adolescence may set an emotional time bomb that will explode later in life. The ego strength necessary to experience adolescence fully may be abnormally slow in developing. Propitious circumstances may belatedly foster that degree of strength after an individual has assumed adult occupational and family obligations. It is not unusual that such a person suddenly finds himself questioning and doubting, seeking the experiences that would crystallize a genuine identity and lead to autonomy, exactly as normally would happen in adolescence. Even though belated "adolescence" of this sort may lead to tremendous new maturity, it is out of phase and untimely. Families and careers are often disrupted, a cost not exacted if adolescence happens at its propitious time.

Even greater, fearful guilt can turn normal periods of asceticism into a life pattern. The motivation toward abstinent life styles and callings usually includes a strong need to maintain repression of sexuality, and decisions to enter such callings are most frequently made in adolescence.

At the opposite pole is the traumatic adolescence of a youngster who does not have the ego strength either to cope with his pubertal drives or to repress them. This may manifest itself in the pseudoheterosexuality of compulsive promiscuity, may be displaced into delinquent antisocial behavior, or may even result in sex crimes. When the oedipal urges are felt to be the most disturbing, an adolescent will not merely separate himself from childhood ties to his parents but will try to remove himself emotionally and sever all constructive ties, sometimes reversing all feelings of love into hate, compulsively forced to espouse only those values that are completely opposite to those of his parents. This maintains his defensive distance but results in incomplete sexual identity and the curtailment of all independent attitudinal choice. He is limited to being an opposite.[30]

A common failure is to prolong adolescence into a life style, sometimes throughout adult life. Such permanent adolescents are lost in uncertainty and self-doubt, clinging desperately to the crises of adolescence as a means of evading adult commitments. The defensive belief in the unresolvable nature of all of life's issues reinforces the claim that adulthood is not worth the effort. There is a mixture of satisfaction and turmoil as such a person finds ingenious ways to combine adult prerogatives with childhood gratifications. In the effort to keep all alternatives open and to avoid finality of choices, he cannot adequately develop and realize any alternative. He has an insatiable need to "share" in a kind of pseudo-intimacy that is basically egocentric and demanding because of his immature capacity for relationships. He is attracted to, and can only attract (until the initial charm wears thin) those who need not an adult partner but a child to indulge and control, one who will permit an irresponsible avoidance of commitment.[31] This particular miscarriage of adolescence has been more common and more dramatically obvious in males, because childlike qualities have been more easily accepted in females, and because male adulthood typically carries the greatest weight of frightening "sink or swim" provider responsibilities.

Late adolescent sexual problems also include unwed pregnancy and venereal disease, on the rise because of increased sexual activity. Many of the same combinations of ignorance and unconscious conflicts as in early adolescence now continue to underlie unwed pregnancies, but late adolescent girls take a more realistic view of the pregnancy itself, their own role in it, and the various possible alternative courses of action. The father of the baby is an important person by this time. Older adolescent girls are often eager for deeper and more permanent commitment, and this introduces a new and usually conscious motivation—the attempt to pressure their boy friends into marriage.[32]

The unmarried father is realistically important in more ways than in the girl's perception of him. He, too, has often reached the stage at which he is yearning for permanency and involvement, and many premature marriages occur out of this unstable blend of maturity and immaturity. Regardless of marriage considerations, the father is often less indifferent and more frequently feels genuine concern about the girl, the fetus, and his responsibility than he may be given credit for. Yet he may not be allowed to give or receive support at this time, forbidden to by his own or the girl's parents. This is a true loss to both partners, because each needs the other's support and the maturing influence of participating in the decision as to alternatives. Whenever possible, unmarried fathers should be included actively in counseling with an unwed adolescent girl.[33]

Premature marriage itself is often a "problem" of late adolescence. "Premature" implies a value judgment, and obviously not all early marriages are premature in the sense of instability, inappropriate motivation, and probable unhappiness, but sadly, those unhappy prognostications are fulfilled in most marriages consummated while the couple is still adolescent. Since identities are incomplete, it is at least as likely that the two will grow more apart than together. Young people who marry while still in high school statistically have lower than average intelligence and grades, and are more likely to be disturbed youngsters from disturbed homes.[34] Unless there is financial help from parents, family responsibilities at this age usually spell financial and educational suicide for one or both partners. Either alternative has ominous overtones. Teenage (not strictly adolescent) marriages have an astronomical divorce rate, estimated at two to four times as high as that for marriages begun in the twenties.[35]

One of the major sexual motivations for premature marriage is unwed pregnancy. A conservative figure is that fully 50 percent of teenage brides are pregnant at their wedding, and some estimates run as high as 90 percent.[36] Authorities are in full agreement that young marriages prompted by pregnancy have little chance of success.[37] One overall figure cited is an 80 percent divorce rate for those who marry by the age of eighteen when the bride is pregnant.[38] "Fetal glue" is notoriously undependable for holding a couple together.

A second sexual motivation for marriage—the desire for ready access to sex without guilt—results in marriages predicated upon physical attraction alone and undertaken during that uniquely human phase of transient insanity called infatuation, when the tunnel vision of the two lovers conveniently blocks out all other considerations but genital urgency. Infatuation does not last, but incompatible personality traits and life goals frequently do. As more young people come to accept active sexuality and genuinely have less guilt over it—not merely denying their unconscious guilt—this basis of poor marital judgment should diminish, but sexual prohibitiveness and guilt still are stark realities for the majority of middle-class adolescents, regardless of how frequently they defy the taboos. Sympathetic and conflicted parents, themselves supportive of their adolescents' sexual needs but unable to break through their own inhibitions enough to help the youngsters out of the traditional morality, sometimes foster premature marriage. It is too often a maladaptive solution prompted by sincere but misguided empathy.

As can be expected, the closer an adolescent comes to the time for adult sexual function, the more clearly will crippling conflicts and incapacities begin to take their toll. By no means will all of those who eventually develop deviant forms of sexual behavior express them overtly during late adolescence. Some youngsters will strive valiantly against their conflicts in order to feel and to appear normal. Many others will be relatively or completely sexually inactive, unable to enjoy increasing sexuality as their peers do and unwilling to act upon their homosexual desires. Their preferences emerge only in masturbatory fantasies, and trouble them deeply. But by late adolescence, many preferential or exclusive homosexuals have admitted their preferences, and quite a few have "come out," especially in college or university environments.

One of the peaks in pedophilia, or sexual offenses against children, occurs in mid to late adolescence, when a boy cannot bring himself to make sexual advances toward a girl his own age.[39] Exhibitionism becomes more frequent in late adolescence, betraying the same failure of gratification from more normally appropriate sexual outlets.[40] (Some studies indicate a peak incidence of exhibitionism among very early pubescent boys,[41] but it can be questioned whether this is actually any more indicative of genuine disturbance than any of the other fairly chaotic sexual behavior of that time.) Any and all substitutions for natural heterosexuality, including fetishism, transvestism, and sadomasochism, emerge as sexual outlets that compensate for dammed-up heterosexuality.

Paraphilias, or disorders of sexual object preference, are more frequent in or even virtually limited to males.[42] There are no exceptions. The reasons for this universally greater male vulnerability is that male sexual differentiation is more complex, male sexual function is more dependent upon learning, and male sex identity is more difficult to achieve because a boy must first disidentify from a female—his mother. Therefore, learning and rearing deficits can take a greater toll. Only the female capacity for erotic pleasure is as vulnerable to mislearning as is male heterosexual function. As late adolescence ends, the proportion of male victims of disruptive psychosexual development influences begins to become distressingly apparent.

What Puberty Accomplishes

This and the two preceding chapters have dealt with adolescence, the second cycle of psychosexual development, that is precipitated in one way or another by puberty.

Briefly restated, the universal tasks of adolescence in *any* culture are (1) to shift from the family of origin to a different family of procreation, (2) to shift from the position of being nurtured to that of providing nurture for others, and (3) to attain the capacity for productive social participation and for mature heterosexual love. As detailed at the beginning of this chapter, adolescence will have ended—whether or not those basic tasks have been fully or ideally met—with the achievement of stable emotional and behavioral patterns, committed life roles, firm sexual identity, an internalized value system, and a reasonable balance between biological drives, conscience, and ego.

A perusal of these sets of criteria reveals that they do not coincide. It is evident that adolescence may end without its tasks being accomplished, and it may end with an infinite variety of adaptive or maladaptive character structures, personality patterns, and emotional states jelled into an adult life style. Or it may not end at all.

I have frequently referred to the *Sturm und Drang* of adolescence as normal and its absence as a sign of truncated development. This deserves a closer look. Do adolescents really need to go through a period of significant turmoil in order to benefit maximally from their adolescence?

There have been two studies, one by Daniel Offer and another by Roy R. Grinker, Sr., of male adolescents who were characterized by minimal adolescent upheaval and were considered normal and healthy because they had no diagnosable psychiatric disorders and were subjectively satisfied with their function. They also showed a uniformly low incidence of any form of heterosexual activity. A few girls were included in Offer's study, but the findings apply essentially to boys. Careful consideration of the reports reveal some significant ego deficits and unresolved conflicts. These adolescents are nonchallenging sons with a strong sense of filial obedience, whom their parents describe as compliant and right-thinking. They tend to be mother-dominated, and reveal clear evidence of unresolved oedipal conflicts when they describe their reasons for a lack of heterosexual activity. They are usually confused and contradictory in their sexual attitudes, with little capacity for introspection or creativity. College follow-up studies reveal them to be still struggling to shed their child status in their mother's eyes, and they are prone to depression then and in later life.[43]

Another way of looking at health—considering it to imply optimal ego growth—is to study the adolescence of those who have achieved the level of principled, or what has been called post-conventional, moral thought. This level is characterized by autonomous ethical principles which have validity apart from the authority of the people or groups who hold them, and by an awareness of the relativism of personal values. Such principled judgment involves universal principles of justice, equality of human rights, and respect for the dignity of every individual—in contrast to conventional morality, defined as a "good boy" need to behave so as to gain approval, and a commitment to authority, fixed rules, and the maintainment of the existing social order without question. Postconventional morality can be achieved only after the ability for abstract thinking comes into existence.

Studies suggest that as few as 10 percent of those over age sixteen in the United States have achieved the level of principled thought. Typically, those who have achieved it have gone through the turmoil of struggling for an autonomous identity and a period of nihilistic doubting and questioning of everything.[44] The achievement of this level of ego maturity and autonomy requires a rebellious adolescence in order to free one's initiative from authority-related guilt. Research has found adult emotional health (not only ego growth) to be correlated with a troubled and troublesome adolescence.[45]

There are those—adults and adolescents alike—who will opt for conventionality, belonging, and acceptance because the spectre of moral anarchy and the fear of their own impulses is too great. It must be emphasized, however,that the freedom to question anything does not imply inevitably rejecting everything. It means only that whatever one accepts of the existing or traditional social mores is accepted because one wishes to accept it, not because one is afraid to oppose it. Retaining the late childhood level of conventional morality by avoiding adolescent turmoil appears to exact a high price in adult rigidity and inhibited initiative and creativity.

Adolescent turmoil, then, is not as grave a sign as is adolescent quiescence. Turmoil for its own sake is not the issue, however, because some forms of disturbed adolescence reflect serious psychopathology. Nor do I suggest that any society should set about arbitrarily to frustrate its adolescents so as to produce turmoil. Rather, turmoil can be considered a normal reaction to puberty in any culture that imposes a long delay between puberty and the readiness for adult sexual responsibilities, and that forces adolescents to experiment and to make choices by offering a rich variety of adult alternatives. Rebellious turbulence is probably "necessary" in the sense that it indicates that a youngster has not foreclosed his choices but is experiencing his adolescence in a manner most conducive to genuine identity formation, autonomy, and ego maturation.

The paradigm of adolescent rebellion in our culture is active heterosexuality. Are there any indications that intercourse during adolescence may be a valid and constructive expression of revolt against tradition, or is it merely a self-damaging misplacement of energies, a hollow pseudo-adulthood? If this is not an all-or-none issue, are there any recognizable distinctions between constructive and destructive adolescent intercourse?

It has been suggested that overt sexuality during early adolescence can have many of the dire consequences postulated for sexuality during latency. Psychiatric and psychoanalytic child development literature is replete with descriptions of the impairment of ego maturation, object constancy, and the capacity for sublimation, traceable to early sexual gratification. It is maintained that since the ego is still immature and the unconscious is still enmeshed in oedipal wishes, intercourse is premature and will fixate the ego at immature narcissistic levels devoid of involvement and contaminated with infantile conflicts, and that full heterosexual gratification should therefore be postponed until ego maturation and sexual identity are firm and complete.[46]

It is realistic to point out that real sexual identity is impossible until it is based upon real experimentation with new situations and challenges. Thus it is entirely reasonable to wonder whether sex identity and ego growth can take place adequately as a result of anticipatory fantasy alone. There is also good reason to believe that adolescents can learn from mistakes, hurts, and anxieties, as well as from successes, which casts doubt upon the theory of the inevitability of emotional damage from immature sexual experimentation and less-than-ideal experiences.[47]

The most reasonable approach is to study whole population samples and see what correlations may exist between adolescent intercourse and various criteria of health or disturbance. Nearly everyone knows one or many people who led an active adolescent sex life and who seem not to have been damaged, who perhaps even benefited from it. But that is a shaky basis for conclusions—seldom do we know the details of our friends' sex lives and conflicts. Kinsey found that the earlier and more frequently a woman had orgastic experience, especially from premarital intercourse, the more likely and frequent was orgastic response in marriage.[48] But orgasm is not all there is to adult sexual health. Cross-cultural data indicates that sexually permissive societies show fewer adult sexual dysfunctions and deviations than are found in restrictive societies.

A study of representative United States adolescents relating sexuality to other aspects of function and life style found that teenagers fall naturally into several broad and enlightening behavioral categories. The sexually inexperienced are conservative and conformist, and generally still regard themselves as children. The sexual beginners who are heterosexually active in petting short of orgasm and are still virgins are the most religious and politically conservative group, have the most stable and happy parental relationships, and make the lowest average school grades of any group except sexual adventurers.

Among those actively engaged in intercourse, the sexual adventurers ("promiscuous") are a dysfunctional group. They make the lowest grades, have the poorest parental relationships, and are generally dissatisfied with themselves and their lives, including their sex lives. They are more willing to exploit a partner, only 46 percent consistently use contraceptives, and only about one-third of the girls are satisfied with their orgastic response.

The other sexually active group is called serial monogamists without marriage. While some may have had several partners, they remain committed to one for considerable time. Half have been together a year or more. They feel love for, and loved by, their partners, and most claim to be satisfied with their sex lives, with slightly over half the girls usually orgastic. They have more frequent sex than even the adventurers, and 66 percent always use contraceptives. They average the highest grades of all groups, and the vast majority wish for a closer rapprochement with their parents over their sexuality.

The characterizations of the different groups hold true regardless of age. Even thirteen-year-old serial monogamists (of which there are a few) have the qualities described. Naturally, the proportion of serial monogamists increases with age, since they are clearly the most mature group.[49] By any criteria of ego strength and capacity for relatedness they have achieved more than the average teenager showing any other described pattern of sexual behavior, and are least impaired in directing their energies toward learning. The sexual beginners and sexually inexperienced sound suspiciously like the perennial children who have so far refused adolescence. One can assume that most of them will eventually shift to some pattern of activity that includes intercourse later in adolescence or as adults. Another group may adopt total monogamy and thus be unlike either serial monogamists or adventurers. One can further speculate that sexual beginners may be struggling with guilts and anxieties of a specifically sexual nature to such an extent that other important aspects of their lives suffer, such as school.

The weight of reason and evidence is that full sexual activity in adolescence is not necessarily damaging, and can be healthy and beneficial. This conclusion does not conform to conventional morality, but concepts of health or illness cannot be circumscribed by any one set of moral rules. Emotional health is related to values in that it cannot exist in the absence of some socially viable value system, but an internally evolved value system which is a product of maturity is a different matter from externally imposed moral laws which deny the right to autonomous decision making. While there are moral attitudes that would label all unmarried adolescent intercourse as evil, there is no way to label it all deleterious to emotional health.

What is essentially at issue is neither age nor morals, but maturity. It is clear that some felicitous conditions in the family and the rearing of certain adolescents promote an early level of maturity and capacity for relatedness that makes them able to handle the emotional involvements of intercourse very well. They misuse it and each other minimally, and are free to use their energies and explore their capacities in other areas of their lives. It is equally clear that such a degree of maturity is painfully lacking in many adolescents— probably the majority. They are either unprepared to use sex healthily when they become active, or must squander their energies in a struggle against unnecessary emotional obstacles.

That either-or summation is oversimplified. Some adolescents, particularly those who pet to orgasm and are mutually concerned for one another's well-being, may be able to postpone intercourse very healthily. Maturation is so variable in timing that many of those slow to start, or who are engaged in a disruptive struggle, will emerge with healthy sexuality. Perhaps those who use their sexuality well went through some of the same conflict earlier. The conclusion to be drawn, I believe, is that much of the self-damaging conflict and inappropriate destructiveness attributed to full adolescent sexual expression must be unnecessary, a pathogenic aspect of our culture. Society presumably could work toward lessening the unnecessary obstacles to healthy adolescent sexual experience.

Our middle-class culture makes of adolescence a uniquely stressful and difficult time, and not only in the sexual sphere. Since no particular past or present culture's institutions and social norms are eternal or sacred, ours must be recognized as nothing more than one more arbitrary, blindly put together hodgepodge of the past. Ill-conceived cultural norms can create their own unique problems, and adolescence may be one of ours. Some aspects of adolescent stress may derive from the caprice of social tradition instead of being an inevitable part of growing up in a technologically advanced culture.

At the same time that our culture increases the difficulties facing adolescents, it also increases the potential rewards. Compared with cultures in which adult roles are sharply limited in number or accessibility, ours offers a rich choice. For those adolescents with genuine access to that richness of choice, the rewards of unlimited possible achievement offer maximum opportunity for self-actualization. But choice is more difficult than following a predestined course, and induces conflict and turmoil. Cultures without the conditions that produce those kinds of stress also do not produce maximum ego growth or emotional maturity. Nothing is free; the higher the stakes, the fewer winners and the more casualties.

Psychosexual development does not end with adolescence, though most of its formative influences have had their strongest effects by now. If there seems to be an overwhelming array of potentially disruptive influences during the preadult years, leaving little room for the emergence of true health, that is true. Nothing is to be gained by denying it. The combination of the unmatchable intricacy of human psychodynamics with both the complex demands and idiosyncratic mores of our culture assures that no one emerges really unscathed. It is axiomatic that our culture makes it impossible to grow to adulthood completely free of sexual "hangups"; there are only differences in how many, what kinds, and how severe.

Perfect mental health in general, and sexual maturity in particular, are imaginary ideals—like infinity, approachable but not achievable. Luckily, the variations in the degree to which everyone falls short of the ideal are very wide. Enough people emerge into the new relative equilibrium of sexual adulthood in reasonable condition, able to enjoy their sexuality and able to make the sexuality of others enjoyable, to make the rearing effort worth while. Perhaps, with the instrumental effectiveness available to them as adults, they will even try to modify the unnecessary and pathogenic social norms for the benefit of their own children.

The Third
Cycle

TEN

Young Adulthood: Pairing and Mating

Psychosexual development is not complete upon the attainment of adulthood. It is a lifelong, conception-to-death process, normally in continuous modification. A few authorities have called attention to this fact, and the concept is gaining more widespread acceptance, but the predominant assumption has traditionally been that one's sexuality has developed by adulthood and remains essentially unchanged except by the toll of years thereafter. One goal of this book is to expand that limited and constricting assumption and to demonstrate that sexuality is a vital aspect of living throughout the life cycle. There is no reason to believe that what is good cannot evolve into something even better, or that something distorted or inhibited cannot become healthier and more gratifying, long after adolescence.

Psychosexual development throughout adult life is the third cycle of human sexuality. The normal march of environmental, psychological, and biological events allows and enforces still another and more highly integrated working through of psychosexual issues reminiscent of both childhood and adolescence.

For clarity, young adult sexuality will be discussed separately from marriage, but this is a false separation. The average girl, for example, marries during or immediately after adolescence, so that these two facets of early adulthood are concurrent. In most instances, characteristics of young adult sexuality continue to be expressed by young marrieds even when they had been single for a number of years. It is the frequency with which both men and women remain single, yet increasingly lead active sex lives, that justifies the arbitrary distinction. The separation is also a reflection of the seemingly universal order in which an adult member of any society assumes responsibilities. Despite the many obvious exceptions, the normative progression is responsibility for self, spouse, offspring, and society itself.

The sexual uncertainties, doubts, and experiments of adolescence do not come to an abrupt end, ever. Young adults are busy synthesizing and harmonizing what they experienced and learned in adolescence. This means that they continue to try out and test the validity of those experiences in more and more committed relationships. Erik Erikson—one of those who have clearly understood the lifelong nature of psychosexual and psychosocial development—characterized this period as that during which a person either developed the capacity for intimacy or took on the defensive personality traits of isolation and self-distancing from others. Erikson's point that one cannot involve oneself as a fully participating member of a twosome until one becomes "oneself" is difficult to challenge.[1]

Occupational identity and choice, a major preoccupation of most young adults, exerts a distinct but indirect influence upon further psychosexual development. The responsibility of family support still rests predominantly on the male, and will probably continue to do so despite the minority who explore alternative sex role styles. Males are acutely aware of this, and it may well be that successful occupational competition constitutes a more meaningful test and validation of manhood for many men than does excellence in sexual participation. This means that while a bachelor may date and have affairs with a variety of young women, he will probably eventually marry one who appears to fit with his occupation and its implicit life style and goals. A young corporation lawyer will rarely marry a sexually casual young woman from a rural commune. It is easy to imagine how differently she, compared with a more traditional woman, might interact with him sexually. His own (as well as his wife's) further psychosexual development is thus sharply channeled by the priority of occupation.

Women are affected in a related manner, not only as in the illustration just given, but also because the future of most women is so closely linked to the occupational success of their husbands that that consideration weighs heavily in their choice of mates. Some young women cite this as a reason for remaining unmarried, others for having a separate occupation and remaining childless after marriage, and others for relegating the child's well-being to the lowest family priority in their determination to remain competitively employed and unaffected by the dependence of the child; the latter are, and will likely remain, distinctly a minority. Fully nine-tenths of all women, including those with the best and most liberated education, opt willingly for home and family and the nurturant activities inherent in the traditional division of labor. The valid social goals of feminism notwithstanding, there is little evidence that this will cease to be the dominant pattern in the foreseeable evolutionary future.

While retaining the focus on healthy development in the dominant subculture, it is worth remembering from time to time how variable the different cultural influences and their consequences can be. For instance, lower-class males become heterosexually active much earlier than their middle-class counterparts but tend to remain almost exclusively homosocial.[2] There is little prestige associated with companionable heterosocial life styles, and this reflects itself in different types of marriages, different qualities of sexual interaction, and grossly different resulting attitudes toward sex. Poverty cultures are characterized by marriages in which there is little social companionship or reciprocity, little concern by the man for his wife's sexual pleasure, low levels of female gratification, and conspicuously negative attitudes toward sex by wives.[3] These are consequences of a style of relating sexually, not a consequence of poverty *per se*. Any couple in any subculture or at any socioeconomic level who related in like fashion would suffer comparable personal and interpersonal losses.

The Broadening Sexual Horizon

The sexual behavior of the young adult does not differ a great deal from that of the sexually active adolescent. There is simply more of it, and to some extent it may become more varied. The number of persons with some premarital intercourse experience are increasing, and this is significantly more true of females than males. More females report intercourse with more than one partner than in earlier generations. More males are likely to have their first intercourse with a loved partner than with a prostitute. More couples live openly together without or before marriage. Nonvirginity carries less social stigma.

It is also true that a large proportion of young adults continue to strive toward adherence to traditional restrictive mores, many of them retain those values, and masturbation remains a principal, if not *the* principal, source of orgastic gratification.

The most significant superficial reason for the greater sexual activity of young adults is their greater freedom from parental surveillance and easier access to private surroundings where they can make use of sexual opportunities. Most of them live away from home, some transportation is available, and either the man or the woman can find a place of privacy. A significant part of the feeling of freedom to follow up on sexual opportunity, especially for women, is safe and reliable contraception and, more recently, safe and reliable abortion. I referred earlier to the research demonstrating that the availability of contraceptives had no measurable effect upon modifying a girl's sexual values and therefore did not lead to carefree bedhopping by girls who otherwise would have refrained. That remains true for young adults. The same research also defined the group for whom contraception would influence decision. Women whose already existing value system accepts and approves of nonmarital intercourse are more likely to have intercourse, and to do so more frequently, when they know they are safe.[4] It is apparent to most observers that female sexual standards are becoming less restrictive.

Young adult sexuality is still highly experimental. Relatively few have had the opportunity to try as many sexual practices, free from intrusion, while they were adolescents. As their familiarity with the bodies and the varieties of response and emotions of the opposite sex increases, along with self-knowledge and self-confidence, inhibitions against new and different sexual practices begin to relax. This depends also upon complex intrapsychic processes, but opportunity and familiarity also play an obvious role. Opportunity may be governed not so much by physical freedom as by the emotional attitudes of one or both partners. A man cannot explore the mutual response to oral sex when he is revolted by the presumed unpleasant odor of female genitalia as a result of unconscious associations between the genital opening and feces. In an uncommon reversal of the usual hierarchy of fears and avoidances, a young woman who was once a patient of mine defended herself from penile penetration for months by performing fellatio for her male partners. Nevertheless, young adults usually become more and more experienced in the varieties of sexual practices. In the process they may both expand the range of their sexual enjoyment and also discover those sexual activities which, for whatever reasons, they prefer (or are unconsciously compelled) to avoid.

Not all young adults are sexually secure and confident. Many are still proving their masculinity or femininity through sex. The desire for variety in experience is a human characteristic that is neither abnormal nor in any way limited to sex. It is a strong motive behind the wish for a period of less permanent commitments in perfectly healthy young men and women. So is the determination to exercise the best possible judgment in choosing a mate. But insecurity is a more imperative pressure that impels the scalp collectors of both sexes. Male fears of inadequate performance and inability to satisfy the woman, female fears of the ability to attract and hold a man, irrational fears of homosexuality, equating virility or attractiveness with the number of women one can seduce or the number of men one can sleep with—all these, plus even more pernicious conflicts, may underlie compulsive sexuality.

It is a common complaint of single young women that bachelors want nothing but sex and that, in a gathering of singles, the young women feel as though they are impaled on a meat rack for inspection, but this is an inaccurately one-sided complaint. A few visits to busy singles' cocktail lounges in large cities makes it clear that both "meat" and "meat inspectors" come in both sexes. The newly awakening sexual equality of women—a good thing in itself—prompts a number of women to emulate some of the predatory qualities so long resented in men.

This increasing equality has introduced a new quality of anxiety about performance into female sexuality—that of orgastic response. When the anxiety does exist it can be a more private anxiety than the performance anxiety in a male, because he cannot possibly hide an episode of impotence or premature ejaculation. This does not mean that anxiety and diminished self-esteem are not eating away destructively at many nonorgastic women. One effect of this anxiety can be a ceaseless and frantic search for the "right" partner who will be able to gratify her. Some women may unluckily have known only self-preoccupied, importunate men who had little concern about arousing them, but often the woman is seeking an external solution for an intrapsychic problem, an unconsciously determined inhibition that only a change in herself will release.

It should scarcely be necessary to affirm women's equal right to orgastic pleasure, or to suggest that essentially the only women, in the past or now, who claim not to care whether they are orgastic, are those whose natural responsiveness and desire have been destroyed or impaired by distorted psychosexual development. Because human sexual response is so easily disrupted, a temporary price of a woman's knowing she has a right to equal enjoyment will be increased frustration and sexual insecurity until the rearing of girls catches up with a woman's potential. Hopefully, the delay will not be long.

Normal adult male sexual physiology and response is, in comparison with the female, relatively simple. Except for the unconscious struggles with integrating inner and outer genitality, the vicissitudes of which have been manifested since infancy, man's normal function seldom introduces emotional problems and tasks unless his development has gone awry and he has unconsciously forged inappropriate associations between emergency emotions and his normal sexuality.

When female orgasm is a problem, it is almost entirely an artificially produced one. It is true that an orgasm is more likely to arouse intrapsychic apprehension in a woman because of her greater sense of bodily vulnerability and the greater risk, seemingly, of entrusting herself to the penetrating man during the orgastic loss of control. But, as is demonstrated by many past and present societies, as well as by countless individuals in our own society, no healthy woman will fail to be responsive unless her capacity to respond is interfered with. Orgastic response is a normally occurring animal phenomenon.

A part of the problem concerns the differentiation between clitoral and vaginal orgasm. Because early psychoanalytic theory failed to recognize that girls have a normal feminine psychosexual development fully correlated with their appropriately female anatomy, clitoral orgasm was labeled as immature and vaginal orgasm as mature. One consequence has been that several generations of women have had deep concern about whether they had clitoral or vaginal orgasms, and have felt distressing sexual insecurity if they could not be sure of the vaginal "maturity" of their orgasms.

It is easy to dismiss this misconception on the physiological level. Research at the Reproductive Biology Research Foundation in St.

Louis, Missouri, has proved beyond question that every woman's physiological response to orgasm is identical, no matter how the orgasm is achieved. Whether an orgasm is stimulated by fantasy, nongenital stimulation (such as caressing the nipples), clitoral masturbation, or intravaginal intercourse, all the same things happen in the same sequence in a woman's body. There are no sexual nerve endings in the vaginal wall more than an inch or so beyond the vaginal introitus. Moreover, the in-and-out motion of intravaginal intercourse inevitably produces movement of the soft and flexible adjacent perineal tissues so that the clitoris is directly stimulated by the friction of its own hood moving to and fro—even when the partners studiously avoid manipulating the clitoris in any way.[5]

The issue is not that simple, however; orgasm is an integrated, total body and emotional response, not merely a series of physiologic events. Many women who are fully aware of the fallacy of two different kinds of physiologic orgasm report clearly different subjective responses and genital sensations arising from clitoral masturbation and from orgastic intercourse with a loved partner. The description of such differences are numerous, knowledgeable, and convincing.

To account for this discrepancy, two factors must be considered. First, a woman's feeling about orgasm, her subjective response to it, is emotional. Orgasmic physiology triggers that response, which may not even be sensed as pleasant. An entirely normal physiologic orgasm may arouse anxiety, guilt, and even displeasure in a sufficiently conflicted woman. Therefore what she feels is not determined by physiology alone. Second, the physiology itself is intensely internal, involving strong muscular contractions of the uterus, vagina, and other pelvic structures. In tracing psychosexual development it has been seen that acceptance of internal sexual sensations poses a significant intrapsychic problem which some women do not resolve satisfactorily. Because of fear or resentment, there are women who value only those sensations over which they can exert the greatest control—the clitoral sensations—and some women are mentally capable of blocking all conscious awareness of the full inner pelvic sensations.

Thus, while there is only one kind of orgasm physiologically, there are various sensory and emotional perceptions of orgasm. The terms clitoral and vaginal are best avoided because of their history of misuse, but it is valid to recognize that the major perceptual variations in women's orgastic response reflect their predominantly externalized or internalized subjective focus. There are often typical emotional and characterological distinctions between the women who prefer, or are limited to, one or the other focus. Women who are unconsciously afraid of their inner sexuality, afraid or resentful of yielding to a man enough control and "power" over their sexual response so as to allow themselves to be fully responsive to intravaginal intercourse, and women who retain a competitively masculine quality of true penis envy, will generally be limited to sensing the external component of their orgastic sensations. They may even prefer masturbation to coitus because it avoids their fears and gives them total control. During masturbation they may be able to relax enough to enjoy their full body response, something they cannot permit themselves during intercourse.

Women who lack such fears and have intercourse with men whom they love and trust (both consciously and unconsciously) report a preference for coital orgasm that involves full awareness of the strong inner sensations and the mutual loss of control. They can often describe distinctly different sensations from clitoral masturbation. Even though they may know their own erotic responses more thoroughly and be more easily able to achieve masturbatory orgasm, they prefer the mutual involvement of loving intercourse. The greater importance of the emotional component of orgastic response is demonstrated by the fact that women whose uterus had been removed but who had previously developed the freedom and preference to enjoy the full pelvic response to coitus continue to report the identical pleasure and response.

Another issue of female physiology that affects a woman's sexuality is the menstrual cycle with its shifting quantities and gradients of the two principal ovarian hormones, estrogen and progesterone. A woman's period is customarily counted from the first day of menstrual flow, but the easiest way to comprehend the basic hormonal fluctuations and interactions is to regard the flow itself as the final phase of the cycle.

During or toward the end of the menstrual flow, one (occasionally more) of the thousands of Graafian follicles—microscopic cystlike structures near the surface of the ovary, each of which contains an ovum—begins to mature. As it ripens, it produces increasing amounts of estrogen, which causes the endometrium (the lining of the uterus) to thicken and become more vascular in early preparation for possible implantation of a fertilized ovum. At about mid-cycle, most commonly eleven to fourteen days after the onset of flow, ovulation occurs with the rupture of the follicle and the release of the ovum into the peritoneal cavity, whence it will be drawn into the fallopian tubes. Beginning at the time of ovulation, a different part of the follicle begins to grow and to produce both progesterone and additional estrogen. Progesterone furthers and completes the proliferation of the endometrium so that it may sustain the life of an implanted conceptus and provide nourishment for it. When fertilization of the ovum fails to occur, the ruptured follicle begins to deteriorate, with the gradual diminution of both progesterone and estrogen. Approximately twenty-eight days following the onset of the previous flow, estrogen has returned to its lowest level in its normal cyclic variations, and progesterone production abruptly ceases. It is the withdrawal of progesterone that causes the breaking down and sloughing off of the endometrium. The blood, tissue fluid, and bits of tissue which had composed the endometrium is the material that constitutes the menstrual flow itself.

It has long been known that the moods and sexual interests, even the emotional stability, of many women fluctuate predictably with their menstrual cycle. Typically, the women who do suffer emotional distress related to their periods are most vulnerable from a few days before menstruation begins to the time when the flow is almost over. This period of no more than a week constitutes at most 25 percent of a woman's life during her reproductive years, yet a series of studies have documented an amazing concentration of female dysfunction occurring at this time. During this 25 percent of each month, to cite but a few examples, occur 49 percent of all crimes committed by female prisoners, 45 percent of punishments meted out to school girls, 53 percent of suicides, and 46 percent of admissions to mental hospitals.[6] On advanced examinations, the pass rate of female students was 13 percent lower.[7] The British Road Research Laboratory reports that 60 percent of women's traffic accidents also occur during the same phase.[8]

The combination of psychological and physiological reasons for this clustering of female dysfunction is not fully known. In a study of 103 American women, it was reported that premenstrual distress and behavior disorders were suffered only by those women who had had conflict with their mothers and whose mothers had not prepared them healthily for menarche. Emotional factors impaired their welcoming and valuing womanhood and conditioned them to respond to menstruation with fear and depression.[9]

In addition to psychological factors, there also definitely appear to be correlations between the cyclic endocrines and the so-called premenstrual syndrome. It is known that progesterone has a calming and antidepressant effect. The weight of evidence indicates that the most probable physiological correlate of the distressing symptoms is the dropping of progesterone to a low level as menstruation approaches, and particularly its very sudden extinction usually about twenty-four to forty-eight hours before menses begin. This explanation is compatible with the analogous combination of suddenly diminished progesterone and high incidence of psychiatric disorders characteristic of the period immediately following childbirth.[10]

What is known still leaves many unanswered questions. Does every woman who has premenstrual emotional distress have a history of a poor relationship with her mother relating to her menarche? While that proposition appears oversimplified, it is true that the existing hormonal explanations are inadequate to account for the many women who are usually untroubled by premenstrual distress. Whatever the physiological mechanisms, they can operate only in concert with a woman's developmental and emotional state. And however widely emotional factors may vary, cyclic menstrual endocrinology is the normal physiology of all women of reproductive age. The result is that these normal female hormonal fluctuations, through interactions not yet understood, can disrupt the emotional balance of those women who, for whatever reasons, are susceptible. This poses tasks of emotional coping that are unique to women and also constitutes one of the remarkably few normal physiological disadvantages that weigh more heavily upon women than upon men.

Of still greater interest are the effects of the cyclic hormone changes upon sexual desire and attitudes. The most exhaustive and painstaking research yet undertaken on this correlation has shown that women's active heterosexual interests typically mount throughout the first half, or estrogenic phase of the cycle, reaching a peak at the time of ovulation when both hormones are at a high level. During the second half, or progesterone phase, women become more calm and introspective, less active heterosexually but more receptive in general mood and therefore perhaps more receptive to intercourse, despite their less active heterosexual preoccupations. There may also be a secondary peak of heterosexual interests just before menstruation and during the early part of the flow.

In other words, there is reason to recognize an innate, hormonally determined, psychological form of "heat" that coincides in perfect appropriateness with ovulation, in the human female, less intense but analogous to the heat, or estrus period, of lower animals. This must not, of course, be taken too literally. Humans can be aroused at any time, and sexual arousal is highly dependent upon both learning and circumstances. In a woman with intense heterosexual anxieties, the period of her most intense inner heterosexual drive could manifest itself behaviorally as anger toward men and fearful avoidance of sexual activity. Considerations such as these probably explain why various other investigators, evaluating essentially conscious perceptions of sexual desire and overt sexual activity, have sometimes reported other timings for peak sex drive, or have even been unable to detect a consistent variation. But at an inner level reflecting sexual motivation, female psychosexuality seems to fluctuate in fitting harmony with, and to be determined by, a woman's endocrine and reproductive status. It is at this unconscious level, underlying that of overt behavior, that the most intriguing emotional correlations between biology and psychosexual state may be discerned.

The same research project kept meticulous note of unconscious emotions and needs as revealed through dreams and associations during analysis. Estrogen may be considered a hormone of preparation. At the same time that it is preparing the endometrium for possible pregnancy, it is preparing the woman to become pregnant by increasing her heterosexual drive. Dreams during the preovulatory phase reflect her increasingly active heterosexual preoccupations, which are also of an increasingly mature nature. It is not only the absolute amount of hormone, but also its gradient—whether increasing or declining—that influences a woman's inner psychosexual state. At the highest levels of production of both estrogen and progesterone, immediately after ovulation, one sees evidence of the most mature levels of emotional and ego integration that are accessible to a specific individual.

Progesterone is the hormone of pregnancy—it is produced in greatest amount during pregnancy and is required for successful maintenance of pregnancy—and may be characterized as relating to oneself and one's inner space. During its peak production in the days following ovulation, heterosexual tension diminishes and is replaced by receptive and retentive tendencies and narcissistic bodily interests. A woman's dreams typically relate to mother, mothering, being loved and cared for, pregnancy, enclosed and filled spaces. This is the period of incipient pregnancy, when the fertilized ovum has begun cellular division and development; it does not normally reach the uterus and implant until four to six days after fertilization. The correlation is an obvious one between maximal endocrine and uterine readiness for pregnancy and gestation to begin, the emotional preoccupation with one's body, and an attitude of receptivity and nurturance.

Without fertilization and implantation to interrupt the cycle, estrogen and progesterone regression is paralleled by a regression in emotional concerns to earlier psychosexual developmental levels. Dream material evidences a continued receptivity at more and more passive and dependent levels, with the return of oral and anal phase concepts and emotions appearing more frequently. The premenstrual increase in heterosexuality is more reflective of an infantile "care for me" level than of active adult sex drive. With the cessation of progesterone production and the onset of the menses, oral and anal fantasies from the earliest levels of infantile psychosexuality predominate the unconscious processes. Just as the highest levels of combined estrogen and progesterone production are paralleled by intrapsychic evidence of the highest degree of integration of psychosexuality, the lowest hormone levels correlate with unconscious emotional responses at the earliest and least integrated psychosexual levels.[11]

Overt behavior may mask these intrapsychic fluctuations. Unconscious concerns at an infantile level do not mean that women cannot function at entirely effective and adult levels in their daily social and professional lives, despite those intrapsychic shifts. But these studies provide a clear illustration of how our minds and bodies function in an inseparably interrelated harmony. In women whose emotional preparation for mature and confident womanhood has left them vulnerable to dysfunction, the emotional regression of the premenstruum-menstruum phase offers substantial understanding of the clustering of dysfunction into this part of the cycle.

One intrapsychic prerequisite for mature adult sexuality is coming to terms comfortably with one's parental images. I use the term *parental images* because everyone's perception of his parents is a composite of the real mother and father as they actually were, plus the unconscious fantasies and misperceptions that have remained in his unconscious ever since infancy. These images persist as internalized percepts with which one must make peace even when one or both parents are deceased. As long as a person harbors conscious or unconscious sexual conflicts concerning his parents—be it guilt, bitterness and blame, inappropriate idealization, rebelliousness, or continued oedipal desire—his sexuality will to some degree be colored, limited, and distorted as a result.

This *sine qua non* for mature sexuality holds true regardless of how genuinely inadequate or destructive the parents were, as was the case for many of the girls at a state reformatory where I once served as consultant. For that unhappy population a typical set of parents might consist of an alcoholic prostitute mother and a series of drug-addicted pimps in the father role. These are extreme examples and the conflicts usually presented an insurmountable ego task, but most of the girls persisted in a desperate effort to perceive their parents as caring and good. It is necessary, despite the realistic shortcomings of parents, that an adult come to realize that no matter what influences his parents once exerted, he is now independent and need no longer be subject to their aberrations. For some people, intensive psychotherapy may be required to achieve that realization, for only then will a person be free to love maturely.

Another reflection of the state of resolution of infantile fantasies and conflicts is in the freedom and variety of foreplay activities. Oral-genital play, breast kissing and sucking, anal stimulation, the pleasure in looking, the enfolding quality of snuggling and cuddling, mouthing of the whole body, even nonhurtful forms of mild restraint and dominance play are adult expression of very early infantile and childhood psychosexual stages and their accompanying preoccupations and fantasies. Their psychosexual origins imply no disorder unless they become preferred or exclusive ends in themselves.

The freedom to enjoy the gamut of foreplay pleasures depends upon freedom from the inappropriate anxieties, guilts, and hostilities that once were associated with unconscious fantasies in the original phases of development. The man who is obsessed by an unconscious image of a vagina with teeth will have considerable apprehension about fellatio—the stimulation of his penis by the mouth of his female partner. A woman who felt inadequately nurtured by her mother and never developed an inner willingness to feel motherly may be repelled by oral caresses of her breasts and nipples. Both sexes, and men in particular, achieve an emotional acceptance of their inner sexuality only with true maturity, and continued conflict brings anxiety to any foreplay that calls attention to internal organs and sensations.

A final resolution of such conflict is necessary for unconstrained heterosexual enjoyment. The willingness to lose control of oneself in orgasm is accompanied by a temporary loss of the sense of oneself as a separate entity, and a consequent merging with one's partner. This totality of participation is possible only when each lover has achieved an anxiety-free identification of a part of himself with a part of the other; it is then that masculine-feminine differences become fully complementary and reinforcing. As one young woman with a securely functioning sexual identity told me, "I've learned every bit as much about myself as a woman from guys as I have from other women."

Conflict between the sexes is timeless and ubiquitous. Many such conflicts are the result of disturbed psychosexual development, but there are possibly also innate, inescapable sources of animosity between the sexes that only felicitous rearing can diminish, though perhaps never fully eliminate, because no rearing can be perfect or conflict-free. Perhaps the best evidence for this view is the biological inevitability of female mothers. However warm and loving a mother, all the interactions of discipline, power, dependency, frustrated love, and the necessity to disidentify from her in order to achieve a masculine sex identity leave indelible scars in the unconscious of a boy. It is possible that he never feels entirely equal to or free of her power, as evidenced by the ubiquity of the incest taboo. And "mother" is man's female prototype. For their part, women sometimes patronize men, forgetting that men are not all little boys in need of mommy's care.

A second innate source of strife lies in man's essential vulnerability, both physically and psychologically, in comparison with women. The higher death rate and disease susceptibility of males and their more frequent failure in successful heterosexual function has been well documented. It is not too fanciful to consider that there lurks in man an inner sense of his many weaknesses, for all his physical strength and bravado, that breeds fear and sometimes hostility.

It is common physiologic knowledge that the scrotal sac and testicles retract when a male experiences anxiety. One study that measured the degree of scrotal retraction in response to various subjects and questions verified the extreme sensitivity of scrotal responses as indicators of anxiety. It was further found that scrotal retraction was greater for repressed anxiety than for consciously felt anxiety. In every male studied, the greatest scrotal retraction occurred when the subject of bowel training was discussed; the second greatest came in reaction to the question, Who has more to enjoy sex with, man or woman? Even at the conscious level, the most frequent answer was "girls." The men denied conscious anxiety over either of these subjects and were often totally unaware of the vigorous activity of their scrotal sac.[12] Bowel training is of course associated with a dominance-submission struggle with the powerful mother; the conviction that woman is more sexually powerful implies repressed but intense and easily activated anxiety over her presumed advantage.

A third innate basis of sex antagonism is the recurring issue of male anxiety over internal sexual sensations. When that anxiety is not resolved, men may reject not only their imagined inner "femaleness" but females as well.[13]

A final built-in facet of the battle of the sexes is both a likely contributory cause and a weapon in its expression. This is the universal, biologically determined physical size and strength of males, and the corollary—their testosterone-related greater physical and competitive aggressiveness.[14] Man is prone to use his aggressive strength in a disagreement unless he has achieved a high degree of freedom from his primitivity, and woman's lesser strength may evoke resentment, hostility, and counterattack with her own uniquely devastating weapons. In addition, all the other sources of stress between the sexes has undoubtedly prompted males to resort to physical strength to resolve conflicts in their own favor.

None of the wellsprings of antagonism between the sexes, even if innate, is impervious to the gentling effects of good rearing; it is the inappropriate responses to these sexual differences that result in unnecessary strife and antipathy. It may seem discouraging that mankind has historically fallen short in moderating its own irrationalities, but individual family focus upon rearing sensitive and compassionate adults is a more viable hope than the vain belief that sociological reforms will somehow modify innate sexual differences and thus produce worldwide psychosexual utopia. Unnecessary sources of discord between the sexes are far more numerous, and probably far more disruptive in the lives and loves of individual couples, than any innate undercurrents of tension and discord.

Some sexual dysfunction among healthy adults is normal and expectable, and does harm only when it is fearfully assigned an undue importance. No woman, however relaxedly responsive, need expect to be equally arousable or orgastic on every occasion. Fatigue, cyclic fluctuations of desire, preoccupation with other interests, and simply varying levels of interest are normal even with a dearly loved partner. People are not robots with pushbutton responses.

Men are even less able than women to perform at will. While men are not subject to the influence of cyclic hormones, all the other influences that can produce differing levels of readiness and responsiveness are equally applicable. Transient episodes of impotence, or intercourse without ejaculation or orgasm are entirely normal, not catastrophic. Such experiences are especially common after too much alcohol, and are only significant if the excessive drinking is a problem. The excitement of infatuation, long abstinence, or a new involvement may result in ejaculation so quickly as to disappoint both partners—again, not a problem unless it becomes the rule.

An understanding acceptance of such normal variability of response, however capricious it may seem, reassures a lover that his humanness and his own level of need are respected. This is a quality traditionally less well-developed in men than in women. But as women become more naturally active sexually, the burden of consideration will shift more to them. In any situation where there is equal freedom to enjoy sex, males are at a physiological and psychological disadvantage.

Love, Marriage, and Other Human Peculiarities

It is not known whether species other than humans love. Some species, such as wolves and geese, mate for life and demonstrate unmistakable care for their mates. I may be accused of anthropomorphizing, but one of the most poignantly touching photographs of mutual bliss that it has been my pleasure to see was of a mother and infant gorilla. In any event, love, in contrast with simple genital lust, is inextricably related to learning. This is a function of the cerebral cortex. Man's ratio of cortex to other portions of the brain is incomparably greater than that of other animals—so much so that the differences may be considered qualitative. In this sense, love, as we know it, is a human peculiarity.

Love is not the same as infatuation (being "in love"). Mature sexual love, the capacity to invest both sexual and tender feelings in the same person and to hold that person's well-being as important as one's own, will hopefully characterize a permanent relationship between a couple, especially if children become involved, but a measured and rational quality is seldom the overriding character of strong, initial attraction. While it is a fallacy to regard romantic infatuation as invariably neurotic—research has shown that the capacity for romantic involvement indicates a healthy personality[15] —those so affected do show some temporary distortions of perception and judgment. In general, the physical and emotional attraction is overwhelming, the loved person is idealized, and there is a marked resistance to granting importance to whatever faults the person has or to the potentially irreconcilable incompatibilities that may exist. Few people realize the extent to which a potential partner will likely change their lives.

Since most people have had a number of romantic involvements, experience often operates as a screening process, but the impulse to fall in love is almost entirely unconscious. When the superficial reasons are stripped away, people in love almost invariably admit that they do not know why they feel as they do—and it is most common for people to marry while they are still in love. It is sobering and a bit eerie to realize that one of the most momentous decisions in one's life is governed by the unconscious.

The determinants are a confluence of innate drives and unfinished business of earlier psychosexual development. The innate drives are, in part, those of lust and species survival. A formal cultural institution such as marriage is probably a very late addition in the evolution of *Homo sapiens*. It is reasonable to speculate that throughout most of man's evolution attraction, coupling, and reproduction followed quickly and naturally upon one another. The basic innate urge in attraction or infatuation is a biologic one of genital lust and propagation of the species. It is only quite recently (as evolutionary time is measured) that the period of falling in love has been separated from the more serious business of raising a family. The innate drives can account only for an indiscriminate pursuit of any available partner; in no way can they account for the nearly ubiquitous need to be in love (as opposed to mere gratification of desire) or the qualitatively different degree to which a human being is attracted to just one, or at most a very few, among the hundreds of members of the opposite sex met in a lifetime.

The need to love and be loved is an effort to repair the never-forgotten symbiosis with the mother during infancy. That symbiosis minimized infant sexual differences, and the need to regain it applies to both sexes. That earliest loss was survived, obviously to the necessary benefit of both mother and child, but it left scars, a sense of being only part of a whole, and an eternal need to seek completion in a lasting and loving union with another person. Because the fetal brain is organized to respond more readily to someone of the opposite sex, women seek that reunion with a man, even though the original symbiosis was with a woman. Popular idioms attest to the folk knowledge of love as repairing the sense of incompleteness: expressions such as "my other half" and "you make me feel whole again" could be multiplied endlessly. The adoring gaze of the lover reenacts that of the all-admiring mother of infancy.

Selective infatuation is probably determined by parental models and internalized images. Selectivity in this sense refers to an unanticipated, often sudden and intense attraction, seen in its most exaggerated form as love at first sight. Conscious selection of a mate may sometimes proceed from practical criteria and one can purposefully attempt to minimize the influence of spontaneous infatuation. Parents who were rejecting or hated may determine an attraction to their opposites. There is an ominous prognosis if the attraction is based on an unconscious need to gain the parent's love exactly as it was given in childhood, since no member of the opposite sex can fulfill that need. But in a reasonably healthy and happy family, children learn to love the qualities and characteristics of the opposite sex that give them pleasure, support, and security, and they grow up hoping to find those qualities in someone else.

After the final resolution of the oedipal strivings, when the threat of wanting the actual person of mother or father no longer drives young people away from their parents, their preferences often return quite closely to the original. Girls often marry men much like their fathers, and because of their less harsh repression of oedipal desires, they may well be conscious of the preference. There was much more than turn-of-the-century sentimentality to the popular song, "I Want a Girl Just Like the Girl That Married Dear Old Dad." Because for most people the oedipal attachments never entirely lose their association with painful emotions, the resemblances are usually not obvious. Just as in dreams, in which the association between the unconscious emotion and the images are usually obscure and disguised, the resemblance between one's beloved and the parent may be tangential and outside the lover's awareness. The setting in which a person is first seen, a peculiar body mannerism, or a unique phrase or vocal intonation may forge an associative link that immediately sets that one person apart as someone special, even before a meeting has occurred. It is the unconscious nature of the resonance with the primary parental model that gives the spontaneous "falling in love" phenomenon its mysterious quality and renders it inexplicable.

The inner motivations to marry are virtually the same as those to pair and to love and be loved. For most people, permanence and dependability rank very high in their needs, even when they are not planning to have children. It is not mutual love alone, but love in the context of permanence that can restore the lost symbiosis of infancy. In fact, all the issues aroused in the family triangle have been left unfinished, even though the major internal conflicts associated with them may have been satisfactorily resolved. Dependency needs change their character but are never fully renounced, and their remnants remain unfulfilled. The child at five, and later in adolescence, learns to give up his wish for sexual possession of his parent, but he still needs someone to fill the void.[16]

All such loose strands are pulled together and fulfilled on a new level in a permanent heterosexual relationship. That new level, accessible only to adults, is mutual interdependence. The restoration of interrupted completeness and the recovery of dependency gratifications is mutual; each partner has found his own sexual love object who finally replaces the original. The permanent heterosexual commitment completes the previous developmental cycles by achieving gratification of what had been left unsatisfied during earlier development. Simultaneously, it initiates the last cycle by embarking upon a new version of the same situation—an intensely interdependent relationship between two people that will enforce further psychosexual development in each.

There are many social pressures and motives for marriage that have nothing to do with innate processes or unconscious needs. These vary widely both within and across cultural boundaries, and sometimes do violence to any reasonable concepts of psychosexual development and readiness, as in child bride customs. These pressures can be powerful and can override inner emotional considerations, but in cultures which permit individual adult preferences and feelings of being in love to determine the timing and choice of a mate, innate and unconscious factors are operative.

Marriage can be expected to bring about further modifications in the personality structure and sexuality, assuming that neither partner is bound up in rigid defenses that preclude change. Because the relationship recapitulates infantile and dependency needs and gratifications, it is an ideal milieu in which repression of infantile sexuality can be loosened. Each person senses a push to give freer rein to practices derived from infantile sources. The relationship eases the remnants of the punitive childhood superego. Since the spouse actually represents the parent(s) in important unconscious ways, that spouse's active interest in and enjoyment of sex acts to countermand the original parental prohibitions and thus to provide guilt-free access to all the component expressions of sexuality.

The characteristics of the primitive drives and the consciences of marital partners can reinforce each other in ways other than mutual expansion. Two people with highly restrictive consciences may well be attracted, in part, because each wants the other's help in keeping anxiety-provoking drives in check. A man with intense guilt over what he regards as dangerous and uncontrollable sexual behavior may choose a strict, motherly woman to augment his inadequate control. A young woman whose libertine life style represents a lifelong effort to overthrow her conscience and to deny the validity of any values or restraint, may choose a free-sex swinger whom she knows (or hopes) will not interfere with her impulsive gratification of every urge.

Ego maturation is strongly augmented in a good marriage. Mature adult sexuality implies the capacity and willingness to care for another, but caring which can be abandoned at will is of a different quality than caring within a legal and responsible commitment in which there are strong and varied motivations to keep the relationship workable. The step has been taken forward from responsibility for oneself to responsibility for one's mate. Each partner's ego must expand to include the other's welfare and individuality. True complementarity enforces diminution of egocentricity. The well-being of each is linked to that of the other, so that there can be no gain to one if the other loses. Thus marriage not only recaptures mother-infant union, but begins inexorably to recapitulate the next steps of increased individuation. Pleasure in each other's pleasure and self-actualization go beyond symbiosis and are similar to the mother and the infant reinforcing each other's needs and pleasures through a mutuality of give and take.

Marital interdependence must not be confused with the interaction of two dependent people. Mutual dependence, if it is a persistent life style rather than a temporary but normal period of diminished resources, can be draining. In this case, each needs the other so desperately that he is afraid to give even though he may be well able to do so, for fear the other will grow away from him. Interdependence is a process of enriching, cherishing and fostering each other's autonomy and growth, knowing that as a result each has more to give the other; one is hardly likely to grow away from anyone so supportive. Mature persons know that winning the other is but the prologue to keeping the other.

Unique abilities and special interests must be fostered and maintained. This is especially true for a wife not only because a woman's qualities may be neglected in a male-oriented world— women in Western culture are probably less restricted and derogated than in the majority of other cultures, present or past—but because most women willingly put other pursuits aside in the interest of mothering and homemaking. Their personalities must not wither in the process, nor be left impoverished when their children's maturation leaves them freer. For a woman committed to her husband and family as well as to her own dignity and self-realization, the reinforcement and encouragement provided by her husband is probably more meaningful—because of the loving complementarity—than that of women's organizations or her employer or public applause.

Through the operation of an emotional mechanism known as transference, parental behaviors and expectations will express themselves in a marriage. A husband, for example, will unwittingly transfer some of his own attitudes toward his mother onto his wife and will expect her to express some of his mother's attitudes toward him. He may unrealistically expect to be criticized for interest in sexy magazines or movies when, in fact, his wife finds them equally enjoyable. Parental transference is as applicable to women as to men—perhaps even more so if a woman's choice of husband is openly determined by a man's similarity to her father. Transference is benign if the parental relationships were sound, but it can result in considerable confusion when neither knows what is happening, and it can be deadly if there has been severe unresolved conflict with a parent. Many a partner is frustrated to the point of despair when he finds himself treated with a fury he neither provoked nor could prevent, caught in unconscious repetition of a battle he cannot understand, call off, or win.

The same process of parental identification expresses itself when one or both partners acts the role of parent. This may happen in response to sensing the transferred parental expectations of the other, or because of the identification with one's own parent. Again, the entire range from benign to malignant manifestations depends upon the kind and appropriateness of the parenting that is being expressed. Either spouse may need to retreat at times from autonomously functioning responsibility and replenish himself with some nurturant parental care. Either spouse may get sick to death of decisions and welcome letting the other take over for awhile.

Young married couples differ in important, but sometimes subtle, ways from their unmarried peers. Statistically, married couples have considerably more sex than unmarried couples, probably for no more esoteric reason than that sexual availability and privacy are usually maximal. But the very act of marrying introduces potential stresses that do not apply to affairs.

Most first marriages are undertaken with a maximum of idealism and a minimum of common sense, and at least the belief in sexual fidelity even when one realizes it is seldom practiced. Many newlyweds with a reasonable amount of previous sexual activity are uncomfortably aware of their mutually self-imposed limitation. Since they generally undertake this limitation willingly and in good faith, their concerns initially often focus upon how their partner will respond to it. How serious this stress becomes depends a great deal upon how openly thoughts and attitudes about sex are communicated. In the absence of adequate communication, performance anxiety may plague them both. Not wanting the partner to miss the free life or regret its loss, anxiety to please the other takes the place of spontaneous enjoyment. Either one, but the wife especially, may fear expressing any normally varying levels of interest, and be afraid to turn the other down.

At the opposite pole are those who relax from the good behavior of courtship into more insensitive and self-centered selves. The still considerable remnants of the double standard contribute to different manifestations of the "now I can be myself" syndrome. Men may begin to be importunate in their sexual demands, feeling that they now have a right to gratification whenever they want it, with less concern for the woman's pleasure. Women, no longer having to "catch" a husband with sex, may feel freer to refuse sexual overtures or plead some form of indisposition. Clearly, this pattern is more characteristic of women who have not achieved an adult level of sexual enjoyment and participation before marriage. But even the most sexually healthy woman who finds herself married to a suddenly inconsiderate man (unless one wishes to regard such a union as unlikely, since the woman's maturity of judgment would have to be suspect), may turn to withholding sex out of resentment. From this point on, their sex relationship turns into one of barter, hostility, and struggle for control—one of the desert wastelands of human sexuality.

The above extreme is just that, an extreme. But in less dramatic expression it produces one of the most difficult kinds of sexual stress in marriage. It is a natural thing, and the mark of considerate people, to want to please one another. Courtship, assuming the couple are in love and infatuated with each other, heightens their desire to please to what may be its peak intensity. No exploitiveness or wish to deceive the other may play the slightest role in the steady, mutual, unwitting deception that goes on in perfectly "normal" courtships. The partners see in each other what they want to see. They believe, because each so much wants to believe, in each other's assurances of the willingness and ability to change or discard any distressing attributes—ones that have now become as unacceptable to the possessor as to the partner in the new light of this wonderful relationship. And each is entirely sincere, because pleasing the other is so important, in the belief that any annoying traits in the marvelous other are minor and can easily be adjusted to, or that one can learn to like some of the things the other does or desires—things that are really profoundly distasteful—because love is potent enough to enable such change. None of this may come to pass, no matter how genuinely felt, but courtship is often too short for the unintentional deception to emerge.

After marriage, and usually only gradually, the reality of how difficult it is to change emotionally determined sexual attitudes begins to dawn upon the couple. When the differences are significant, each feels a puzzling mixture of guilt and resentment, while at the same time becoming increasingly frustrated. On the one hand, each was honestly self-confident of the capacity to modify the attitudes or the preferences that are now discovered to be surprisingly refractory. And on the other hand, each accepted the other's assurances that some particular personal idiosyncrasies and patterns of behavior would be quite acceptable, but now finds them being resented and criticized. Neither realized the power of unconsciously determined sexual attitudes.

The situation just described is dishearteningly common, and perhaps the more saddening because it both arises so innocently and is largely avoidable. It illustrates one more of the problems already chronicled as resulting from failure or inability to communicate one's honest sexual thoughts and attitudes. Any lasting union requires enormous compromise, negotiation, and growing together —sexuality is only one important area in which this is unavoidable. Courtship is the time for the utmost honesty in all things, not only sex. Today the majority of married couples report premarital intercourse with one another, and it is my clinical experience that it is far better so.

Sex for its own sake can be good clean fun, but I am referring to more than that when I seriously recommend premarital sex as frequently beneficial. Obviously a mutually caring and considerate relationship, expressed in every interaction as well as sexually, is a basic prerequisite. Then, building upon that foundation, a *sexual* courtship must include learning to communicate openly the most intimate of emotions and attitudes, if it is to be helpful. It is the wisest, albeit the hardest, time to take such risks. If courtship is prolonged and the couple lives together over an extended period prior to marriage, there is much more opportunity to know each other in depth, to shed the artificiality of dating behavior, to develop sexual honesty, and to discover any truly irreconcilable incompatibilities.

Living together before marriage is not new but may be increasingly significant. In one sizable university study, approximately one-fifth of the students were currently living in a sexual relationship with someone of the opposite sex. Moreover, four-fifths of the students accepted the idea and said they would do so themselves if given the opportunity. Sexual availability was the major motive for males, future marriage the major motive for females. However, only a small proportion of those actually living together professed future marriage plans.[17] Even without marriage plans, such a relationship can be an unparalleled learning (as well as pleasure) experience. Individual gains can be carried into a later marriage and can contribute both to better judgment in the selection of a mate and better communication in the crucial interpersonal issues.

Of course, neither premarital intercourse nor living together is necessary for the tasks inherent in making sexual and interpersonal adjustment. There are far too many genuinely good marriages in which neither played a part, and living together does not elicit all of the interactional and intrapsychic stresses inherent in a legally binding commitment. Both kinds of sexual behavior are probably quite natural, although for many couples who neither have premarital sex nor live together, the decision to refrain may contain elements of sexual inhibition or guilt that will surface after marriage takes place. And to the extent that the less inhibited behaviors represent a growing capacity—or even only the desire—to permit sexuality to become a more natural part of life, they can be used in constructive ways.

Some of the problems in sexual communication go back to the early failure to be provided with sexual words and the early learning that sexual talk was taboo. Other problems arise in ignorance of sexual anatomy and the feelings of shame that began with bodily prudery and the prohibition of childhood sexual explorations. Intercourse alone is a poor remedy. The majority of married men and women lack the most rudimentary knowledge of each other's sexual anatomy or function. Some of the unwitting deception that goes on in courtship follows upon the fact that one may not even know one's own attitudes until one is able to verbalize them.

Some ramifications of the double standard contribute to poor sexual communication. Men are supposed to know about sex. Ever since their earliest teenage lying braggadocio, for boys to admit ignorance is unthinkable. As they become men, they are taken in by their own nonsense. They begin to believe it—and so do women. It may not take long for a perceptive woman to discover how untrue this really is, but both will still be saddled with the man's falsely based masculine self-esteem. He is afraid to ask because he fears the woman will lose respect for him, and she is afraid to initiate such a discussion for fear he will interpret it as an attack upon his masculinity. When he *is* relatively knowledgeable, he may hesitate to educate the woman and to broaden the woman's sexual expression because of a mental stereotype that women are easily offended by "grossness." When the woman is the more experienced of the two, she must cope with the double fear of losing the man's respect and arousing his anxiety over invidious comparison with other lovers. Short of the kind of healthy childrearing that fosters open sexual discussion, I know of no remedy but to risk the relationship by insisting upon mutual honesty. The possible wounds are usually less crippling than those inflicted by the failure to talk.

Some couples enter marriage with the naïve assumption that their idiosyncratic preferences and expectations are self-evident and universal and will naturally be shared by the spouse. Unless the partners have almost identical subcultural backgrounds (and even that is no guarantee) they will face rude shocks and major problems of marital adaptation. Marriage inevitably carries different implications for virtually every human, since the unique relationship between one's own father and mother is initially accepted as the norm.

Sexual inexperience and the sometimes allied issue of different levels of sexual drive open additional areas of marital stress. Statistical research offers no definitive answers to the question of the effects of premarital sexual experience upon marital "happiness" or "success"—the words are in quotation marks because these concepts are impossible to define. Some researchers have found a slight but statistically unreliable correlation between premarital chastity and professed satisfaction with marriage, particularly on the part of women,[18] but these findings, in addition to their questionable statistical validity, are impossible to interpret. The results may simply reflect that sexually conservative couples are also those who believe that marital durability, at whatever cost to themselves or their children, is the most significant measure of success. The consensus of clinical experience in marital therapy indicates that the most successful outcome of some marriages is divorce.

Some studies clearly relate premarital sexual experience with greater satisfaction in marriage.[19] Kinsey found that premarital orgastic sexual activity is positively correlated with marital orgastic response. In a follow-up of the same large population sample, it was further shown that there was also a definite correlation between women's frequency of orgasm in marriage and their judgment of happiness in marriage.[20]

The mere occurrence or nonoccurrence of coitus or other sexual activity before marriage is not the sole or most relevant consideration; more determinative are such factors as the presence or absence of guilt-producing rearing and religious standards, individual readiness and ego strength, circumstances of premarital activity, and the relationship between the partners. There is documentation that the quality of the interpersonal relationship is possibly the most significant factor in how premarital intercourse will be integrated into later sexual and marital adjustment.

The subject of marital satisfaction has been drastically modified by cultural changes. Formal and supposedly permanent marriage has been the expected norm from a time early in the evolution of our culture, when the average adult life expectancy was no more than thirty to forty years. Not divorce but the Grim Reaper kept most marriages relatively brief. With current life expectancy nearing seventy years, and the average age of marriage slightly over twenty, the continued goal of marital permanency means that a couple must expect to live with each other and like it for forty or fifty years.

Equally important is the shift in the principal goal of marriage. From essentially economic, survival, and procreative goals in which the romantic aspect was minimized, the change has been to personal happiness and self-actualization involving intimacy and a high degree of companionship. The more time two people must spend together, and the more they expect from one another, the more difficult it becomes to achieve and maintain these goals. As marriage has currently evolved, its implicit expectations are demonstrably beyond the capacity of many people, especially when they enter a marriage with the blithe expectation that each will always be able to fulfill every kind of need—sexual and otherwise—of the other.

Sexual needs themselves can vary widely. Unconscious factors probably play the major role, but there is reason to credit the existence of constitutional differences in sex drive as well.[21] Such differences can become the basis of real misery for both spouses, especially when the difficulties come as a post-marriage surprise. Both partners are subject to mounting resentment and self-doubt, one resenting the other's seeming indifference or the escalating accusatory quality in his or her sexual demands. The less motivated spouse begins to have more and more self-doubts with a corresponding decrease in sexual self-confidence. The more strongly motivated spouse, already resentful, also begins to have self-doubt; males in particular eventually come to blame themselves for some vague incapacity to be "man enough" to arouse their wives. Thus the double standard tallies up still more victims through its classic dictum that there are no such beings as frigid women, only inept men.

Marital sexuality cannot be discussed without touching upon extramarital sexuality, even though it is not possible to assign it a specific role in normal psychosexual development. More has probably been written upon the subject of infidelity than upon the entire process of psychosexual development. As with most other items of sexual behavior, figures are worthless except to confirm the obvious—that it is a very common phenomenon. Investigating in the late forties and early fifties, Kinsey found that by age forty, half of the married men and a quarter of the married women had had at least one experience of extramarital intercourse. Within subgroups the percentages varied greatly in relation to differing social and economic factors. For example, extramarital intercourse was lowest among the most highly educated men, but highest among the most educated women.[22] No comparably broad up-to-date studies are available, but the most informed opinion holds that percentages have risen significantly.

The most interesting question of all may well be whether or not extramarital intercourse is normal. I must answer with a somewhat qualified yes. It is normal according to our basic definition of species normality, in that marital infidelity by the species as a whole would not inevitably dictate that the species could not survive. It is normal in that sexually monogamous permanent marriage places an unnatural restriction upon the human animal's biologically normal desire and capacity for sexual variety. Sexual monogamy has not proved to be an achievable goal in any society that has tried to enforce it—a strong testament that such demands run counter to normal human nature. Its normality is attested to by the exaggerated moral sanctions against it in sexually repressive societies—one does not build a fortress to contain a flea. Its normality is given further tacit acknowledgment by the infrequency of infidelity being cited as the major cause for dissolving a marriage (except in courts of those states or societies in which it is the only legal grounds for divorce). And, of course, normal infidelity can occur as a result of genuine deprivation. Marriage counselors and psychotherapists are in strong agreement that while there are certainly exceptions, other qualities and benefits of marriage are of such greater importance that most partners will go to great lengths to pretend ignorance or to ignore evidences of infidelity even when they do not like it. Some will openly condone various limited types of infidelity. It is only when other, more vitally interpersonal aspects of the relationship are lacking that most marriages will be in serious trouble.

Regarding extramarital sexual adventure as normal in the broad sense described is not to be misread as either indiscriminate approval or encouragement. It is merely a statement that normal characteristics of our species do not yield readily to the demands of individual cultural mores that attempt to curtail them. It is equally true that any specific instance of infidelity may have its roots not in normal human tendencies, but in every kind and level of intrapsychic and interpersonal immaturity or emotional disorder. The existence of inappropriate motivations similarly cannot justify a blanket condemnation of sex outside of an existing marriage.

Balancing the normal aspects of extramarital sexuality is the fact that there are potent, inherent needs to seek completion of oneself in a close, dependable, lasting, and to some extent possessive relationship with a mate. These innate needs operate at both individual and child-rearing, family-maintaining levels.

The major reason for infidelity is probably the normal desire for variety. When actual deprivation of marital sex exists, a second basic reason becomes the normal desire for sexual gratification. Whether or not any particular husband or wife acts upon these normal desires, however, brings into play an infinitely complex variety of emotional and social influences that range from simple opportunity, to life-style ideology, to the capacity for commitment, to the felt security of that commitment, and to the most obscure unconscious psychopathology.

Those who are most healthy emotionally are also those with the fullest capacity for intimate involvement with and enduring commitment to another person, and subsequently to offspring. Those whose innate propensities were least disrupted and who have benefited from the most constructive psychosexual child rearing are also those who will choose that quality of commitment and give it highest priority. Genuine mutual commitment and sexual exclusiveness, however, are not synonymous.

The emotional rewards of adult interdependence and of finding the completion of oneself in the relationship with another person are precious achievements. When infidelity would be seen as hurting that bond, the rewards are strong enough to override the natural desire for variety, but the desire itself does not necessarily signal a deterioration of the relationship. The sexually secure partners to a genuinely mutual commitment can both value their relationship deeply enough, and be sufficiently accepting of human nature, not to be threatened by varying degrees of sex outside their marriage. In marriages of such an emotional quality, it is only when one spouse's commitment shifts outside the relationship that the bond is violated and the marriage no longer rewarding.

Marriages which are held together or even strengthened by the extramarital sex of one or both partners are well known. Whether this is seen as healthy or unhealthy is likely to reflect only an arbitrary subjective judgment unless a great deal is known about the reasons for inadequate sexual gratification within the marriage, the couple's priority of values and responsibilities, and the quality of the other crucial aspects of their interpersonal relationship.

There are a significant number of people, married and unmarried, who swap partners, involve themselves in group sex, advocate sex freedom in or out of marriage, form communes of varying degrees of sexual casualness, enter into semiformalized group marriages—in general, who seek alternatives to traditional marriage. Many of them are opportunistic, exploitive, emotionally disturbed, hypocritical, incapable of lasting commitment, or hedonistic "hippie" types. But it must not be taken for granted that all such persons are emotionally disturbed; none of the relevant research on alternatives to traditional marriage have revealed a grossly disturbed population. One major study of mateswappers in the Midwest found a population that, with the exception of their highly ritualized and secretive swapping activity, was uniformly a virtual caricature of "square" WASPs, whose conservatism was epitomized by the fact that 60 percent were Wallace supporters in the 1968 presidential election.[23] Groups studied by other researchers were, of course, sometimes quite different, but assuming the sincerity and at least average mental health of many people exploring alternative sex-marriage life styles, what does it mean?

First a distinction must be made. Sex is not marriage, any more than sex is automatically love. The limitation of sex to marriage is artificial and culturally arbitrary, even though many are satisfied with that arrangement and there are innate forces favoring a durable, dependable dyadic relationship of one's own. There is no definitive data proving that the benefits and rewards of a genuinely committed marriage, including the sexual ones, are necessarily destroyed or vitiated by sex occurring outside the marriage; that depends entirely upon personal preferences, tolerances, and degree of possessiveness. Rather, there is reason to believe that lifelong sexual exclusiveness is perhaps an unnatural burden which a large portion of people cannot or will not live up to. This could suggest that sexual monogamy may be more of a threat than a bulwark to marital stability.

Considerations such as these motivate many of the idealistic seekers after social change. At the very least, a widely reported complaint is boredom within the sexual confines of marriage. Some not only believe that sexuality should be a freely enjoyable activity, but that its separation from the exclusive province of marriage would in fact strengthen marriage.[24] Some sociologists tentatively agree. One explanation suggested is that extramarital sexuality in all its forms is a desperate attempt to maintain permanent dyadic marriage, as more and more comes to be unrealistically expected of it and despite its unnatural restrictiveness.[25] Another explanation sees mateswapping and group sex activities as a newly emerging culturally institutionalized safety valve, akin to prostitution in Victorian times. By providing an outlet for socially deviant desires for variety and for the acting out of exotic sexual fantasies, traditional marriage is preserved because it does not have to be broken up in order to satisfy those urges.[26]

Those who seek to establish what are in effect extended families—group marriages and relatively permanent communes— are motivated in part by the wish for greater sexual freedom and in part by a genuine belief that the nuclear family is inadequate and that a broader, freer experience of human intimacy and relatedness will make better people of themselves and their children. The ramifications of these family experiments are discussed in the next chapter.

In addition, both the idealists and those who indulge in the various forms of open extramarital sex simply for recreation report a number of consciously felt personal gains. These include enhancement of one's sexual self-esteem, loss of inhibitions and taboos that limited their previous sexual enjoyment in their marriages, more sex education than they have ever had before, a sense of human contact and acceptance that being nude together—with or without sex—is felt to enhance, and a revitalization of their own marriages.[27] These are conscious reports, of course, and it is too early for long-term effects, personal or marital, to have been assessed. Relatively few direct casualties have yet found their way into the published studies, although one researcher reported that he could not objectively observe evidence of the benefits that the participants anticipated. Casualties mentioned include loss of sexual self-esteem by not being able to live up to one's grandiose adolescent sexual fantasies (affecting mostly males), being sexually rejected for whatever reasons, jealousy, and seriously damaged male egos resulting from the discovery not only that their wives and girl friends can go on pleasuring each other in homoerotic encounters long after the males are exhausted but that as many as two-thirds of the women in the study came to prefer the lesbian experiences to sex with their husbands.[28]

There may be an evolutionary basis on which to speculate that the seekers after alternative sex and marriage styles may be underestimating the power of possessiveness and jealousy, though most claim to feel it (consciously) very little. Possessiveness can be an intolerable burden when pathologically extreme or one-sided, but it may have had positive—even imperative—survival value throughout the millions of years of evolution of mankind as a species. Any animal breeder knows that temperament and "personality" traits can be bred into or out of animals just as physical traits can. One may assume that *Homo sapiens* at least started out with individuals having all degrees of possessiveness toward their mates. But in the exigencies of survival in the hostile environment typical for evolving mankind throughout all but a tiny recent fraction of his existence, different degrees of jealous possessiveness would also confer different survival potentials. The female and her offspring were incapacitated and vulnerable throughout most of her lifespan and their childhood. She and her progeny, for their very survival, needed to keep the male provider and, if necessary, fight to keep other females from usurping him. If she failed, or if she simply had an inadequate possessive drive to make the effort successful, she and her children stood less chance of living to propagate further. Her genes would not enter the gene pool of her tribe or of *Homo sapiens* in general.

The same reasoning applies to males. While they did not require females for their own survival once past their childhood, anthropology and ethology alike testify to the normal animal requirement of aggressive possessiveness to get and keep a mate. In precisely the same way, those males without such qualities would be less likely to propagate, and thus their genes would similarly not enter the gene pool of evolving man. Eons of selective propagation of humans with the requisite possessive and aggressive qualities would inevitably produce a species in which those qualities are innate. One may observe the process still clearly in operation. If one assumes, as clinical evidence demonstrates, that one causative factor underlying some obligatory homosexual development is a fear of competing with other males for a woman, then to whatever extent the lack of heterosexual aggressiveness in a homosexual may be genetically determined, their genes are not passed on to progeny and into the gene pool.

It is not known to what extent humans can learn to control and eliminate their possessiveness and jealousy. Some can and do, and perhaps more could. It is known that those traits are nearly universal and are likely to have an innate component, and it is also known how slowly evolutionary changes occur. Whether such qualities are valued or not, they still exist. Whether they continue to serve constructive human ends is unknown and perhaps questionable. Their presence is one determinant that will cause open sexual freedom within marriage and all forms of multilateral sexual relationships to remain socially exceptional behavior for the foreseeable future. Although perfectly valid and possibly progressive, the ability to abandon total sexual exclusiveness in a healthy manner will characterize only the one who is capable of forming a genuine commitment with another person, and at the same time is sexually secure enough not to need to "own" the physical affections of his or her spouse.

The sincere advocates of change are obviously reacting against marriage and family life as they knew it. Their primary source of learning about the gratifications and disappointments of marriage was their experience with their parents' marriage. Later, but with less impact, observations of their friends' parents' marriages and ultimately those of their peers added some influence. It is axiomatic that no one will want to change something good. A person whose parents really enjoyed one another will want the kind of relationship that they had. If they valued sexual monogamy, he will likely value it, too, though he will also be open to reevaluating it in the light of the mounting burdens and tasks forced upon the partners to an exclusive dyadic marriage.

Those who seek something "better" are revealing a great deal about what they experienced at home—in effect, that it was not good enough. Either they could see their parents' dissatisfactions and hostilities, or felt these hostilities and dissatisfactions turned upon themselves. If they have already tried marriage and found it wanting, the likelihood is that they did not have the family training to know how to choose a mate appropriately or how to make marriage work. Many such people are not emotionally damaged to the point that they are incapable of intimacy and commitment. It is only that their parents did not help them to see the rewards in traditional marriage, and they seek it in the configurations of other relationships.

The simple truth of these observations is not a defense of the status quo of traditional sexually monogamous marriage. There are many examples of disastrous cultural institutions that perpetuate themselves if they somehow satisfy enough people. Sexual exclusiveness may well be so unnatural a restriction that it is a major cause of marital boredom, disharmony, and unhappiness—the very reason many children are left with a jaundiced view of marriage. The separation of sexual possessiveness from the enormously positive aspects of the marriage commitment is probably a valid progressive goal, if evolution can be unlearned. Nothing is psychologically free. Enough people find the satisfaction of the innate need for the reunion and self-completion in an exclusive twosome so great as to be willing to accept the price. Enough children experience happy enough homes that nearly all still want the same for themselves.

Among the sincere proponents of alternative forms of marriage are those who do have some defective or inhibited capacity for intimacy and commitment and adult dependability. They hope fervently that a new or different form of relationship will release their own capacities and bring them what they have missed. Some are successful; I have known a few. Some learn all the right words and go through as many of the right motions as they can grasp, yet remain as desperately empty as before; I have known more than a few.

Finally there are those who not only have difficulty with intimacy but who actively repudiate marriage and heterosexual involvement in any form, or who go through the motions of marriage but cannot find adequate pleasure in it. The avoidance of marriage (in any of its forms) or the relegation of marriage or heterosexual relatedness to a low priority is usually due to fear, most often unconscious. Among women, some pathogenic influences in psychosexual development have induced a fear of the wife-mother role.[29] In men, similar factors operate to engender anxiety over the husband-father role, or there is fear of the power and dominance of a woman, or of the competition necessary to get a wife and to provide successfully for her and a family.

Naturally, the rationalizations available are endless, and often contain enough truth with which to fool oneself. For marriage-avoidant women, the most popular rationalization is that men are selfish, power-hungry, subjugators of women. Some are, but if this were the rule, it cannot account for the fact that fully 90 percent of even the best educated women look forward eagerly to a traditional marriage and family. One must look deeper. In an unusually extensive study of 15,000 female college graduates it was found that less than 10 percent deviated from that traditional expectation. More importantly, it was found that difficulties in relationships with and between parents were very closely correlated with socially deviant attitudes toward heterosexuality and marriage. Discord in the family of origin was found to be related to a low commitment to the family role.[30]

Obviously not everyone must marry to feel satisfied and happy with life, or to function with the utmost of effectiveness and emotional stability. Health is a balance of more forces and influences than can be numbered, and it will never be definable by any single set of criteria. But heterosexual commitment (whether in formal marriage or otherwise) is the species norm. At the same time, it is the culmination of biological, cultural, and intrapsychic development so complex and so delicately vulnerable to disruption that virtually everyone falls short of its ideal achievement, and some are rendered unable to achieve it at all. Even those who are truly happy without it reveal that in some manner beyond their control this avenue was closed to them, and not by their own adult, rational choice. It is simply that they have the emotional health and ego strength to make a stunningly successful adaptation to their handicap.

Erikson has defined the ideal of adult sexual love and intimacy: "Mutuality of orgasm with a loved partner of the opposite sex with whom one is able and willing to share a mutual trust and with whom one is able and willing to regulate the cycles of work, procreation, [and] recreation, so as to secure to the offspring, too, a satisfactory development." [31] That is a tall order.

ELEVEN

Parenthood

Nowhere is it as clear as during parenthood that psychosexual development continues throughout normal sexually active adult life. Parenthood is a psychobiological process that ends only with the parent's or the child's death, but discussion here will be limited to the time children are still at home and under some degree of parental control. Parenthood will be considered to begin technically with conception, or, psychologically, when a woman becomes aware that she is pregnant. At every stage of a developing child's life—including when he is in the womb—his existence, behavior, and the stages through which he is passing reawaken corresponding emotional processes in his parents.

Much of the parent-child psychodynamic interaction has already been detailed in discussing the child's phases of psychosexual development; now there is a shift in focus from the parents' effects upon the child to the child's effects upon the parents. The reawakened emotions appropriate to each phase are by no means mere echoes; they precipitate further change and significant emotional growth in the parents, and the psychosexual development that can only occur under the impetus of pregnancy, childbirth, and very early parenthood is a major increment of emotional maturation.

I will proceed from certain basic assumptions, the most obvious being the innateness of the procreative drive. I consider that a built-in drive for preservation and propagation of any species is self-evident. I mention it in part because of the growing sociological vogue to deny all innate behavioral components in man and to state that postnatal learning has erased every vestige of biological determinacy.

The drive for preservation and propagation is also useful as an illustration that the lack of universality of any specific behavior pattern in no wise compromises its innateness. Not everyone becomes a parent. This was true even before socioecological pressures of overpopulation began to be exerted. Whether through seeming autonomous choice or through avoidance, it is evident that any species-innate drive may be denied expression in any number of individuals. Faulty rearing alone is sufficient to subvert innate propensities. As an example in a totally different area, although self-preservation is a most powerful innate drive that few would gainsay, many people become so depressed as to kill themselves.

A second basic assumption is the universality of the family. This is less obvious because of the many superficially divergent forms of family structure evident in different cultures, but if the family is defined to include adult male(s), adult female(s), and children, then it can be seen as a universal sociological unit, perhaps one of the chief defining characteristics of mankind.[1] Subcultural exceptions, as in the sizable proportion of ghetto black families in which adult males have little permanent, ongoing roles, are but socioeconomically determined distortions of the norm.

The third basic assumption is that maternalism and, perhaps to a lesser extent, paternalism are innate. This issue raises the most question in some people's minds despite the invariable fact that normal animals are biologically prepared to do what they must do. More doubt attaches to paternalism than to maternalism—woman must nurture what she alone can produce because she alone can do so, especially through the long evolutionary history of mankind.[2] While the role of possessiveness in survival (as outlined in the previous chapter) is speculative, the role of maternalism is imperative. There can be no question that the offspring of females devoid of innate nurturant maternalism would have an infinitely high infant mortality rate, and maternalism would come to dominate the gene pool of surviving and procreating females.

Paternalism is more difficult to account for, and probably has weaker innate roots. It has been reasoned that the principal basis upon which males originally became permanent members of the nuclear family was their constant, nonseasonal sexual interest in the females. While the bonds that thus evolved, involving aggressive possessiveness, undoubtedly operated to benefit both mother and children, there is little reason on those bases to assume a sentimental male interest in his offspring. One of the functions of the incest taboo is to preclude natural paternal hostility, at least to male offspring.[3]

One must look to the earliest mother-infant symbiosis, and to the little child's later identification with the mother, to discover the probable sources of what might be called innate paternalism. Even the male infant's earliest identity is female during the period that he is unaware of any differentiation between himself and his mother. As he develops self-esteem while taking in his mother's good feelings toward him as she cares for him and meets his oral needs, he also incorporates her giving quality.[4] His later envy of her ability to create a child passes as a developmental phase, but those giving feelings remain a part of his total unconscious structure. The identical interactions also contribute to maternalism in females.

Fatherhood provides a man the opportunity to express those maternal qualities that early became part of himself. They show as he "mothers" his wife through her adaptations to pregnancy and early motherhood, and as he "mothers" his child. These paternal-maternal qualities in a man must be recognized as far more fragile and disruptible than those of women, however. Since they arise in the postnatal relationship with the mother rather than from characteristics innate to the species, they are heavily dependent upon the quality of that relationship. Inadequate mothering will mean that no such qualities are internalized, and the lack of inborn roots renders paternal tenderness far more vulnerable to the caprices of cultural sex role training. Hence the less obvious and less frequent expressions of paternalism than of maternalism in almost any cultural setting. The different origins and roots in the two sexes serves to emphasize the more solid and durable groundings of innate maternalism.

An issue frequently raised throughout this discussion of the child's psychosexual development is the relationship of innate masculine and feminine characteristics to different qualities of mothering and fathering. Those distinctions have often been described in a way that has led to a distinction between the mother's presumed "expressive-affective" role and the father's "instrumental" role. These terms probably refer to valid masculine-feminine differences, as long as it is understood that such differences are a matter *only* of degree; neither is the exclusive property of either sex. "Expressive-affective" refers to woman's greater capacity for interpersonal sensitivity and emotional responsivity, and it is considered that because of these qualities, her family role is more that of providing for the love and emotional well-being of her children. "Instrumental" denotes the man's role in teaching, disciplining, acculturating, and providing for his children—the ways in which he is instrumental in helping them bridge the transition from the "I am loved because I exist" family to the "I am loved and rewarded, depending upon what I am like" outside world.[5]

While these qualitative sex distinctions are probably accurate as they apply to the normal intrapsychic propensities and tendencies, serious question has been raised about their applicability to the nuclear family in our technological society. In preindustrial societies, in which both mother and father were usually equally accessible to their children, they likely could and did interact in accord with natural psychological differences, but in our society, most fathers are seldom home. Mothers must perform most of the instrumental tasks and roles, especially with the younger children; during the father's brief times with children, he is more likely to take the opportunity to be playful and affectionate with them—an expressive role.[6]

These facts have both serious repercussions and thought-provoking implications. The repercussions upon the children include potential sex role confusions, since they experience their parental models functioning in ways that may feel alien to their own developing inner sexual identities. The parents, too, may feel their roles as alien, the mother finding it difficult to be a firm, consistent, and calm disciplinarian, and the father sensing a vague emptiness in his family function, as though there is really no place for him—no opportunity to fulfill the role for which he is best suited.

The implications involve how children in our culture are prepared for parenthood. If boys and girls are socialized in the direction of their natural proclivities—a practice which can be found in all societies[7]—then they are not prepared for the role reversal many will find required of them. Typical and intuitively wise socialization prepares them far better for successful function in marital interactions than in parenthood. There are as yet no answers to this dilemma, though some sociologists suggest that boys and girls be socialized into different sex roles that are more adaptive to contemporary family conditions. As always, a model of psychosexual development and identity that regards children as totally malleable to the influence of training is fallacious. How children are to be prepared for roles that do violence to innate sex distinctions, without concomitantly inflicting unanticipated psychological damage, is a task for the future.

Preparation for both parenthood and marriage is generally spotty in our culture. The theme of discontinuity between child-rearing practices and adult sexual function applies here with dramatic specificity. Cultural mores provide parents with few if any guidelines to help them teach their children how to become effective parents. Although the deficit is slowly being remedied, sex and family life education is not regarded as a crucially required part of the curriculum in any but a pitifully few schools. Pregnancy offers a very short time to begin learning about parenthood, even when the prospective parents recognize the need to learn and when learning facilities are available to them.

Social changes exert still further influences that undermine effective parenthood. This has become especially evident to parents who spent part of their adolescence in the 1960s or early 1970s, when the emphasis on "here and now" was most popular. Impatience and the demand for immediate gratification or change, whether in social, political, economic, or sexual spheres, was regarded at least by many young people as a virtue. Impatience as a personality trait is a time bomb to bring either into marriage or to parenthood. Children cannot respond or learn or become just what one wants of them "right now." [8] Neither can one's own responses, nor those of one's spouse, do anything other than follow the measured pace of all major developmental processes.

The disappearance of the extended family as the dominant familial structure in our culture has also contributed both to the stress and the unpreparedness of parenthood. When many members and generations of a family live as an emotionally and physically close-knit unit, everyone learns about parenting within the ongoing progression of generations around him. Family and caretaking responsibilities are widely shared even among the children, and there is help available when a woman suddenly becomes a mother.

The isolated nuclear family lacks those advantages. The new mother must suddenly assume the full duty of caring for an infant—a job for which she may be realistically unready and inept. There are few people on hand to share responsibilities or to fulfill divergent roles. No small part of the added stress in such families is the necessity that each partner fill all the roles and fulfill all the needs that in an extended family may be distributed among a number of people. The near impossibility of the isolated nuclear family's subserving all the functions of the extended family is attested to by increasing divorce rates and experimentation with alternative marriage and family styles.

Extended families tend to preserve tradition whereas nuclear families allow more rapid adaptation to changing social conditions.[9] My intent here is not to discuss the pros and cons, but to emphasize that family structure is in a position to exert a strong influence upon both the nature and the ease or difficulty of psychosexual development.

It is an illustration of the power of the innate reproductive drive that it can so often overcome the obstacles of poor preparation and excessive demands. Despite formidable psychological and practical hazards, a reasonable proportion of mothers still manage to love and nurture their children so as to impart trust and self-worth to them; fathers still manage to provide for and to nurture both their wives and their children and to find some way to fulfill an adequate portion of their instrumental roles; parents still manage to present a model of interaction that provides some preparation by example.

Conception and Pregnancy

There is an old wives' tale that a woman cannot become pregnant unless she has an orgasm; this belief has resulted in countless shocked teenage girls when they learn why they have missed a period or two.

Old wives' tales have had an interesting history. With the coming of the scientific era and the understanding of realistic cause and effect, all such folk mythology fell into disrepute; but with increased sophistication and wisdom, people began to wonder why such "nonsense" got started in the first place. They began to learn that mankind had survived the incredible odds of scientific ignorance and a hostile environment because prescientific man had been a careful and often accurate observer. Old wives' tales have become a fruitful stimulus for research. This one is no exception; although women do not have to have an orgasm in order to conceive, the reason for the belief is worth investigating.

Normal physiology facilitates whatever function an organ system is designed to perform. In the study of subhuman mammals, for example, it has been found that the hormone oxytocin, produced by the hypothalamus and stored in the pituitary gland, has a functional role both in parturition (giving birth) and in conception, through its action upon the muscles of the vagina, uterus, and fallopian tubes. Its mode of action, however, is quite different in the two different circumstances. When it is released at the time of parturition, it produces peristaltic waves of contraction in the uterine muscles in an expulsive direction, pushing the fetus out and causing birth. Coitus also causes the release of oxytocin, but its action upon the same muscles is exactly the opposite. It produces peristaltic waves in the vagina, uterus, and tubes in the direction from outside toward inside, thus facilitating sperm transport and conception.[10]

The extensive research into human sexual physiology carried out at the Reproductive Biology Research Foundation also found that some of the anatomical and physiological events accompanying female orgasm facilitated fertilization. In brief, these consist in the early stages of sexual excitation of a swelling of the outer third of the vagina which acts to grip the penis, and also functions as a kind of stopper to prevent the escape of seminal fluid. At the same time the inner portion of the vagina expands and the uterus retracts upward in such a way as to provide a more effective seminal receptacle. These changes occur with excitement alone, regardless of whether the woman has an orgasm.

With orgasm, there are strong contractions of the outer third of the vagina which aid in the full expulsion of all semen from the penis. The expanded vaginal receptacle remains expanded, and immediately following orgasm the uterus descends rapidly, immersing the cervical os (mouth) in the seminal pool. (These descriptions apply to intercourse with the woman supine.) Without orgasm, descent of the uterus is markedly slower. Also in the absence of orgasm, the pelvic blood vessels remain engorged, and the pelvic and perineal tissues remain congested and swollen. When chronic, this condition is known to diminish the chances of conception. This research was unable to detect any reverse peristaltic action or negative uterine pressure analogous to that in other animals.[11] More recent research in Britain, using highly sensitive techniques of measurement which were also less disruptive of the sexual involvement of the couple, has provided evidence to fill this gap in physiological logic. A sudden negative pressure, or suction, was found to develop following female orgasm, which could be expected to coincide with immersion of the cervical os in the seminal pool. There is some evidence that this negative uterine pressure may also be due to the action of oxytocin.[12]

Thus human female orgasm does facilitate sperm transport and conception, though it is clearly not a necessary prerequisite. It is only logical that human reproductive physiology should be similar rather than contrary to that of other mammals. Orgastic response is correlated with healthy psychosexual development. Disturbance and unconscious conflicts can impair or destroy woman's capacity for orgasm. So even in conception itself, the quality of psychosexual development exerts a facilitating or inhibiting influence.

The first pregnancy is for most women probably the most important point of transition in their entire life cycle. This one event turns a marriage into a family. It also, on a deep emotional level, turns a wife into a woman. Finally, and for the first time, she has achieved parity with her own mother—the fulfillment of all her childhood wishes and fantasies—in a far more significant manner than marriage alone could accomplish. Similarly, the father-to-be has equalled his father, an emotional event possessing the same enormous conscious and unconscious gratifications as those felt by his wife. These remarks assume that the pregnancy will be carried to normal completion—miscarriage or other gestational disaster would largely shatter these intrapsychic gains—but the beginning psychosexual implications of parenthood do not wait upon success-ful delivery; they are felt and coped with from the earliest knowledge of pregnancy.

Essentially, pregnancy, birth, and early parenthood are the woman's drama. The increasing emphasis in contemporary society upon the husband's participation throughout the whole experience could not be more constructive and is long overdue, but there is no escaping the fact that the developing fetus is literally a part of the woman's body, an absolutely unique experience with which her husband can at best only empathize.

Pregnancy reawakens a woman's emotions—and emotional con-flicts—about her own mother more strongly than any event other than actually having and nurturing her own newborn. Her ability to anticipate motherhood as a true fulfillment will depend largely upon the nonverbal, empathic messages she picked up in the process of her own mothering. The quality of her anticipation will also be strongly colored by what she saw of the dignity and recognition that her father accorded her mother's childbearing and child-rearing role, and her husband's attitudes also add an important dimension.

It requires a healthy psychosexual development to have a healthy pregnancy. I have proposed as a principle that such health is unlikely in this culture, and that few if any adults escape some damaging conflicts that may surface at various times. This depends upon general factors such as the amount of stress a person is under, and also upon individual factors such as the specific association between the nature of the conflict and the particular sexual life events at the moment. Pregnancy is one of the critical times for the emergence of hidden conflicts.

Any number of unresolved conflicts can interfere with a woman's emotional and physical comfort and even with the course of the pregnancy and the health of the fetus. Some unconscious conflicts are so severe as to cause psychogenic infertility or habitual abortion. Minor conflicts may not disrupt the pregnancy but may seriously affect the well-being of both mother and fetus; most of them have been mentioned in tracing the possible future disturbances consequent upon disturbed psychosexual development during the various stages. For example, a high degree of residual oedipal guilt could reawaken in a woman the fantasy that the child she is carrying is her father's.

One of the more common psychosomatic disorders of pregnancy, which varies from mild to fatal, is morning sickness *(hyperemesis gravidarum)*. Most authorities believe there is an important physiological element in this symptom as a result of the massive biochemical changes accompanying pregnancy to which the body must become adapted. While the exact pathophysiology is unclear, the probable basis is the particular woman's sensitivity to the metabolic breakdown products of the gonadal hormones—perhaps specifically progesterone, which is at a peak circulating level during pregnancy.

There is also a general consensus that, in the absence of specific organic disease, persistent vomiting of some severity has a strong psychogenic component and reveals an unconscious wish to get rid of the fetus.[13] While the conflicts leading to unconscious rejection of pregnancy may arise from many possible sources, this specific symptom is clearly associated with the childhood fantasy of oral impregnation and gestation literally in the stomach. The fantasy goes: since the unwanted baby got in the stomach by eating, vomiting will get rid of it.[14] If vomiting during pregnancy can be shown to be related to the high progesterone level, then there is an association with the progesterone phase of the menstrual cycle. It is under the influence of progesterone that oral tendencies and unresolved oral conflicts are revived, thus adding impetus to the vomiting, the bizarre appetites, and the loss of appetite—additional symptoms sometimes seen in pregnancy as psychophysiological manifestations of conflict.[15]

Habitual abortion is another psychosomatic disruption of pregnancy with dynamics quite specific to the pregnant state. It is obvious that a variety of physical disorders and disease states can of themselves be incompatible with completed pregnancy. Nonetheless, various psychiatric studies of habitual aborters disclose highly disturbed family backgrounds and certain frequently shared psychosexual disorders. One typical psychiatric profile of a habitual aborter reveals a physically or emotionally unavailable father in childhood with whom the daughter could not experience and work through affectionate feelings for a man, and a domineering, rejecting mother who had negative attitudes toward sex and pregnancy. The daughter became overly dependent upon her mother, a relationship obviously filled with covert hostility. When the daughter became pregnant, her hostility to her mother made motherhood unacceptable. Also, the negative attitudes toward sex that she had absorbed made her fear that the pregnancy would result in rejection by her parents and her husband. The significance of emotions in the combination of psychological and physical factors implicated in spontaneous abortion is demonstrated in the fact that there has been approximately 80 percent success in producing viable pregnancies in habitual aborters who are willing to undergo psychotherapy.[16]

Stress, whether physically traumatic or emotional, produces in the body massive biochemical changes designed to resist the effects of that stress. When the stress is prolonged, as may be the case in chronically unresolved unconscious conflicts, the physiological effects eventually cause a variety of diseases.[17] It is known that the placenta is not an effective barrier against the passage of stress-induced metabolites and hormones from the maternal circulation into the fetal circulation. There is a broad literature attesting to the deleterious effects of maternal stress upon fetal development and viability, and upon later childhood characteristics. The maternal stress may or may not be related to conflict directly associated with the pregnancy.

Habitual abortion and premature births are more common with maternal stress, and children hospitalized for psychiatric disorders often show a history of having been premature. Maternal stress may lead to fetal hyperactivity and, in turn, hyperactive children;[18] fetal hyperactivity is also closely correlated with neonatal feeding problems and gastrointestinal instability.[19] Illegitimate pregnancies have a greater risk of being stillborn and there is evidence that maternal stress is a factor here. Women who were reared without a father have a higher than normal percentage of stillbirths and early infant mortality.[20] In experiments with rats maternal stress feminized and demasculinized male offspring, but data on such specific sexual effects of maternal stress on human fetuses is not available.[21]

Various psychosomatic diseases and addictions that attest to emotional disturbance in the mother also have deleterious effects upon the fetuses. Obesity and diabetes mellitus[22] pose distinct threats to the developing fetus. Drugs can cross the placenta and may affect the undeveloped tissues and systems of the fetus even more than they affect the mother. A 32 percent incidence of severe disease, malformation, and neonatal death has been reported in children born of alcoholic mothers.[23] Habitual smoking with inhalation must be regarded as both an addiction and a symptom of psychiatric disorder, since no one who knowingly takes poison by mouth can expect to be considered emotionally healthy. Smoking mothers have fewer pregnancies, more abortions, higher infant mortality, more stillbirths and premature infants than nonsmoking mothers, and their newborns show an increased incidence of respiratory difficulties.[24] The rate of fetal growth is retarded by smoking.[25]

Rejection of pregnancy is not always unconscious or conflicted. For some women pregnancy is an unmitigated disaster. It may come at an unwanted time, it may interrupt educational or career plans of higher priority, there may be practical problems, such as poverty or an anticipated divorce, a woman may recognize her inability to cope with mothering without more help—the reasons are endless, and the fact that they are often rationalizations to cover an impoverishment of maternalism is irrelevant to the woman's real distress. Adequate contraception and the recent availability of safe, inexpensive, legal abortion have reduced or relieved a large part of the traditional irreversibility of pregnancy, but there are still many women whose moral or religious values, or fears and guilts, close off such avenues, and many of those whose bodies fail to respond with a convenient spontaneous abortion suffer serious distress or simply fall apart under the unwanted pressure of motherhood.

Men, too, have unconscious psychodynamic responses to pregnancy. Pregnancy can revive a man's unresolved conflicts, ranging from angry rivalry growing out of the original envy of the mother to guilt over publicly visible results of his sexuality, to fear of reprisal based upon repressed oedipal desires. Some of a man's more seriously disruptive negative responses may be taken out on his wife. Some men experience an awakening rivalry with the coming child; these are usually men whose marital relationship is contaminated by a pathological amount of infantile dependency upon their wives, whose pregnancy is felt as a distinct threat. They may openly resent the pregnancy, turn hostile and rejecting, and, possessed by the fantasy that they are being deserted, seek extramarital relationships both in retaliation for the imagined desertion and in search of additional nurturant supplies. Such a man may also reject his wife because of unconscious incestuous guilt. As long as he had only a wife, he could keep his mother and wife emotionally separate, but once his wife becomes a mother, the inappropriate association becomes an equation and he can no longer tolerate his sexual interest in her. The devastating emotional desertion experienced by many pregnant wives frequently has such unconscious roots.

The logical progression of ideas and reasoning dictates that normal psychosexual responses be explored before disturbed ones, but an unavoidable disadvantage inherent in this logic is that discussion often seems to end on a sour note. This impression is augmented by the fact that normal responses tend to be simpler whereas conflicted responses are snarled and intricate lybyrinths. I think it better to reassure too often rather than too seldom that whatever the issue—in this instance, pregnancy—it is usually negotiated with reasonable success and continued growth. As long as one recognizes that conflict is inevitable, that total emotional maturity is an impossible ideal, and that the possibility of increasingly mature development extends throughout life, then the struggles and stumbles and vicissitudes—whether actual experiences in life or as described in a book—can be taken in stride and turned to advantage.

Childbirth and Early Parenthood

The experience of labor and childbirth has some unusually close connections with both prior and subsequent psychosocial development.[26] Cross-cultural studies have shown that in societies with relaxed and accepting sexual attitudes, labor and birth tend to be short and painless, whereas in sexually repressive societies they are prolonged and painful. Obviously the quality of a woman's sexual rearing and attitudes will have a direct influence upon her childbearing experience; one progressive movement in that direction has been called childbirth without fear. The major psychological advantages are to free the mother to anticipate with pleasure not only the birth but her own active role in it—the obstetrician becomes more of an assistant. Of similar importance is the equal involvement of the husband in the prenatal preparation and at least passive participation in the birth itself. The preparation for participatory unanesthetized delivery often constitutes the best developmental sexual training a couple has had, and will pay emotional dividends far beyond facilitating parturition.

Childbirth also triggers caretaking behavior and increased sexual responsiveness. Women who have borne children are more sexually responsive in general and also more erotic during early pregnancy. The increase in normal wifely caretaking will be directed toward the father as well as maternally toward the child, to the degree that he is regarded as part of the experience.

Further, cultures which show an easy handling of maternal functions such as childbirth and nursing are also more accepting of the normal sexual components of mothering. This includes pleasure in genital stimulation of the infant and acceptance of the directly erotic pleasure the mother feels while nursing. Women have reported orgasm during nursing.

All these responses are closely interwoven and, in turn, relate to others. An accepting attitude toward sexuality seems related to a positive position about breast-feeding. Conversely, breast-feeding mothers are more tolerant toward sexual matters, and show the quickest return and highest level of heterosexual interest in their husbands. Also, sexual excitement stimulates the flow of milk.

There are certain consistent threads of constructive psychosexual development during early parenthood that are mutually reinforcing: (1) The more positive the attitudes toward sexuality, the easier and more effectively functioning are all the operations and processes of early motherhood. (2) The more guilt-free the sexuality of the mother, the more effective are her maternal functions. (3) The more relaxed her maternal functions, the more caring and lovingly sexual she is with her mate. (4) The more she is able to enjoy the physiologically normal erotic responses between her infant and herself, the firmer and more loving the bond that will probably evolve. Growing out of all these positive and pleasureful interactions, it is inconceivable that the infant would fail to achieve the beginnings of positive body and sexual self-concepts or that the mother and the father would not discover new pleasures and reach new levels in their existing psychosexual development. These interactional processes correlate closely and well with the unconscious psychodynamics of this phase of parenthood.

Perhaps only the mother's direct stimulation of her infant's genitals strikes a potentially questionable chord. The probability is that there is no intrinsic, inevitable damage from such sex play— there might even be intrinsic benefit if contradictory social expectations and cultural mores did not override it. It is a questionable practice in *this* culture, however, because it would likely set off a type of psychosexual process in the infant which the society could only turn into conflict and emotional pain. Frankly sexual maternal stimulation would unmistakably convey the message that overt sexual excitation and play is good and acceptable. As the youngster grew, this would unquestionably be acted out in overt sex play. Unless this society were to make the sharp attitudinal switch necessary for childhood sex play to be fully accepted, there

could be difficulty. Such a youngster might feel himself or herself to
have been betrayed and misled by the mother, or indeed to have
been overstimulated by her in the sense that the youngster might
imagine that the mother intended the youngster's sexuality to be
focused upon her.

Any consideration of the psychosexual aspects of early parenthood demands an understanding of the physiological consequences
of breast-feeding or its lack. Breast-feeding has undeniable advantages for both the infant, and the mother. Suckling stimulates the
release of oxytocin, necessary for the milk "letdown reflex" which
increases the flow of milk to the nursing infant. If nursing is begun
immediately after birth, the oxytocin produces strong uterine
contractions. This is physiologically beneficial in that the contractions clamp down upon the uterine blood vessels which are
simultaneously being stimulated to contract, thus helping to prevent
excessive uterine bleeding; the contraction of both uterus and blood
vessels facilitates separation and expulsion of the placenta; and the
uterus more quickly regains its normal, prepregnancy size. The
latter effect occurs even if suckling does not begin immediately
after delivery.[27] Thus even on a physiological level, mother and
infant genuinely need one another for optimal health and development.

The pituitary hormone prolactin is primarily involved in milk
production, and its production is stimulated by continued suckling,
which exerts some inhibitory effect upon ovulation, but that effect is
neither total nor dependable. While it is statistically more difficult
for a nursing mother to become pregnant, there is absolutely no
security in considering lactation and breast feeding to be an
adequate form of contraception.

In considering the immediately perinatal period, it must be noted
that one physiological event attending childbirth often has disturbing consequences. As I pointed out in discussing the psychobiology
of the menstrual cycle, there is a relationship between emotional
disorders and the sudden extinction of progesterone in a woman's
system. At no time in a woman's life is there so sharp and massive a
decrease in progesterone as following delivery. Progesterone is
produced during pregnancy at a rate as high as ten times that
during the second half of the menstrual cycle. The rate of change

differs among different women, but about 30 percent show a drop of about three-quarters in only a few days following delivery.[28]

The postpartum period is notorious for the frequency of emotional disorders even in the healthiest of women, varying from mild "postpartum blues" to serious depressions and psychoses. This is yet another example of the inseparability of biological and psychological factors. While the decrease in progesterone is strongly supported by research, countless mothers do not suffer postpartum distress. Those who do may possess a genetically determined hypersensitivity to the endocrine changes, but many are probably women whose unconscious conflictual responses to motherhood add their weight to the biochemical influences, combining to overwhelm their capacity to cope.

The intrapsychic growth that normally takes place in the interaction between healthy infants and emotionally healthy parents is one of the most strikingly integrated phenomena available to study. The intensity of the psychosexual maturation produced and *required* in the new parents, and the relatively short period in which the adaptations must occur, make of early parenthood, like puberty, one of the normally most conflictual periods in the life cycle. Therefore it has the potential for both enormous strides and a peak incidence of emotional breakdown.

The crucial intrapsychic factors here are the parents' identification with their child, and the fact that they receive from the child emotionally as well as give to him. The child's part of the interchange has been fully described, but the original description could not do justice to the true reciprocity. The mother is usually the parent more deeply involved.

Essentially, the mothering capacity arises from two primary sources. One is the innate quality of the reproductive drive and of maternalism; this correlates with the mother's desire to give. The other is derived from her earliest oral relationship with her own mother; this reactivates her need to receive and underlies her ability to identify with her infant. This earliest stage is one of symbiosis—a condition of truly mutual need—although this usefully descriptive term is technically inaccurate because the infant's need is absolute whereas the mother's is relative.

Ideally, as the infant gradually incorporates a sense of worth and trust from the mother's loving care and feeding, a parallel process is occurring in the mother. As a mother sees her infant thrive, grow, and respond to her ministrations with pleasure and well-being, her identification with him through her own oral phase permits her to incorporate aspects of herself from him. The good thriving infant is taken in and made part of herself, reflecting and validating her quality as the good succoring mother. These are new components to her self-image and psychosexual development, not merely echoes of her early development. An infant cannot identify with his mother in the same way that she can identify with him, because she has been there and he has not. Her identification with him and with her own mother, now on a functional level for the first time, permits her to add new facets to her sexual identity and further increments to her ego maturation. The varying attitudes of love, ambivalence, and rejection that she incorporated as an infant become enmeshed in the dynamics of her own mother-infant identification in two ways: they influence her confidence in her motherliness, and they help determine how she unconsciously expects her infant to respond to her. Such conflicts are not necessarily fixed indelibly; the mother is far from the same person she was as an infant, and her own maternal experience provides an additional stage upon which those old conflicts may be reenacted, reworked, and sometimes resolved. It is easy to see that inadequate or poor mothering may reproduce itself generation after generation and contribute to related manifestations such as rejection of motherhood or its validity and importance.

New fathers also continue their psychosexual development in much the same way and from many of the same intrapsychic sources, although they necessarily remain somewhat peripheral, especially if there is a nursing unit of mother and infant. A man's original female identification and later envy of his mother, and the role of his own oral symbiotic relationship with her, reawakened by his wife's pregnancy, begin to mobilize his nurturant qualities and facilitate his identification with his infant so that in the parallel giving and receiving interaction the father also incorporates new ego and psychosexual aspects of himself.

In addition to the specifically psychosexual components, some related developmental processes begin in this early stage of parenthood. One critical interaction centers around a child's negative responses to his parents. These are inevitable and begin early. Infants cannot possibly always be happy; they are sometimes sick, sometimes fussy, sometimes uncooperative—and they begin while quite young to imitate their parents. Since parents, too, are humanly fallible and subject to bad days and irritable moods, they sometimes see negative or unacceptable aspects of themselves reflected by their infants. When the infant is old enough to reach the "no" stage, yet another level of negativism and separateness is introduced.

The self-esteem and security of parents must be sufficient so that they respond to these negative expressions without a profound modification of their love for their children; this is especially difficult if they learned negative concepts from their own parents' responses to analogous situations. An illness or fussiness should arouse no more than normal maternal concern in order to discover and remedy its cause. Unflattering imitations should provide feedback that the parent may recognize ruefully but use in the continual process of self-modification. "No!" should stimulate the beginning and ever-shifting balance between benevolent parental discipline and broadening areas of childhood autonomy.

Suppose a parent had learned in his own infancy to regard himself as a bad person through incorporating a parent's negative responses to certain behavior. If good-nurturing-mother can be taken in and equated with good-worthwhile-self, so can bad-rejecting-mother be equated with bad-unloved-self. Under these circumstances, the inescapable identification that each parent makes with his infant can wreak havoc; the baby's negative response reawakens the parent's negative self-concept. Not only does the parent then reciprocally incorporate an increasingly destructive self-image through identification with the infant, but also identifies the child with his own unconsciously perceived bad self. The stage is set for disastrous self-fulfilling mutual expectations throughout development, in which the child lives "down" to his internal unlovable self-image acquired through identification with that aspect of the parents, and the parents perceive the child as unlovable as a result of the unconscious equation in which unloved (parent) self equals unloved child.

A second early issue of far-ranging import is the infant's

delegation of omnipotent status to his parents. This is probably a universal developmental phenomenon, unrelated to social factors except through subsequent complications that can be added by the degree to which a particular culture fosters authoritarian and omnipotent parental roles. It is possible that the infant, in his helplessness, *must* see his parents as omnipotent in order to value their love and to develop a sense of trust and self-worth.

Parents accept this omnipotent role for several reasons. Again through identification, their own infantile omnipotence has been stirred. Also, it allows them to feel equal with—perhaps better than—their own once-perceived (but long since demoted) omnipotent parents. It gives them confidence to undertake the awesome task of rearing and teaching a child, even with the hope that they may do a better job than their parents.

Omnipotence, however imaginary, is heady stuff. Parents must recognize its fantasy nature and be prepared to relinquish the pretense of perfection. They must allow their children to discover their mistakes and human frailties without suffering a debilitating loss of self-esteem. Either the dogged effort to cling to omnipotent authority or the inability to maintain self-respect as imperfections become known represents stagnated emotional development in parents and will paralyze that of their children.[29]

Once the critical period of pregnancy and early parenthood have been taken into account, it becomes feasible to telescope somewhat, to touch more briefly upon the subsequent adult psychosexual development as it parallels that of the child. Not that it is less complex or less important to full sexual self-actualization in adulthood—on the contrary, people who live a normal life span are sexually interactive adults much longer than they are active parents of children living at home—but because parental needs and responses have already been largely covered in the discussion of childhood psychosexual development. It is necessary mainly to restate and reinforce the mental shift of focus from the parents' effect upon the child to the child's effect upon the parents.

Each stage of a child's psychosexual development reawakens the emotions of the same period in each parent's childhood. The dual identification with one's child and one's parents continues at the same time that a person must carry out his parental responsibilities in real life. I wish to emphasize especially that it is the unique quality of the dual identifications and real life function that characterizes parenthood as a stage. It is an emotional constellation of maturational forces available only to parents. At no other time and under no other circumstances is there the sheer quantity of emotional opportunities to put together a more psychosexually integrated self. In identification with the child the parent relives the emotions and fantasies and tasks of each particular stage. And there now becomes accessible a quality of identification with his own parents possible only to those who share the same emotional tasks. Simultaneously the parent must blend these new qualities of mind-expanding awarenesses with the practical task of rearing a unique child in his own unique social setting. Living in three concurrent worlds is the essential quality of parenthood, and it offers opportunities for unparalleled new increments of maturity and new facets of personality structure. The pitfalls are commensurate with the opportunities.

In toddlerhood, parents reassess their own sense of autonomy and body (now life) mastery. It is difficult to grant their children something they do not have themselves. The fairly natural privacy of most young couples in our society may be threatened for the first time by a mobile toddler. If parents have not fully established their own autonomy, they may find themselves unexpectedly puzzled and indecisive about where to help the child establish limits and guidelines while still fostering the child's appropriate self-determination. The toilet training of this period provides new impetus, especially for women, to accept their genitals more fully as their hygienic functions reinforce the difference between elimination and sexuality. The young couple who still have not established an appropriate degree of independence from their parents may find themselves stirred into renewed, intensified conflict with them— and possibly into a healthy resolution of the conflict—by pressure of the revived intrapsychic issues of autonomy.

The oedipal period, obviously, can be stressful because it is one of the high points of psychosexual conflict. Partly because it is biologically natural and partly through identification with their children, parents find themselves erotically responsive to the child of the opposite sex. Some parents are sufficiently self-aware to be conscious of it; others are prone to vague anxieties that express themselves in disorganized and sometimes rejecting responses to their children. The thrust of genital interest and the increased incidence of masturbation are a challenge to parents not already comfortable with overt sexuality or the sexual undertones in all human relationships, including familial. Until faced with his daughter's sexuality and his spontaneous response to it, a man may not understand the mutuality and the anxiety in his own childhood oedipal relationship with his mother. This recognition may facilitate the development of the qualities of empathy and ego control that will allow him to foster his little girl's femininity while neither subtly reciprocating sexually nor having to push her away emotionally to defend himself from guilt. The same growth influences are available to mothers of sons.

Throughout early childhood, boys' fathers have repeated opportunities to overcome residual homosexual anxieties. Unless discouraged, little boys are exuberantly affectionate with both parents. A son's physical affection, and the stirring of erotic response that affectionate display by a child of either sex can produce, may reawaken repressed and guilt-ridden memories. A father then has the opportunity to reevaluate his guilts and fears; he may now realize that his own father had been standoffish and anxious, thereby preventing him from learning that affection between males is compatible with masculinity. I have emphasized males because our society does not make it as difficult for women to show affection for each other.

During a child's latency period, parents must learn to withstand their first dethroning. Other people become important, comparisons begin, and contrasts between the outside world and parental versions of it become both more available and more comprehensible to the youngster's mental capacity. For some parents in isolated nuclear families this may be the first major test of their self-respect in the face of vanishing omnipotence.

The sociosexual aspect of latency provides even more opportunity for growth. All children can be merciless parodists, and in the latency stage this quality often blossoms. It is disconcerting to see oneself unexpectedly in a living mirror. Some parents experience a sense of shocked and embarrassed self-recognition when they overhear their children at play—especially when the play includes make-believe family relationships. Harsh tones of voice, sarcastic and hurtful phrases, demeaning attitudes by one sex toward the other all may have a sudden familiar ring. Children may treat one another in ways they have learned at home which are uncomfortably recognizable to their parents, or they may simply confront their parents with the results of their broadened observations and comparisons. As children become aware of alternative interpersonal styles, they may demand to know why in their home girls are valued more or less than boys or may challenge the parents' ways of treating one another.

Surprisingly often, this may be the first time a parent catches a glimpse of himself as he may appear in the eyes of other people. Except in specialized situations, such as encounter groups, adults are not prone to confront each other with their faults. A married couple may become so inured to each other's character manifestations that they take them for granted. Even if undesirable traits are a source of frequent dissension, it is easy to build defenses against expected accusations, but the mirrors provided by young children can often penetrate these barriers. They come from an unexpected source, they have the added emphasis of caricature, and they are often too ingenuously direct to be ignored. The revelations they provide constitute another opportunity for reworking and change.

Puberty and adolescence constitute the most prolonged and intense pressure toward further parental psychosexual maturation. This is a period of marked and fluctuating regression for the youngsters, and their regressions revive corresponding regressions in parents. Any remaining sexual conflicts and inappropriate attitudes of the parents are flushed into the open. Some parents begin to act (perhaps for the first time) like adolescents. The upheaval may affect siblings and other relatives, even grandparents. Just as the first time around, out of this potentially constructive kind of regression and the second "adolescent" reworking of intrapsychic sexual emotions at a now higher level of ego development, parents can also emerge with gains. Further psychosexual development at this stage of life usually manifests itself in the integration of healthier reciprocity in sexual relations and in a broader acceptance of sexuality as a normal and good part of life.[30] All too obviously, many families do not have the emotional capacity to make use of this unparalleled opportunity.

The discussion of adolescence has detailed the ways in which the sexual attitudes and adaptive capacity of the parents are challenged,

flouted, defied, and shredded by the adolescent in his effort to find
his own values and to test those of his parents. That unique parental
intrapsychic complex of real function plus dual identification with
both older and younger generations continues to furnish the
opportunity for further growth. I will briefly discuss only two of the
more significant typical issues: the parents' sense of being replaced
by their youngsters and the parents' reaction to adolescent sexuality.

It is not easy to be replaced. Yet that, inevitably, is what begins to
happen to parents during their children's adolescence. With the
conscious intellectual mind one may realize that this is not entirely
so. Adolescents are untried and untrained, at best apprentices to an
adult world in which their parents are at the peak of their
effectiveness; despite the socioeconomic and political impact of the
youth culture, true power is wielded by the late middle-aged. But
these facts do not eliminate the *sense* of being replaced. Perhaps
this is because parents see adolescents with their entire productive
lives before them, knowing that their own lives are now limited. I
think, however, that the problem for parents hits more deeply, at
the primitive and archaic unconscious roots of self-esteem—sexual
body image. In a society that equates youth and physical attractiveness, there are relatively few parents of adolescents who meet the
stereotyped standards as well as their blossoming teenage children,
and this is true regardless of the cultural fad. Time inevitably takes
a toll of skin texture, supportive tissues, muscle tone, stamina, and
ultimately health—the physical self. The day does come when a son
can whip his father. Parents' sexual stamina is seldom equal to that
of their youngsters.

These generalizations are subject to all kinds of exceptions—with
a less strenuous life style, premature aging of women is no longer
typical; the man who keeps himself in condition can be a beautiful
physical specimen in middle life; couples who have continued to
grow sexually could teach their adolescents much about sexual
enjoyment—but the blow delivered by burgeoning adolescence
cannot be denied. A man's lifelong vulnerability in masculine
esteem makes him an easy target for depression; a woman's special
sensitivities are the fear of fading beauty (whether it is happening or
not) and the approaching loss of procreative ability.

This combination of realizations and concerns can stimulate psychosexual development as well as precipitate maladaptive defenses and solutions. A successful parental job into which one has put one's best is an achievement of top order, a source of psychosexual pride that can be gained in no other way, and at no earlier stage in life. The recognition of increasing sexual understanding and finesse, and the steady growth of the capacity for the kind of interpersonal relationship in which sexual expression is an ever deeper and more multifaceted pleasure is likewise an accomplishment for which time and experience are indispensable.

Coping with adolescent sexuality offers another potential for parental development, although not many parents seize upon this opportunity with enthusiasm. The initial reaction of most parents has some of the unconsidered quality of a knee-jerk reflex: "Don't do it!" Research indicates that adult attitudes toward adolescent sexual behavior are not related to parental age. Parents' attitudes are not determined by their having been reared at an earlier period but are correlated with whether or not their children are postpubescent. That is, parents of the same age express more liberal sexual attitudes if their children are still below the age of pubertal changes, and childless adults of similar age express even more permissive attitudes. The issue seems to be that the parents of adolescent children consider themselves responsible for the sexuality of others—their children.[31] In addition, parents are increasingly more disapproving of more intimate sexual involvement, such as intercourse as compared with petting.

These differences seem defensible enough; the "knee-jerk" characterization might seem prejudicially harsh but for two major considerations. The first is that the predominant tendency in parents is to deny that adolescents have either the right or the capacity to assume responsibility for their own sexuality; the second is parental hypocrisy. This is a common adolescent battle cry, but there has been little direct study of it. What there is, is corroboratory. In the only small study to focus directly upon this issue, it was found that parents would permit themselves sexual activity that they would deny to their adolescents.[32] Indirect evidence, however, is considerable. As early as 1953, Kinsey found that most white males and nearly 50 percent of white females had had premarital intercourse.[33] No study of parental attitudes toward the sexual activity of their own adolescents reveals even a near approximation of that same degree of permissiveness.[34]

The reasons for this apparent hypocrisy are unclear. It is not that those parents who experienced premarital intercourse have lived long enough to discover its destructive effects on their lives, because there is no statistically significant correlation between premarital intercourse and reported marital happiness. The most reasonable hypothesis is that most adults have never fully resolved their unconscious sexual conflicts and guilts, so that they have not come fully to accept their own behavior. When their adolescents stir disapproval by their real or anticipated sexual behavior, the parents express their own continuing guilt and anxiety. Particularly if a parent has failed to resolve his oedipal guilts, the identification with the adolescent reanimates his inner need for a severe superego, which is then expressed by his efforts to prohibit their sexual activity.

The same identifications can also operate beneficially. Through successful interaction with a child during both the original and the adolescent oedipal dilemma, a parent may become intrapsychically more secure as he discovers that oedipal wishes are not as powerful as he once believed and that his original guilt and anxiety were grossly excessive. In the process, the remnants of his childishly punitive superego soften its harsh strictness, permitting a more objective view of both his own and his child's sexuality.

This kind of further development may occur spontaneously during felicitous parenthood, but parents, like children, do not necessarily mature unless forced to. Force, on this issue particularly, is exactly what many adolescents apply. They demand explanations for the hypocrisy they perceive and insist that parents validate their positions. In some families this becomes an impasse that can destroy the relationship. For parents with the basic ego strength to reconsider and modify previously insufficiently explored value systems, it can be a mind-expanding experience. They may retain many of their personal standards but will come out of the experience with a greater appreciation of the existing plurality of values, more respect for their adolescent's responsible questioning, and a sharply diminished blind dogmatism.

Special Situations

Not everyone marries. Not everyone becomes a parent. Not all families are composed of the husband's and wife's biological offspring. Not all families remain constituted of the same members. Not all parents have normally developing children to grow with. All these variations affect the psychosexual development of the adults involved.

Stepparents have some unique tasks that are by no means limited to psychosexuality. If the real parent is alive and involved, there are general issues that may reflect themselves in the sexual area of both the stepparent and the child. When planning that involves the child and philosophies of child rearing must be shared with another mother or another father, serious differences may exist. Usually the parent with whom the child lives has pragmatic final authority, but this does not spare him the necessity of validating, questioning, and defending his attitudes. As always, this can produce parental growth. But when the child sides with the absent parent, some of the normal supports for successful resolution are missing. With the possible exception of the stepparent who assumed his role when the child was an infant, the facilitatory dynamics of mutual identification will usually be diminished if not missing. The lack of a shared childhood may multiply misunderstandings and problems of communication. The stepparent's attitudes are doubly challenged at the same time that he (and the child) are at a disadvantage in working through the differences.

The very necessity of having to work harder to come to terms with the situation may result in enhanced gains for both stepparent and child, but the stepparent will not always prevail, even when to do so would be appropriate. Changes in the legal philosophy of child custody are making it easier for a child to decide to move back with his real parent, and that decision is increasingly respected by the courts. If the decision is a willful and "childish" one, the chief loser will be the child, though the decision will also tax the rejected stepparent's sexual security.

The stepparent and spouse may be in disagreement over various sexual issues, and children are prone to exploit the differences. In the instance of a stepchild, there may be the added complication of the real parent's oversensitivity to the spouse's response to the child and possibly ill-advised overprotection by the real parent. The resulting fray may scar all participants, but in the end the child may have done the couple an unwitting service. Without the child having attempted to play one against the other, the differences could have been ignored. Their resulting nonresolution would have deprived both parents of more meaningful sexual communication and a richer mutuality of enjoyment.

A specifically sexual problem for a stepparent is the absence of the natural incest taboos. This is usually a minor issue when the child is only four or five years old, but it can mushroom into major proportions at adolescence, and obviously it can affect both parties. Both stepparent and adolescent have probably incorporated sufficiently the cultural prohibitions so that overt sexual activity is unlikely, but coping with the desires may require more emotional effort than if the parent were the natural one. The lack of innate components comes into play and weakens controls in a stepparent when there is a combination of sexual dissatisfaction in the marriage and a strong attraction to the adolescent. Successful control leaves a stepparent feeling stronger but may exact a draining price of guilt and further marital disruption. Only rarely are these struggles talked out between man and wife unless the attraction becomes obvious enough to force discussion.

The psychosexual dilemmas faced by adoptive parents are similar to those of stepparents, and the same considerations apply. Most obvious is the same kind of potentially explosive oedipal attraction —although the word "explosive" may be no more than ethnocentric bias: such nonblood relationships are not taboo in all cultures. In my personal practice there was a case of a man who divorced his wife and married his adopted daughter. She had been adopted when a teenager and their age difference was eighteen years. They have remained happy for the several years of their marriage, and follow-up information from various additional sources reveal no developing problems. This certainly constitutes an exception in our middle-class culture. The long-term outcome cannot be predicted, but this case offers a striking precaution against dogmatism.

An opposite problem may be posed by an adolescent adoptee who expresses his need to distance himself from his parents by idealizing his unknown, real parents. This can be a devastating weapon against insecure adoptive parents because it is, by definition, unanswerable. The only internal defense is a secure identity.

Couples usually adopt because one or both are infertile. An infertile adult in a sexually repressive culture has a unique intrapsychic burden. He must somehow free himself from the ubiquitous guilts aroused by all the sexual activity against which he heard such dire warnings, plus the guilts aroused by all of his unacceptable fantasies. His guilt is likely to be reinforced by the myth that masturbation will cause sterility and by early religious training which has inculcated a belief in divine punishment especially fitting to the sin. Such guilt can erode sexual self-confidence and the security in one's masculinity or femininity. It is a major victory to surmount reproductive incapacity and retain or attain relatively unimpaired sexual identity.

The fact (undisputed by most authorities) that a very high percentage of infertility is psychogenic raises an interesting dilemma. The capacity to beget or conceive a child would not and could not be totally prevented by emotional conflicts acting upon the reproductive system unless there were serious conflicts relating specifically to the reproductive function—for example, childbirth, maternity, or fatherhood.[35] Yet it is sometimes possible to relieve the block temporarily by some such superficial intervention as hypnosis.[36] In some instances conception then occurs though there has been no change in the conflicted psychosexuality that had previously prevented it.

A potentially ethical and philosophical question arises, for both the couple and the physician, when such a couple seeks noncurative medical intervention such as hypnosis so that they can conceive. Practically, it may be possible, but what should the physician recommend? I have treated a number of psychogenically infertile persons and find them generally unprepared emotionally for parenthood. Their bodies are telling them something to which they should listen. The conflicts may be relatively minor or quite deep. My recommendation is that they seek psychotherapy so as to overcome the conflicts interfering with fertility. If they have a relatively minor problem, it should respond quickly and easily; if not, they may require therapy as extensive as psychoanalysis. In any event, they will correct their conflicted psychosexual development and will probably be better parents.

Illnesses, deaths, and other family disruptions will also affect the psychosexual development of parents. Any unexpected misfortune that is in any manner associated with sexuality can awaken unresolved unconscious guilts and fears and rouse fantasies of punishment for some sexual "misdeed." This sequence can attend such distressing circumstances as stillbirth, the birth of a malformed or defective child, the chronic illness or death of a child, or the chronic illness or death of a spouse. Since few people are free of unconscious sexual conflict, there are almost inescapable intrapsychic burdens attendant upon such conditions; their intensity varies according to the ego strength and psychosexual maturity of the parent.

It is particularly distressing when the effect of guilt is so intense that the parent seeks some means of expiation. The husband or wife may become depressed, lose sexual interest, and withdraw. The mother of a defective child may turn so much of her attention to that child that the rest of the family is emotionally deprived. All grief must end eventually, and the normal emotional and sexual needs of each parent must ultimately be met. I have found a component of sexual guilt surprisingly common in the complex of emotional responses to a family disaster. Real catastrophes are unhappy tasks, to be coped with as best one can. It is not expected that parents would normally grow sexually as a result of catastrophes, but almost any misfortune may fortuitously result in unexpected forms of maturation.

Discussion of parenthood would be incomplete without consideration of those who choose not to have a child. Remaining childless has been rendered quite practical with the advent of effective contraception, and much more easy to rationalize in the face of world overcrowding, diminishing resources, and deteriorating social environment. The time may not be far distant when procreation will no longer be solely at a specific couple's option. Nevertheless, the issue cannot simply be dismissed as either a matter of individual choice or of ecological-economic necessity; there are intrapsychic components that relate it inextricably to psychosexual development.

Some scientific truths are more emotionally freighted with prejudice and vested interest than others—an example would be Galileo Galilei's insistence upon a peripheral terrestrial position in the solar system at a time when man's divine centrality was religious dogma. Contemporaneously inflammatory in some circles is the matter of innate versus socially learned propensities, in the foolish assumption that it could ever be a simple either/or question. The heat this issue generates justifies repeating that any inborn human tendency can be modified by learning experiences and that humans can adapt to almost any deprivations. Human adaptability includes the capacity to be happy, to feel fulfilled, and to function admirably in areas outside of those that have been disrupted (though not all people have that much ego strength), but the adaptation, however successful, inevitably leaves its imprint upon other aspects of the mind and spirit. It is only the imperfection of our empathic and perceptive microscopes that allows the consequences at times to remain invisible.

That stated, I take the position that the procreative drive is innate. To "choose" to forgo it is not a totally free choice; it is a "choice" made because the option of parenthood has somehow been rendered unattractive. Any of the true reasons underlying the rationalized choice may be unconscious—it is this fact that is often so galling. Most people loathe the idea that any of their decisions and attitudes are determined by influences about which they know nothing.

The clearly inappropriate avoidance of parenthood due to sexual guilt or fear is the least difficult to comprehend; there are dozens of ways in which any individual may be deflected through emotional conflict from accepting and fulfilling a parental role. A special case might be pressed for those who adopt a celibate religious calling, but whatever their sincerity or human goodness, they do not demonstrate qualitatively different emotional processes. They are human, with human psychodynamics. An exhaustive inquiry into the subject reveals the same needs and psychosexual vicissitudes and conflicts—they simply resolve them in their own special way.[37]

The roots are more difficult to trace in people who feel no conflict about their decision and who even accept and function well in other expressions of sexuality. The large study of college women to which I referred in the previous chapter, which indicated disturbed family backgrounds in the 10 percent of educated women who tended to avoid marriage as a first choice, focused particularly upon the rejection of the family and maternal role by this same group of women. While the study readily recognized the number of questions that cannot be answered by existing research, some thought-provoking observations and speculations were made.

This 10 percent, the "young feminists," showed a much higher level of career than marriage commitment and choose predominantly masculine-identified professions. They were uninterested in domesticity, wanted few or no children, and were willing or eager to delegate the care of children to others. They were highly vocal in the demand for free child care facilities. Such women, in order to succeed in the life styles they prefer, must have a high energy level and considerable psychological toughness and aggressiveness. The study calls careful attention to the similarity in personality between such women and those exposed to excess androgen during fetal development. It is speculated that small, as yet undetectable, androgen/estrogen imbalances in favor of androgen may, in part, account for these typically masculine traits, including the lack of interest in maternalism. Since most of this large sample of young women were unmarried and childless at the time of the study, it was pointed out that such nonmaternal attitudes as the demand for child care centers were probably as much a reflection of personal preferences as an altruistic concern for other women with children.

Among these same young women, an element of psychological distancing from intimacy with infants was noted, as well as an ambivalence toward pregnancy and childbirth. Warmth and close bodily intimacy with the mother during infancy is absolutely necessary in learning to cope with intimacy. It is reasonable to suppose that these young women, regardless of the speculative role of androgenization in their development, are also the products of emotionally impoverished mothering. The result is their own similar impoverishment, now expressed in rejection of the mothering role.

One might assume that this 10 percent are those who are bright and perceptive enough to recognize changed social conditions and inequities in cultural role valuation, and who decided to do something about it. But if theirs were entirely a rational decision, then one would expect to find no definitive differences in the family backgrounds that would set them apart from the other 90 percent of female graduates. The very close correlation between early family discord and the rejection of the family role strongly suggests a causal relationship that links negative attitudes toward maternalism with psychosexual maldevelopment.[38]

This brings us to the matter of day care and other child care facilities—their meaning and value and, more pointedly, their value to whom? Obviously it is not a monolithic issue. It is not even a debatable one in the vast number of cases of dire economic need. Unless many a mother is freed to work, the whole family will subsist at a poverty level, if at all. It *does* become debatable when the mother's occupation is optional and her children are still quite young, in the sense that she has alternatives open to her.

Much depends upon the quality and policies of the center. Many centers are staffed by transient young people wishing only an interim job on the way to other jobs. There are vacations, rapid staff turnover, shift changes—all resulting in a multitude of seemingly (to the child) undependable adults. Small children do not respond well to this kind of multiple handling. In such settings children are inadvertently being taught insecurity and mistrust. They are learning *not* to be able to count upon the steady availability of a loving mother or mother surrogate, with whom they can develop basic trust. In Czechoslovakia, which was among the first nations to utilize day care extensively, and where its effects have been available for study over a number of years, child care facilities for children under the age of four have been discontinued because it was found that younger children were being severely damaged emotionally.[39]

The American psychoanalyst Helene Deutsch recalls her many decades of experience unequivocally:

> Motherhood is a tyrannical full-time emotional task; part-time motherhood is a compromise that hurts both masters: professional work and motherhood.
>
> There are women who, through their unusual gifts and their capacity to adjust, seem to have fulfilled both tasks successfully. I have been happy to know them, and have often referred to them as good examples in support of my belief that the conflict can be solved. In a number of cases, however, I have been able to gain some insight into the adolescence of their children. The shock of these revelations has led me definitely to give up my optimistic view.[40]

The weight of evidence is that women who insist that child care centers for young children are as good as mothers are unwittingly revealing a great deal about their own mothers. They do not know what it is like to be mothered properly, and consequently their own maternalism is stunted and undeveloped; for such women, a good child care center probably could do as good a job with their child as they could. However, it might be wiser all around for women without the inner drive called maternalism, and without the capacity to find a truly unique joy in the mother-infant symbiosis, to avoid becoming mothers.

Contemporary technological society places so many extra burdens upon individuals and families that a variety of efforts have been made to devise alternatives to the nuclear family which might hopefully be more adaptive to current social realities. The Israeli kibbutzim represent an extended social experiment in family deemphasis and child rearing. The successful lives of the majority of sabras indicate clearly that children can be reared communally, but two minor trends are worth noting. The first is that there is, in the second and third generation of kibbutzniks, a resurgence of desire to grant more primacy to the nuclear family and some pressure for increased responsibility by the biological parents for the rearing of their children. There has been an expressed longing by some kibbutz women for more traditional maternal roles and a disinclination to exercise their sociosexual equality in executive and authoritative roles within the kibbutz.[41]

The second trend involves the personality type of adolescent and adult that results from the communal style and highly regulated form of kibbutz child rearing. A highly biased, almost proselyting recent study admiringly equated the health of kibbutz adolescents with the "normal" adolescents described by Offer and Grinker (see chapter 10)—those who gave evidence of not having experienced the ego maturation possible as a result of adolescent turbulence but maintained a latency child adaptation throughout that period.[42] If there is reason to see maturational potential in an adolescence characterized by *Sturm und Drang*, then there is also reason to question some of the consequences of structuring this quality out of adolescent experience. This cannot be labeled a "good" or "bad" result. Such value judgments are unwarranted, except in terms of the quality of adult character valued and fostered by a given society. The result, however, does illustrate the determinative nature of different kinds of parenting.

While communes are not new on the world scene, their present upsurge, with its characteristically freer sexual ambience, is too recent for an authoritative assessment of relative successes and disadvantages. Some preliminary and informal observations suggest that pregnant women and young mothers do derive some of the lost benefits of mutual support and task assistance. Particularly in rural communes, the children, most especially boys and most noticeably in latency, seem to benefit from the closer daily association with their fathers and other working and contributing adult males. The larger peer group and the frequently permissive attitude toward childhood sex play awaits evaluation with time.

On the other hand, the very availability of surrogate mothers permits feckless reproduction by immature young women who subsequently desert their children emotionally. The children usually survive, and may receive adequate mothering by others, but their ultimate emotional impairment appears inevitable. Psychiatric clinics have begun to see an influx of sexually disturbed four- and five-year-olds whose difficulties seem to arise from neglect of their intensified oedipal psychosexual vulnerabilities in those communes characterized by open and free adult sexuality and casual sleeping and partner arrangements.[43] Total sexual casualness, an aspect of a minority of communes, results in children for whom there is no clear legal paternal responsibility.

Some investigators are more sanguine than others about the viability and future of multilateral sexual involvements which often constitute an informal group marriage. Apparently a minority manage to hold together for at least a few years, though most disintegrate. Sex role tasks, and sexual jealousies and preferences, despite overt professions of nonpossessiveness, play an important part in reported conflicts. Sexual motivations loom large in a person's decision to adopt this life style.[44]

In view of the data on psychosexual development assembled thus far, there appear to be at least five factors that would seriously undermine the effectiveness of this life style as a true substitute for the natural extended family. The first is the absence of a full spread of generations; this, of course, may evolve with time. The second is the frequent fluidity of relationships and legal bonds and responsibilities. With the relative freedom from culturally sanctioned and biologically real kinship ties, long-term commitments and loyalties are less dependable. The third is the likelihood that many participants, by their very choice of a multilateral sexual life style, reveal difficulties in the areas of intimacy, commitment, and family responsibility—difficulties that would operate detrimentally in *any* family style. The fourth is that many of the young adults, particularly the males, who are attracted to such life styles are themselves victims of serious problems in the area of dealing with authority. Consequently, there is often great ambivalence and inconsistency in applying the appropriate discipline young children must have in order to internalize reasonable guidelines and controls. Most important is the absence of the biological basis for the incest taboo if the father is unknown. Since the cohesiveness of the family structure is rooted in this universal taboo, its amelioration or absence alone lends a poor prognosis.

Erikson, in his emphasis on the recognition of psychosexual development as a lifelong continuum, characterized the years of early parenthood as those in which people either achieve a sense of generativity or lapse into a state of emotional stagnation. Generativity involves the expansion of ego interests and emotional maturity necessary to concern oneself with establishing and guiding the next generation. Obviously this level of mature adult function is not limited to those who are biologically parents. Many people, through a combination of personal circumstances and special gifts, express their generativity through a variety of socially productive functions of unique and altruistic value. Where this quality fails to develop— and it may certainly fail in persons who have biologically produced children—a sense of emotional impoverishment sets in. One often sees in such a person an intense self-concern, as though that person were his own only child. The lack of generativity also may reflect a lack of trust in the worth of mankind, which is necessary in order to welcome a child as a valuable privilege and responsibility.[45]

By the time the last of their children are well into adolescence, most parents have lived more than half their lives. Development, now, must take on a new meaning. In most common usage, positive development connotes a process that is ever broadening and enlarging, constantly on an upward path. That is now too limited a concept. A healthy adult woman in her forties may find her still-developing sexuality becoming enriched beyond her fondest hopes in terms of interpersonal relatedness and fulfillment—but she is also at or near the end of her procreative function. Development must be seen as embracing all appropriate adaptive flexibility to changing circumstances. It is the quality of keeping constructive pace with reality, even—or perhaps especially—when that reality entails a diminution of certain aspects of sexuality.

It would be arrogant and unwarranted to pass premature judgment upon any efforts to cope with the culturally unprecedented tasks of parenthood while adaptively modifying the family to fit unforeseen social changes for which adequate preparation was impossible. Such caution is appropriate even in the instances of avoidance of parenthood, despite the evidence that such avoidance is most often motivated by misrearing and unconscious psychosexual conflict. Mankind's ability to outsmart itself has never been more evident than in his learning to propagate so prolifically, to extend life so effectively, and to decrease infantile mortality so dramatically that parenthood must now become more a public than a private concern. For mankind to survive, parenthood and family size cannot long remain a matter of personal decision.

The modification demanded in the very psychobiological roots of the species is the most wrenching in recorded history. Never before has the whole of humanity, as a species, been required—very suddenly—literally to alter some of its basic species characteristics in order to survive. Ecological necessity, however imperative, will not accomplish it; it will somehow have to be enforced. Propagative freedom must be regulated long before there is any possibility of an evolutionary reduction of the reproductive drive. What will be available to fill the gap? The answer does not currently exist.

TWELVE

The Middle and Later Years: New Dimensions of Sex

The two final periods in the human sexual life span are, for many people, longer than any of those already traversed. Their onset is more varied, both psychologically and chronologically, and their extent is almost totally uncertain.

The middle years arrive when the children begin to leave home and are functioning as independent adults and starting their own families; they extend until one's productivity and self-sufficiency begins significantly to wane. The late years are those that remain. It is virtually impossible to assign meaningful time spans to these periods. Menopause might be considered to define the onset of middle age for females; there is no comparable event for males.

An enormous amount of further psychosexual development continues after active parenting has ceased. This makes it important to focus with special emphasis upon these (usually) postreproductive years. The vital place of sexuality in the lives of older adults is only recently and hesitantly being recognized. Our culture has been as negative and repressive toward sexuality in older people as toward that in children and adolescents. Older people have largely been victims of the cultural values they helped devise, and of their own earlier expectations that sex will have relatively little place in their later lives. Many have forfeited a most sustaining aspect of those years. Both they and society at large stand badly in need of corrective education.

Late Middle Age—A Final Peak

What I have chosen to call the middle years corresponds in most people's minds to later middle age. Initiated by the menopause in women at an average age of around fifty, and considering a similar age as the beginning in men, it is obviously somewhat arbitrary to correlate the middle years with the time when one's children leave home. Many couples who married in their teens, while still in their late thirties saw their children begin to depart. Others, who by

416

preference or long professional preparation postponed marriage, still have most of their children at home. Still others, with children of widely-spread ages or children from more than one family or marriage, may have both married children and children in primary school. But it is probably more the rule than the exception that three events occur in most parents' lives at approximately this age: at least some of their children have left home; they are becoming grandparents; and the wife is experiencing the end of her reproductive capacity. These are important spurs either toward further psychosexual development or toward premature decline.

By and large—sexuality aside for the moment—these are peak years of productive and creative endeavor. Youthful enthusiasts and firebrands notwithstanding, the bulk of social prestige, power, and authority are wielded by those between the ages of fifty and seventy. Barring illness or other disability, the release from active parenting permits the combination of experience, knowledge, and vigor to reach a zenith of many years' duration. This can be especially true for women, who may start entirely new lives or return to careers even if their principal endeavor has up to now been child rearing. Erikson's criteria of generativity versus stagnation applies as fully now as during the most active period of parenting. It is now that the final dimension in the series of adult responsibilities—self, mate, offspring, society—is most fully assumed.

As true and typical as are these social achievements of the middle years, there are some obstacles in the way of a comparable peak of psychosexual development. Some are physiological, and while most of them are unnecessary and pose only mythological hazards, as long as they are misunderstood they will wreak havoc. The most dramatic is menopause (the gradual cessation of the menses). A distinction should be made here between two terms that are sometimes used with confusing interchangeability: menopause and climacterium. Menopause is the biological regression of procreative capacity. The climacterium is the period of psychosocial response to menopause.

There is nothing imaginary or mythical about menopause. As the age of menarche has been steadily decreasing, the age of menopause has been gradually increasing. The present average age of about fifty is variously quoted as approximately four years later than fifty years ago[1] and nearly ten years later than the average at the turn of the century.[2] There is apparently no correlation in the individual between the ages of menarche and menopause, and the normal age range for menopause is thirty-five to fifty-five.

Ovarian function actually begins a slight decline before the age of thirty, as attested by a gradually lowering rate of conception and higher fetal mortality and maldevelopment as women pass into their mid-thirties and beyond. Menopause itself is first manifested by anovulatory periods and then irregular periods with either scanty or increased flow, or both in unpredictable sequence. These changes are not due to a decrease of the gonadotropic hormones FSH and LH but to an increasing ovarian insensitivity to their stimulation. Ovarian estrogen decreases gradually as the hormone-producing tissues atrophy, and as a rule eventually reaches a level no higher than that of women whose ovaries have been removed. The remaining naturally produced estrogen comes from the adrenals and may vary in amount considerably from one woman to another.

Other changes occur in direct consequence of the withdrawal of estrogen, and probably of progesterone as well. The endometrium atrophies in the absence of cyclic hormonal stimulation, so that menstruation ceases. The uterus becomes smaller, and as the time passes the other genital tissues and the breasts become smaller and less firm. The vaginal walls become thinner and more friable, the cellular lining of the vagina changes character, and some involution of the high degree of pelvic vascularity results in less ready lubrication upon erotic stimulation. One of the most prominent subjective symptoms is "hot flashes," most often affecting the head and neck, and accompanied by profuse sweating. Their cause is not fully known but is probably related to a vasomotor instability (unpredictable dilation and contraction of blood vessels) caused by the hormonal fluctuations. Other symptoms may be fatigue, irritability, and headache.[3]

The catalog of physiologic changes consequent upon menopause is enough to make it seem that it should be genuinely dreaded, except for several important considerations. Principal is the fact that only about 15 percent of women suffer menopausal symptoms of any severity at all.[4] The great majority make the transition to nonprocreative physiology with ease. Furthermore, the decrease in circulating estrogen is both gradual and quite variable from person to person.[5] Since the symptoms are closely linked to available estrogen, the processes of physiologic aging also vary widely in their onset and rapidity of progress. Finally, the effects of the menopause are among the easiest and most successfully treated when they do occur, simply by replacing the estrogen, either orally, by injection, or by implantation of slow-release pellets. All methods are thoroughly successful.

Authorities differ sharply over whether replacement estrogen should be used routinely after menopause if there are no clear contraindications, or whether it should be instituted only upon the appearance of symptoms clearly linked to estrogen deficiency. One concern has been the speculative role of estrogen in increasing the likelihood of certain forms of cancer, but the consensus of modern clinical authority is that valid evidence is lacking. Despite differences in medical management, no woman's body can remain forever impervious to the deprivation of the sexual hormones. It is indefensible to withhold hormone treatment of the physiologic changes, because they can seriously impair sexual function and enjoyment, and thus at least indirectly affect emotions and relationships.

In contrast to the effects of menopause, the supposedly comparable "male climacterium" has a thoroughly questionable physiologic basis. There is definitely no sudden decline in testosterone production or reproductive capacity at any age. While much has been written about an analogous syndrome of fatigue, hot flashes, weakness, and nervousness, there is virtually no basis for believing that the male climacterium is a normally occurring phenomenon. Some researchers suggest there is a very gradual diminution in the number of testicular cells capable of producing testosterone that occurs throughout adulthood and extends into quite old age, and also that testosterone levels slowly fall.[6] Others find no evidence whatsoever of any decline in testosterone at any age.[7]

Significant loss of testosterone production apparently occurs only in specific disease of the organs (brain structures and testicles) responsible for its production. These conditions can be diagnosed biochemically, and only then is testosterone replacement to be regarded as properly indicated therapy. In such relatively rare circumstances, the results can be as dramatic as estrogen replacement. Many physicians, believing that middle-aged and elderly patients complaining of diminishing potency are truly low in testosterone, use it fairly routinely, and report frequent subjective improvement in those patients. Testosterone has a number of rejuvenating effects upon the brain and body generally; it is most likely that the patients' responses are to this rather temporary physical and psychological boost than to the replacement of genuinely deficient androgens. Since there are greater potential hazards to the indiscriminate use of testosterone than to that of estrogen, its place in routine therapy is questionable.

This does not mean that males do not age sexually. They do, but much more slowly than is generally thought, and usually for general physical reasons rather than specific hormonal ones. The differences have begun to manifest themselves by latter middle age, but are not really striking and certainly not debilitating. The general changes, which progress only *very* gradually with advancing age, include primarily the taking of a longer time for the penis to erect; greater necessity for physical stimulation, rather than pure mental excitement, to produce erection; a longer period of stimulation before orgasm and ejaculation; an increasing incidence of intercourse without ejaculation; less powerful expulsion of semen; more rapid loss of erection after orgasm; and a longer refractory period before erection can again be attained.

Women, for all their relatively abrupt menopausal changes, show far fewer normal results of aging, providing any estrogen deficit is corrected. As in males, the normal anatomical and physiological responses to excitation and orgasm may not take place to the same extent, may take longer to occur, and last for a shorter time.[8] It must be emphasized that such consequences of aging are barely, if at all, noticeable in the early part of the age span under discussion.

If psychosexual development has proceeded healthily, this period of life may well be the richest and most fulfilling of all. Women often feel a new surge of vitality and sense of freedom, a new depth of personal identity when, still healthy and attractive, their obligatory parenting roles are largely terminated. Even though the issue of unwanted pregnancy is no longer a major one for most women, those whose personal attitudes or morals precluded contraception are now also freed of the burden of that apprehension. If their sexual relationships have been good ones, more women have by this time shed their inhibitions and conquered unconscious conflicts, and thus become more fully responsive than at earlier periods in their life. These factors, combined with woman's inherently great capacity for sexual arousal, make for a stronger sexual drive than the woman may ever have felt before.

It is probable that relatively few men of fifty to sixty years can match the sexual stamina of a willing and interested partner—the peak of male sexual capacity is reached usually in the late teens and early twenties—but they may well possess advantages that can more than offset their slightly declining capacities. Ideally, they are not so importunate as to be preoccupied with sex for its own sake and chiefly for their own gratification. The relationship with a partner as a whole person takes precedence over sex alone. They have sufficient experience to have more sensitively learned a woman's responses and thus are able to achieve more pleasure for them both.[9] It has been found that longer foreplay and longer intravaginal intercourse correlate definitely with a larger proportion of women having more frequent orgasm.[10]

There continue to be intrapsychic and interpersonal factors that can be integrated so as to achieve new levels of psychosexual development. As in the period of more active parenting, each new experience of a now-adult son or daughter reawakens the analogous emotions in the parents. The identification with the children is very strong, especially when they are forming their own marriages and producing their own families. The reciprocal psychobiological involvements continue, allowing the parents a further opportunity to rework the conflicts they had when they were at that stage and, hopefully, to resolve more fully some of the omnipresent unfinished emotional business.

This period involves learning to cope with being replaced, with not being needed. There can be no question that older parents and grandparents are often deeply and sincerely needed, but an ever lessening need, the gradual replacement, the eventual reversal of roles, is inexorably taking place. The change is reflected in the fact that as soon as one marries, the parent is no longer the legal next of kin. Mothers usually experience the greater wrench in letting go, especially in the intense identification with a child-bearing daughter. The adjustment is not easy, and carries the potential for jealousy and other destructive interactions as well as for growth.

Grandparenting is itself a new role and a new task. Grandparents may enjoy their grandchildren more than they did their own children. The usually decreased personal responsibility for the youngster's rearing and its outcome allows their love to be less contaminated by anxiety and uncertainty. Since the objects of that love are less threatening to grandparents' self-concepts, their love can approach unambivalence. The children in turn can benefit from this undemanding love; there is security in being loved without always deserving it, and the child's answering response reassures the grandparents that they, too, are still loved and needed. Finally, grandchildren help to gratify the never-quite-relinquished uncon- scious wishful fantasy of omnipotent immortality.[11]

A woman's emotional responses are as closely tied to the physiology of menopause, and as sensitively reflective of earlier emotional influences, as they are to any other major hormonal change during her life cycle. Menopause poses a unique and difficult adaptive task, since it is a regressive biological phenome- non. As in other areas involving the often obscure and complex role of biological influences in psychosexual development, hard data are scarce, but many factors point to parallels between the menopause and the premenstrual and postpartum periods.

All three states share the condition of low amounts of the sex hormones, particularly progesterone. All three are remarkable for their high incidence of emotional disorder—most often depression. The lack of progesterone has been implicated in the occurrence of premenstrual and postpartum distress, and it is likely implicated at this time also. Low levels of female gonadal hormones likewise seem associated with regressive emotions and attitudes such as feeling helpless and needing to be cared for, and oral defenses such as overeating. This is a frequent tendency among menopausal and postmenopausal women, so that when ego strengths are lowest, the effort to resist a gain in weight adds a still further frustration.

It has been noted that this potentially difficult period is one for which woman's biology has fortuitously provided her with much preparation. The hormonal cycles of the menstrual periods give women repeated opportunities to develop their ego capacity to cope with periods of low gonadal hormones. In this manner, a woman's accomplishments and the adaptive qualities of her ego developed during the reproductive period can sustain her at menopause. A great deal of emotional energy is spent by the ego in coping with the repeated hormonal cycles and with the tasks of childbirth and motherhood. The final postmenopausal leveling off allows the ego to turn its powerful adaptive abilities to other pursuits. Major social and professional contributions are made by women who can focus their learned ego strengths onto nonmaternal interests. In this way the climacterium is a potentially positive psychosexual developmental phase.[12]

For all the possibility that these could be the truly golden years of sexuality for healthy adults, it is obvious that for many they are not. As people age, sexual difficulties come increasingly to possess a component of chronic physical illness, but many of the difficulties are entirely psychogenic, and some are the consequences of widespread misconceptions and cultural wrongheadedness.

Foremost is the task of coping with one's own and society's expectation that sex should retain little interest for those past reproductive age. That this is patently false is demonstrated by the high frequency of middle-aged sexual flings and remarriages. Also, we are considering now only the front end of the aging period, when cultural prohibitions do not exercise their full force. But our Christian and Victorian heritages have steadfastly influenced the association of sex with reproduction, with the quite explicit exclusion of sex in the premarital and postreproductive years. A discouraging number of vital middle-aged people accept as true that they should lose their interest in sex, and their expectaction becomes a self-fulfilling one.

The remainder of the many psychogenic sexual conflicts that beset the middle aged arise either from the breakdown of shaky and inadequate defenses against never-resolved conflicts under the pressure of aging and replacement, or from what might be called existential dilemmas. The latter reflect an unacceptance of the inevitable—age. There is an inordinate fear of losing one's sexual attractiveness and capacity, and the fear often either makes it come true or produces ill-considered and even grotesque behavior in the effort to retain or recapture sexual youth. This may take the form of multiple extramarital affairs, or fairly overt competition with one's grown children for the attentions of their dates or spouses. There is an increased divorce rate at this period. Many men become "swinging bachelors" for a while and eventually remarry women half their age. This trend is not as noticeable among women, but it is difficult to know whether this represents sound judgment or the strong cultural sanctions against wives being markedly older than their husbands.

Being freed both of the responsibilities for minor children and of concerns about pregnancy is a genuine release—often a release from any number of unhappy prisons. Many realistically inappropriate marriages have been held together, whether wisely or not, "for the sake of the children." The couple may have tried their best, though unsuccessfully, to improve their relationship. Once the rationale of "the children" is past, the mutually sustaining quality of the marital relationship becomes much more important, since once again the couple will be alone together. Thus what had been unsatisfying but somehow tolerable now becomes unbearable. It is not always an irrational grasp at fading youth, or a failure to try together, that results in a rash of divorces at this time. It is often that personal convictions about an intact family make this the first time that one or the other partner feels free to consider breaking up the marriage. With the increasing options open to both men and women of middle age, the decision to try it alone and to risk growing old perhaps in solitude may have been carefully thought out. Whether or not a better remarriage results for either partner, the decision often turns out to be a wise one.

While extramarital involvements may express a whole gamut of misused sexuality, they may also represent realistic efforts to cope with real problems. They are often a successful means of keeping a marriage together when the marriage has not been sexually fulfilling but preserved because other aspects of the relationship are rewarding. By late middle age, one partner may have a chronic disease that takes a toll of sexual capacity; unless one wishes to assume the puritan position that sex is only permissible within marriage, an affair may be the healthiest way to avoid a split which might do more real damage to both than the often imaginary damage so typically ascribed to the "evil of adultery."

There are many typically neurotic sexual disturbances that surface, intensify, or continue into middle age. A spouse who has never enjoyed the "duty" of sex—this has usually been the wife—will use aging or often the menopause as an excuse to give up sex completely. Such a situation often results in extramarital flings.

The marriage of one's children revives the echoes of unresolved oedipal feelings. Whereas with mature parents this affords further opportunity for resolution and a still closer rapport with grown children, it may also lead to bitter rivalry and the inability to welcome the new son- or daughter-in-law into the circle of one's love. The rivalry now is reversed. Another way of expressing the broader emotional content of the oedipal rivalry is that the fantasied victorious rival is the one who is at the stage of life in which there is the greatest likelihood of satisfaction of the sex drive. Since so many older parents neither recognize nor use their genuine sexual advantages, it is they who now envy their children. Sometimes this reverse oedipal situation is acted out when middle-aged men divorce and marry young women no older than their daughters.[13]

Rivalry and the emotional distress and depression that accompany it are not always oedipally rooted. Family authority is sometimes difficult to relinquish. Mother-in-law jokes reflect common conflicts. Fathers want to retain their status as principal provider and will sometimes stifle their sons even when it is totally unnecessary because in reality the fathers are still at the height of their productivity. As time passes, these roles, too, reverse, and it may be difficult for a son to empathize with this once- (or still-) powerful man who now needs from his son just what the son needed as a boy from the father—love, admiration, and respect.

Mothers are particularly prone to depression when they are faced with an "empty nest." This may be true even of women who have their own rewarding interests and activities and who encouraged their children's independence. There are ambiguous and conflicting attitudes toward a mother in contemporary American culture: Devote your whole life almost totally to the children as long as they are at home, but leave them almost totally alone once they are grown. This discontinuity is poor preparation for the transition. A study of hospitalized, depressed, late-middle-aged women indicated that there are different forms this conflict may take. Those women who followed the traditional model of total focus on home and family, with few outside friends or activities, were in overt conflict with their children over the amount and quality of emotional interaction with them. Conflict became their only means of contact but could not ward off the severe depressive reaction to the feeling of loss. In contrast, the conflict and the persistent need for the original closeness was unconscious in the more independent and autonomy-fostering women. Their serious depressions surfaced when circumstances such as their own or family illnesses caused them to have to relinquish their substitute objects and activities. While both types of women may be vulnerable to such depressions, there was a significant difference. Those women who had cultivated stronger personal identities for themselves and their children had a distinctly better prognosis for emerging from their depression.[14]

Menopause may at times precipitate either real sexual dysfunction or psychiatric disorders not obviously associated with sexuality. The involutional genital changes caused by estrogen deprivation can transform intercourse into a painful and unpleasant experience for even the most willing of women. The narrowing of the vagina and the thinning of its walls; the diminished pelvic vascularity that decreases lubrication—these and other results of estrogen depletion seriously impair sexual function and pleasure. Happily, the changes do not occur precipitously in the majority of women, and they are almost immediately reversible with hormone replacement. Unhappily, decades after this simple therapy became known, many women are still allowed to suffer this unnecessary impairment, due partly to their own ignorance or reticence to seek relief, and partly to the neglect of attention to the sexual needs of older women by poorly prepared and sexually inhibited physicians.

The physiological and endocrine changes of menopause are insufficient by themselves to account for the severe psychopathology that occurs with greater frequency at this time. Prior emotional disorder, characterological constrictions and distortions, or unstable ego defenses and maladaptive modes of coping are prerequisite for severe menopausal disorders such as depressive and paranoid psychoses. Research is in general agreement that estrogen therapy is spectacularly unsuccessful in relieving any but the physical symptoms.[15] Nonetheless, it would be illogical artificially to separate the mind and the body; they are an integrated and functioning unit at all times. Clinical evidence clearly links low levels of sex hormones with regression and weakened ego strength, and consequent emotional vulnerability, though this may have more to do with low progesterone than estrogen. Its role in postmenopausal disorders is less documented than in those of the premenstrual and postpartum periods. Still, it would be prudent to include progesterone—a quite safe substance—in hormone replacement therapy as an adjunct to the necessary psychiatric management and psychotherapy because of the beneficial effect of both hormones together on general ego function.

Finally, in assessing the sexual problems of later middle age, one cannot overlook the reality factors, such as the increasing incidence of chronic illness and the higher mortality rate of men as compared with women, which produces a shocking disparity in spouse survival: by the age of sixty-five, 20 percent of married men will have lost their wives and 50 percent of women will have lost their husbands.[16] The differential sharply determines the remarriage prospects of either sex. Sustained sexual responsiveness into old age becomes largely academic in the absence of willing and involved partners.

In general it may be said that the principal psychodynamic issues affecting the psychosexual development of persons in later middle age are those associated with the exciting potential for expanded sexual freedom and function, with coping with the empty nest and being replaced, with grandparenting, and with the loss of procreative potential by women.

Illness and Sexuality

Illness of any seriousness has some effect upon sexuality, however slight, both because one's vitality is sapped and because illness is unconsciously perceived as a threat to one's body image and integrity. Some illnesses attack the sexual organs directly. Certain of the chronic illnesses, both local and systemic, usually have their onset during middle age and produce altered sexual function either directly or through side effects. In some instances sexuality is adversely affected not by genuine pathology but by popular misconceptions or medical mismanagement.

Cardiac and circulatory diseases are probably the class of systemic chronic illnesses that affect the largest number of middle-aged and elderly people, males significantly more than females—although the proportion of females is increasing, probably as a result of more cigarette smoking among women and of the increasing number of women entering high-stress jobs and professions. Some of these conditions do have an effect on sexuality, and the exercise of intercourse may occasionally pose a threat, but both the effects and the threat generally have been vastly overestimated.

Coronary artery disease, which leads to "heart attack," or myocardial infarction (in which some greater or lesser portion of the heart muscle suddenly dies from insufficient oxygen), has long been thought a condition that warrants great caution against the exertion of intercourse. Since exertion causes the heart to pump harder and faster, it requires more oxygen. If the vessels of the heart are so narrow as already to have failed to supply enough oxygen, exertion might bring on another infarction. Physicians were usually taught to recommend a very slow return to sexual activity, or even abstinence, for patients who have suffered an infarct. The rationale was seemingly supported by the earlier studies of the direct effects of sexual activity upon the function of the heart, which found that during intercourse and orgasm, heart rates increased as much as 100 beats per minute and blood pressure elevated as much as 2 to $2\frac{1}{2}$ times normal.[17] But these studies were heavily weighted with adolescents and young adults, in whom it is reasonable to assume that intercourse is indeed a relatively prolonged and athletic endeavor.

Careful recent research on middle-aged, long-married couples has found their sexuality to be much more subdued. Intercourse typically causes no more exertion, and therefore no more extra work for the heart, than walking up a single flight of stairs—it was actually less than that expended in ordinary professional activities or a heated discussion at the dinner table. These findings help explain the extreme rarity of deaths from infarctions during intercourse, and also the fact that the great majority of deaths occur during extramarital affairs and marriages to much younger women —situations in which the level of exertion may be considerably higher.[18]

Therefore it is not only unnecessary but harmful to restrict sexual activity very long or very stringently in all but unusual cases. Sexual activity has such emotional importance to most people's self-esteem that deprivation would often be a greater stress and therefore a more serious danger than the level of exertion. Despite the availability of definitive research, there remain both popular and medical misconceptions about the exaggerated dangers of sexual exertion. Either a postcoronary patient or his spouse may be afraid to return to sexual intercourse for fear it may precipitate another, perhaps fatal, infarction. They are often reticent about bringing up this concern with their physician, and he compounds the problem by omitting mention of it in his counseling or by urging great caution. Naturally, the appropriate rate of return to any activity must be determined in each individual case, but sexual activity should never be ignored and need not be especially restricted.

Peripheral vascular diseases (such as arteriosclerosis) which narrow the arteries or weaken their walls may sufficiently impair the blood flow to the penis and the nerves involved in erection as to cause impotence. Data is lacking on the effects on females. Surgical correction using natural or artificial arterial grafts may provide dramatic relief, but because of the very close proximity of the affected vessels and the nerves necessary for ejaculation, it may be impossible to avoid severing the nerves, thus creating another problem (loss of ejaculatory capacity) while correcting the impotence.[19] Since these vascular diseases also weaken arterial walls and typically affect the vessels throughout the body, there is always the slight possibility that increased blood pressure with exercise may cause a stroke, but the likelihood is exceedingly rare.

These same vascular conditions are also associated with most cases of high blood pressure. Some authorities recommend more passive and less strenuous sexual activities for patients with severe uncontrolled hypertension, but others can find little basis for such strictures, probably for the same reasons applicable to coronary patients. Here, too, the treatment may cause more sexual difficulty than the illness, though it is seldom safe to avoid treatment of severe hypertension on that basis. All the known antihypertensive drugs exert their beneficial effects through action on the same nerves necessary for sexual function in the male. Again, effects on female function are unreported. Thus all such agents have been reported to produce varying degrees of impotence, and orgastic and ejaculatory dysfunction. Most males seem to tolerate moderate doses, however, without dysfunction, and they should not be led to expect difficulties because the fear itself may be enough to cause dysfunction.[20] In extremely severe cases, nerves may have to be removed (an operation called a "sympathectomy") to relieve the hypertension as a life-saving measure. The lower down along the vertebrae the sympathectomy is done, the greater the likelihood of loss of ejaculatory capacity. In the few female cases reported, sympathectomy apparently did not diminish orgastic response.[21]

The other major systemic chronic disease associated with sexual dysfunction is diabetes mellitus. Diabetes is not unique to middle age, and younger diabetics also show increased sexual impairment. Impotence in diabetics increases with age, however, with more than 70 percent of male diabetics impotent by age sixty-five. Sex drive usually persists long after sexual function is lost, but gradually subsides.[22] Diabetes in women also produces loss of orgastic response in a significant proportion. Nearly 50 percent of previously orgastic women have become nonorgastic by the time they have had diabetes for twenty years.[23]

The means by which diabetes interferes with sexual function is not fully understood, but the evidence strongly indicates that in some way the disease impairs the nerves necessary for performance and for response.[24] However, diabetes does not inevitably impair sexuality. While every person complaining of recent onset of impotence or orgastic inability should be tested for diabetes (the sexual symptoms are often the first sign), by no means should diabetics be warned to expect sexual difficulty. For one thing, unrecognized and therefore previously untreated diabetics may regain sexual function with proper treatment. More important, the suggestion creates anxiety which then often creates the problem. Those patients who are dysfunctional will benefit from careful explanation that the cause is physical, because that is less damaging to their sexual self-esteem.

Among chronic diseases of specific organs, those affecting the prostate gland of the male are often associated with sexual difficulties—sometimes factually and sometimes through misinformation. The prostate becomes increasingly subject to pathology with age, the three most common chronic conditions being chronic congestion (swelling due to tissue fluids and vascular engorgement), benign prostatic hypertrophy (increase in size due to actual growth but not cancerous), and cancer of the prostate.

Prostatic congestion does not affect sexual function. In fact, it is often brought on or aggravated by inadequate orgastic gratification or sexual abstinence.[25] However, it is often used by the patient as an excuse for existing impotence or to rationalize his decreasing sexual interest. It is easily treated by prostatic massage, after which some men regain potency on the basis of their belief that the prostatic condition was the cause. But since that is untrue, massage will not permanently alter existing sexual problems.[26]

Neither benign hypertrophy nor cancer of the prostate in itself causes potency disorders. It is the fact that both usually require surgery which makes them of importance in the sexuality of middle-aged and elderly men. As with other surgery in the perineal and pelvic area, the interference with the nerves controlling the sexual function is the critical factor. In this instance, the issue is one of alternative surgical techniques involving the direction from which the surgeon approaches the prostate. Benign hypertrophy requires less extensive surgery and allows the surgeon more alternatives. As long as he does not operate from an incision in the perineum, potency is seldom affected. However, any prostatic removal interferes with ejaculation by disrupting the nerves which close the sphincter at the neck of the bladder. The man is perfectly capable of intercourse and orgasm, but the semen is propelled back into the bladder instead of out through the penis—a condition called retrograde ejaculation.

Cancer of the prostate, as is true of all cancer, requires much more extensive removal of tissue and also limits the surgeon's alternatives for approach. The usual route is through the perineum, and this approach results in almost 100 percent loss of potency. Even minor prostatic surgery, like that for benign hypertrophy, takes the same toll if the perineal route is employed,[27] and when other approaches are used, the amount of tissue removal and nerve destruction has essentially the same effects.

There is some authoritative disagreement with the near total impotence following perineal or radical surgery on the prostate. Some studies report a higher rate of retained potency.[28] In some, however, successful intercourse once in the year following surgery is rated as proof of potency. Nonetheless, the possibility that even a few men will remain capable of intercourse should bring caution when discussing the possible effects of surgery for prostatic cancer. The retrograde ejaculation should be explained, so as to avoid anxiety when it occurs.

Another common cause of sexually disruptive surgery among older people, especially males, is cancer of the rectum or lower bowel, which requires massive removal of pelvic tissue and nerves, plus disruption of some of the blood supply to the genitals. It is not surprising that somewhat more than 75 percent of men become impotent after this surgery.[29] It is reported that women generally retain their sexual function.[30]

This kind of surgery requires extensive counseling about sexual function because it typically involves closing off the rectum and providing a means for emptying the bowel contents through a colostomy, an opening in the abdominal wall through which the large intestine empties into a carefully fitted bag that requires regular emptying, cleaning, and reattachment. Patients are often intensely self-conscious about this and often avoid sexual activity out of fear of offending the partner. Both the patient and the spouse need extended and sensitive discussion of the facts about the colostomy and also of their sexual attitudes and apprehensions. This often clears the way for continued sexual interaction at whatever level is possible following the surgery.

Of the chronic diseases specific to women, those requiring surgery on the reproductive or secondary sex organs may have sexual side effects. It is noteworthy, however, that regardless of the disease or the surgical procedure, almost all debilitating sexual results are emotional. Statistics make it clear that if orgastic response existed prior to surgery, it is rarely lost afterward. This is true no matter how extensive the surgery, including removal of uterus, tubes, ovaries, pelvic and perineal nerves, major and minor labia, and the clitoris. As long as enough of the vagina remains to permit some penetration, sexual gratification will normally survive any such surgery.[31]

The major problem to be considered is the woman's emotional response to the surgery, which includes the unconscious meaning she attaches to the organs involved. While the most radical removal of all pelvic sex organs except the vagina does not usually destroy sexual response, the simple removal of the uterus alone may precipitate serious disruption of sexual function and even neurotic illness. This type of emotional complication is not unique to women. With any surgery upon, especially removal of, any of the sex organs, there is possible damage to sexual self-esteem. A woman whose uterus has been removed may consider herself no longer a complete woman, or sexually valuable and desirable. She may unconsciously perceive the surgery as punishment for some past sexual behavior or fantasies. She sometimes imagines her strength and vitality diminished so that she is weaker and more vulnerable.[32]

Disfiguring surgery, such as removal of the labia and clitoris due to cancer, and including removal of one or both breasts, imposes further emotional burdens. These constitute more direct and realistic assaults upon sexual body image. They impose more severe fears of loss of sexual attractiveness and desirability. The more that physicians are aware of the potential emotional conflicts and disruptive responses, the more easily the latter can be avoided by preoperative discussion in which misconceptions can be dispelled and anxieties aired.

In any consideration of the sexual effects of chronic illness, it must be emphasized that the inappropriate fear of sexual dysfunction is often more damaging than the illness itself and that sexual function tends to persist more often among those who had an active sex life before the illness than among those who did not.

I have referred to the important counseling role of the physician, and also have suggested that he often falls very far short in this role. The first allusion is obvious. The second may be surprising but it is not an expression of subjective bias. Very few medical schools offer even rudimentary courses in the emotional aspects of illness. Only in the last decade are some medical schools beginning to offer any course in human sexuality, and in my personal experience only a few are barely adequate or better. Thus, physicians are usually no better trained in the human and emotional aspects of sexuality than are educated laymen.

Sex is emotionally charged for most people in our culture, including doctors. They are as likely as anyone to have emotional conflicts about sex and to be embarrassed discussing it. Research has shown that the nature and the rigors of medical training tend to attract people who are particularly prone to be sexually conservative and rigid.[33] Some studies have corroborated that many doctors regard themselves and others as uncomfortable discussing sex with their patients. Fewer than 50 percent of physicians frequently ask questions about sexual history or function; those who do ask find pertinent sexual concerns in over 50 percent of their patients, while those who do not are told of the significant sexual material by less than 10 percent.[34]

It is obviously necessary both that physicians be better prepared to work with the sexual aspects of illness and that patients be more ready to bring their concerns to their doctors' attention. This is particularly true with the middle aged and elderly who avoid sexual problems as a result of fear and misunderstanding.

Actual treatment of sexual dysfunction may be neglected when sexual matters are ignored by both doctor and patient. There are a number of therapeutic possibilities open to the knowledgeable physician, either through medical procedures or through very simple guidance. Even estrogen replacement after menopause may be neglected if the patient and physician both avoid the subject, possibly because they both assume that sex should no longer be important.

Surgery affecting the size of the vagina need have no disturbing effect upon sexual relations if estrogen levels are kept adequate and dilators are used to bring the size back to normal. Males who are impotent can now have semiflexible silicone splints inserted in their penis by a minor surgical procedure and thus be enabled to continue intercourse indefinitely. Since erectile capacity is sometimes lost without the sex drive or orgastic response being lost, this simple operation may restore full pleasure to both partners. When an illness genuinely requires severe restriction of activity and exertion, couples can be counseled about modifying their roles so as to permit more passivity for the ill one, or about noncoital means of stimulation such as manipulation or oral-genital sex.

Such counseling requires an understanding and sexually accepting physician, and also may involve more time to open up the patients' attitudes and perhaps help remove some inhibitions. Counseling applies in many other situations. A completely impotent or unresponsive partner need not stop giving the other sexual pleasure through noncoital means when he is helped to accept the idea. In the many instances in which a partner is unavailable or unwilling, masturbation should be discussed. If guilt and shame can be alleviated, there is no reason why this gratification should not be available. Flagging interest can sometimes be revitalized through the use of "pornography," better referred to as sexually explicit books, photographs, and movies. If one accepts the rightness and healthfulness of sexual activity at any age, then there can be no rationale for avoiding any nonharmful means of helping in its accomplishment.

The Final Years

In contrast with the upward and expanding emotional movement characteristically possible in later middle life, there can be no denying that old age for the vast majority involves a genuine decline in most of their physical, mental, and emotional functions. It is impossible to specify an age when one begins to become old, but sixty-five is a widely used average. After that age, for most people, the principal emotional and psychodynamic concerns focus upon the various facets of decline. They must cope with lessening physical strength and abilities, with slowing mental capacities, with the gradual shift from independence to dependence, and with the various increments of personal freedom and autonomy that are lost along with all those processes.

There are many exceptions to such a portrait of aging, and everyone knows of some. There are men and women who could not be considered aged even at ninety, but even they, unless they die of illness or accident while still displaying their peculiar vigor, will someday begin to find themselves having to cope with the same characteristic concerns.

It must not be assumed that the aged *cannot* cope; decline in any real sense is barely beginning. The ego strengths people have achieved through the years do not desert them until brain deterioration becomes significant. The task of accepting with dignity the narrowing scope of function and activity is one of the major tasks in the life cycle, but the progressive simplification of life style that usually accompanies aging also means that not so much is required. The elderly can devote more of themselves to the enjoyment of the "now" and to accepting the finiteness of everything, including themselves.

One of the pleasures of the "now" most emphatically includes continued capacity for sexual activity. This has not been widely understood or acknowledged. In a study of attitudes toward the elderly among university students, every student questioned indicated that sex for most old people is negligible, unimportant, ended, negative, distasteful, or taboo.[35] The fact of continued sexual activity and pleasure for the majority of elderly people, however, is undeniable.

A number of studies corroborate the fact that age alone is not a major factor in the loss of sexual desire or capacity for either sex. While the statistics vary to some extent, there is general consensus that up to the age of seventy or seventy-five, 55 to 65 percent of males are still potent and active.[36] Most studies report a fairly sharp decrease in sexual activity after that age, but the largest study yet reported differs sharply, finding that 48 percent of men between the ages of seventy-five and ninety-two claim to be having satisfactory coitus.[37] Most of the existing data concerns males; when females have been included, it appears that a smaller proportion of elderly women report active sexuality.

There are a number of reasons to look beyond the aging process to understand the majority of instances in which sexuality ceases to be a part of the elderly person's life even though he is not affected by a sexually debilitating illness. The Reproductive Biology Research Foundation, which produced the data on the physiological aspects of sexual aging, has also provided knowledge about the preservation and restoration of sexual function in the aged. The research subjects left the unequivocal conclusion that orgastic sexual response need not be lost even into the ninth decade. Those persons treated when elderly for sexual dysfunction—and it must logically be assumed that restoring sexual function to an elderly person is more difficult than its preservation—provide even more dramatic proof of the same fact. Persons in their sixties and above were capable of regaining full orgastic function in intercourse even after the dysfunction had been of several decades' duration.[38]

This being true, and differentiating the chronic illnesses that often accompany aging from the uncomplicated aging process itself, the causes of sexual decline must largely consist of situational and psychological influences. Clinical experience underlines the powerful effect exerted by cultural taboo and negative expectations. Physicians, clergymen, family members, all often reinforce the asexuality of age. It is more difficult to escape the dictates of the society one helped build than it is, as in the case of an adolescent, to escape when the sanctions are imposed by a society one had no part in forming. Hospitals, institutions, and homes for the aged also tacitly maintain the taboo by segregating men and women. Even the senescent, in whom social judgment and discretion are deteriorating, often still have sexual desires, and have a right to them. There is no defensible reason why an attendant happening upon masturbatory or coital behavior should respond in any way other than to close the door.

The unavailability of partners is possibly the major reason for sexual inactivity. Elderly people often lead isolated lives even when technically in the company of others. Cultural taboos again often act as a deterrent against admitting desire and seeking a partner, and personal conflict and guilt may frequently inhibit even masturbatory pleasure.

When brain function begins to deteriorate, senescence and senility contribute to the reality of sexual loss. These conditions are the terminal part of the aging process, but even they do not affect sexual capacity so much as they do the means and likelihood of sexual expression. Diminished mental function means less effectiveness in seeking or attracting a partner and the inability to bring a competent mind to bear upon one's own or one's partner's needs. Full-blown senility usually also means loss of mobility and social contact with others because of the necessity for almost total custodial care.

In senescence, one occasionally finds cases of indiscrete sexuality such as public masturbation, and of disapproved behavior, as in exhibitionism and sexual advances toward children. These latter sexual expressions reflect diminished judgment and childishness, and are extremely rare. The public outcry at such incidents when they occur are more an expression of the cultural taboo of sex for old persons than of real danger to the child. The old men are surely the most harmless of "offenders." Their sexual behavior is almost invariably at the childlike level of looking and fondling, and is motivated by a need for simple human closeness. No child, intelligently handled by responsible adults, need be emotionally damaged by such an occurrence.

A combined situational and psychological cause of premature sexual decline is the lack of an active sex life in the formative and adult years. There are obvious psychological elements in the degree of sexual activity or inactivity, but this then constitutes a situational reality that does not typically lend itself to reversal. The relationship has been unanimously noted by all investigators who have inquired into it. An active and enjoyable sex life in old age depends upon having established such a pattern earlier. There is even some indication that active sexuality is associated with prolonged vigor and delayed senescence, but its causal relationship is undetermined. It could well be that such activity is but one facet of the unusual physical, mental, and social vitality that characterizes all those who manage to stay the advance of years for so much longer than most.

All the discussion and data about continued sexuality in old age is not meant to deny the obvious fact that various aspects of male sexual performance do wane with advancing years. One of those changes is the diminishing sense of the imperative need and inevitability of ejaculation. It is not only unfortunate but destructive that ejaculation has generally come to be regarded as the sign of a successful sexual encounter by both men and women alike. The crucial fact is that potency is not measured by ejaculation but by erectile capacity, and that facility for erection is never lost at any time as a function of simple aging.

In the ordinary course of events in which misconception or conflict does not complicate aging sexuality, a man will usually require more stimulation and time to achieve erection, but he can surely do so. The erotic pleasure of intercourse is thoroughly rewarding, and he does not feel the inner demand to ejaculate that is felt by young men. He may ejaculate only once in several experiences of intercourse, and be completely satisfied. After he has pleased his partner, he can more readily become erect again if he has not ejaculated. But if ejaculation is considered the only acceptable goal, either or both partners will feel he has failed when it does not occur. Fear of failure is the surest guarantee of impotence that exists. When the female partner feels she has failed by not affording her man an ejaculation, and therefore presses for that outcome at every experience of lovemaking, she compounds his feeling of failure and he tends to withdraw to protect his self-esteem from further blows. If this simple concept were more widely understood, it could preserve the sexual happiness of countless elderly people.[39]

Dynamically, there continue to be psychosexual processes in operation that can still be considered developmental, in that they represent a progressive adaptation to the realities of life. Aged people who have been parents have an ever expanding number of persons and generations with which to identify. Children, grand-children, great-grandchildren, even nieces and nephews and other collateral relatives, all provide additional opportunities for healthy pride, vicarious self-fulfillment, and a sense of meaningful extension into the future—a kind of immortality that is neither fantasy nor delusion. The greater dependency of old age creates problems in inverse proportion to the firmness of family ties. Whereas some of one's progeny may have been disappointing, others reinforce one's basic value as having been able to contribute something worthwhile to the world. Elderly parents who have outlived their families often have a more difficult time. They, like those who never had children, must manage to find meaning and dignity in the memory and continuing awareness of other contributions to their world and the people around them. A proud old age is dependent upon a balance of satisfaction with what one has produced.

Not everyone is fortunate enough to live out his life with the relatively unimpaired mentality necessary to retain both ego mastery over aging and a sufficient degree of autonomous compre-hension and personal interaction. Either lifelong emotional and ego deficits or the physiological deterioration of senescence overtake many. The progress of deterioration has been likened to a reversal of the developments of adolescence. The strength of the sexual drive tends to diminish and along with it the pressure toward fulfillment. A greater portion of sexual strivings return to need for simple affection and the gratification of dependency as in childhood. Ego capacities and higher cognitive functions regress to simpler modes. Independence shrinks and the aged may again have to be obedient to caretaking persons or be rejected, much like children. Physical aging narrows the differences between the sexes.[40] Ulti-mately, magical thinking may once again take over, and the aged child will believe and insist that his own children be able to solve all problems and banish all distress.

Not all old people drift into the blurring mists of senility. Unknown constitutional and genetic factors as well as improving health care make it possible for more and more of the elderly to remain alert and participating members of their families and communities until illness ends their lives before the onset of debilitating senescence. Those whose minds remain capable of the task face the ultimate crisis of healthy identity. Erikson has defined these final alternatives as ego integrity versus despair. Ego integrity is not simple to describe, as it represents the culmination of an entire emotionally successful lifetime. It implies an understanding that there is somehow an order and meaning to one's life despite vicissitudes, inconsistencies, and failures. It is an acceptance of the one and only life cycle one has—not necessarily because it was the best possible, but simply because it was the only. It is a life cycle forged as an accident of one moment of history in one arbitrary culture and one unique family of rearing, interacting with one person's biological limits and the psychological flexibilities and alternatives available. It represents the best one could do, and it is unnecessary either to take full responsibility for its course or to despair over its imperfections.[41]

A full and rewarding sexuality throughout life is a prime ingredient of the quality of final integrity and the dignity it can impart. That sexuality has varied throughout the psychosexual cycles, and with those ever-changing and varying qualities have come differing nuances of pleasure and fulfillment. Old age is no exception, and the accidents of illness and death cannot rob a life of its intrinsic uniqueness. A final depth of sexual discovery which has to wait patiently upon the arrival of the late years is that fullness of sharing that can come to two people for whom each is in truth the other's world.

> We shall not cease from exploration
> And the end of all our exploring
> Will be to arrive where we started
> And know the place for the first time.[42]

Reference Notes

Index

Reference Notes

INTRODUCTION

1. J. P. Scott, "Critical Periods in Behavioral Development," *Science* 138 (1962): 949.
2. Walter B. Cannon, *The Wisdom of the Body* (New York: Norton, 1932).
3. Sandor Rado, "Emergency Behavior, With an Introduction to the Dynamics of Conscience," *Psychoanalysis of Behavior: Collected Papers* (New York: Grune and Stratton, 1956), p. 214.
4. Robert J. Stoller, *Sex and Gender: On the Development of Masculinity and Femininity* (New York: Science House, 1968).

1. LIFE IN THE WOMB

1. Ingeborg L. Ward, "Prenatal Stress Feminizes and Demasculinizes the Behavior of Males," *Science* 175 (1972): 82.
2. This chapter summarizes thousands of research studies by hundreds of scientists over a number of decades, and separate documentation would be intrusive and unwieldy. Fortunately, there are a few published articles and books that contain documented overviews of most of this area of research. The reader who wishes to pursue specific data will find comprehensive bibliographies to the original work in one or more of the following sources: R. K. Burns, "Role of Hormones in the Differentiation of Sex," in *Sex and Internal Secretions*, edited by William C. Young, 3d ed. (Baltimore: Williams and Wilkins, 1961), I: 76; Warren J. Gadpaille, "Research Into the Physiology of Maleness and Femaleness," *Archives of General Psychiatry* 26 (1972): 193; Alfred Jost, "Problems in Fetal Endocrinology: The Gonadal and Hypophyseal Hormones," *Recent Progress in Hormone Research* 8 (1953): 379; John Money and Anke A. Ehrhardt, *Man and Woman: Boy and Girl* (Baltimore: Johns Hopkins University Press, 1972).
3. Irvin D. Yalom, Richard Green, and Norman Fisk, "Prenatal Exposure to Female Hormones," *Archives of General Psychiatry* 28 (1973): 554.
4. Phyllis Greenacre, "Further Notes on Fetishism," *Psychoanalytic Study of the Child* 15 (1960): 191.

5. Irving Bieber et al., *Homosexuality: A Psychoanalytic Study* (New York: Basic Books, 1962), chap. xi; Lawrence J. Hatterer, *Changing Homosexuality in the Male: Treatment for Men Troubled by Homosexuality* (New York: McGraw-Hill Book Company, 1970), p. 469; Harvey E. Kaye et al., "Homosexuality in Women," *Archives of General Psychiatry* 17 (1967): 626; Albert Ellis, "The Effectiveness of Psychotherapy with Individuals Who Have Severe Homosexual Problems," *Journal of Consulting Psychology* 20 (1956): 191.

6. Milton Diamond, "A Critical Evaluation of the Ontogeny of Human Sexual Behavior," *Quarterly Review of Biology* 40 (1965): 147.

7. Albert Ellis, "Constitutional Factors in Homosexuality: A Re-Examination of the Evidence," in *Advances in Sex Research*, ed. Hugo G. Beigel (New York: Hoeber Medical Division, Harper and Row, 1963), chap. xix.

2. ALL-ENCOMPASSING INFLUENCES

1. Ashley Montagu, *Touching: The Human Significance of the Skin* (New York: Columbia University Press, 1971), pp. 43–72, 254–260; Richard V. Yazmajian, "Biological Aspects of Infantile Sexuality and the Latency Period," *Psychoanalytic Quarterly* 36 (1967): 203.

2. Erik H. Erikson, *Childhood and Society* (New York: Norton, 1950), pp. 70, 220.

3. Antonio Ciocco, "Sex Differences in Morbidity and Mortality," *Quarterly Review of Biology* 15 (1940): 59; Harry Bakwin, "The Sex Factor in Infant Mortality," *Human Biology* 1 (1929): 90; Barton Childs, "Genetic Origin of Some Sex Differences Among Human Beings," *Pediatrics* 35 (1965): 798.

4. T. C. Washburn, D. N. Meadearis, Jr., and B. Childs, "Sex Differences in Susceptibility to Infections," *Pediatrics* 35 (1965): 57.

5. Montagu, *Touching*.

6. Ibid., p. 73.

7. Erikson, *Childhood and Society*, pp. 67–76.

8. Ibid., pp. 74–75, 219–222.

9. René A. Spitz, *The First Year of Life* (New York: International Universities Press, 1965), pp. 150–156.

10. Karen Horney, *Our Inner Conflicts* (New York: Norton, 1945), pp. 40–41; Harry S. Sullivan, *Conceptions of Modern Psychiatry* (New York: Norton, 1940).

11. Henry B. Biller, *Father, Child, and Sex Role* (Lexington, Mass.: Heath, 1971).

12. Sigmund Freud, *New Introductory Lectures on Psycho-analysis* (New York: Norton, 1933), pp. 153–185.

13. Judith S. Kestenberg, "Vicissitudes of Female Sexuality," *Journal of the American Psychoanalytic Association* 4 (1956): 456–457; Marjorie C. Barnett, "Vaginal Awareness in the Infancy and Childhood of Girls," *Journal of the American Psychoanalytic Association* 14 (1966): 130.

14. Phyllis Greenacre, "Special Problems of Early Female Sexual Development," *The Psychoanalytic Study of the Child* 5 (1950): 124–126; Jan Langman, *Medical Embryology*, 2d ed. (Baltimore: Williams and Wilkins, 1969), pp. 173, 273.

15. Marjorie Brierley, "Specific Determinants in Feminine Development," *International Journal of Psycho-analysis* 17 (1936): 164–165; Greenacre, "Early Female Sexual Development."

16. William H. Masters and Virginia E. Johnson, *Human Sexual Response* (Boston: Little, Brown, 1966), pp. 27–168.

17. Marjorie C. Barnett, " 'I Can't' versus 'He Won't'," *Journal of the American Psychoanalytic Association* 16 (1968): 589–590.

18. Robert J. Stoller, "The Sense of Femaleness," *Psychoanalytic Quarterly* 37 (1968): 42.

19. Karen Horney, "The Denial of the Vagina," *International Journal of Psycho-analysis* 14 (1933): 61–62; Melanie Klein, *The Psycho-analysis of Children* (London: Hogarth Press, 1954), pp. 288–289.

20. Judith S. Kestenberg, "Phases of Adolescence: With Suggestions for a Correlation of Psychic and Hormonal Organizations, Part I: Antecedents of Adolescent Organizations in Childhood," *Journal of the American Academy of Child Psychiatry* 6 (1967): 455.

21. Alfred C. Kinsey, Wardell B. Pomeroy, and Clyde E. Martin, *Sexual Behavior in the Human Male* (Philadelphia: Saunders, 1948), p. 177.

22. Ibid., p. 176.

23. Alfred C. Kinsey et al., *Sexual Behavior in the Human Female* (Philadelphia: Saunders, 1953), pp. 102–107.

24. Sigmund Freud, "The Dissolution of the Oedipus Complex," *Standard Edition of the Complete Psychological Works of Sigmund Freud* (London: Hogarth Press, 1961), XIX, 178.

25. Spitz, *First Year of Life*, 50–52.

26. Kestenberg, "Female Sexuality," 459.

27. Arthur E. Gillman and Arlene R. Gordon, "Sexual Behavior in the Blind," *Medical Aspects of Human Sexuality* 7 (June 1973): 48.

28. Anita I. Bell, "Some Observations on the Role of the Scrotal Sac and Testicles," *Journal of the American Psychoanalytic Association* 9 (1961): 261.

29. Horney, "Denial of the Vagina," 62–63.

30. Kestenberg, "Female Sexuality," 453, and "Outside and Inside, Male and Female," *Journal of the American Psychoanalytic Association* 16

(1968): 457; Phyllis Greenacre, "Anatomical Structure and Superego Development," *American Journal of Orthopsychiatry* 18 (1948): 636, and "Early Physical Determinants in the Development of the Sense of Identity," *Journal of the American Psychoanalytic Association* 6 (1958): 612.

31. Lewis M. Terman, "Psychological Sex Differences," in *Manual of Child Psychiatry*, ed. Leonard Carmichael (New York: Wiley, 1962) p. 954; Howard A. Moss, "Sex, Age, and State as Determinants of Mother-Infant Interaction," *Merrill-Palmer Quarterly* 13 (1967): 22; Richard Q. Bell and Joan F. Darling, "The Prone Head Reaction in the Human Newborn: Relationship with Sex and Tactile Sensitivity," *Child Development* 36 (1965): 943.

32. E. S. Schaeffer and N. Bayley, quoted in Robert J. Stoller, *Sex and Gender* (New York: Science House, 1968), p. 13.

33. Moss, "Mother-Infant Interaction," 22.

34. J. D. Call, quoted in R. Stoller, *Sex and Gender*, p. 13; Bertrand Cramer, "Sex Differences in Early Childhood," *Child Psychiatry and Human Development* 1 (1971): 137–138.

35. Lois B. Murphy, *The Widening World of Childhood* (New York: Basic Books, 1962), p. 346; Susan Goldberg and Michael Lewis, "Play Behavior in the Year-Old Infant: Early Sex Differences," *Child Development* 40 (1969): 29.

36. Robert R. Sears, Eleanor E. Maccoby, and Harry Levin, *Patterns of Child Rearing* (Evanston, Ill.: Row and Peterson, 1957), pp. 253–254, 403–404.

37. Biller, *Sex Role*, p. 41.

38. John L. Hampson and Joan G. Hampson, "The Ontogenesis of Sexual Behavior in Man," in *Sex and Internal Secretions*, ed. William C. Young, 2d ed. (Baltimore: Williams and Wilkins, 1961), II, 1401.

39. John Money and Anke A. Ehrhardt, *Man and Woman: Boy and Girl* (Baltimore: Johns Hopkins University Press, 1972), p. 146.

40. Hampson and Hampson, "Sexual Behavior in Man," 1416–1417.

41. Montagu, *Touching*.

42. René A. Spitz, "Hospitalism: An Inquiry into the Genesis of Psychiatric Conditions in Early Childhood," *Psychoanalytic Study of the Child* 1 (1945): 53.

43. Sigmund Freud, "Three Essays on the Theory of Sexuality," *Standard Edition of the Complete Psychological Works of Sigmund Freud* (London: The Hogarth Press, 1953), VII, 223.

44. René A. Spitz, "Autoerotism: Some Empirical Findings and Hypotheses on Three of its Manifestations in the First Year of Life," *Psychoanalytic Study of the Child* 3/4 (1949): 85.

45. Kestenberg, "Outside and Inside," 467.

46. Warren J. Gadpaille, "Innate Masculine-Feminine Differences," *Medical Aspects of Human Sexuality* 7 (February 1973): 141; Ralph R. Greenson, "Dis-identifying from Mother: Its Special Importance for the Boy," *International Journal of Psycho-analysis* 49 (1968): 370.

47. Robert J. Stoller, "Symbiosis Anxiety and the Development of Masculinity," *Archives of General Psychiatry* 30 (1974): 164.

48. Stoller, *Sex and Gender*, 108–125.

49. Robert J. Stoller, "Etiological Factors in Female Transsexualism: A First Approximation," *Archives of Sexual Behavior* 2 (1972): 47.

50. Lawrence Kohlberg, "A Cognitive-Developmental Analysis of Children's Sex-Role Concepts and Attitudes," in *The Development of Sex Differences*, ed. Eleanor E. Maccoby (Stanford, Calif: Stanford University Press, 1966), p. 82.

51. Roy G. D' Andrade, "Sex Differences and Cultural Institutions," in *The Development of Sex Differences*, ed. Eleanor E. Maccoby (Stanford, Calif: Stanford University Press, 1966), p. 174.

52. Mabel Blake Cohen, "Personal Identity and Sexual Identity," *Psychiatry* 29 (1966): 1.

53. Theodore Lidz, "Psychoanalytic Theories of Development and Maldevelopment: Some Recapitulations," *American Journal of Psychoanalysis* 27 (1967): 115.

54. Gadpaille, "Innate Differences," 141.

55. Greenacre, "Early Physical Determinants," 612.

56. Herman Roiphe, "On an Early Genital Phase," *Psychoanalytic Study of the Child* 23 (1968): 348; Eleanor Galenson and Herman Roiphe, "The Impact of Early Sexual Discovery on Mood, Defensive Organization, and Symbolization," *Psychoanalytic Study of the Child* 26 (1971): 195.

57. Erik H. Erikson, *Identity and the Life Cycle, Psychological Issues*, Vol. I, No. 1 (New York: International Universities Press, 1959), pp. 55–65.

58. Ruth Benedict, "Continuities and Discontinuities in Cultural Conditioning," in *A Study of Interpersonal Relations*, ed. Patrick Mullahy (New York: Hermitage Press, 1949), p. 297.

3. WHO OWNS A CHILD'S BODY?

1. Selma H. Fraiberg, *The Magic Years* (New York: Scribners, 1959).

2. Judith S. Kestenberg, "Phases of Adolescence: With Suggestions for a Correlation of Psychic and Hormonal Organizations, Part I: Antecedents of Adolescent Organization in Childhood," *Journal of the American Academy of Child Psychiatry* 6 (1967): 443–457.

3. Fraiberg, *Magic Years*, pp. 91–102.

4. Erik H. Erikson, *Childhood and Society* (New York: Norton, 1950), pp. 76–81, 222–224; and *Identity and the Life Cycle, Psychological Issues*, Vol. I, No. 1 (New York: International Universities Press, 1959), pp. 65–74.

5. E. Kuno Beller and Peter B. Neubauer, "Sex Differences and Symptom Patterns in Early Childhood," *Journal of the American Academy of Child Psychiatry* 2 (1963): 417; Bertrand Cramer, "Sex Differences in Behavior of Children between Three and Seven," *Psychosocial Process* 1 (1970): 60.

6. Bertrand Cramer, "Sex Differences in Early Childhood," *Child Psychiatry and Human Development* 1 (1971): 133.

7. Warren J. Gadpaille, "Innate Masculine-Feminine Differences," *Medical Aspects of Human Sexuality* 7 (February 1973): 141; Weston LaBarre, *The Human Animal* (Chicago: University of Chicago Press, 1964), pp. 208–219.

8. Sandor Rado, *Adaptational Psychodynamics: Motivation and Control* (New York: Science House, 1969), pp. 128–140; Fraiberg, *Magic Years*, pp. 146–176, 242–282.

9. Herman Roiphe, "On an Early Genital Phase: With an Addendum on Genesis," *Psychoanalytic Study of the Child* 23 (1968): 348.

10. M. N. Searl, "A Note on the Relation Between Physical and Psychical Differences in Boys and Girls," *International Journal of Psychoanalysis* 19 (1938): 50.

11. James E. Moore and Diane G. Kendall, "Children's Concepts of Reproduction," *Journal of Sex Research* 7 (1971): 50.

12. Judith S. Kestenberg, "Vicissitudes of Female Sexuality," *Journal of the American Psychoanalytic Association* 4 (1956): 453, and "Outside and Inside, Male and Female," *Journal of the American Psychoanalytic Association* 16 (1968): 457.

13. Marjorie C. Barnett, "Vaginal Awareness in the Infancy and Childhood of Girls," *Journal of the American Psychoanalytic Association* 14 (1966): 129.

14. Karen Horney, "The Denial of the Vagina," *International Journal of Psycho-analysis* 14 (1933): 68.

15. Barnett, "Vaginal Awareness," 129.

16. Ibid.

17. Horney, "Denial of the Vagina," 57.

18. Kestenberg, "Outside and Inside," 457.

19. Anita I. Bell, "Some Observations on the Role of the Scrotal Sac and Testicles," *Journal of the American Psychoanalytic Association* 9 (1961): 261; Anita I. Bell et al., "Interdisciplinary Study: Scrotal Sac and Testes. Psychophysiological and Psychological Observations," *Psychoanalytic Quarterly* 40 (1971): 415.

20. Anita I. Bell, "Bowel Training Difficulties in Boys: Prephallic and Phallic Considerations," *Journal of the American Academy of Child Psychiatry* 3 (1964): 577.

21. Paul Kramer, "Early Capacity for Orgastic Discharge and Character Formation," *Psychoanalytic Study of the Child* 9 (1954): 128; Marjorie C. Barnett, "'I Can't' versus 'He Won't'," *Journal of the American Psychoanalytic Association* 16 (1968): 588.

22. Anna Freud, *Normality and Pathology in Childhood* (New York: International Universities Press, 1965), pp. 93–107, 157–158.

23. Jules Henry, "The Social Function of Child Sexuality in Pilagá Indian Culture," in *Psychosexual Development: In Health and Disease*, ed. Paul H. Hoch and Joseph Zubin (New York: Grune and Stratton, 1949), pp. 91–101; Clellan S. Ford and Frank A. Beach, *Patterns of Sexual Behavior* (New York: Harper and Row, 1951), pp. 188–192.

24. Robert J. Stoller, "The Sense of Maleness," *Psychoanalytic Quarterly* 34 (1965): 207, and "The Sense of Femaleness," *Psychoanalytic Quarterly* 37 (1968): 42; John Money and Anke A. Ehrhardt, *Man and Woman: Boy and Girl* (Baltimore: Johns Hopkins University Press, 1972), chaps vii and viii.

25. Henry B. Biller, *Father, Child, and Sex Role* (Lexington, Mass.: Heath, 1971), pp. 6–7.

26. Edith Jacobson, "The Development of the Wish for a Child in Boys," *Psychoanalytic Study of the Child* 5 (1950): 139; P. J. van der Leeuw, "The Preoedipal Phase of the Male," *Psychoanalytic Study of the Child* 13 (1958): 352; James A. Kleeman, "Genital Self-Discovery during a Boy's Second Year: A Follow-up," *Psychoanalytic Study of the Child* 21 (1966): 358; John B. Nelson, "Anlage of Productiveness in Boys: Womb Envy," *Journal of the American Academy of Child Psychiatry* 6 (1967): 213.

27. John H. Gagnon, "Sexuality and Sexual Learning in the Child," *Psychiatry* 28 (1965): 212.

28. Theodore Lidz, *The Origin and Treatment of Schizophrenic Disorders* (New York: Basic Books, 1973), pp. 56–65.

29. John H. Gagnon, "Female Child Victims of Sex Offences," *Social Problems* 13 (1965): 176.

30. Karl Abraham, "Contributions to the Theory of the Anal Character," *Selected Papers of Karl Abraham* (New York: Basic Books, 1953), p. 370; Ernest Jones, "Anal-Erotic Character Traits," *Papers on Psycho-Analysis* (London: Balliere, Tindall and Cox, 1950): p. 413; Otto Fenichel, *The Psychoanalytic Theory of Neurosis* (New York: Norton, 1945), pp. 278–284.

31. Phyllis Greenacre, "Anatomical Structure and Superego Forma-

tion," *American Journal of Orthopsychiatry* 18 (1948): 636; Bell, "Role of the Scrotal Sac and Testicles," 226–228.

32. Eleanor E. Maccoby, "Sex Differences in Intellectual Functioning," in *The Development of Sex Differences*, ed. Eleanor E. Maccoby (Stanford, Calif.: Stanford University Press, 1966), p. 25; Steven Goldberg, *The Inevitability of Patriarchy* (New York: Morrow, 1973), chap. viii.

33. Kestenberg, "Outside and Inside," 457.

34. Roy G. D'Andrade, "Sex Differences and Cultural Institutions," in *The Development of Sex Differences*, edited by Eleanor E. Maccoby (Stanford, Calif.: Stanford University Press, 1966), p. 174.

35. Kestenberg, "Outside and Inside," 458.

36. Eleanor Galenson and Herman Roiphe, "The Impact of Early Sexual Discovery on Mood, Defensive Organization, and Symbolization," *Psychoanalytic Study of the Child* 26 (1972): 196.

37. Beller and Neubauer, "Sex Differences and Symptom Patterns," 417.

38. Unless otherwise noted, full references to the bulk of original research into the various influences of mothers and fathers on the sex identity of their children may be found in Biller, *Father, Child, and Sex Role.*

39. E. Mavis Hetherington, "Effect of Fathers' Absence on Personality Development in Adolescent Daughters," *Developmental Psychology* 7 (1972): 313.

40. Seymour Fisher, *The Female Orgasm* (New York: Basic Books, 1973), p. 231.

41. Harvey E. Kaye et al., "Homosexuality in Women," *Archives of General Psychiatry* 17 (1967): 626; Eva Bene, "On the Genesis of Female Homosexuality," *British Journal of Psychiatry* 111 (1965): 815.

42. Malvina W. Kremer, "Identity Formation in Male and Female Adolescent Homosexuals," in *Science and Psychoanalysis*, Vol. XV: *Dynamics of Deviant Sexuality*, ed. Jules H. Masserman (New York: Grune and Stratton, 1969), p. 51.

43. Carlfred B. Broderick, "Preadolescent Sexual Behavior," *Medical Aspects of Human Sexuality* 2 (January 1968): 28.

44. Theodore Lidz, "Psychoanalytic Theories of Development and Maldevelopment: Some Recapitulations," *American Journal of Psychoanalysis* 27 (1967): 115.

45. Emmett J. Holt, Jr., and Rustin McIntosh, *Diseases of Infancy and Childhood* (New York: Appleton-Century-Crofts, 1936), p. 780.

46. Meredith F. Campbell, ed., *Urology*, 3 vols. (Philadelphia: Saunders, 1954), pp. 1595–1597.

47. René A. Spitz, "Autoerotism Re-examined: The Role of Early

Sexual Behavior Patterns in Personality Formation," *Psychoanalytic Study of the Child* 17 (1962): 283.

48. Kramer, "Orgastic Discharge and Character Formation," 134–138.

49. Anna Freud, *Normality and Pathology*, pp. 16, 19.

50. Ibid., pp. 7–8; Spitz, "Autoerotism Re-examined," 304–313; Annie Reich, "The Discussion of 1912 on Masturbation and our Present-Day Views," *Psychoanalytic Study of the Child* 6 (1951): 80.

51. Ford and Beach, *Sexual Behavior*, pp. 178–198, 266; Money and Ehrhardt, *Man and Woman*, pp. 117–145.

52. Harry F. Harlow and Margaret Kuenne Harlow, "Social Deprivation in Monkeys," *Scientific American* 207 (1962): 137.

53. Ford and Beach, *Sexual Behavior*, pp. 180–184.

54. Joseph Shepher, "Mate Selection Between Second Generation Kibbutz Adolescents and Adults: Incest Avoidance and Negative Imprinting," *Archives of Sexual Behavior* 1 (1971): 294.

55. M. Prywes, *Medical and Biological Research in Israel* (New York: Grune and Stratton, 1960), p. 111; David Rapaport, "The Study of Kibbutz Education and its Bearing on the Theory of Development," *American Journal of Orthopsychiatry* 28 (1958): 587; Bruno Bettelheim, "Personality Formation in the Kibbutz," *American Journal of Psychoanalysis* 29 (1969): 3.

56. Gagnon, "Female Child Victims," 176.

57. Melvin Lewis and Philip M. Sarrel, "Some Psychological Aspects of Seduction, Incest, and Rape in Childhood," *Journal of the American Academy of Child Psychiatry* 8 (1969): 606; Charles William Wahl, "The Psychodynamics of Consummated Maternal Incest," *Archives of General Psychiatry* 3 (1960): 96/188.

58. Gagnon, "Female Child Victims," 176; Lauretta Bender and Abram Blau, "The Reaction of Children to Sexual Relations with Adults," *American Journal of Orthopsychiatry* 7 (1937): 500; Lauretta Bender and Alvin Eldridge Grugett, Jr., "A Follow-up Report on Children Who Had Atypical Sexual Experience," *American Journal of Orthopsychiatry* 22 (1952): 825; Alalay Yorukoglu and John P. Kemph, "Children Not Severely Damaged by Incest with a Parent," *Journal of the American Academy of Child Psychiatry* 5 (1966): 111.

59. Augusta Rasmussen, "Die Bedeutung sexuelle Attentate auf Kinder unter 14 Jahren für die Entwicklung von Geisteskrankheiten und Charakteranomalien," *Acta Psychiatrica et Neurologica* 9 (1934): 351.

4. THE RICHES OF FANTASY

1. James A. Kleeman, "Genital Self-Discovery during a Boy's Second Year: A Follow-up," *Psychoanalytic Study of the Child* 21 (1966): 371.

2. Sigmund Freud, "On the Sexual Theories of Children," *Standard Edition of the Complete Psychological Works of Sigmund Freud* (London: Hogarth Press, 1959), IX, 205.

3. Eleanor Galenson and Herman Roiphe, "The Impact of Early Sexual Discovery on Mood, Defensive Organization, and Symbolization," *Psychoanalytic Study of the Child* 26 (1971): 195.

4. Katherine Wood Hattendorf, "A Study of the Questions of Young Children Concerning Sex: A Phase of an Experimental Approach to Parent Education," *Journal of Social Psychology* 3 (1932): 37; Jacob H. Conn, "Children's Reactions to the Discovery of Genital Differences," *American Journal of Orthopsychiatry* 10 (1940): 747, and "Sexual Curiosity of Children," *American Journal of Diseases of Children* 60 (1940): 1110, and "Children's Awareness of the Origins of Babies," *Journal of Child Psychiatry* 1 (1948): 140; Jacob H. Conn and Leo Kanner, "Children's Awareness of Sex Differences," *Journal of Child Psychiatry* 1 (1947): 3; Richard A. Gardner, "Sexual Fantasies in Childhood," *Medical Aspects of Human Sexuality* 3 (October 1969): 121; James E. Moore and Diane G. Kendall, "Children's Concepts of Reproduction," *Journal of Sex Research* 7 (1971): 42.

5. Conn, "Sexual Curiosity," 1110.

6. Erik H. Erikson, *Childhood and Society* (New York: Norton, 1950), pp. 74–75.

7. William G. Niederland, "Early Auditory Experiences, Beating Fantasies, and the Primal Scene," *Psychoanalytic Study of the Child* 13 (1958): 471.

8. Ibid.

9. Kleeman, "Genital Self-Discovery," 364.

10. Ibid., 376.

11. Judith S. Kestenberg, "On the Development of Maternal Feelings in Early Childhood," *Psychoanalytic Study of the Child* 11 (1956): 257, and "Vicissitudes of Female Sexuality," *Journal of the American Psychoanalytic Association* 4 (1956): 463–467.

12. Conn, "Origins of Babies," 140.

13. Edward Weiss and O. Spurgeon English, *Psychosomatic Medicine*, 2d ed. (Philadelphia: Saunders, 1949), pp. 511–521.

14. Hans and Shulamith Kreitler, "Children's Concepts of Sexuality and Birth," *Child Development* 37 (1966): 375–376.

15. Moore and Kendall, "Children's Concepts," 55–56.

16. Erikson, *Childhood and Society*, pp. 49–54.

17. Kreitler and Kreitler, "Sexuality and Birth," 371–372.

18. Moore and Kendall, "Children's Concepts," 54–55.

19. Edith Jacobson, "Development of the Wish for a Child in Boys," *Psychoanalytic Study of the Child* 5 (1950): 139.

20. Kleeman, "Genital Self-Discovery," 374.

21. Gregory Zilboorg, "Masculine and Feminine," *Psychiatry* 7 (1944): 288–290; Daniel S. Jaffe, "The Masculine Envy of Woman's Procreative Function," *Journal of the American Psychoanalytic Association* 16 (1968): 532.

22. Iago Galdston, "The Psychopathology of Paternal Deprivation: The Rise and Decline of Fatherhood," in *Science and Psychoanalysis*, Vol. XIV: *Childhood and Adolescence*, ed. Jules H. Masserman (New York: Grune and Stratton, 1969), p. 14.

23. Selma Fraiberg, "Enlightenment and Confusion," *Psychoanalytic Study of the Child* 6 (1951): 326–328.

24. Sigmund Freud, "Analysis Terminable and Interminable," *Standard Edition of the Complete Psychological Works of Sigmund Freud* (London: Hogarth Press, 1964), XXIII, 233–234.

5. THE IMPOSSIBLE WISH

1. Sigmund Freud, "The Interpretation of Dreams," *Standard Edition of the Complete Psychological Works of Sigmund Freud* (London: Hogarth Press, 1953), IV, 255–264.

2. Warner Muensterberger, "On the Biopsychological Roots of Social Life," *Psychoanalysis and the Social Sciences* 4 (1955): 7; Franz Alexander, "Educative Influences of Personality Factors in the Environment," in *Personality: In Nature, Society, and Culture*, ed. Clyde Kluckhohn and Henry A. Murray, 2d ed. (New York: Knopf, 1954), p. 421.

3. Abram Kardiner, *The Individual and His Society: The Psychodynamics of Primitive Social Organization* (New York: Columbia University Press, 1939), pp. 445, 479–481; Abram Kardiner et al., *The Psychological Frontiers of Society* (New York: Columbia University Press, 1945), p. 374.

4. Dorothy Eggan, "The General Problem of Hopi Adjustment," in *Personality: In Nature, Society, and Culture*, ed. Clyde Kluckhohn and Henry A. Murray, 2d ed. (New York: Knopf, 1954), p. 276.

5. Kardiner, *The Individual*, pp. 445, 479–481.

6. Muensterberger, "Biopsychological Roots," 7; Weston LaBarre, *The Human Animal* (Chicago: University of Chicago Press, 1954), pp. 121–125.

7. Sigmund Freud, "Totem and Taboo," *Standard Edition of the Complete Psychological Works of Sigmund Freud* (London: Hogarth Press, 1955), XIII, 1; David Lester, "Incest," *Journal of Sex Research* 8 (1972): 268; Yehudi Cohen, *The Transition from Childhood to Adolescence* (Chicago: Aldine, 1964), chaps. vii and viii.

8. LaBarre, *Human Animal*, pp. 110–131.

9. Donald Stone Sade, "Inhibition of Mother-Son Mating among Free-Ranging Rhesus Monkeys," in *Science and Psychoanalysis*, Vol. XII: *Animal and Human*, ed. Jules H. Masserman (New York: Grune and Stratton, 1968), p. 18.

10. Erik H. Erikson, *Childhood and Society* (New York: Norton, 1950), pp. 81–87.

11. Judith S. Kestenberg, "Phases of Adolescence: With Suggestions for a Correlation of Psychic and Hormonal Organizations, Part I: Antecedents of Adolescent Organizations in Childhood," *Journal of the American Academy of Child Psychiatry* 6 (1967): 443–457.

12. Irving Bieber, "Olfaction in Sexual Development and Adult Sexual Organization," *American Journal of Psychotherapy* 13 (1959): 851; Michael G. Kalogerakis, "The Role of Olfaction in Sexual Development," *Psychosomatic Medicine* 25 (1963): 420.

13. Erikson, *Childhood and Society*, pp. 224–225.

14. Kate Friedlaender, "Children's Books: And their Function in Latency and Prepuberty," *American Imago* 3 (1942): 129.

15. Erik H. Erikson, *Identity: Youth and Crisis* (New York: Norton, 1968), pp. 276–278.

16. Jose Barchilon, "Development of Artistic Stylization: A Two Year Evolution in the Drawings of a Normal Child," *Psychoanalytic Study of the Child* 19 (1964): 256–259.

17. Marjorie C. Barnett, "Vaginal Awareness in the Infancy and Childhood of Girls," *Journal of the American Psychoanalytic Association* 14 (1966): 138.

18. Kurt Freund et al., "The Female Child as a Surrogate Object," *Archives of Sexual Behavior* 2 (1972): 119.

19. John H. Gagnon, "Female Child Victims of Sex Offenses," *Social Problems* 13 (1965): 182–183.

20. Margaret L. Meiss, "The Oedipal Problem of a Fatherless Child," *Psychoanalytic Study of the Child* 7 (1952): 216; Peter B. Neubauer, "The One-Parent Child and His Oedipal Development," *Psychoanalytic Study of the Child* 15 (1960): 286.

21. Frank E. Crumley and Ronald S. Blumenthal, "Children's Reactions to Temporary Loss of the Father," *American Journal of Psychiatry* 130 (1973): 778.

22. Erikson, *Childhood and Society*, p. 225.

23. Sigmund Freud, "The Dissolution of the Oedipus Complex," *Standard Edition of the Complete Psychological Works of Sigmund Freud* (London: Hogarth Press, 1961), XIX, 171.

24. Robert J. Stoller, "Symbiosis Anxiety and the Development of Masculinity," *Archives of General Psychiatry* 30 (1974): 164.

25. Karen Horney, "The Denial of the Vagina," *International Journal of Psycho-analysis* 14 (1933): 67–68; Marjorie C. Barnett, " 'I Can't' versus 'He Won't'," *Journal of the American Psychoanalytic Association* 16 (1968): 593–596.

6. RELATIVE TRANQUILLITY

1. Sigmund Freud, "Three Essays on the Theory of Sexuality," *Standard Edition of the Complete Psychological Works of Sigmund Freud* (London: Hogarth Press, 1953), VII, 177.

2. Clellan S. Ford and Frank A. Beach, *Patterns of Sexual Behavior* (New York: Harper and Row, 1951), p. 190.

3. Alfred C. Kinsey, Wardell B. Pomeroy and Clyde E. Martin, *Sexual Behavior in the Human Male* (Philadelphia: Saunders, 1948), pp. 162–181; Alfred C. Kinsey et al., *Sexual Behavior in the Human Female* (Philadelphia: Saunders, 1953), pp. 102–116.

4. Glenn V. Ramsey, "The Sexual Development of Boys," *American Journal of Psychology* 56 (1943): 217.

5. Judith S. Kestenberg, "Phases of Adolescence: With Suggestions for a Correlation of Psychic and Hormonal Organizations, Part I: Antecedents of Adolescent Organizations in Childhood," *Journal of the American Academy of Child Psychiatry* 6 (1967): 457–459.

6. Weston LaBarre, *The Human Animal* (Chicago: University of Chicago Press, 1954), pp. 210–211.

7. Richard V. Yazmajian, "Biological Aspects of Infantile Sexuality and the Latency Period," *Psychoanalytic Quarterly* 36 (1967): 203.

8. Erik H. Erikson, *Identity and the Life Cycle, Psychological Issues*, Vol. I, No. 1 (New York: International Universities Press, 1959), p. 78.

9. Erikson, *The Life Cycle*, pp. 82–88.

10. Berta Bornstein, "On Latency," *Psychoanalytic Study of the Child* 6 (1951): 279.

11. Joseph Shepher, "Mate Selection among Second Generation Kibbutz Adolescents and Adults: Incest Avoidance and Negative Imprinting," *Archives of Sexual Behavior* 1 (1971): 294.

12. Harry B. Lee, "A Critique of the Theory of Sublimation," *Psychiatry* 2 (1939): 239.

13. Lauretta Bender and Joseph B. Cramer, "Sublimation and Sexual Gratification in the Latency Period of Girls," in *Searchlights on Delinquency: New Psychoanalytic Studies*, ed. K. R. Eissler (New York: International Universities Press, 1949), p. 53.

14. Anna Freud, "Certain Types and Stages of Social Maladjustment," in *Searchlights on Delinquency: New Psychoanalytic Studies*, ed. K. R.

Eissler (New York: International Universities Press, 1949), p. 193; Berta Bornstein, "Masturbation in the Latency Period," *Psychoanalytic Study of the Child* 8 (1953): 65; Paul Kramer, "Early Capacity for Orgastic Discharge and Character Formation," *Psychoanalytic Study of the Child* 9 (1954): 128.

15. Judith S. Kestenberg, "Outside and Inside, Male and Female," *Journal of the American Psychoanalytic Association* 16 (1968): 468–472.

16. Lili Peller, "Reading and Daydreams in Latency, Boy-Girl Differences," *Journal of the American Psychoanalytic Association* 6 (1958): 57; Kate Friedlaender, "Children's Books: And their Function in Latency and Prepuberty," *American Imago* 3 (1942): 129.

17. Judith S. Kestenberg, "Vicissitudes of Female Sexuality," *Journal of the American Psychoanalytic Association* 4 (1956): 471.

18. Anita I. Bell, "Some Observations on the Role of the Scrotal Sac and Testicles," *Journal of the American Psychoanalytic Association* 9 (1961): 277–278; Phyllis Greenacre, "Anatomical Structure and Superego Development," *American Journal of Orthopsychiatry* 18 (1948): 636.

19. Selma Fraiberg, "Technical Aspects of the Analysis of a Child with a Severe Behavior Disorder," *Journal of the American Psychoanalytic Association* 10 (1962): 338, and "Some Characteristics of Genital Arousal and Discharge in Latency Girls," *Psychoanalytic Study of the Child* 27 (1972): 439.

20. Anna Freud, "Social Maladjustment," p. 193.

21. Irving Bieber et al., *Homosexuality: A Psychoanalytic Study* (New York: Basic Books, 1962), chap. vii; Peter and Barbara Wyden, *Growing Up Straight: What Every Thoughtful Parent Should Know about Homosexuality* (New York: Stein and Day, 1968).

22. Carlfred B. Broderick, "Socio-sexual Development in a Surburban Community," *Journal of Sex Research* 2 (1966): 1.

23. Selma Fraiberg, *The Magic Years: Understanding and Handling the Problems of Early Childhood* (New York: Scribners, 1959), pp. 235–241.

7. COUNTDOWN TO THE BIOLOGICAL IMPLOSION

1. Some useful overviews exist, with full references to original studies and specific data. Only material not included in these sources will be specifically referenced either in this chapter or in the following two chapters on early and late adolescence: James M. Tanner, *Growth at Adolescence*, 2d ed. (Oxford: Blackwell Scientific Publications, 1962); Herbert Rowell Stolz and Lois Meek Stolz, *Somatic Development of Adolescent Boys* (New York: Macmillan, 1951); Nathan B. Talbot et al.,

Functional Endocrinology from Birth Through Adolescence (Cambridge, Mass.: Harvard University Press, 1952); Lawson Wilkins, *The Diagnosis and Treatment of Endocrine Disorders in Childhood and Adolescence*, 2d ed. (Springfield: Charles C. Thomas, 1957); Charles W. Lloyd, "The Ovaries," in *Textbook of Endocrinology*, ed. Robert H. Williams, 4th ed. (Philadelphia: Saunders, 1968), p. 459; Charles W. Lloyd, ed., *Human Reproduction and Sexual Behavior* (Philadelphia: Lea and Febiger, 1954), chaps. i, ii, and v; Judith S. Kestenberg, "Phases of Adolescence: With Suggestions for a Correlation of Psychic and Hormonal Organizations, Part I: Antecedents of Adolescent Organizations in Childhood," *Journal of the American Academy of Child Psychiatry* 6 (1967): 443–460, and "Part III: Puberty Growth, Differentiation, and Consolidation," *Journal of the American Academy of Child Psychiatry* 7 (1968): 108.

2. Geoffrey W. Harris, "The Development of Neuroendocrinology," in *Frontiers in Brain Research*, ed. John D. French (New York: Columbia University Press, 1962), p. 191.

3. Judson J. Van Wyk and Melvin M. Grumbach, "Disorders of Sex Differentiation," in *Textbook of Endocrinology*, ed. Robert H. Williams, 4th ed. (Philadelphia: Saunders, 1968): 559.

4. Edna H. Sobel, discussing Lytt I. Gardner, "Biochemical Events at Adolescence," in *Pediatric Clinics of North America: Symposium on Adolescence*, Vol. VII, No. 1 (1960), p. 25.

5. Harvey Peskin, "Pubertal Onset and Ego Functioning," *Journal of Abnormal Psychology* 72 (1967): 1.

6. Judith S. Kestenberg, "Phases of Adolescence: With Suggestions for a Correlation of Psychic and Hormonal Organizations, Part II: Prepuberty Diffusion and Reintegration," *Journal of the American Academy of Child Psychiatry* 6 (1967): 577; Peter Blos, "Preadolescent Drive Organization," *Journal of the American Psychoanalytic Association* 6 (1958): 47; Reuven Kohen-Raz, *The Child from 9 to 13: The Psychology of Preadolescence and Early Puberty* (Chicago: Aldine, 1971), pp. 103–132.

7. Warren J. Gadpaille, "Homosexual Activity and Homosexuality in Adolescence," in *Science and Psychoanalysis* Vol. XV: *Dynamics of Deviant Sexuality*, ed. Jules H. Masserman (New York: Grune and Stratton, 1969), p. 60, and "Homosexual Experience in Adolescence," *Medical Aspects of Human Sexuality* 2 (October 1968): 29.

8. Alfred C. Kinsey, Wardell B. Pomeroy, and Clyde E. Martin, *Sexual Behavior in the Human Male* (Philadelphia: Saunders, 1948), p. 162; Alfred C. Kinsey et al., *Sexual Behavior in the Human Female* (Philadelphia: Saunders, 1953), pp. 107–114.

9. Kinsey, *Human Male*, pp. 161–162, 172, 667–778.

10. Glenn V. Ramsey, "The Sexual Development of Boys," *American Journal of Psychology* 56 (1943): 217.

11. Carlfred B. Broderick, "Social Heterosexual Development Among Urban Negroes and Whites," *Journal of Marriage and the Family* 27 (1965): 200.

12. Kinsey, *Human Male*, 172–173.

13. Carlfred B. Broderick, "Heterosexual Interests of Suburban Youth," *Medical Aspects of Human Sexuality* 5 (March 1971): 98.

14. Robert C. Sorénsen, *Adolescent Sexuality in Contemporary America* (New York: World Publishing Co., 1973), pp. 189, 197.

15. Broderick, "Suburban Youth," 95.

16. Carlfred B. Broderick and George P. Rowe, "A Scale of Preadolescent Heterosexual Development," *Journal of Marriage and the Family* 30 (1968): 97.

17. Blos, "Drive Organization," 49.

18. Kate Friedlaender, "Children's Books: And their Function in Latency and Prepuberty," *American Imago* 3 (1942): 129.

19. Judith S. Kestenberg, "Outside and Inside, Male and Female," *Journal of the American Psychoanalytic Association* 16 (1968): 457.

20. Helene Deutsch, *The Psychology of Women: A Psychoanalytic Interpretation*, Vol. I (New York: Grune and Stratton, 1944), chap. i.

21. Judith S. Kestenberg, "Vicissitudes of Female Sexuality," *Journal of the American Psychoanalytic Association* 4 (1956): 473–474.

22. Judith S. Kestenberg, "Menarche," in *Adolescents: Psychoanalytic Approach to Problems and Therapy*, ed. Sandor Lorand and Henry I. Schneer (New York: Paul B. Hoeber, 1961), p. 19.

23. Erik H. Erikson, "Sex Differences in the Play Configurations of Preadolescents," *American Journal of Orthopsychiatry* 21 (1951): 667, and *Identity: Youth and Crisis* (New York: Norton, 1968), chap. vii.

24. Friedlaender, "Children's Books," 129.

25. Mary Cover Jones and Paul Henry Mussen, "Self-Conceptions, Motivations, and Interpersonal Attitudes of Early- and Late-Maturing Girls," *Child Development* 29 (1958): 491; Margaret Siler Faust, "Developmental Maturity as a Determinant in Prestige of Adolescent Girls," *Child Development* 31 (1960): 173.

26. Jones and Mussen, "Early- and Late-Maturing Girls," 491.

27. Kinsey et al., *Human Female*, pp. 246, 276, 521, 554.

28. Paul Henry Mussen and Mary Cover Jones, "Self-Conceptions, Motivations, and Interpersonal Attitudes of Late- and Early-Maturing Boys," *Child Development* 28 (1957): 243.

29. Kinsey, *Human Male*, pp. 297–326.

30. Peskin, "Pubertal Onset," 1; Mary Cover Jones, "The Later Careers of Boys Who Were Early- or Late-Maturing," *Child Development* 28 (1957): 113, and "Psychological Correlates of Somatic Development," *Child Development* 36 (1965): 899.

31. Yehudi Cohen, *The Transition from Childhood to Adolescence* (Chicago: Aldine Press, 1964), chaps. vii and viii.

32. Ira L. Reiss, "The Influence of Contraceptive Knowledge on Premarital Sexuality," *Medical Aspects of Human Sexuality* 4 (February 1970): 71.

33. Tanner, *Adolescence*, facing p. 29.

34. Natalie Shainess, "Psychiatric Evaluation of Premenstrual Tension," *New York State Journal of Medicine* 62 (1962): 3573.

35. Warren J. Gadpaille, "Infertility and Amenorrhea in the Hysterical Character," in *The Collected Award Papers* (Port Chester, New York: The Gralnick Foundation, 1966), p. 131.

36. Blos, "Drive Organization," 47.

37. Phyllis Greenacre, *Trauma, Growth, and Personality* (New York: International Universities Press, 1952), chap. x.

8. EARLY ADOLESCENCE

1. Erik H. Erikson, *Identity and the Life Cycle, Psychological Issues,* Vol. I, No. 1 (New York: International Universities Press, 1959), pp. 89–94.

2. Anke A. Ehrhardt, K. Evers, and John Money, "Influence of Androgen and Some Aspects of Sexually Dimorphic Behavior in Women with the Late-Treated Adrenogenital Syndrome," *Johns Hopkins Medical Journal* 123 (1968): 115.

3. Eugene E. Levitt and Albert D. Klassen, "Public Attitudes Toward Sexual Behaviors: The Latest Investigation of the Institute for Sex Research," (Paper delivered at the Annual Convention of the American Orthopsychiatric Association, New York, May 29, 1973).

4. Jon P. Alston and Frances Tucker, "The Myth of Sexual Permissiveness," *Journal of Sex Research* 9 (1973): 34.

5. Levitt and Klassen, "Public Attitudes."

6. Richard K. Greenbank, "Are Medical Students Learning Psychiatry?" *Pennsylvania Medical Journal* 64 (1961): 989.

7. Ira L. Reiss, *The Social Context of Premarital Sexual Permissiveness* (New York: Holt, Rinehart and Winston, 1967), pp. 142–143.

8. Warren J. Gadpaille, "Adolescent Sexuality and the Struggle over Authority," *Journal of School Health* 40 (1970): 479.

9. John H. Gagnon, "Sexuality and Sexual Learning in the Child," *Psychiatry* 28 (1965): 212.

10. Erikson, *Identity*, pp. 90–91.

11. Lawrence Kohlberg and Carol Gilligan, "The Adolescent as a Philosopher: The Discovery of the Self in a Postconventional World," *Daedalus* 100 (1971): 1051.

12. Margaret Siler Faust, "Developmental Maturity as a Determinant in Prestige of Adolescent Girls," *Child Development* 31 (1960): 173; E. G. Everett, quoted in Dorothy J. Eichorn, "Biological Correlates of Behavior," in *Child Psychology, National Society for the Study of Education, Yearbook* No. 63, pt. 1 (Chicago: University of Chicago Press, 1963), p. 4.

13. Peter Blos, *On Adolescence: A Psychoanalytic Interpretation* (New York: Free Press, 1962), p. 90.

14. Robert C. Sorensen, *Adolescent Sexuality in Contemporary America* (New York: World Publishing Co., 1973), p. 441.

15. Alfred C. Kinsey, Wardell B. Pomeroy, and Clyde E. Martin, *Sexual Behavior in the Human Male* (Philadelphia: Saunders, 1948), p. 500.

16. Glenn V. Ramsey, "The Sexual Development of Boys," *American Journal of Psychology* 56 (1943): 224.

17. Alfred C. Kinsey et al., *Sexual Behavior in the Human Female* (Philadelphia: Saunders, 1953), p. 141.

18. Sorensen, *Adolescent Sexuality*, p. 441.

19. Ibid., pp. 171–186.

20. Daniel Offer, *The Psychological World of the Teenager* (New York: Basic Books, 1969), p. 83.

21. Ramsey, "Sexual Development," 228.

22. Sorensen, *Adolescent Sexuality*, p. 441.

23. Harold T. Christensen and Christina F. Gregg, "Changing Sex Norms in America and Scandinavia," *Journal of Marriage and the Family* 32 (1970): 616.

24. Warren J. Gadpaille, "Homosexual Activity and Homosexuality in Adolescence," in *Science and Psychoanalysis*, Vol. XV: *Dynamics of Deviant Sexuality*, ed. Jules H. Masserman (New York: Grune and Stratton, 1969), p. 60, and "Homosexual Experience in Adolescence," *Medical Aspects of Human Sexuality* 2 (October 1968): 29.

25. Kinsey et al., *Human Female*, pp. 502–509.

26. Kinsey, Pomeroy, and Martin, *Human Male*, pp. 667–678.

27. Carlfred B. Broderick, "Socio-sexual Development in a Suburban Community," *Journal of Sex Research* 2 (1966): 1.

28. *The Report of the Commission on Obscenity and Pornography* (Washington: United States Government Printing Office, 1970), pp. 232–243.

29. Edith Jacobson, "Adolescent Moods and the Remodeling of Psychic Structures in Adolescence," *Psychoanalytic Study of the Child* 16 (1961): 164.

30. Judith S. Kestenberg, "Phases of Adolescence: With Suggestions for a Correlation of Psychic and Hormonal Organizations, Part II: Prepuberty Diffusion and Reintegration," *Journal of the American Academy of Child Psychiatry* 6 (1967): 577.

31. Helene Deutsch, *Selected Problems of Adolescence* (New York: International Universities Press, 1967), pp. 77–83.

32. Anna Freud, *The Ego and Mechanisms of Defence* (New York: International Universities Press, 1946), p. 152.

33. Ibid., pp. 149–193.

34. Terese Benedek, *Studies in Psychosomatic Medicine: Psychosexual Functions in Women* (New York: Ronald Press, 1962), p. 329.

35. Judith S. Kestenberg, "Menarche," in *Adolescents: Psychoanalytic Approach to Problems and Therapy*, ed. Sandor Lorand and Henry I. Schneer (New York: Paul B. Hoeber, 1961), p. 19, and "Outside and Inside, Male and Female," *Journal of the American Psychoanalytic Association* 16 (1968): 457; Marion Hart and Charles A. Sarnoff, "The Impact of the Menarche: A Study of Two Stages of Organization," *Journal of the American Academy of Child Psychiatry* 10 (1971): 257.

36. Group for the Advancement of Psychiatry, *Normal Adolescence: Its Dynamics and Impact* (New York: Scribners, 1968), pp. 95–99.

37. James Anthony, "The Reactions of Adults to Adolescents and Their Behavior," in *Adolescence: Psychological Perspectives*, ed. Gerald Caplan and Serge Lebovici (New York: Basic Books, 1969), p. 54.

38. S. A. Szurek, "Concerning the Sexual Disorders of Parents and Their Children," *Journal of Nervous and Mental Diseases* 120 (1954): 369; Adelaide M. Johnson and S. A. Szurek, "The Genesis of Antisocial Acting Out in Children and Adults," *Psychoanalytic Quarterly* 21 (1952): 323.

39. Weston LaBarre, "Changing Mores in American Society," (Paper delivered at the American College of Psychiatrists, New Orleans, La., February 1, 1969).

40. Seymour Fisher, *The Female Orgasm: Psychology, Physiology, Fantasy* (New York: Basic Books, 1973), pp. 96–115, 230–238, 258–262, 404–408.

41. Sherry Lynn Marcus Hatcher, "The Adolescent Experience of Pregnancy and Abortion: A Developmental Analysis," *Journal of Youth and Adolescence* 2 (1973): 53.

42. Robert W. Kistner, *Gynecology: Principles and Practice*, 2d ed. (Chicago: Year Book Medical Publishers, 1971), pp. 125–127.

9. LATE ADOLESCENCE

1. Group for the Advancement of Psychiatry, *Normal Adolescence: Its Dynamics and Impact* (New York: Scribners, 1968), pp. 62–63, 93–94; Peter Blos, *On Adolescence: A Psychoanalytic Interpretation* (New York: Free Press, 1962), pp. 128–158.

2. Erik H. Erikson, *Identity and the Life Cycle, Psychological Issues*,

Vol. I, No. 1 (New York: International Universities Press, 1959), pp. 89–94.

3. Erik H. Erikson, *Identity: Youth and Crisis* (Norton, 1968), pp. 156–158.

4. E. G. Everett, quoted in Dorothy J. Eichorn, "Biological Correlates of Behavior," in *Child Psychology, National Society for the Study of Education, Yearbook* no. 63, pt. 1 (Chicago: University of Chicago Press, 1963), p. 4.

5. Margaret Siler Faust, "Developmental Maturity as a Determinant in Prestige of Adolescent Girls," *Child Development* 31 (1960): 173.

6. Mary Cover Jones and Paul Henry Mussen, "Self-Conceptions, Motivations, and Interpersonal Attitudes of Early- and Late-Maturing Girls," *Child Development* 29 (1958): 491.

7. Harvey Peskin, "Pubertal Onset and Ego Functioning," *Journal of Abnormal Psychology* 72 (1967): 1.

8. Mary Cover Jones, "The Later Careers of Boys Who Were Early- or Late-Maturing," *Child Development* 28 (1957): 113, and "Psychological Correlates of Somatic Development," *Child Development* 36 (1965): 899; Paul Henry Mussen and Mary Cover Jones, "The Behavior-Inferred Motivations of Late- and Early-Maturing Boys," *Child Development* 29 (1958): 61; Peskin, "Pubertal Onset," 1.

9. Calvin F. Settlage, "Cultural Values and the Superego in Late Adolescence," *Psychoanalytic Study of the Child* 27 (1972): 74.

10. Warren J. Gadpaille, "Innate Masculine-Feminine Differences," *Medical Aspects of Human Sexuality* 7 (February 1973): 141.

11. Steven Goldberg, *The Inevitability of Patriarchy* (New York: Morrow, 1973), pp. 74–99.

12. Group for the Advancement of Psychiatry, *Normal Adolescence*, pp. 28–34.

13. Carl Feinstein, "Peer Group Formation and Adolescent Rebellion," unpublished paper prepared for GAP Committee on Adolescence, 1972.

14. Commission on Population Growth and the American Future, *Population and the American Future* (New York: Signet, 1972).

15. Robert C. Sorensen, *Adolescent Sexuality in Contemporary America* (New York: World Publishing Co., 1973), p. 441.

16. Harold T. Christensen and Christina F. Gregg, "Changing Sex Norms in America and Scandinavia," *Journal of Marriage and the Family* 32 (1970): 616.

17. Sorensen, *Adolescent Sexuality*, p. 249.

18. Ira L. Reiss, *The Social Context of Premarital Sexual Permissiveness* (New York: Holt, Rinehart and Winston, 1967); Lester A. Kirkendall, *Premarital Intercourse and Interpersonal Relationships* (New York: Julian

Press, 1959); William Simon, Alan S. Berger, and John H. Gagnon, "Beyond Anxiety and Fantasy: The Coital Experiences of College Youth," *Journal of Youth and Adolescence* 1 (1972): 203.

19. Christensen and Gregg, "Changing Sex Norms," 616.

20. Alfred C. Kinsey, Wardell B. Pomeroy, and Clyde E. Martin, *Sexual Behavior in the Human Male* (Philadelphia: Saunders, 1948), pp. 402–414, 595–609; Kirkendall, *Premarital Intercourse*, pp. 256–257; Simon, Berger, and Gagnon, "Beyond Anxiety," pp. 217–220.

21. Sorensen, *Adolescent Sexuality*, p. 220.

22. Theodore Lidz, *The Person: His Development Throughout the Life Cycle* (New York: Basic Books, 1968), pp. 342–359.

23. Alfred C. Kinsey et al., *Sexual Behavior in the Human Female* (Philadelphia: Saunders, 1953), pp. 651–672.

24. Volkmar Sigusch et al., "Psychological Stimulation: Sex Differences," *Journal of Sex Research* 6 (1970): 10; Gunter Schmidt and Volkmar Sigusch, "Sex Differences in Responses to Psychosexual Stimulation by Films and Slides," *Journal of Sex Research* 6 (1970): 268; Gunter Schmidt, Volkmar Sigusch, and Siegrid Schäfer, "Responses to Reading Erotic Stories: Male-Female Differences," *Archives of Sexual Behavior* 2 (1973): 181.

25. Kinsey et al., *Human Female*, pp. 353, 598, 714–716; Kinsey, Pomeroy, and Martin, *Human Male*, p. 226.

26. William H. Masters and Virginia E. Johnson, *Human Sexual Response* (Boston: Little, Brown, 1966), chap. xvii.

27. Judith S. Kestenberg, "Outside and Inside, Male and Female," *Journal of the American Psychoanalytic Association* 16 (1968): 457.

28. Masters and Johnson, *Sexual Response*, pp. 119–120.

29. Theodore Lidz, "Psychoanalytic Theories of Development and Maldevelopment: Some Recapitulations," *American Journal of Psychoanalysis* 27 (1967): 115.

30. Anna Freud, "Adolescence," *Psychoanalytic Study of the Child* 13 (1958): 264–275; Blos, *On Adolescence*, pp. 217–244.

31. Blos, *On Adolescence*, pp. 219–223.

32. Sherry Lynn Marcus Hatcher, "The Adolescent Experience of Pregnancy and Abortion," *Journal of Youth and Adolescence* 2 (1973): 53.

33. Irene M. Josselyn, *Adolescence* (New York: Harper and Row, 1971), p. 112.

34. Lee G. Burchinal, "Trends and Prospects for Young Marriages in the United States," *Journal of Marriage and the Family* 27 (1965): 243; Alan E. Bayer, "Early Marriage in the United States," *Medical Aspects of Human Sexuality* 7 (August 1973): 208.

35. Thomas P. Monohan, "Does Age at Marriage Matter in Divorce?" *Social Forces* 32 (October 1953): 81.

36. Burchinal, "Young Marriages," 246.

37. Ibid., 250–252; Bayer, "Early Marriage," 208; Mary Steichen Calderone, "The Married Teenager," *Journal of the International College of Surgeons* 43 (1965): 442.

38. [Philip M. Sarrel], *Teenage Pregnancy: Prevention and Treatment, SIECUS Study Guide No. 14* (New York: Sex Information and Education Council of the United States, 1971), p. 6.

39. J. W. Mohr, R. E. Turner, and M. B. Jerry, *Pedophilia and Exhibitionism* (Toronto: University of Toronto Press, 1964), pp. 38–45.

40. Paul H. Gebhard et al., *Sex Offenders: An Analysis of Types* (New York: Harper and Row, 1965), p. 809.

41. Mohr, Turner, and Jerry, *Pedophilia and Exhibitionism*, pp. 121–127.

42. Kinsey, Pomeroy, and Martin, *Human Male*, p. 610; Kinsey et al., *Human Female*, pp. 446–509, 642–689.

43. Daniel Offer, *The Psychological World of the Teenager* (New York: Basic Books, 1969), and "Sex and the Normal Adolescent," in *Adolescent Psychiatry* Vol. II, ed. Sherman C. Feinstein and Peter L. Giovacchini (New York: Basic Books, 1973), pp. 165–171; Daniel Offer and Judith L. Offer, "Growing Up: A Follow-up Study of Normal Adolescents," *Seminars in Psychiatry* 1 (1969): 46; Roy R. Grinker, Sr., " 'Mentally Healthy' Young Males: Homoclites," *Archives of General Psychiatry* 6 (1962): 405.

44. Lawrence Kohlberg and Carol Gilligan, "The Adolescent as a Philosopher: The Discovery of the Self in a Postconventional World," *Daedalus* 100 (1971): 1051.

45. Harvey Peskin, "Multiple Prediction of Adult Psychological Health," *Journal of Counseling and Clinical Psychology* 38 (1972): 155.

46. Peter Blos, "The Generation Gap: Fact or Fiction?" in *Adolescent Psychiatry* Vol. 1, ed. Sherman C. Feinstein, Peter L. Giovacchini, and Arthur A. Miller (New York: Basic Books, 1971), p. 5; Deutsch, *Problems of Adolescence*; and "The Contemporary Adolescent Girl," *Seminars in Psychiatry* 1 (1969): 99; Sherman C. Feinstein, "Effects of Pregnancy on Adolescent Sexual Development," in *Adolescent Psychiatry* Vol. II, ed. Sherman C. Feinstein and Peter L. Giovacchini (New York: Basic Books, 1973), p. 189; Josselyn, *Adolescence*; Malvina W. Kremer, "The Adolescent Sexual Revolution: Introduction," in *Adolescent Psychiatry* Vol. II, ed. Sherman C. Feinstein and Peter L. Giovacchini (New York: Basic Books, 1973), p. 160; Leo A. Spiegel, "A Review of Contributions to a Psychoanalytic Theory of Adolescence," *Psychoanalytic Study of the Child* 6 (1951): 375.

47. Warren J. Gadpaille, "Adolescent Sexuality: A Challenge to

Psychiatrists," *Journal of the American Academy of Psychoanalysis* 3 (1975) (in publication).

48. Kinsey, *Human Female*, pp. 385–391, 405–407.

49. Sorensen, *Adolescent Sexuality*, pp. 147–186, 217–282.

10. YOUNG ADULTHOOD

1. Erik H. Erikson, *Identity and the Life Cycle, Psychological Issues* Vol. I, No. 1 (New York: International Universities Press, 1959), p. 95.

2. William Simon and John H. Gagnon, "On Psychosexual Development," in *Handbook of Socialization Theory and Research*, ed. David A. Goslin (Chicago: Rand McNally, 1969), p. 744.

3. Lee Rainwater, "Marital Sexuality in Four Cultures of Poverty," *Journal of Marriage and the Family* 26 (1964): 457; and "Some Aspects of Lower Class Sexual Behavior," *Journal of Social Issues* 22 (April 1966): 96.

4. Ira L. Reiss, "The Influence of Contraceptive Knowledge on Premarital Sexuality," *Medical Aspects of Human Sexuality* 4 (February 1970): 71.

5. William H. Masters and Virginia E. Johnson, *Human Sexual Response* (Boston: Little, Brown, 1966), pp. 56–67.

6. Katharina Dalton, *The Premenstrual Syndrome* (Springfield, Ill.: Charles C. Thomas, 1964); Carlos Neu and Alberto DiMascio, "Variations in the Menstrual Cycle," *Medical Aspects of Human Sexuality* 8 (February 1974): 164.

7. Katharina Dalton, "Menstruation and Examinations," *Lancet* 2 (1968): 1386.

8. Quoted in Lionel Tiger, "Male Dominance? Yes, Alas. A Sexist Plot? No." *New York Times Magazine*, 25 October 1970, p. 134.

9. Natalie Shainess, "Psychiatric Evaluation of Premenstrual Tension," *New York State Journal of Medicine* 62 (1962): 3573.

10. David A. Hamburg, Rudolf H. Moos, and Irvin D. Yalom, "Studies of Distress in the Menstrual Cycle and the Postpartum Period," in *Endocrinology and Human Behaviour*, ed. Richard P. Michael (London: Oxford University Press, 1968), p. 94.

11. Terese Benedek and Boris B. Rubinstein, "The Correlations Between Ovarian Activity and Psychodynamic Process," *Psychosomatic Medicine* 1 (1939): 245, 461.

12. Anita I. Bell, Charles F. Stroebel, and Deborah D. Prior, "Interdisciplinary Study: Scrotal Sac and Testes: Psychophysiological and Psychological Observations," *Psychoanalytic Quarterly* 40 (1971): 415.

13. Judith S. Kestenberg, "Outside and Inside, Male and Female," *Journal of the American Psychoanalytic Association* 16 (1968): 458.

14. Steven Goldberg, *The Inevitability of Patriarchy* (New York: Morrow, 1973).

15. William M. Kephart, "Evaluation of Romantic Love," *Medical Aspects of Human Sexuality* 7 (February 1973): 92.

16. Theodore Lidz, *The Person: His Development throughout the Life Cycle* (New York: Basic Books, 1968), chap. xiii.

17. Ibithaj Arafat and Betty Yorburg, "On Living Together Without Marriage," *Journal of Sex Research* 9 (1973): 97.

18. Lester A. Kirkendall, *Premarital Intercourse and Interpersonal Relations* (New York: Julian Press, 1959), chap. ix; David F. Shope and Carlfred B. Broderick, "Level of Sexual Experience and Predicted Adjustment in Marriage," *Journal of Marriage and the Family* 29 (1967): 424.

19. E. W. Burgess and Paul Wallin, *Engagement and Marriage* (Philadelphia: Lippincott, 1953), pp. 366, 370–372.

20. Paul H. Gebhard, "Factors in Marital Orgasm," *Journal of Social Issues* 22 (April 1966): 88.

21. Alan J. Cooper, "Factors in Male Sexual Inadequacy: A Review," *Journal of Nervous and Mental Diseases* 149 (1969): 337; Alan J. Cooper et al., "Androgen Function in 'Psychogenic' and 'Constitutional' Types of Impotence," *British Medical Journal* 3 (1970): 17; John Johnson, "Androgyny and Disorders of Sexual Potency," *British Medical Journal* 2 (1965): 572.

22. Alfred C. Kinsey et al., *Sexual Behavior in the Human Female* (Philadelphia: Saunders, 1953), pp. 436–438.

23. Gilbert D. Bartell, "Group Sex Among the Mid-Americans," *Journal of Sex Research* 6 (1970): 113.

24. Nena O'Neill and George O'Neill, *Open Marriage: A New Life Style for Couples* (New York: Evans, 1972).

25. Jetse Sprey, "Extramarital Relationships," *Sexual Behavior* 2 (August 1972): 34.

26. Duane Denfeld and Michael Gordon, "The Sociology of Mate Swapping," *Journal of Sex Research* 6 (1970): 85.

27. George C. and Nena O'Neill, "Patterns in Group Sexual Activity," *Journal of Sex Research* 6 (1970): 101; James R. and Lynn G. Smith, "Co-Marital Sex and the Sexual Freedom Movement," *Journal of Sex Research* 6 (1970): 131; Larry L. and Joan M. Constantine, "Sexual Aspects of Multilateral Relations," *Journal of Sex Research* 7 (1971): 204.

28. Bartell, "Group Sex," 113.

29. Toby Bieber, "Women's Resistance to Marriage," *Medical Aspects of Human Sexuality* 5 (February 1971): 64.

30. Alice S. Rossi, "Maternalism, Sexuality, and the New Feminism," in *Contemporary Sexual Behavior: Critical Issues in the 1970s*, ed. Joseph

Zubin and John Money (Baltimore: Johns Hopkins University Press, 1973), p. 145.

31. Erik H. Erikson, *Childhood and Society* (New York: Norton, 1950), pp. 230–231.

11. PARENTHOOD

1. Weston LaBarre, *The Human Animal* (Chicago: University of Chicago Press, 1954), chap. vii.

2. Ibid., pp. 104–109.

3. Ibid., p. 104.

4. Terese Benedek, "The Organization of the Reproductive Drive," *International Journal of Psycho-analysis* 41 (1960): 1.

5. Theodore Lidz, *The Person: His Development throughout the Life Cycle* (New York: Basic Books, 1968), pp. 57–63.

6. Alice S. Rossi, "Transition to Parenthood," *Journal of Marriage and the Family* 30 (1968): 26.

7. Steven Goldberg, *The Inevitability of Patriarchy* (New York: Morrow, 1973), chaps. iv and v.

8. Clark E. Vincent, "Side Effects on the Family from Liberalized Sexual Attitudes," *Medical Aspects of Human Sexuality* 7 (June 1973): 80.

9. Lidz, *The Person*, pp. 63–67.

10. Marcel Heiman, "Reproduction: Emotions and the Hypothalamic-Pituitary Function," *Fertility and Sterility* 10 (1959): 162.

11. William H. Masters and Virginia E. Johnson, *Human Sexual Response* (Boston: Little, Brown, 1966), pp. 68–126.

12. C. A. Fox, H. S. Wolff, and J. A. Baker, "Measurement of Intra-Vaginal and Intra-Uterine Pressures During Human Coitus by Radio-Telemetry," *Journal of Reproduction and Fertility* 22 (1970); 243.

13. J. P. Greenhill, *Obstetrics*, 11th ed. (Philadelphia: Saunders, 1955), pp. 367–370.

14. Edward Weiss and O. Spurgeon English, *Psychosomatic Medicine: A Clinical Study of Psychophysiologic Reactions*, 3d ed. (Philadelphia: Saunders, 1957), pp. 382–383.

15. Terese F. Benedek, "Sexual Functions in Women and Their Disturbance," in *American Handbook of Psychiatry*, Vol. i, ed. Silvano Arieti (New York: Basic Books, 1959), p. 727.

16. David Rothman, "Habitual Abortion and Sexual Conflict," *Medical Aspects of Human Sexuality* 7 (July 1973): 56.

17. Hans Selye, *Stress* (Montreal: Acta Endocrinologica, 1950).

18. Antonio J. Ferriera, "Emotional Factors in Prenatal Environment," *Journal of Nervous and Mental Diseases* 141 (1965): 108.

19. Lester Warren Sontag, "The Significance of Fetal Environmental Differences," *American Journal of Obstetrics and Gynecology* 42 (1941):

996, and "Differences in Modifiability of Fetal Behavior and Physiology," *Psychosomatic Medicine* 6 (1944): 151.

20. William H. James, "The Effect of Maternal Psychological Stress on the Foetus," *British Journal of Psychiatry* 115 (1969): 811.

21. Ingeborg L. Ward, "Prenatal Stress Feminizes and Demasculinizes the Behavior of Males," *Science* 175 (1972): 82.

22. Lawrence E. Hinkle, Jr., and Stewart Wolf, "Studies in Diabetes Mellitus: Changes in Glucose, Ketone, and Water Metabolism During Stress," in *Life Stress and Bodily Disease, Research Publications: Association for Research in Nervous and Mental Diseases* vol. xxix (Baltimore: Williams and Wilkins, 1950), p. 338.

23. Kenneth L. Jones and David W. Smith, "Recognition of the Fetal Alcohol Syndrome in Early Infancy," *Lancet*, November 3, 1973, p. 999.

24. Alton Ochsner, "Influence of Smoking on Sexuality and Pregnancy," *Medical Aspects of Human Sexuality* 5 (November 1971): 78.

25. Ferriera, "Prenatal Environment," 108.

26. The detailed research on the psychobiological aspects of childbirth, maternal sexuality, lactation, and breastfeeding is considerable. Unless otherwise noted, and to avoid excessive referencing, the reader will find extensive bibliographies in two recent overview articles: Niles Newton, "Interrelationships between Sexual Responsiveness, Birth, and Breast Feeding," in *Contemporary Sexual Behavior: Critical Issues in the 1970s*, ed. Joseph Zubin and John Money (Baltimore: Johns Hopkins University Press, 1973), p. 77; Alice S. Rossi, "Maternalism, Sexuality, and the New Feminism," in *Contemporary Sexual Behavior: Critical Issues in the 1970s*, edited by Joseph Zubin and John Money (Baltimore: Johns Hopkins University Press, 1973), p. 145.

27. Ashley Montagu, *Touching: The Human Significance of the Skin* (New York: Columbia University Press, 1971), pp. 78, 86–88.

28. David A. Hamburg, "Effects of Progesterone on Behavior," in *Endocrines and the Central Nervous System, Research Publications: Association for Research in Nervous and Mental Diseases* vol. xliii (Baltimore: Williams and Wilkins, 1966), p. 251.

29. Terese Benedek, "Parenthood as a Developmental Phase," *Journal of the American Psychoanalytic Association* 7 (1959): 389.

30. Kent Ravenscroft, Jr., "Normal Family Regression at Adolescence," *American Journal of Psychiatry* 131 (1974): 31.

31. Ira L. Reiss, *The Social Context of Premarital Sexual Permissiveness* (New York: Holt, Rinehart and Winston, 1967), pp. 142–143.

32. Frank R. Wake, "Attitudes of Parents Towards the Pre-Marital Sex Behavior of Their Children and Themselves," *Journal of Sex Research* 5 (1969): 170.

33. Alfred C. Kinsey et al., *Sexual Behavior in the Human Female* (Philadelphia: Saunders, 1953), pp. 286–287, 330, 333.

34. Jon P. Alston and Frances Tucker, "The Myth of Sexual Permissiveness," *Journal of Sex Research* 9 (1973): 34; Robert R. Bell and Jack V. Buerkle, "Mother and Daughter Attitudes to Premarital Sexual Behavior," *Marriage and Family Living* 23 (1961): 390; Eugene E. Levitt and Albert D. Klassen, "Public Attitudes Toward Sexual Behavior: The Latest Investigation of the Institute for Sex Research" (Paper delivered at the Annual Convention of American Orthopsychiatric Association, New York, May 29, 1973).

35. Warren J. Gadpaille, "Amenorrhea and Infertility in the Hysterical Character," in *Collected Award Papers* (Port Chester, N.Y.: Gralnick Foundation, 1966), p. 131; David Rothman, Alex H. Kaplan, and Elizabeth Nettles, "Psychosomatic Infertility," *American Journal of Obstetrics and Gynecology* 83 (1962): 373; A. E. Rakoff, "Endocrine Factors in Psychogenic Amenorrhea," in *Endocrinology and Human Behaviour*, ed. Richard P. Michaels (London: Oxford University Press, 1968), p. 139; Weiss and English, *Psychosomatic Medicine*, pp. 187–194.

36. Flanders Dunbar, *Emotions and Bodily Changes* (New York: Columbia University Press, 1954), pp. 511–512, 537–541.

37. Weston LaBarre, *The Ghost Dance: Origins of Religion* (Garden City, N.Y.: Doubleday, 1970).

38. Rossi, "Maternalism," p. 145.

39. Derek Miller, "Adolescence and Schizophrenia," paper presented at the Annual Meeting of the American Society for Adolescent Psychiatry, Dallas, Texas, April 30, 1972.

40. Helene Deutsch, *Selected Problems of Adolescence* (New York: International Universities Press, 1967), p. 130.

41. Menachem Gerson, "Women in the Kibbutz," *American Journal of Orthopsychiatry* 41 (1971): 566; A. I. Rabin, "Some Sex Differences in the Attitudes of Kibbutz Adolescents," *Israel Annals of Psychiatry and Related Disciplines* 6 (1968): 62.

42. Julius Zellermayer and Joseph Marcus, "Kibbutz Adolescence: Relevance to Personality Development Theory," *Journal of Youth and Adolescence* 1 (1972): 143.

43. Richard W. Brunstetter, "Growing Up 'Organic'—Developmental Aspects of Childhood in a Commune," (Paper delivered at the meeting of the Southern Psychiatric Association, New Orleans, La., October 1972).

44. Larry L. and Joan M. Constantine, "Sexual Aspects of Multilateral Relations," *Journal of Sex Research* 7 (1971): 204; Sheldon Salzberg, "Is Group Marriage Viable?" *Journal of Sex Research* 9 (1973): 325.

45. Erik H. Erikson, *Identity: Youth and Crisis* (New York: Norton, 1968), pp. 138–139.

12. THE MIDDLE AND LATER YEARS

1. E. Stewart Taylor, *Essentials of Gynecology*, 4th ed. (Philadelphia: Lea and Febiger, 1969), p. 483.

2. Committee on Human Sexuality of the American Medical Association, *Human Sexuality* (Chicago: American Medical Association, 1972), p. 80.

3. Charles W. Lloyd, "The Climacteric and the Menopause," in *Human Reproduction and Sexual Behavior*, ed. Charles W. Lloyd (Philadelphia: Lea and Febiger, 1964), chap. xvii; Taylor, *Gynecology*, p. 483.

4. J. P. Pratt, quoted in Edward Weiss and O. Spurgeon English, *Psychosomatic Medicine: A Clinical Study of Psychophysiologic Reactions*, 3d ed. (Philadelphia: Saunders, 1957), p. 377.

5. Robert W. Kistner, *Gynecology: Principles and Practice*, 2d ed. (Chicago: Year Book Medical Publishers, 1971), pp. 658–660.

6. A. Albert, "The Mammalian Testis," in *Sex and Internal Secretions* Vol. I, 3d ed., ed. William C. Young (Baltimore: Williams and Wilkins, 1961), p. 332; Sheldon J. Segal, "The Testis: Physiology," in *Human Reproduction and Sexual Behavior*, ed. Charles W. Lloyd (Philadelphia: Lea and Febiger, 1964), p. 67.

7. C. Alvin Paulsen, "The Testis," in *Textbook of Endocrinology*, 4th ed., ed. Robert H. Williams (Philadelphia: Saunders, 1968), p. 413; Weiss and English, *Psychosomatic Medicine*, p. 404; Charles W. Lloyd, "Gonadal Failure in the Adult Male," in *Human Reproduction and Sexual Behavior*, ed. Charles W. Lloyd (Philadelphia: Lea and Febiger, 1964), chap. xx.

8. William H. Masters and Virginia E. Johnson, *Human Sexual Response* (Boston: Little, Brown, 1966), pp. 223–270.

9. James Leslie McCary, "Sexual Advantages of Middle-Aged Men," *Medical Aspects of Human Sexuality* 7 (December 1973): 138.

10. Paul H. Gebhard, "Factors in Marital Orgasm," *Journal of Social Issues* 22 (April 1966): 88.

11. Terese Benedek, "Parenthood During the Life Cycle," in *Parenthood: Its Psychology and Psychopathology*, ed. E. James Anthony and Terese Benedek (Boston: Little, Brown, 1970), p. 185.

12. Terese Benedek, "Climacterium: A Developmental Phase," *Psychoanalytic Quarterly* 19 (1950): 1.

13. Leo Rangell, "The Return of the Repressed 'Oedipus'," in *Parenthood: Its Psychology and Psychopathology*, E. James Anthony and Terese Benedek (Boston: Little, Brown, 1970), p. 325.

14. Eva Y. Deykin et al., "The Empty Nest: Psychosocial Aspects of Conflict Between Depressed Women and their Grown Children," *American Journal of Psychiatry* 122 (1966): 1422.

15. Weiss and English, *Psychosomatic Medicine*, pp. 375–382; Benedek, "Climacterium," 1; Taylor, *Gynecology*, pp. 486, 489, 493–494.

16. Group for the Advancement of Psychiatry, *Psychiatry and the Aged: An Introductory Approach*, GAP report no. 59 (New York: GAP, 1965), p. 539.

17. Alfred C. Kinsey et al., *Sexual Behavior in the Human Female* (Philadelphia: Saunders, 1953), pp. 597–599; Masters and Johnson, *Sexual Response*, pp. 34–36, 174–176.

18. Herman K. Hellerstein, "Sexual Activity in the Postcoronary Patient," *Medical Aspects of Human Sexuality* 3 (March 1969): 70; George X. Trimble, "The Coital Coronary," *Medical Aspects of Human Sexuality* 4 (May 1970): 64.

19. Jere W. Lord, Jr., "Peripheral Vascular Disorders and Sexual Function," *Medical Aspects of Human Sexuality* 7 (September 1973): 34.

20. Wilbur W. Oaks and John H. Moyer, "Sex and Hypertension," *Medical Aspects of Human Sexuality* 6 (November 1972): 128; Elliot J. Howard, "Sexual Expenditure in Patients with Hypertensive Disease" (with commentary by Ray W. Gifford), *Medical Aspects of Human Sexuality* 7 (October 1973): 82, 90.

21. Lord, "Peripheral Vascular Disorders," 34.

22. Alan Rubin, "Sexual Behavior in Diabetes Mellitus," *Medical Aspects of Human Sexuality* 1 (December 1967): 23; Max Ellenberg, "Impotence in Diabetics: A Neurologic Rather than an Endocrinologic Problem," *Medical Aspects of Human Sexuality* 7 (April 1973): 12.

23. Robert C. Kolodny, "Sexual Dysfunction in Diabetic Females," *Medical Aspects of Human Sexuality* 6 (April 1972): 98.

24. Ellenberg, "Impotence in Diabetics," 12.

25. Alex L. Finkle, "The Relationship of Sexual Habits to Benign Prostatic Hypertrophy," *Medical Aspects of Human Sexuality* 1 (October 1967): 24.

26. B. Lyman Stewart, "Inflammatory Causes of Impotence," *Medical Aspects of Human Sexuality* 7 (June 1973): 158.

27. Richard D. Amelar and Lawrence Dubin, "Sex After Major Urologic Surgery," *Journal of Sex Research* 4 (1968): 265; Bruce G. Belt, "Some Organic Causes of Impotence," *Medical Aspects of Human Sexuality* 7 (January 1973): 152.

28. Alex L. Finkle, "Sex After Prostatectomy," *Medical Aspects of Human Sexuality* 2 (March 1968): 40; Isadore Rubin, "Sex and the Aging Man and Woman," in *Human Sexuality in Medical Education and Practice*, ed. Clark E. Vincent (Springfield, Ill.: Charles C. Thomas, 1968), pp. 339–340.

29. William C. Bernstein, "Sexual Dysfunction Following Radical

Surgery for Cancer of the Rectum and Sigmoid Colon," *Medical Aspects of Human Sexuality* 6 (March 1972): 156.

30. Isadore Rubin, "Sex and the Aging," p. 544.

31. Gray H. Twombly, "Sex After Radical Gynecological Surgery," *Journal of Sex Research* 4 (1968): 275; John W. Huffman, "Sexual Reactions After Gynecologic Surgery," *Medical Aspects of Human Sexuality* 3 (November 1969): 48.

32. Marvin G. Drellich, "Sex after Hysterectomy," *Medical Aspects of Human Sexuality* 1 (1967): 62.

33. Harold I. Lief et al., "A Psychodynamic Study of Medical Students and Their Adaptational Problems," *Journal of Medical Education* 35 (1960): 696; John W. Mudd and Richard J. Siegel, "Sexuality—the Experience and Anxieties of Medical Students," *New England Journal of Medicine* 281 (1969): 1397.

34. Ira B. Pauly and Steven G. Goldstein, "Physicians' Ability to Treat Sexual Problems," *Medical Aspects of Human Sexuality* 4 (October 1970): 24, and "Prevalence of Significant Sexual Problems in Medical Practice," *Medical Aspects of Human Sexuality* 4 (November 1970): 48.

35. Peggy Golde and Nathan Kogan, "A Sentence Completion Procedure for Assessing Attitudes Toward Old People," *Journal of Gerontology* 14 (1959): 355.

36. Gustave Newman and Claude R. Nichols, "Sexual Activities and Attitudes in Older Persons," *Journal of the American Medical Association* 173 (7 May 1960): 117; Eric Pfeiffer, Adriaan Verwoerdt, and Hsioh-Shan Wang, "Sexual Behavior in Aged Men and Women," *Archives of General Psychiatry* 19 (1968): 753; Alex L. Finkle et al., "Sexual Potency in Aging Males," *Journal of the American Medical Association* 170 (18 July 1959): 113; Joseph T. Freedman, "Sexual Capacities in the Aging Male," *Geriatrics* 16 (1961): 37.

37. Isadore Rubin, "Sex Over 65," in *Advances in Sex Research*, ed. Hugo G. Beigel (New York: Harper and Row, 1963), p. 138.

38. William H. Masters and Virginia E. Johnson, *Human Sexual Inadequacy* (Boston: Little, Brown, 1970), chaps. vii and viii, and *Sexual Response*, chaps. xv and xvi.

39. Masters and Johnson, *Sexual Inadequacy*, pp. 322–324.

40. Theodore Lidz, *The Person: His Development throughout the Life Cycle* (New York: Basic Books, 1968), p. 477.

41. Erik H. Erikson, *Childhood and Society* (New York: Norton, 1950), pp. 231–233.

42. T. S. Eliot, "Little Gidding," *Four Quartets*, in *The Complete Poems and Plays: 1909–1950* (New York: Harcourt, Brace and World, 1952), p. 145.

Index

relation to antisocial behavior, 203

relation to fantasies, 13, 127

sexual, 19, 84, 115, 116, 119, 185, 189, 192, 194, 202, 263–266, 269, 281, 296–297, 329–330, 374, 393–394

See also Judeo-Christian culture

Reproduction, knowledge of, 91, 106, 129

Reproductive Biology Research Foundation, 348–349, 386, 436

female orgasm studies, 348–349, 386

sexual function of the aged, 436

Romance, 359–360, 370

Scrotal retraction. *See* Testis, retraction as a source of anxiety, as a sign of anxiety, and in relation to toilet training

Scrotum

awareness of by infants, 52, 54

awareness of by toddlers, 92–94, 97, 125

embryology, 31

maturation at puberty, 222–224, 259–260

pain from prolonged sexual stimulation, 324

Self-determination, drive for

toddler years, 16, 78, 80, 104, 399

oedipal stage, 177–181

adolescence, 275, 278

Self-esteem

infancy, 382

oedipal stage, 176, 184

latency, 208

preadolescence, 252

adolescence, 292, 302, 327

young adulthood, 347, 368, 374–375

parenthood, 295, 397, 402

middle and later years, 428, 432, 438

Self-hate, origin of, 46

Semen, 19, 247, 292, 386

Senescence, 437–440

Senility, 437, 439

Serial monogamy. *See* Monogamy, serial

Sex antagonism, 63–64, 177–178, 231, 253, 356–358, 365–366

Sex chromosomes, 26–30, 38

Sex, determination of. *See* Fetal development

Sex drive

in anal-muscular phase, 116, 118

in phallic-oedipal phase, 154, 158, 160, 176

in latency, 188–191, 195, 201, 203

in prepuberty, 234

in preadolescence, 237

in puberty, 261

in adolescence, 269, 280, 289, 292, 311

in parenthood, 297

in middle years, 421

in later years, 436

fluctuations during menstrual cycle, 352–354

hormonal basis of, 159, 261

in marriage, 370

male-female differences, 320–321, 421

mastery of, 292, 323

Sex education

home, 56, 97–100, 102, 129–130, 151–152, 171–172, 219, 244–246, 265, 299, 374

peer group, 198

school, 189, 244–245, 265, 299–300, 384

sources of misinformation, 99–101, 127–130, 151–160, 205

Sex hormones. *See* Androgens; Estrogen; Progesterone; Testosterone; Gonadotropins

About the Author

Warren J. Gadpaille, M.D., is a psychoanalyst in private practice with adults and adolescents in Denver, Colorado, and is
affiliated with the Porter-Swedish Hospital complex. He is also an
adjunct professor at the University of Northern Colorado, teaching graduate courses in psychosexual development and maldevelopment, and consultant for the Jefferson County School District sex education program. He has been a member of the
Committee on Adolescence of the Group for the Advancement of
Psychiatry since 1957, is on the Executive Board of the American
Association of Sex Educators and Counselors, and has lectured
and published widely on the subject of sexual development.

DATE DUE

JUL 20 '75			
OCT 05 '74			
APR 9 1981			
FEB 1 8 1982			
MAY 2 5 1990			